The Huguenots and French Opinion, 1685-1787

The Enlighten[ ] on Toleration

D0792596

Geoffrey Adams

The decision of Louis [ ]
thus liquidate French [ ]
intellectual communit[ ]
the Huguenots. This [ ]
After the death of the [ ]
the Protestant minorit[ ]
leading thinkers such [ ]
Voltaire. By the mid[ ]
liberal clerics, lawye[ ]
Encyclopedists in urg[ ]
who were seen to be l[ ]
in 1787, thanks to ir[ ]
included Malesherbes [ ]
ary Rabaut Saint-Éti[ ]
issued an edict of tole[ ]
modest bill of civil an[ ]

Adams' illuminating v[ ]
tory of toleration; it e[ ]
mentalités, and it of[ ]
"reform from above"[ ]

Geoffrey Adams is a To[ ]
at the University of Ch[ ]
taught at Waterloo L[ ]
University), Elmira C[ ]
1962, at Concordia U[ ]
researching the civic [ ]
Dreyfus Affair.

Editions SR / 12

EDITIONS SR

Volume 12

The Huguenots and French Opinion, 1685-1787

The Enlightenment Debate on Toleration

Geoffrey Adams

Published for the Canadian Corporation for Studies in Religion/Corporation Canadienne des Sciences Religieuses by Wilfrid Laurier University Press

1991

This book has been published with the help of a grant from the Humanities and Social Sciences Federation of Canada, using funds provided by the Social Sciences and Humanities Research Council of Canada.

We acknowledge the support of the Canada Council for the Arts for our publishing program.

We acknowledge the financial support of the Government of Canada through the Book Publishing Industry Development Program for our publishing activities.

Library and Archives Canada Cataloguing in Publication

Adams, Geoffrey, 1926–

    The Huguenots and French opinion, 1685–1787 : the enlightenment debate on toleration

(Editions SR ; 12)
Includes bibliographical references and index.
ISBN 978-0-88920-217-7 (cloth)
ISBN 978-0-88920-209-2 (paper)
ISBN 978-0-88920-904-6 (e-book)

1. Huguenots – France – History. 2. Religious tolerance – France – History – 18th century. I. Canadian Corporation for Studies in Religion. II. Title. III. Series.

BX9454.2.A33 1991   272.40944   C91-095690-1

© 1991 Canadian Corporation for Studies in Religion/
      Corporation Canadienne des Sciences Religieuses

This printing 2014

Printed in Canada

Cover design by Connolly Art & Design

Cover image: *Grand Dieu qu'allois-je dire? . . . o mon Pere! mon Pere!*, courtesy of the Bibliothèque National de Paris.

The Huguenots and French Opinion, 1685–1787: The Enlightenment Debate on Toleration has been produced from a manuscript supplied in camera-ready form by the author.

for
Jack
and for
Reford and Natalie

Contents

PART ONE
THE REVOCATION IMPOSED, 1685-1715

PART TWO
THE REVOCATION ATTACKED, 1715-1760

PART THREE
THE REVOCATION UNDONE, 1760-1787

List of Illustrations

xi

Acknowledgements

Attempts to trace the social impact of ideas are bound to be at one and the same time fascinating, complex, and subtle. Those of us who were fortunate enough to study under the late Louis Gottschalk at the University of Chicago were inevitably drawn to such studies while being solemnly forewarned of the risks involved. The theme of the present work— the change in French intellectual attitudes towards the Huguenots between the Revocation of the Edict of Nantes and the Revolution and the concomitant increase in support for religious toleration—was directly inspired by Professor Gottschalk's teaching.

It was my good fortune to begin research in France while Emile-G. Léonard was in the process of completing his monumental history of Protestantism. Although he was at first rather startled that a Canadian graduate student might be interested in the fortunes of his eighteenth-century co-religionists, Professor Léonard ended up offering much useful advice and a number of helpful scholarly tips; his successor, Daniel Robert, was equally forthcoming at a later date. The custodians of the French Protestant Library in the rue des Saints-Pères were invariably courteous and supportive. Early on in my excursions to the Bibliothèque Nationale and the Archives Nationales, I came to appreciate the sympathetic interest and the extraordinary bibliographical awareness of their personnel.

My colleagues at Concordia University in Montreal have been in every way supportive. I owe a quite special debt of gratitude to the late Cyril O'Keefe, S.J., as well as to Robert Tittler and Lionel Rothkrug, who offered many valuable suggestions about structure and style. Jean-Paul Coupal helped reduce a rather bulky manuscript to more manageable dimensions while working on his doctorate. Ezio Cappadocia, a fellow-student at Chicago, now at McMaster University, provided a number of useful technical as well as textual suggestions. Gwen Holden and Jean MacDougall turned scruffy notes into polished manuscript which was in turn transformed into 'camera-ready' text by the computer wizardry of Gerald Lancaster and Andrew Francis.

I feel a particular debt of gratitude to my colleague Jack Lightstone of the Religion Department at Concordia, to William James of Queen's University and to David Jobling of Saint Andrew's College in Saskatoon for acting on my behalf with the Canadian Corporation for Studies in Religion. Michael Carley and his associates in the Canadian Federation for the Humanities provided vital moral as well as financial support. Sandra Woolfrey and the staff at Wilfrid Laurier University Press gave the manuscript a great deal of time and attention; their warm reception of the text (and of its author) was particularly welcome at the final stage of production.

Funding as well as encouragement for this radically revised and expanded version of a doctoral dissertation written at an earlier stage in my life came from Reford and Natalie MacDougall who share my passion for

France and my interest in the many battles waged there in behalf of toleration in all its forms.

Those who read the text at various stages in its development have helped me correct a number of errors of fact as well as lapses in judgement. It goes without saying that they can in no way be called to account for any flaws that remain in what follows.

Permission to reproduce the engravings used in the text has been kindly given by the Bibliothèque Nationale de Paris, except the illustration on p. 60, which is reproduced courtesy of Roger Viollet, and the illustration on p. 294, reproduced courtesy of the Société Louis XVI.

This book has been published with the help of a grant from the Canadian Federation for the Humanities, using funds provided by the Social Sciences and Humanities Research Council of Canada.

Introduction

A little over a generation ago, Lucien Febvre, who had already established his reputation as an historian of *mentalités*, urged his Protestant colleague Emile-G. Léonard to write a general study of the French Calvinist community for the public at large. There was a need for such a work, Febvre argued, in order to modify the cruelly caricatural portrait of the Huguenots—no doubt based on ignorance, prejudice and centuries of popular preaching, which still lingered on in the French popular consciousness. A citizen of the Reformed faith was still perceived as "un dur, un coriace, peu maniable...assez intraitable sur l'argent. D'un moralisme insupportable à l'esprit gaulois."[1]

Léonard took up the challenge and in 1953 produced a concise analysis, part history, part sociology, in which he pointed out that, because of differences in geography, class background and cultural inheritance (not to mention bitter internal squabbles over dogma and church structure), France's Calvinists were just as diverse in their lifestyle and ideology as their Catholic neighbours.

It would be difficult to gauge the impact of Léonard's book on the public it was designed to persuade, but it is clear that in the decades since its publication the anti-Protestant prejudice about which Febvre was so concerned has disappeared as a factor in French public life. Three centuries after the Revocation of the Edict of Nantes, France's Calvinists are fully integrated into the national life as (among other things) their high visibility in the governing Socialist party during the 1980s attests.[2]

As a scholar steeped in Renaissance culture, Lucien Febvre should have known that the anti-Protestant prejudice which he deplored in twentieth-century France had its origin as much in the impressive intellectual support it found during the early years of the *Réforme* as in the furious declamations of local priests or the blind ignorance of the mob. As early as 1542, Rabelais had identified Protestant *prédestinateurs* as lying somewhere between *abuseurs* and *imposteurs* on his scale of infamy.[3] His contemporary Montaigne was even more categorical, condemning as highly dangerous the Protestant commitment to translate the Scriptures into French and place them in the hands of the unreflecting mass; the Reformers' defence of freedom of conscience, he added, would lead sooner or later to the justification of armed rebellion and thus to the subversion of the state. Montaigne's summary of what he saw to be the tragic but inevitable consequences of Luther's heresy anticipates the indictment brought against the Protestant Reformation a century later by Bossuet:

> This incipient malady might easily degenerate into an execrable atheism because the masses, without the capacity to judge things as they really are, let themselves be swept away by the tide and are easily deceived by outward

appearances. Once they have been mandated to mock and contradict opinions
which they used to hold to with great devotion, even when it is a question
of their very salvation; once they have been induced to cast in doubt or leave
in the balance certain key articles of faith, they will throw off every single
element of their creed; from then on, they will believe nothing unless they
have reached their own personal judgment in the matter and given their own
private consent to it.[4]

Anti-Protestant prejudice in the France of the Ancien Régime was not,
then, just a question of ignorance, popular fury, or priestly incitement, as
Febvre had supposed; it was an eminently respectable attitude. Not
surprisingly, when Louis XIV revoked the Edict of Nantes by which his
ancestor Henri IV had granted the Reformed a charter of civil as well as
religious rights, the French intellectual establishment not only applauded the
decision but provided a generous series of rationalizations in support of the
attempt to liquidate heresy by decree.

The present study begins with an examination of the negative myths
concerning the Calvinists which brought the Sun King to propose, and most
contemporary French thinkers to justify, a law designed to extirpate heresy
and make France all-Catholic. In the chapters which follow, an analysis is
made of the shifts and changes in intellectual attitudes towards the
Huguenots between 1686 (when the poet Fontenelle and the military
engineer Vauban voiced oblique criticism of the Revocation) and 1787,
when the monarchy, prodded by an almost unanimous intellectual
community, accorded the Reformed a measure of civil and religious liberty.
Separate chapters are devoted to the views of such key figures as Voltaire,
Montesquieu, Prévost, and Rousseau. The attitudes of other key thinkers
such as Diderot, d'Alembert, Marmontel, Morellet, and Beaumarchais are
examined in some detail as are the views of two key members of the
Huguenot 'internal emigration-' Laurent-Angliviel de La Beaumelle and
Louis de Jaucourt. An examination is made of the sympathetic interventions
on behalf of the Calvinist cause made by members of the government
beginning with Machault d'Arnouville in the early 1750s and resumed
during the administrations of Choiseul, Turgot, Malesherbes, Necker and
Loménie de Brienne. The support given Protestant litigants caught in the
toils of the law by defence attorneys and magistrates is noted, as is the
increasingly sympathetic attitude of liberal priests and representatives of the
Jansenist constituency during the second half of the eighteenth century.

While a number of monographs has been devoted to analyzing the
attitudes of individual thinkers towards the Huguenots during the
Enlightenment (Voltaire has benefited from an understandably concentrated
attention in this regard), there have been few attempts to examine the shifts
in outlook vis-à-vis the Calvinists on the part of the French intellectual
community at large between the Revocation and the Revolution.[5] The

present work attempts to fill this gap. It does not pretend to be a history of French Calvinism in the eighteenth century nor is it an examination of the relationship between the Protestant minority and the French administration between 1685 and 1787; these matters have been well and fully treated in standard works to which the interested reader may turn.[6] Inevitably, however, some analysis of the internal evolution of the Reformed churches and of the policy decisions affecting the Huguenots reached at Versailles between 1685 and 1787 is indispensable if the changes in attitude on the part of France's intellectuals during the Enlightenment are to be seen in context.

The century of shifting opinions concerning the Reformed divides itself logically into three periods: 1) the final thirty years of Louis XIV's reign, during which the Revocation policy was given all but universal support while the Huguenots went into exile or were driven underground; 2) the first four-and-a-half decades of the reign of Louis XV when the repressive policies of the Sun King came under attack by men of Voltaire's generation while the Calvinists effected a remarkable spiritual revival; 3) the period 1760-1787, at the end of which the ministry, dominated by men who were converts to the philosophes' agenda on the toleration issue, accorded the Protestants a measure of civil and religious liberty.

1. Emile-G. Léonard, *Le protestant français* (Paris, 1953), p. 1.

2. The presence of a substantial number of Protestants in the various Socialist ministries which have governed France during the last decade clearly attests to this development. Cabinet members of Reformed background during this period include: Gaston Defferre, Georgina Dufoix, Lionel Jospin, Pierre Joxe, Louis Mexandreau, Nicole Questiaux, and Michel Rocard.

3. Rabelais, *Prologue to Pantagruel*, ed. V. L. Saulnier (Geneva, ed 1965), 1, 57 (var.).

4. Montaigne, *Essais*, ed. M. Rat (Paris, 1958), II, p. 12, p. 116.

5. Very general studies are offered in G. Bonet-Maury, *Histoire de la liberté de conscience en France depuis l'édit de Nantes jusqu'à juillet 1870* (Paris, 1900); A. Matagrin, *Histoire de la tolération religieuse* (Paris, 1905); S. T. McCloy, *The Humanitarian Movement in Eighteenth-century France* (Lexington, 1957). But there is nothing as comprehensive as Arthur Herzberg's provocative *The French Enlightenment and the Jews* (New York, 1968).

6. The best account of the spiritual evolution of the French Calvinists during the Enlightenment is given in Emile-G. Léonard, *Histoire ecclésiastique des Réformés français au XVIIIe siècle* (Paris, 1940). The complex relationship between the Huguenots and the French monarchy is examined at length in J. Dedieu, *Le rôle politique des Protestants français 1715-1794* (Paris, 1921) and *Histoire politique des Protestants français 1715-1794* (2 vols.; Paris, 1925). Good summaries of this relationship are to be found in B. C. Poland, *French Protestantism and the French Revolution* (Princeton, 1957), pp. 3-82 and in S. Mours and D. Robert, *Le Protestantisme en France du XVIIIe siècle à nos jours, 1685-1970* (Paris, 1972), pp. 11-174.

PART ONE

THE REVOCATION IMPOSED, 1685-1715

LE ROY DE FRANCE.

l'Home immortel Chef de la S.te Ligue.

Mon soleil parsa force eclaira l'heretique.
Il chassa tout d'un coup les brouillards de Calvin:
Non pas par un Zele divin.
Mais afin de cacher ma fine Politique.

Realpolitik under a mask of piety: A Protestant caricature of Louis XIV at the time of the Revocation.

CHAPTER I

The Edict of Fontainebleau:
The Rationalization of Intolerance

When Louis XIV began his personal reign in 1661, France's religious minorities were probably better off than any in Europe. The Reformed, in particular, enjoyed a large measure of civil and religious freedom derived from the Edict of Nantes promulgated by Henri IV in 1598. In 1629, when Cardinal Richelieu signed the Peace of Alais with Protestant rebels who had taken up arms against the crown, he deprived the Huguenots of the military guarantees which had been accorded them in 1598 but agreed that they should retain basic civil and religious rights.

Following his accession, Louis XIV reversed the policy of his predecessors and, urged on by the Catholic clergy, adopted a number of measures aimed at the slow extinction of French Calvinism.[1] One by one, the King rescinded the rights remaining to the Protestants after 1629 on the assumption that, by slowly reducing the margin of freedom left to them, he might persuade them to convert through self-interest. Then, in 1676, he put the ex-Huguenot, Paul Pellisson, in charge of a *Caisse des Conversions* which had been set up to reward Protestants willing to abjure their faith. Meanwhile, at a somewhat loftier level, Versailles encouraged an ecumenical dialogue between Catholic and Calvinist theologians in the hope that the Reformed would more readily convert if they could be persuaded that the gap between their own creed and that of the national church was no longer unbridgeable. Finally, and most drastically, a policy of proselytizing at gunpoint was adopted by a number of government officials, first in 1681, then again in May, 1685, when Intendant Foucault of Béarn initiated the *grande dragonnade* which swept through the major strongholds of Huguenot power in southern France.

By the 1680s, the apparent success of this multi-faceted campaign to liquidate heresy created the illusion in the King's mind that French Calvinism was indeed moribund. In the meantime, developments inside and outside France persuaded him that the moment had arrived to deliver the *coup de grâce* to the Reformed, something the Assembly of the Clergy, meeting between October 1681 and June 1682, pressed him to do.

Before he took concrete legislative action to annihilate heresy, Louis had to overcome a major moral and political dilemma: how was he to reverse the policy of his ancestor Henri IV which had evidently been designed to guarantee the Reformed a permanent place in French society? This dilemma was resolved when the *Conseil de conscience*, a consultative committee on religious affairs which the King had created in 1666, ruled in 1684 that the 'irrevocable' Edict of Nantes could in fact be rescinded.

The formalization of the King's resolve to extirpate the Calvinist heresy came with the promulgation of the Edict of Fontainebleau, given the royal signature on October 17, 1685, and ratified five days later by the Paris parlement. The preamble of the edict established the rationale for what was to follow: Henri IV had granted the Edict of Nantes merely as an interim measure "in order to be better able, as he had all along resolved, to bring back into the church those who had so casually strayed from it."[2] The vast majority of the Huguenots, the text continued, including the best and most substantial elements among them, had already been converted. Strict adherence to the new law would bring this noble task to swift and certain completion.

In addition to revoking all the rights which had earlier been granted the Huguenots, the Edict of Fontainebleau set forth measures by which all physical and spiritual traces of heresy would be erased. Calvinist churches were to be levelled, and all forms of public worship in the Reformed rite were forbidden. Huguenot pastors were summoned to abjure and declare themselves Catholic, following which they would be allowed to retain their status as doctors of theology; any minister who stayed in France without repudiating his faith would be condemned to row on the King's galleys. Calvinist schools were to be closed, and children born to Huguenot parents were henceforth to be baptized and educated in the Catholic faith.

A four-month period of grace was granted those Huguenots who had already fled France so that they might return and repossess their citizenship by declaring themselves Catholic; failure to take advantage of this amnesty, however, would result in property confiscation. Those who sought refuge abroad following the issuance of the new edict were to be severely penalized, men being subject to galley-service, women to imprisonment without reprieve. Relapsed heretics would be dealt with under what were already harsh existing statutes.

In Article XII of the Edict of Fontainebleau, which was to be the subject of conflicting interpretation for the best part of a century, Louis XIV made it clear that while the Huguenots were waiting upon God's grace to aid them in the sometimes difficult process of conversion, they would be permitted to retain their property and to engage in private commerce. By implication, this article assured the Calvinists of a limited freedom of conscience, the right to hold on to their inner convictions until they were fully persuaded of the truth of Roman doctrine.

Two other pieces of legislation passed in 1685 suggest that there was some concern in the King's mind about the civil rights of unrepentant Calvinists at the time of the Revocation. An *arrêt du conseil* signed on September 15, 1685, specified that, where Calvinists were no longer permitted to worship, they might marry in the presence of a civil magistrate named by the local intendant;[3] a royal declaration of December 11, 1685, stipulated that close relatives or neighbours of a deceased Calvinist were to report the death to the local judge, who would make appropriate burial arrangements.[4]

During and after the Revocation, supporters of the King's policy helped rationalize it by levelling a volley of charges against the Huguenots. For the pious among them, the Calvinist heresy was above all a deadly pollutant, corrupting the nation's soul; as schismatics or *"frères separés"*, the Reformed were seen to require forcible reintegration into the national church. Heresy apart, the other elements in the indictment brought against the Protestants were formidable enough.[5] Critics insisted that Protestant doctrine seemed everywhere to go hand-in-hand with republican ideas. They added that France's Calvinists had engaged in treason and subversion against the state. They suggested that the less sophisticated among the Reformed were inclined towards mindless fanaticism, while their intellectual and spiritual elites tended to be latent deists or, worse still, utterly indifferent in matters of faith. They insisted that the Huguenots were undeserving of freedom because wherever Europe's Protestants had been in the ascendancy, they had persecuted Catholics as well as other dissenters. Finally, they maintained that the Reformed stood aloof from the cultural values and ideals which made seventeenth-century France a paragon among nations.

The allegation that Huguenots were heretics was of course incontrovertible, at least from the Catholic perspective. On the other counts against them, the evidence was suggestive enough to provide their enemies with powerful polemical arguments. On the political front, it could be argued that the structure of the Reformed churches, loosely federal and based on the elective principle, had been bound sooner or later to serve as a model for the radicalization of European politics, whether in Geneva, Edinburgh or Cromwell's England.[6]

In practice, the political outlook of the Huguenots shifted in response to their acceptance or repudiation by the crown. Following the Saint Bartholomew's Day Massacre in 1572, some Calvinist apologists had advocated popular sovereignty and the establishment of republican institutions; and during the 1620s at La Rochelle, a group of Huguenot grandees had passed a resolution urging that the French constitution be modelled on that of Protestant Holland. From 1629 until the accession to the throne of Louis XIV, however, the relationship between the Huguenots and the Crown seemed almost idyllic. There were no Calvinist participants to speak of in the civil war known as the Fronde (1648-52); and the triumph of Protestant republicanism in England during the same period served only to incite France's Calvinists to make an even greater display of their devotion to the Catholic prince who governed them.[7] It should be noted, however, that during the funeral oration which he preached in 1659 for Charles I's widow, Henrietta Maria, Bossuet fulminated against the Puritans across the

Channel for loosening the bonds of obedience which had held English
society together for centuries;[8] and the Oratorian Richard Simon, echoing
this sentiment, charged that French Calvinist theologians openly and
consistently disseminated republican propaganda.[9] As though to lay such
allegations to rest, the Huguenot Elie Merlat published a *Traité sur les
pouvoirs absolus des souverains* (just two months before the Revocation) in
which he argued that disobedience in a subject is defensible only if it arises
directly out of matters binding upon Christian consciences.[10]

Following the Revocation, Huguenots in exile provided new
ammunition for the charge that France's Calvinists were latent republicans:
Pierre Jurieu found arguments for popular sovereignty both in Scripture and
in French constitutional precedent, causing his fellow refugee Pierre Bayle
to denounce his "ill-considered republican outlook."[11]

Behind the allegation of republicanism, some critics of the Protestants
saw something even more disturbing—a general antinomianism, the
senseless infatuation with *nouveautés* which Montaigne had already detected
in sixteenth-century subscribers to Calvinist doctrine.[12] Equally alarming to
other observers was *l'esprit d'indépendance*,[13] a refusal to accept higher
authority of any kind, which they saw to be an integral part of the Protestant
mentality.

The third accusation levelled against the Calvinists was that they had
engaged in treasonous activities against the state—during the sixteenth-
century wars of religion and again in the 1620s, and that their continued
presence carried with it the risk of future subversion, particularly when
France was at war with her Protestant neighbours. In some ways even more
damaging was the allegation that the Reformed had extorted the Edict of
Nantes from Henri IV by force of arms.

The published views of Jurieu in exile after the Revocation gave this
charge of subversion further credibility. Jurieu was convinced that the
survival of European Protestantism was linked to the destiny of William of
Orange, whose aim was to do battle with Louis XIV and Catholic reaction;
and the provocative tract—*L'Accomplissement des prophéties* (based on an
inspired reading of Revelations)—which Jurieu composed for the edification
of France's beleaguered Calvinists contained an unmistakable invitation to
sedition.[14]

The fourth basis upon which the Huguenots were indicted was their
alleged susceptibility to fanaticism. It was one of the central contentions of
Bossuet that, because the Protestants had been deprived of the props to faith
furnished by tradition, the Church Fathers and papal authority and because
they were as a result dependent for doctrine upon personal readings of
Scripture and the uncertain inspiration of individual consciences, they were
bound sooner or later to lapse into all kinds of extravagant heresies.[15]
Following the Revocation, which deprived them of properly instructed

pastors, the less sophisticated elements in the Huguenot population were bound to give Bossuet's allegation new credibility.

The fifth charge levelled at the Calvinists, that they were latent deists, seems at first glance to be at variance with the accusation that they were capable of fanaticism. How could the Huguenots be at one and the same time mindless zealots and practitioners of rational religion? The answer lies in a close analysis of the theological training of the Reformed pastorate. Before the Revocation, candidates for the ministry were often given a "liberal" version of Calvinist doctrine at the Reformed seminaries at Saumur and Sedan. Following the death of Louis XIV, Antoine Court, the orchestrator of the underground Calvinist revival which began during the Regency, saw to it that candidates for this illegal pastorate were given a sophisticated intellectual preparation in Lausanne, where the faculty held advanced theological views. Paradoxically, the intellectual cultivation which Court encouraged in those who were preparing to preach the gospel back in France exposed these men to the charge that they were just as detached from Calvinist orthodoxy as those of their co-religionists who had embraced apocalyptic versions of the Gospel following the Revocation[16]

The sixth, and in many ways the most vexing, of all the arguments used to justify the proscription of the Huguenots was that they were themselves intolerant. Certainly, the evidence that leading Calvinist theologians had sanctioned intolerance was not hard to find. Calvin's own *Defensio orthodoxae fidei* (1554) was an apologia for the most severe punishment of dissenters;[17] and his collaborator, Théodore de Bèze, had denounced as diabolical the plea of the liberal Sebastian Castellio for the toleration of all but atheists.[18] In the age of Louis XIV, Jurieu's fulminations against deviant members of his own church both in France before the Revocation and later in Rotterdam were proof enough that the repressive urge was still strong within the Reformed community, and Bossuet could take pleasure in pointing out that France's Protestants were presumptuous to demand toleration from Catholic regimes when their co-religionists elsewhere in Europe denied fundamental rights to non-conformists.

The situation of England's (and more particularly Ireland's) Catholics during the Revocation crisis and throughout the eighteenth century provided an irresistible propaganda opportunity for defenders of the Edict of Fontainebleau. The Huguenots, such apologists pointed out, had little or no chance of making a convincing case for their own emancipation as long as British Protestants were trying to extirpate Catholicism by ruthless economic as well as political means.[19]

Cases of generalized Protestant repression of Catholics were to identify and exploit; instances of Calvinist authorities putting non-conformists to death could also be cited as evidence that there was Protestant as well as Catholic intolerance in post-Reformation Europe. Bossuet (among others) pointed to the tragic fate of Michael Servet, burned at the stake in Calvin's Geneva for refusing to recant his anti-Trinitarianism. The Bishop of Meaux also noted that, with the exception of such marginal sects as the Anabaptists and Socinians, Christians of all persuasions had consistently practiced what they felt was righteous intolerance.[20]

Stung by such criticism and convinced that there was indeed bigotry and intolerance inside his own communion, Pierre Bayle tried in vain to persuade his fellow Huguenots to strengthen the case for their toleration by denouncing Calvin's treatment of Servet and thereby championing the rights of conscience (including *conscience erronnée*) which had been implicit from the beginning in the teachings of the sixteenth-century Reformers.[21] The seventh charge levelled against the Calvinists had to do with what we might now call mentalities. Their critics argued that, by leaving the resolution of serious moral dilemmas to the judgment of private consciences, the Reformed had opened the way to the erosion of all ethical standards; in implicitly denying that there were any absolute norms of behaviour, they encouraged licentiousness of all kinds, including divorce and the breakdown of the family. At the same time, paradoxically, *le petit troupeau* as the Huguenot minority sometimes defined itself, was condemned for adopting a self-righteous outlook, an attitude of moral superiority which alienated it from the majority.[22]

Finally, there was the prejudice against the Huguenots engendered by their seemingly disproportionate wealth. Like many minorities which have been formally excluded from public life, the Reformed often sought compensation for this discrimination by committing themselves vigorously to the world of private business. As recent scholars have established, the thousands of Reformed who remained in France after 1685 made a vital contribution to the commercial and financial boom of the eighteenth century.[23] The result, in terms of public attitudes, was mixed: intellectuals interested in the nation's economic life applauded the Calvinists for their industriousness; Catholic neighbours and in-laws (as well as orthodox apologists of the Revocation system), expressed their open hostility as evidence of Protestant prosperity kept surfacing.

The many grave accusations levelled against them in the late seventeenth century continued to frustrate and inhibit the Huguenots as they pressed the case for their re-admission into French society in the century following the Revocation. Paradoxically, some of their most sympathetic supporters among the philosophes repeated some of these charges against the Reformed, which may well explain the cautious nature of the campaign for Huguenot toleration which they supported through the first half of the eighteenth century. Leading thinkers of the Age of Reason were ready enough to denounce legislation which had increased the power and the pretension of the priesthood and visited severe economic and cultural hardship on France; but their sympathy for the victims of the Revocation was tempered by the conviction that some at least of the charges levelled against the Calvinists were well founded.

---

1. Writers during the Enlightenment sometimes argued that the Revocation decision came as a result of appeals to the King's piety by madame de Maintenon and the Jesuit Père La Chaize, appeals which had a special impact because of the alleged conversion experiences which Louis XIV underwent in 1676 and 1680. V. Voltaire, *Le Siècle de Louis XIV*, ed. Adam (2 vols.; Paris, 1966), II, p. 324. Until recently, Protestant historians have tended to agree with this interpretation. V. E.O. Douen, *La Révocation de l'édit de Nantes à Paris* (3 vols.; Paris, 1894), I, pp. 3-4. Catholic scholars, on the other hand, have insisted that the King's principal aim was political, the elimination of a latently republican sect which threatened France's unity. V. J. Orcibal, *Louis XIV et les Protestants* (Paris, 1951), p. 94.

   During the last generation, leading French Calvinist scholars have come to accept the view that the Revocation was politically motivated. V. E. Labrousse, *"Une foi, une loi, un roi?" La révocation de l'édit de Nantes* (Paris, 1985), p. 107; J. Garrisson, *L'Edit de Nantes et sa révocation* (Paris, 1985), pp. 7-8. The 'ecumenical' mood in which Protestant as well as Catholic scholars are now able to reflect upon all aspects of the Revocation was dramatically demonstrated during a colloquium held on the premises of the French Protestant Library in Paris during the tercentennial observation of the Edict of Fontainebleau in October 1985. The views of the Reformed were represented at that colloquium by (among others) Elisabeth Labrousse, Pierre Chaunu, Pierre Bolle, Philippe Joutard and Janine Garrisson. Catholic scholars present included Jean Delumeau and Jacques LeBrun. During this intellectual exchange, Chaunu even suggested that Louis XIV may have been too ill during the fall of 1685 to make a rational judgment concerning the status of the Reformed! V. P. Chaunu, "La décision royale?: un système de la Révocation," "La Révocation de l'édit de Nantes et le protestantisme français en 1685," *Actes du colloque de Paris* (15-19 October 1985), *SHPF* (Paris, 1986), pp. 13-29.

   No doubt also influenced by this 'ecumenical' outlook, Bernard Dompnier has argued that there was a great deal of peaceful co-existence between Catholics and Huguenots in the pre-Revocation period, including frequent mixed marriages. B. Dompnier, *Le venin de l'hérésie. Image du protestantisme et combat catholique au XVIIe siècle* (Paris, 1985), pp. 137-68. Jean Queniart, another modern Catholic student of the Revocation, has pointed out that men and women of the two conflicting faiths were forced by circumstances to dwell together and frequently did so peaceably; where there was tension, it tended to come from members of Catholic religious orders. Jean Queniart, *La Révocation de l'Edit de Nantes. Protestants et catholiques en France de 1598 à 1685* (Paris, 1985), p. 75.

   An excellent summary of developments affecting the French Reformed community between the Edict of Nantes and its Revocation is offered in Elisabeth Labrousse, "Calvinism in France, 1598-1685," in Menna Prestwich (ed.),

International Calvinism, 1541-1715 (Oxford, 1986), pp. 285-314. Mme Labrousse includes in this summary an analysis of the internal evolution of Huguenot society, a study of the shifting relationships between Calvinists and Catholics as well as a review of changes in attitude towards the Reformed on the part of church and state.

2. *Edit du Roy, du mois d'octobre 1685, portant révocation de celui de Nantes; et défenses de faire aucun exercice public de la R.P.R. dans son Royaume*, L. Pilatte (ed.), *Edits, Déclarations et Arrests concernans la Religion P. Reformée 1661-1751* (Paris, 1885), p. 240.

3. *Arrest du Conseil, du 15 septembre 1685, concernant les Baptêmes et les Mariages de ceux de la R.P.R.*, ibid., p. 236.

4. *Déclaration du Roy, du 11 décembre 1685 pour établir la preuve du jour de decez de ceux de la R.P.R.*, ibid., pp. 257-59.

5. Elisabeth Perry has analyzed the tendency of seventeenth-century Catholic writers to shift the focus of their attack on French Calvinism from the theological and doctrinal to the political ground. V. E.I. Perry, *From Theology to History. French Religious Controversy and the Revocation of the Edict of Nantes* (The Hague, 1973), pp. 7-8, 39, 76-82, 196-200.

6. C. Nicolet in *L'idée républicaine en France* (Paris, 1982), pp. 49-51, rejects the view that French Protestantism played a role in the evolution of republican ideology but notes that the myth of Huguenot republicanism, invented by seventeenth-century critics of Calvinist toleration, was readily adopted by later Protestant thinkers such as Madame de Staël and Benjamin Constant and that it held sway for much of the nineteenth century among both Reformed and liberal writers.

7. The traumatic impact of the English Civil War on French Calvinist as well as Catholic opinion is analyzed in J.-M. Goulemot, *Discours, histoire et révolutions* (Paris, 1975). It is clear from an examination of Reformed sermons during this period that the Huguenots were intent on distancing themselves from the radical political ideas associated with their Protestant cousins across the Channel. The many twists and turns in Huguenot political theory between 1534 and 1715 are examined in Myriam Yardeni, "French Calvinist Political Thought, 1534-1715," in Prestwick, *International Calvinism*, pp. 315-37. Yardeni's overall conclusion is that "French Calvinist thought was a literature of combat, a literature concerned with the right to exist, even in the fifty years of false illusions between 1630 and 1680. From this there stemmed its pragmatism and its capacity for rapid adaptation to novel situations" (p. 335).

8. Bossuet, *Oraison funèbre de Henriette Marie de France, reine de la Grande Bretagne, le 16 novembre 1669*, in *Oraisons funèbres* (3d ed.; Paris, 1680), p. 52.

9. Richard Simon to Fremont d'Ablancourt, c. 1680, in *Lettres choisies de M. Simon, où l'on trouve un grand nombre de faits Ancecdotes de Littérature* (3 vols.; Amsterdam, 1730), I, p. 68.

10 Elie Merlat, *Traité du pouvoir absolu des souverains pour servir d'instruction, de consolation et d'apologie aux Eglises réformées de France qui sont affligées* (Cologne, 1685).

11. Pierre Bayle, *Avis important aux refugiés sur leur prochain retour en France, donné pour estrennes à l'un d'eux en 1690* (Amsterdam, 1690).

12. Montaigne, *Essais*, ed. M. Rat (Paris, 1958), II, 12. p. 119.

13. The charge that the Reformed were obssesively preoccupied by '*l'esprit d'independance*' would be taken up up by one of Bossuet's polemical successors in mid-eighteenth century France. V. Abbé Jean Novi de Caveirac, *Mémoire politico-critique où l'on examine s'il est de l'intérêt de l'Eglise et de l'Etat d'établir pour les Calvinistes du Royaume une nouvelle forme de se marier* (n.p., 1756), p. 9.

14. Pierre Jurieu, *L'Accomplissement des prophéties, ou la Déliverance prochaine de l'Eglise* (2 vols.; Rotterdam, 1686).

15. For an exhaustive treatment of Bossuet's critique of Protestant theology, v. Alfred Rebelliau, *Bossuet, historien du protestantisme. Etude sur "l'Histoire des Variations" et sur la controverse entre les Protestants et les Catholiques au dix-septième siècle* (Paris, 1891).

16. For a thorough understanding of the influence of 'philosophic' ideas on the underground pastorate, v. J. Woodbridge, "L'influence des philosophes français sur les pasteurs réformés du Languedoc pendant la seconde moitié du XVIIIe siècle" (typewritten thesis, Toulouse, 1969).

17. John Calvin, *Defensio orthodoxae fidei de sacra Trinitate contra prodigiosos errores Michaelis Serveti* (Geneva, 1554).

18. Theodore Beza, *De Haereticis a civili magistratu puniendis libellus, adversus Martini Belli farraginem et novorum academicorum sectam* (Geneva, 1554).

19. How, it was asked, could the Huguenots make a convincing case for their own rights when their Protestant cousins across the Channel were resorting to cruel economic as well as political means to extirpate Catholicism. This question is fully explored in Bernard Cottret, *La Glorieuse Révolution d'Angleterre, 1688* (Paris, 1988), pp. 121-64.

   An even bolder parallel has been drawn by the modern French Protestant scholar Pierre Chaunu who compares the suffering undergone by the Huguenots in their combat for religious freedom against Louis XIV with those experienced by Catholics of the Vendée against Jacobin radicals during the 1790s: "Camisards et Vendéens, même cause, même courage, même combat," P. Chaunu, "La décision royale," p. 19.

20. J.-B. Bossuet, *Oeuvres* (43 vols.; Versailles, 1815-19), XX, p. 64

21. Two modern scholars have celebrated Bayle's contribution to the struggle for toleration: W. Rex, *Essays on Pierre Bayle and Religious Controversy* (The Hague, 1965) and E. Labrousse, *Pierre Bayle* (2 vols.; The Hague, 1963-64).

22. V. E. Labrousse, "*Une foi, une loi, un roi?*" *La révocation de l'édit de Nantes* (Paris, 1985), p. 53, for a discussion of this paradox.

23. The involvement of the Reformed in French economic life during the Revocation period is examined in S.C. Scoville, *The Persecution of Huguenots and French Economic Development 1680-1720* (Berkeley, 1960). The Huguenots' role in eighteenth-century financial developments is examined in detail in H. Lüthy, *La Banque protestante en France de la Révocation de l'Edit de Nantes à la Révolution* (2 vols.; Paris, 1959-61). Arie Theodorus Van Deursen has examined in depth the ways in which the Huguenots who remained in France after 1685 evaded the laws which precluded them from entering the professions or engaging in commercial or

industrial activity. His conclusion is that Versailles ended up admitting defeat in
these areas and adopted a pragmatic attitude at variance with official policy. The
result was that there were Protestant *maîtres d'écoles*, doctors, lawyers, and officers
in the armed forces as well as in private enterprise of all kinds through the middle
years of the eighteenth century. V. Arie Theodorus Van Deursen, *Professions et
métiers interdits. Un aspect de l'histoire de la révocation de l'édit de Nantes*
(Groningen, 1960).

Forcing consciences in the Sun King's France: A victim's view of the dragonnades.

CHAPTER II

Thunderous Applause, Discreet Dissent:
The Intellectual Reaction to the Revocation

With a very few exceptions, all that was distinguished in the intellectual and spiritual leadership of France—academicians and writers in or near the court, painters, sculptors, and engravers, orthodox and dissident Catholics—joined in celebrating the King's decision to revoke the Edict of Nantes.[1] The reasons for this enthusiasm are not hard to uncover. France's leading thinkers and artists had been conditioned for more than a generation to respect the canons of order, hierarchy, and unity in politics as well as in art. The devout among them had been led to expect the imminent triumph of the Counter-Reformation and the integration of the Huguenots into the Gallican church. The elimination of heresy was thus calculated to satisfy what were felt to be political and aesthetic as well as spiritual needs. The classical sense of restraint led a few of those who first welcomed the Revocation to feel some revulsion at the manner in which the new legislation was implemented; there was an all but unanimous conviction among the nation's leading minds that the King's decision to restore France's unity by decree was a noble one.

Because of its close association with the crown, the Académie française was no doubt bound to become involved in the campaign to uproot and destroy heresy. Paying tribute to the memory of Louis IX in an address to his colleagues in 1681, the Academy's secretary, Jean Doujat, compared the proselytizing methods of the medieval saint-king with those being used by Louis XIV, all to the latter's advantage. His colleagues responded by making their monarch's zeal for the faith the subject of their 1683 award for poetry. Two contestants won the contest ex aequo: Bernard de La Monnaye, who praised Louis for having followed the lead of Clovis and Charlemagne in turning from victory in the field to the higher task of consecrating France to Catholicism, and Charles Du Perier, who ended his tribute to the King's piety with verse containing what was soon to become one of the leitmotives of the reign:

> Et réunis enfin sous une même foi,
> N'ayons qu'un Dieu, qu'un cœur, qu'une Eglise, qu'un Roi.[2]

From 1685 until the end of the century, the Académie offered prizes for works celebrating the eradication of heresy. Typical of the prose which resulted was the praise heaped upon Louis XIV by the abbé Paul Tallement early in 1687. The "noble impatience" of the king had already secured the conversion of some 2 000 000 souls, Tallement trumpeted: by the sheer force of his will, Louis had purged spiritual dissidence forever from his kingdom.[3]

Two of the most distinguished members of the Académie, Jean de La Fontaine and Jean de La Bruyère, applauded the Revocation in works which reached the literate public at large. In the epistle which he wrote in the autumn of 1686 to celebrate the recovery of Louis XIV from a minor operation, La Fontaine developed the by then familiar theme of the warrior-king who, having won his laurels on the battlefield, had achieved with a single stroke of statesmanship the civil peace and order which had eluded his predecessors:

> Il veut vaincre l'erreur: cet ouvrage s'avance,
> Il est fait: et le fruit de ces succès divers
> Est que la vérité règne en toute la France
> Et la France en tout l'univers.[4]

The moralist La Bruyère made his enthusiasm for the Revocation public in a brief passage which appeared in the first edition of his immensely popular *Caractères*, published in 1688. The decision of 1685 was the logical climax to the long, sustained campaign to eradicate heresy which had been opened by Richelieu in the 1620s, he wrote; Louis XIV had brought to the enterprise all the patience and intelligence needed to root out "a religion not only false in itself but subversive of all established authority."[5]

A third well-known academician, Roger de Bussy-Rabutin, who had been exiled from the court shortly after his election to the Académie because of some offensive comments which he made about members of the royal family, nevertheless went out of his way to praise the King's anti-Calvinist policy. Until the nation assimilated the Huguenots and recovered her spiritual unity, Bussy reasoned, she could not hope to fulfil her historic role. Fortunately, Louis XIV had realized that the violence used against the Huguenots in the sixteenth century had misfired by making martyrs of Calvin's partisans, allowing them to expand until they numbered some 2 000 000 souls. The subtler undermining of Protestant strength which had begun with the arrival of Louis XIV on the throne had been admirably organized. The Revocation would surely administer the *coup de grâce* to this alien and subversive minority.[6]

Intellectuals in or near the court were at least as generous as academicians in their support for the King's anti-Calvinist policy. Writing to her cousin Bussy-Rabutin, the inveterate letter-writer Madame de Sévigné expressed unreserved enthusiasm for the King's decision: "Everything about it is admirable. No monarch past or future can possibly outdo it." She went on to report that the gifted Jesuit Bourdaloue was off to the south of France to reinforce the faith of masses of former heretics who had been transformed into instant Catholics by intimidation. "Our dragoons have been excellent missionaries up till now. The preachers who are now being despatched to the scene will complete the task."[7] In advance of the arrival of Bourdaloue in Languedoc, the marquise wrote to the president of the local parlement, urging him to support the proselytizing efforts which would soon be under way. Then, turning her attention to another front in the war against heresy, she wrote a letter of encouragement to her son-in-law, the lieutenant-general of Provence, who was about to set out on an expedition in Dauphiné "to disperse and punish bands of wretched Huguenots who crawl forth from their hovels to pray to God and then disappear like shadows as soon as they see that the authorities are hunting them down and are anxious to exterminate them."[8]

A second prominent figure at court, Mademoiselle de Scudéry, had no difficulty in subscribing to the Jesuit casuistry which allowed so many members of her generation to support the Revocation with an easy conscience. In a letter to a friend, she suggested that the King had already achieved a miracle in his combat against France's heretics, and added: "The compulsion by which he is bringing them back into the church will be salutary for them in the long run. At the very least, it will save their children, who will be brought up in the true faith."[9]

Like their counterparts in the world of letters, France's leading artists exploited the theme of the nation's new-found religious unity partly out of genuine enthusiasm and partly out of a desire to enhance their status at court.[10] Charles Lebrun, who had exercised a virtual dictatorship over the Academy of Painting and Sculpture for a generation, was particularly happy to find an occasion to flatter the king because, since the death in 1681 of his patron Colbert and the ascendancy at court of Louvois, he had fallen into a semi-eclipse. The production of a successful canvas centered on the Revocation provided the perfect occasion to capture the King's eye and to restore his credit at court. The opportunity offered itself when the Oratorians asked Lebrun to furnish a canvas for the ceremonies which they were planning in celebration of the King's recovery from a minor operation in February 1687. The painting which resulted—*L'Eglise victorieuse de L'Hérésie*, was heavy with allegorical meaning. The church, represented by a triumphant female figure carrying a shield on which is emblazoned the portrait of the Sun King, dominates the canvas. Her auxiliaries, Truth and Faith, stand beside her, proud to have shared in her victory. Heresy, a monstrous creature whose forehead crawls with serpents, stares out despairingly at the viewer.

Guy-Louis Vernansal, one of Lebrun's most promising students, managed to exploit the occasion of the Revocation to even greater personal advantage. Membership in the Academy of Painting and Sculpture was accorded him in September 1687, in recognition of a mural devoted to the Revocation which he created for the Salon d'Apollon at Versailles. Louis

XIV dominates the painting, surrounded by Religion, Charity, and Justice who are intent upon overseeing the peaceable execution of his will. Above him stands a venerable matron carrying the host, symbolizing the church. Truth hovers over the scene, borne serenely upon a cloud. Fraud, Hypocrisy, and Heresy cringe, defeated, in the shadows below.

A third member of the artistic establishment, Sebastien Le Clerc, produced a widely circulated engraving depicting the demolition, in November 1685, of the Calvinist church at Charenton, near Paris. Perhaps the most impressive artistic tribute to the Revocation was a splendid bronze fashioned by Antoine Coysevox, a member of the Academy of Painting and Sculpture. Early in 1687, the municipality of Paris commissioned Coysevox to create a statue for the courtyard of the Hôtel de Ville. Coysevox represented Louis XIV in the trappings of a Roman emperor, sword in hand, about to slay two monstrous incarnations of heresy, one sporting bat-wings, the other possessed of hideously contorted features; texts of the major Protestant theologians lie scattered about the statue's base.

The hostility of the First Estate towards the Huguenots was of course as categorical as it was predictable. It is clearly and bluntly expressed in the correspondence between Bishop Bossuet and Jean Rou, a Calvinist lawyer whom he had vainly attempted to convert and who had fled to Holland in 1680 just as the government's anti-Protestant campaign began to intensify. In mid-October 1685, Bossuet wrote to Rou urging him to return to France following the lead of his wife who had turned Catholic in compliance with the royal will.[11] In a bitterly sarcastic reply, Rou thanked Bossuet whose categorical defence of religious repression long before 1685 had given him fair warning of the hazards in store for Huguenots who remained in France after the Revocation.[12] Counter-attacking, Bossuet took up a remark by Rou that true Christians never persecute and asked:

> Would you deny, in face of the express opinion of your own theologians in the matter, that the Republic of Geneva not only could have but was morally bound to condemn Servet to the flames for having denied the divinity of the Son of God?[13]

Quite apart from a natural impulse to prohibit such outrageous doctrines, Bossuet added, Christians were justified in urging the state to punish men such as Servet on the ground that they preached social subversion. Rou countered by suggesting that if his fellow Calvinists were treated as suspect by the civil authority in France it was thanks to the sustained campaign of vilification mounted against them by the French Catholic clergy.[14] Bossuet made no response to this letter, although he was specifically challenged to do so by Rou, who suggested that "this silence...will be looked upon as confession on your part that you have nothing to reply."[15]

Bossuet had in the meantime made his enthusiasm for the Revocation public in the course of the funeral oration for Chancellor Le Tellier which he preached in January 1686. Abandoning the language of ecumenical reconciliation with which he had attempted to win over Calvinist scholars in an earlier day, Bossuet let his words reflect the jubilation which he felt at the thought that France had retrieved her spiritual unity. The Church Fathers, he reminded his audience, had left moving chronicles of the heroic age of early Christianity; but, unlike their seventeenth-century successors, they "had not witnessed, as you have witnessed, the sudden dissolution of an inveterate heresy, the return to the fold of so many lost sheep that our churches are too small to hold them and finally the defection of false pastors who are ready to abandon those whom they have misled without even waiting for the order to do so." In a particularly rhapsodical passage, Bossuet urged his colleagues to make a record of the present King's pious acts for the edification of later generations of Christians:

> Let us salute this new Constantine, this new Theodore, this new Marcian, this new Charlemagne, as six hundred and thirty churchmen saluted his predecessors at the Council of Chalcedonia.[16]

Rather less noble than the bishop's eagerness to do polemical battle with Calvinist theologians was his willingness to exploit the penal legislation directed against suspect 'new Catholics' after 1685. Bossuet urged the strict application of a law which decreed the confiscation of the properties of Calvinists fleeing France and its appropriation to Catholic missionary work;[17] he sanctioned the abduction and confinement of children to insure their instruction in the Catholic faith as well as the arrest of stubborn Huguenot parishioners who refused to give even an external indication of their Catholicism;[18] finally, in response to an attack from Jurieu, Bossuet went so far as to justify the use of the military to help effect conversion, insisting that the horrors visited upon Calvinist laymen during the notorious dragonnades of the late 1680s were as nothing compared with similar Protestant excesses.[19]

Looking back on the late seventeenth century from the perspective of a less theologically partisan age, we may wonder why certain marginal figures within the Catholic communion, the Jansenists in particular, did not see in the King's attack on Calvinism an alarming precedent for their own repression and why, quite apart from such a self-interested motive, they expressed so little compassion for Christians whose religious freedom had been so abruptly extinguished. Superficially at least, the Jansenists seemed logical allies of the Huguenots because of their seemingly parallel views concerning such issues as grace and predestination. But, as early as the 1670s, out of an instinct for self-preservation stronger than charity, they had chosen to demonstrate their orthodoxy by joining the polemical assault on the Huguenots orchestrated by Bossuet. The Jansenist Antoine Arnauld, who had fled to Holland to avoid prosecution by the authorities for his heterodox opinions, had no difficulty in rationalizing the Revocation, for which he found a clear precedent in Saint Augustine's justification of stern measures against the Donatists.[20]

After 1685, the Jansenists plunged into the campaign to ensure the eradication of French Protestantism in order that it should not become an exclusive Jesuit enterprise. Men such as Arnauld and his colleague Pierre Nicole rejected the Jesuit view that it was sufficient to eliminate all physical traces of heresy and to secure from suspected heretics an external submission to the Catholic sacraments. In this insistence that former heretics make a conscious decision to become Catholics, the Jansenists were in effect urging that the Huguenots be given some freedom of conscience. As we shall later see, these scruples helped to bring a theoretical margin of spiritual freedom to the Calvinists in the Declaration of 1698 which was promulgated while the pro-Jansenist Louis-Antoine de Noailles was archbishop of Paris.[21]

The Oratorian Richard Simon, whose 'advanced' biblical criticism alarmed defenders of Catholic orthodoxy, showed no more compassion towards the Huguenots than did his Jansenist contemporaries. One might suppose that a man who stood at the outer edge of Christian scholarly exploration would tend towards tolerance at a time when new exegetical methods seemed to offer the possibility of a meeting of minds between Catholic and Protestant theologians.

The Oratorian scholar made his position concerning the Huguenots crystal clear in a letter written to his Calvinist friend Frémont d'Ablancourt before the Revocation. Heretics lived in France by the King's grace, not by right, he insisted; but when Cardinal Richelieu, trying nevertheless to conciliate them, had sponsored an ecumenical dialogue in which the Genevan version of the Scripture would serve as text and in which all disputes concerning the authority of the Fathers, tradition, and the Councils would be left aside, they had replied by adopting a theological position closer to that of Arminius and Socinus than to that of Calvin and Beza and by flaunting their republicanism.[22]

On March 17, 1687, identifying himself as a 'new Convert,' Simon penned an anonymous reply to the *Lettres pastorales* which were being sent into France by Jurieu in an attempt to sustain the faith of the Huguenots. By inciting his co-religionists to rebel, Jurieu must share the blame for whatever measures the authorities felt obliged to use to keep the peace: "All your speeches and pamphlets tend towards the restoration of the Gospel in France by force of arms...You give men who are no better than rebels the quality of martyrs for Christ."[23] Some of Jurieu's tracts, Simon continued, openly attacked monarchical authority and advocated popular sovereignty while others read like the fantasies of Quakers and fanatics.

Of all the spiritual leaders of French Catholicism in 1685, the gentle aristocratic Fénelon seemed to the Huguenots their most likely friend in adversity. Surely the dove-like archbishop of Cambrai, who was so soon himself to feel the fury of the hawkish Bossuet for flirting with Quietism, was bound by temperament to favour tolerance and compassion over constraint and repression? In fact, the legend of a tolerant Fénelon was for a long time sustained by French Protestant historians[24] before being definitively exploded by the Calvinist historian Douen in 1872.[25] Both in his priestly activities and in his writings, Douen concluded, Fénelon amply demonstrated that he shared the intolerant and repressive instincts of his age. As director of the *Maison des Nouvelles Catholiques* between 1678 and 1688, he was an accomplice in the abduction and forcible conversion of young Calvinist girls; in 1686, he recommended deportation and the taking of hostages as appropriate means of inducing conversion among recalcitrant heretics; and in notes published posthumously, Fénelon indicted the Reformers as the originators of a series of political as well as spiritual catastrophes: "What good has the so-called Protestant reform achieved? It has produced only scandal, disorder, uncertainty of mind, disputatiousness, religious indifference under the guise of mutual tolerance, and, finally, outright irreligion throughout most of northern Europe."[26]

The tiny band of people who viewed the Revocation as a moral or political error knew that open criticism of the King's religious policy was out of the question.[27] Louis XIV was at the height of his power in 1685, determined to use the newly proclaimed spiritual unity of his kingdom as a weapon in the larger campaign to impose French hegemony in Europe. Nevertheless, the poet-essayist Fontenelle ventured an oblique but clearly satirical reference to the Revocation in an anonymous letter published abroad while the military engineer Vauban and the intendant of Languedoc, Henri d'Aguesseau, pleaded privately with the king to modify or rescind the Edict of Fontainebleau.

In the fall of 1684, Fontenelle forwarded to Pierre Bayle, editor of the *Nouvelles de la République des Lettres*, what purported to be a letter recently received from a European travelling in Borneo.[28] At first reading, the letter dealt with the peculiar politics of Borneo, where tradition had it that only women could mount the throne. During the reign of the recently-deceased Mliséo (an anagram for Solime which, in turn, for those in the know, unravelled itself as Jerusalem), all had been unity and harmony, the correspondent reported; but instability had followed Mliséo's death, when rival claims to her domain were put forward by Mréo (Rome) and Eénegu (Genève). At first universally recognized and respected, Mréo had subsequently upset some of her subjects by introducing startling innovations in the island's rituals. Her chief ministers had been forced to turn themselves into eunuchs; magicians in her employ, by transforming bread into an immaterial and thus inedible substance, had caused a serious shortage in that vital staple; and Mréo had further alienated many Borneans by requiring that they pay obeisance to the embalmed bodies of her favourites. These and other extravagances, the description of which allowed Fontenelle to satirize a number of Catholic practices, had prepared the natives to look favourably upon the pretensions of Eénegu, who had thereupon reasserted her claim to the throne, promising if successful to do away with of Mréo's innovations.

Like any child in the direct line of descent, Eénegu had all the obvious physical characteristics of Mliséo, the correspondent pursued. Mréo, however, held one trump card—the dignitaries who attested to the legitimacy of royal offspring were ready to swear that they had been present at her birth, a service which they denied her rival. Thus although Eénegu might resemble in every respect the woman whose succession she claimed, evidence of direct lineage could not be officially authenticated. Not surprisingly in the circumstances, the contest for the succession had degenerated into armed conflict. Recently, the traveller reported, the tide had turned in favour of Mréo, whose troops had surprised a large number of Eénegu's soldiers and had forced from them a formal change of loyalty.[29]

Not seeing that his fellow-writer was denouncing the dragonnades in this passage and, beyond it, the Revocation policy as a whole, the Calvinist editor-in-exile published the letter from Borneo above Fontenelle's signature in the January 1686, issue of his *Nouvelles*. A remorseful Bayle explained this naive editorial lapse two decades later:

> I was completely unaware of the hidden meaning of the letter from Borneo which I published in my *République des Lettres*. No one in this part of the world, not even M. Jurieu or his wife, guessed at its real meaning. We only learned the full purport of the letter when M. Basnage and other refugees informed us later.[30]

However oblique, Fontenelle's criticism of the Sun King's religious policy was bound sooner or later to give offence; his enemies among the *dévots* appear to have used the Borneo letter against him twenty years later when, we are told, he was saved from a sojourn in the Bastille only after the intervention of powerful protectors at court.[31]

Meanwhile, towards the end of 1686, the year in which his letter from Borneo appeared, Fontenelle published his *Histoire des oracles*, inspired by a study of the pagan oracles written by the Dutch Anabaptist Van Dale who had argued that the techniques used by the Roman priesthood closely resembled those of the pre-Christian pagans.[32] The favourable review which was accorded the *Histoires des oracles* in the *Nouvelles de la République des Lettres* must have caused Fontenelle some concern.[33]

In these circumstances, Fontenelle welcomed the opportunity to demonstrate his spiritual conformity offered to him late in 1687 by his former Jesuit teacher, Père Lejay. Lejay had been assigned the task of decorating the gallery in the Collège Louis-le-Grand in which his colleague Père Quartier was to deliver a panegyric on the Revocation. He had conceived a number of allegories in Latin verse on the subject and wondered whether the author of the *Histoire des oracles*, so deft at turning erudite Latin into spirited French, would not find in translating these pious couplets the perfect occasion for covering himself with the authorities.

Lejay had exhausted the rich resources of a baroque inspiration in developing the ten allegorical conceits which would serve as background to the tribute offered to the King by Quartier. In one of these poems, Lejay had Louis XIV, captain of a troubled ship of state, save the vessel by casting off excess cargo; in a second, the Sun King, all-radiance, melts heresy away; in a third, slayer of the Hydra, he redeems the faithful from a multiple threat; in yet another, as stern shepherd, Louis directs watchdogs towards his erring flock, not to attack them, but rather to shield them from rapacious wolves.[34] By translating these pathetic couplets, Fontenelle paid the high cost of intellectual insurance levied on artists in the age of Louis XIV. Years later, he confided to the abbé Trublet that the outrageous verses of Père Lejay which he had agreed to render into French were not worth the compliment of translation, adding: "Let us by all means forget them. Nowadays I am very ashamed of having written them."[35]

Less oblique than the criticism of the Revocation contained in Fontenelle's letter from Borneo were the comments of two highly placed administrators who knew the confessionally mixed nature of French society at first hand. As intendant of Languedoc, the province with the largest Calvinist minority, Henri d'Aguesseau anticipated the coming of the Revocation with a mixture of horror and helplessness. Distressed at the prospect of having to participate in forcible conversions, he urged the Calvinists of Languedoc in 1684 to join the national church in order to save themselves from what was soon to come. His son tells us that the intendant felt honour-bound to resign in protest at the promulgation of the Edict of Fontainebleau.[36]

After returning to Versailles from Languedoc, d'Aguesseau submitted a memorandum to his superiors early in 1686 setting forth his continuing preference for peaceful reunion and his feeling that methods of force would be dangerously counter-productive with the Huguenots: "There is only one real problem which is genuinely to persuade them. All the rest is not conversion but a matter of purely external form. What do we do, then? Teach them, edify them, subject them to genuine instruction in the faith."[37]

By contrast with the solutions to the Protestant question offered by d'Aguesseau, those proposed by the military engineer Vauban were straightforward and simple—the annulment of the Revocation and the restoration of the generous bill of rights given to the Calvinists by Henri IV. Vauban's reactions were above all influenced by his awareness of the serious damage done the French military establishment by the Revocation. As *commissaire des bâtiments du roi*, Vauban had encountered Calvinists committed to prison for attempting to escape the country and talked to Huguenots chained to the King's galleys at Brest.

Vauban made a first vain appeal against the Revocation policy to his superior, War Minister Louvois, on May 28, 1687.[38] Undeterred, he returned to the attack in October 1689, this time with a comprehensive critique of the Revocation decision. Louis XIV had had a glorious opportunity during the peace afforded France by the Truce of Ratisbon (1684) to pursue the campaign of peaceful church reunion. Had such a policy been seriously followed, heresy would have died out within a generation. In any case, methods of constraint would never succeed in these matters and they had proven particularly disastrous since the formation of the League of Augsburg, which gave heretics within the kingdom cause to pray for the triumph of France's Protestant enemies or to lobby them during periods of delicate diplomatic negotiations.

Vauban proceeded to catalogue the losses to the kingdom caused by the Revocation. Some 80 000 to 100 000 Huguenots had emigrated, taking with them 30 000 000 livres. France's artisanal and commercial resources had been seriously depleted. As many as 8 000 or 9 000 sailors, 500 to 600 officers and 10 000 to 12 000 soldiers, "much tougher than those already in their service" had deserted to France's enemies.[39] But quite apart from the cost of the enterprise, it was unlikely that a single genuine convert had been made since no prince, however mighty, could legislate the direction of his subjects' consciences. Instead, impiety, sacrilege, profanation, and spiritual relapse had been the inevitable issue of the King's decree.

Surely the lesson of all this vain persecution was clear, Vauban pursued. Following the St. Bartholomew's Day Massacre, France should have recognized the alternatives that a policy of repression implied: "One is faced by people whom one must either exterminate as rebels and heretics or police as madmen." Should France persist in her present harsh policy, she might provoke a general insurrection by the Huguenots, reinforced by a landing of William of Orange's troops on the coast or even by a rising of those French Catholics who had no particular interest in furthering the Revocation policy and who were bitterly aggrieved against the crown on economic grounds.[40]

Having presented a catalogue of the administration's errors, Vauban made bold to draft a declaration by which Louis XIV would have restored the Edict of Nantes. In exchange for the restoration of their rights, the Calvinists might be charged a 30 sou head tax which would have the added advantage of allowing the government to make an accurate census of the unconverted. Vauban predicted that the promulgation of such a law would also seriously undermine the coalition of Protestant powers against France and produce a diplomatic realignment of German and Swiss states around Versailles.[41]

Having read his subordinate's lengthy submission, Louvois on January 5, 1690, wrote: "I have read your memorandum which contains many good ideas; but, just between us, they are on the whole bit extreme. I shall try in any case to convey them to His Majesty."[42]

In April 1691, following the death of Louvois, Vauban submitted the case for the annulment of the Revocation directly to the king, pointing out that the edict of 1685 had failed in its avowed aim of effecting mass conversion, adding that the Huguenot population of such towns as La Rochelle, Nîmes, and Montpellier had actually increased since 1685! The Calvinists in these and other communities were enjoying what amounted to tacit toleration because of the administration's preoccupation with the war; they were understandably anxious that, when peace returned, the King's wrath should not descend on them. Why not take the initiative and reintegrate them into a nation which they would continue to serve as model citizens? In a careful effort to dispel alarm, Vauban noted that the Huguenots of military age remaining in France were at most 40 000, spread throughout the kingdom, scarcely enough to pose a threat to state security. However, if Louis did not grant them some measure of religious freedom, they would have no other course but to work for his defeat and their own survival as protégés of the Protestant powers.[43]

In May 1693, Vauban made a final appeal to Versailles on behalf of the Protestants.[44] To this third memorandum, he appended the statement of Jacques Le Febvre, a Sorbonne theologian who had defended Calvinist scholars against Arnauld's ferocious polemics in the years before the Revocation.[45] Full freedom of worship should be granted the Protestants, Le Febvre argued, adding that it would be better not to do this in the form of a royal edict, since the Huguenots had some cause to suspect the permanence of the French monarchy's guarantees!

Although he was not persuaded by the appeals put to him so forcefully by Vauban, Louis XIV appreciated the soldierly candour which had inspired them as he made clear in a personal letter of June 13, 1693.[46]

His continuing involvement in the War of the League of Augsburg confirmed Vauban in the opinion that the Revocation had done a profound disservice to France in terms of national defence. In the summer of 1694, having witnessed the shipboard 'conversion' of a well-born Huguenot galley-slave, Vauban could not resist appending a bitter note to the report which he relayed to the Navy Minister on the proselyte's behalf:

On the feast of Our Lady, I was present at the conversion of a gentleman galley slave from the Vivarais who went through all the forms required of him. I promised him that I would relay the news to you of his change of faith which was in fact as sincere as any forced conversion can be.[47]

Although their testimony was to inspire champions of religious toleration during the Enlightenment, neither the satire of Fontenelle, nor the resignation of d'Aguesseau, nor the bold pleading of Vauban, had the slightest chance of modifying the anti-Huguenot policy of Louis XIV. Meanwhile, for established writers and artists, the Revocation offered an occasion to celebrate an act which they genuinely welcomed and to consolidate their standing at court. For the ambitious and for those out of favour, it was an opportunity to flatter the prince and to launch or restore a career. For churchmen, the Edict of Fontainebleau provided reassuring evidence that God had selected a sovereign for France who was ready to use all the powers of the secular sword to effect the undivided commitment of his subjects to the Catholic faith. In their enthusiasm for the Revocation, France's intellectual and spiritual elites not only offered their full support for the King's religious policy; they became eager collaborators in its implementation.

---

1. In 1935, the right-wing Protestant writer Freddy Durrleman published a collection of contemporary as well as subsequent comments on the Revocation. The selections are brief and are presented without critical analysis. Nevertheless, they offer a glimpse into some of the key arguments pro and con the Revocation decision. During the tercentenary commemoration of the Edict of Fontainebleau, the collection was re-edited. C. Bergeal and A. Durrleman, *Eloge et Condemnation de la Révocation de l'Edit de Nantes* (Carrières-sous-Poissy, 1985).

2. Charles Du Périer, *Poème, Pièces de poésies qui ont remporté le prix de l'Académie française depuis 1671 jusqu'à 1747* (Paris, 1747), p. 67.

3. Abbé Paul Tallemant le jeune, *Panégyrique sur l'heureux retour de la santé du Roy, prononcé le 27 janvier 1687, Recueil des Harangues prononcées par Messieurs de l'Académie française dans leurs réceptions, et en d'autres occasions différentes, depuis l'établissement de l'Académie jusqu'à présent* (Paris, 1698), p. 488.

4. La Fontaine, *Epître à Monsieur de Bonrepaux, Oeuvres complètes*, ed. J. Marmier (Paris, 1965), p. 494.

5. La Bruyère, *Les Caractères de Théophraste, traduits du grec, avec les Caractères ou les moeurs de ce siècle, Oeuvres complètes*, ed. J. Benda (Paris, 1951), p. 307. A short passage which appeared in the fifth (1690) edition of Les Caractères suggests that La Bruyère may have developed second thoughts about the Revocation as a result of observing the methods by which it was being applied: "When I reflect upon the painful, dubious and dangerous paths which the King is sometimes obliged to follow in the pursuit of civic peace, including the extreme but necessary methods which he often uses for a sound enough purpose, I know that he must answer to God in matters which affect the happiness of his subjects, that the choice

between good and evil is in his hands and that ignorance will not serve him as an excuse" (ibid., p. 306).

6. Bussy-Rabutin to Madame de Sévigné, November 14, 1685, Roger de Rabutin, comte de Bussy, *Correspondance avec sa famille et ses amis, 1666-1693*, ed. L. Lalanne (6 vols.; Paris, 1858-59), v. pp. 476-77.

7. Madame de Sévigné to Bussy-Rabutin, November 18, 1685, Madame de Sévigné, *Lettres*, ed. Gérard-Gailly (3 vols.; Paris, 1957), III, p. 114.

8. Same to same, March 16, 1689, ibid., p. 388.

9. Mlle de Scudéry to Bussy-Rabutin, November 18, 1685, cited in E. Bersier, *La Révocation. Discours prononcé dans le temple de l'Oratoire à Paris le 22 octobre 1885* (Paris, 1886), p. 37.

10. Hélène Himelfarb has argued that most official artists did not take up the Revocation theme and that they ought therefore to be seen as indifferent rather than full of panegyric fervour about the King's decision. V. H. Himelfarb "Les arts à la rescousse de l'Edit de Fontainebleau? Les paradoxes des Académies royales," *Actes du colloque de Paris*, pp. 335-57. The fact remains that some of France's most prominent painters and sculptors did celebrate the event in their works, and with unambiguous enthusiasm.

11. Bossuet to Jean Rou, October 17, 1685, (Jean Rou), *La Séduction éludée, ou Lettres de M. L'évêque de Meaux à un de ses Diocésains qui s'est sauvé de la Persécution, avec les Réponses qui y ont été faites, et dont la principale est demeurée sans République* (Bern, 1686), p.9.

12. Rou to Bossuet, January 28, 1686, ibid., pp. 14-18.

13. Bossuet to Rou, April 3, 1686, ibid., p. 23.

14. Rou to Bossuet, May 8, 1686, ibid., p. 56.

15. Same to same, June 27, 1686, ibid., p. 76.

16. Bossuet, *Oraison funèbre de Michel Le Tellier, Oraisons funèbres de Bossuet* (Paris, 1959), pp. 167-68.

17. Memorandum of Bossuet to Pontchartrain, March, 1700, *Correspondance de Bossuet*, ed. C. Urbain and E. Levesque (15 vols.; Paris, 1909-1925), XII, pp. 174-75.

18. Bossuet to Monsieur de Nénars, April 2, 1686, ibid., IV, p. 19.

19. Bossuet, *Avertissement aux protestants sur les lettres du ministre Jurieu contre l'"Histoire des variations"*(1689), *Oeuvres* (43 vols.; Versailles, 1815-1819), XXI, p. 324.

20. Arnauld to Prince Ernest, Landgrave of Hesse-Rheinfels, December 13, 1685, Arnauld, *Oeuvres*, ed. G. du Pac de Bellegarde and J. Hautefage (43 vols.; Paris 1775-83), II, p. 585. Jacques LeBrun has pointed out that even the most zealous Jansenists did not make the claims for the rights of individual conscience that were advanced by the Reformed although the logic of their theological position might well have impelled them in that direction. J. LeBrun, "La conscience et la théologie moderne," *Actes du colloque de Paris*, pp. 113-33.

21. The naive assumption on the part of some contemporary Huguenots that one of the aims of the pro-Jansenist playwright Jean Racine in presenting his tragedy *Esther* at court was to make Louis XIV feel a compassionate concern for his afflicted

Calvinist subjects by suggesting a parallel with the sufferings of the Old Testament Jews is definitively laid to rest in J. Orcibal, *Autour de Racine*, I: *La Genèse d' 'Esther' et d' 'Athalie'* (Paris, 1950), p. 41.

22. Richard Simon to Frémont d'Ablancourt, c. 1680, *Lettres choisies de m. Simon, où l'on trouve un grand nombre de faits Anecdotes de Littérature* (3 vols.; Amsterdam, 1730), p. 44, p. 68.

23. Richard Simon, *Lettre de quelques nouveaux convertis de France à Monsieur Jurieu sur ses "Lettres pastorales"* (Paris, 1687), p. 15.

24. Charles Coquerel, *Histoire des églises du désert chez les Protestants de France depuis la fin du règne de Louis XIV jusqu'à la Révolution française* (2 vols.; Paris, 1841), I, p. 661; Napoleon Peyrat, *Histoire des pasteurs du désert depuis la révocation de l'édit de Nantes jusqu'à la Révolution française 1685-1789* (2 vols.; Paris, 1842), I, p. 86.

25. O. Douen, *L'Intolérance de Fénelon, Etudes historiques d'après des documents pour la plupart inédits* (Paris, 1875).

26. Fénelon, *Lettres sur l'autorité de l'Eglise, Oeuvres complètes* (35 vols.; Paris, 1820-30), II, p. 216.

27. Such opposition to the Revocation as was voiced by the French clergy was, predictably, very cautious. Cardinal Le Camus of Grenoble, while not attacking the Edict of Fontainebleau directly, deplored the violence and constraint with which the clergy of his diocese were implementing the new law. He directed the priests under his charge to avoid forcing any of the sacraments on 'new Converts' against their will and to let those whom they might suspect of heresy die in peace, without the deathbed interrogations sanctioned by the courts. Above all, the prelate exhorted his clergy to draw former Huguenots to Catholicism by example. V. *Lettre de monseigneur le cardinal Etienne Le Camus, évêque et prince de Grenoble aux curez de son diocèse, touchant la conduite qu'ils doivent tenir à l'égard des nouveaux convertis* (Grenoble, 1687). This gentle pastoral admonition was approved by Innocent XI in a letter written to Le Camus on October 18, 1687 (ibid., pp. 7-8). Pierre Bolle has noted the contrast between the attitude of Le Camus and that of his Dauphiny colleague, Bishop Daniel de Cosnac, who was ready to sanction whatever methods might be required to extirpate heresy in his diocese. P. Bolle, "Deux évêques devant la Revocation: Etienne Le Camus et Daniel de Cosnac," *Actes du colloque de Paris*, pp. 59-74.

28. Fontenelle's letter from Borneo is obviously inspired in part at least by the account given by Rabelais of Pantagruel's stay among the Papefigues. V. Rabelais, *Pantagruel (1552)* in *Oeuvres*, ed. Marty-Laveaux (5 vols.; Paris, 1868-1902), III, pp. 425-62.

29. Fontenelle, "Extraits d'une lettre écrite de Batavia dans les Indes Orientales, le 27 novembre 1684, contenu dans une lettre de M. de Fontenelle, reçue à Rotterdam par M. Basnage," *Nouvelles de la République des Lettres*, January, 1686, p. 90.

30. Bayle to Desmaizeaux, October 17, 1704, in *Lettres de M. Bayle publiées sur les originaux*, ed. Desmaizeaux (3 vols.; Amsterdam, 1729), III, p. 1006.

YOUNG ENTERRANT SA FILLE

The clandestine burial of Edward Young's Protestant daughter in southern France (1741)

31. Voltaire, *Lettre VII, Sur les Français, in Lettres à S. M. Mgr. le prince de sur Rabelais et sur d'autres auteurs accusés d'avoir mal parlé de la religion chrétienne (1767)* in *Oeuvres* (Moland), XXVI, p. 501.

32. Antonius Van Dale, *De oraculis ethnicorum dissertationes duae* (Amsterdam, 1683). This scholarly work aimed at establishing that the oracles of the Ancients were not to be attributed to the Devil's cunning but to the machinations of pagan priests. Sensing the diversion which such a theme might afford if treated with the lightness of touch which was already his forte, Fontenelle decided to give Van Dale's treatise an elegantly vulgarized Gallic version. The result was his *Histoire des oracles* (Paris, 1686).

33. *Nouvelles de la République des Lettres*, January 1687, pp. 146-64.

34. Père Lejay, *Le Triomphe de la religion sous Louis le Grand, représenté par des inscriptions et des devises, avec une explication en vers latins et françois* (Paris, 1687), p. 97.

35. Abbé Nicolas Trublet, *Mémoires pour servir à l'histoire de la vie et des oeuvrages de M. Fontenelle, tirés du 'Mercure de France' 1756, 1757 et 1758* (2d ed., Amsterdam, 1759), p. 79.

36. Henri-François d'Aguesseau, *Discours sur la vie et la mort, le caractère et les moeurs de M. d'Aguesseau, conseiller d'Etat, Oeuvres complètes* (16 vols.; Paris, 1720), XV, pp. 326-27.

37. Rulhière, *Eclaircissemens historiques sur les causes de la révocation de l'édit de Nantes, et sur l'état des Protestants en France, depuis le commencement du règne de Louis XIV, jusqu'à nos jours* (2 vols.; Paris, 1788), I, pp. 372-74.

38. This letter has been lost but reference is made to the date and by implication to the content in the reply of Louvois to Vauban dated October 13, 1687, cited in *Vauban, sa famille et ses écrits, ses oisivetés et sa correspondance*, ed. Rochas d'Aiglun (2 vols.; Paris, 1910), II, p. 280.

39. Vauban, "Pour le rappel des Huguenots," B.N. Ms. Fr. 7044, fol. 286. Although Rulhière dated this memorandum November or December 1689, a pencilled note in Vauban's handwriting suggests that it was penned and submitted in October of the same year.

40. Ibid., fols. 287, 288.

41. Ibid., fol. 294.

42. Louvois to Vauban, January 5, 1690, Rochas d'Aiglun, *Vauban*, II, p. 317.

43. Vauban, "Addition [au Rappel des Huguenots] du 5 avril 1692," ibid., I, p. 478 ff.

44. Vauban, "Réflexions sur la guerre présente et sur les nouveaux convertis. Du 5 mai 1693," ibid., I, p.483 ff.

45. [Jacques Lefebre], *Lettre de M. Le Fevre, docteur en théologie de la Faculté de Paris, à M. Arnauld, de Paris, ce 25 juillet* 1683 (n.p., n.d.).

46. Louis XIV to Vauban, June 13, 1693, Rochas d'Aiglun, *Vauban*, II, pp. 388-89.

47. Vauban to Jérôme de Pontchartrain, August 20, 1694, ibid., p. 424, n.1.

CHAPTER III

A Three-Way Impasse:
The Huguenots, The Clergy, and The State

The failure of the Edict of Fontainebleau to extinguish French Calvinism posed enormous problems for the three parties most directly affected. For the thousands of Huguenots who chose to remain in France and practise their faith in defiance of the law, the penalties were grim, ranging from death or a life term rowing the King's galleys to confiscation of property or loss of inheritance rights. For the administration, the options were agonizingly difficult: Versailles could keep on trying to liquidate the Reformed faith by applying the full force of the law, at whatever cost, or it could reverse course and offer the Protestants some measure of relief and recognition.[1] Any concessions to the Huguenots were, of course, bound to antagonize members of the First Estate which, having welcomed the Revocation as the triumphant climax to the Counter-Reformation, would insist that the civil arm hold to the commitment made by Louis XIV in 1685.

Calvinist stubbornness, administrative befuddlement, and ecclesiastical intransigence produced decades of tension and frustration for all concerned. What follows in this chapter is a brief recapitulation of the problems faced by priests, Calvinists, and government officials as they tried to police, resist, or modify the terms of the Edict of Fontainebleau after 1685.

It is difficult to gauge precisely the impact of the Revocation on the Huguenot community. At least 200 000 Calvinists (out of some 900 000, or roughly 5 percent of France's population) appear to have fled their homeland in the immediate aftermath of the law. Lesser waves of refugees followed, the last one in 1760, bringing the total number of Protestants who preserved their faith through flight to some 300 000.[2] Of the 700 pastors who were ministering to Reformed congregations in 1685, at least one-sixth, perhaps as many as one-quarter, abjured in order to stay in France; the rest found asylum abroad.

The Calvinists who remained in France were under enormous pressure to convert or at least outwardly to accept the Catholic sacraments. The extent to which they resisted this pressure depended in large part, of course, on their courage; but social status and geography played a significant role in determining compliance with or resistance to the Edict of Fontainebleau.[3]

Where they were in the minority or where the authorities were able to keep them under surveillance, as in most cities, especially in the northern part of France, it was virtually impossible for the Huguenots to avoid external acts of Catholic devotion, sometimes atoned for by domestic worship presided over by the *pères de famille*. In Paris, although it was illegal, Huguenots began turning up at the chapels of Dutch and Prussian embassies soon after the Revocation; those who were wealthy enough could travel to neighbouring Protestant states to worship and have marriages solemnized in the Calvinist rite.

By contrast, in some parts of France, and especially in remote areas of the south which were hard to police, Calvinist worship never ceased. Even before the Revocation, as Huguenot rights were being eroded, the schoolmaster François Vivens and the lawyer Claude Brousson (encouraged by Pierre Jurieu in Amsterdam who began sending a series of *Lettres pastorales* full of millennarian promise back into his homeland in 1684), laid the foundation of what was to become a network of underground churches (*Eglises sous la Croix* or *Eglises du Désert*) throughout southern France. Thus the groundwork for Huguenot survival was set in place even as the Edict of Fontainebleau was promulgated.

As evidence of the persistence of heresy surfaced to embarrass the administration in the decade following the Revocation, the *Conseil d'en haut* launched a wide-ranging inquiry into the Huguenot question. The result was the issuance of an edict dated December 13, 1698, directing all the King's subjects, without exception, to attend mass and receive the eucharist. It should be noted, however, that this new legislation was followed by a confidential *Instruction interprétive* of January 1, 1699, advising secular officials not to use force in compelling suspected heretics to the altar.

The struggle between priests determined to fulfill the promise of the Edict of Fontaintebleau and Huguenots equally determined to hold onto their faith led to outright violence, beginning on July 24, 1702, when a band of *cévenol* peasants murdered the abbé du Chayla, superintendent of missionary activity in the region. Thus began the Camisard revolt, encouraged from abroad by Pierre Jurieu.

Bitterness at the unrelenting tax burden placed on the Camisards undoubtedly played a part in the rising, as recent historians have argued; but it is hard not to see the Camisards as first and foremost religious enthusiasts who felt impelled to profess their faith openly and thus, in part at least, to atone for their parents' passivity at the time of the Revocation.[4]

A peculiar folk religion emerged among the peasants of the Cévennes during this insurrection: visionary adolescents, claiming direct inspiration from the Almighty, transmitted to semi-literate congregations their own very special interpretation of the Gospel, often inducing something close to hysteria in their followers.[5]

Although their ideology might best be described as populist and theocratic, the Camisards were denounced from the beginning as republican; and since their activity was by its very nature subversive, they provided concrete evidence against the Reformed on that count as well. Finally, their religious excesses allowed critics to revive the old allegation of Calvinist fanaticism.

A graphic account of the Camisard rebellion, together with a description of the many persecutions which preceded it, constitutes a major part of *Le Télémaque travesti*, a youthful novel by Marivaux passed by the French censors in 1714 (although not published until 1736, and then only abroad).[6] The central characters of the novel are stand-ins for the original cast of characters in Fénelon's *Télémaque*. Phocion is Marivaux's Mentor, championing justice and mercy for the Huguenots. Brideron, the father of Timante (Télémaque) is the villain of the piece, an army man ready to deploy all the brutal resources at his command in order to bring the Reformed back into the Catholic fold; like those in charge of the *dragonnades*, he billets his men in Huguenot homes, lets them abuse and abduct Reformed children, urges them to defecate inside Calvinist *temples*, and instructs them to shoot to kill when they surprise Protestants going to illegal meetings for worship.

The Huguenots, as Marivaux presents them, remain for a long time passive in the face of these outrages; they make vain efforts to point out to their tormentors that the Reformed are hard working and productive while many of their Catholic neighbours are beggars; they even suggest that they might have considered conversion except for the brutality of the tactics used against them. In the mock-Homeric descriptions of the ensuing Camisard revolt which Marivaux offers the reader, the novelist condemns atrocities committed by both sides but notes that religious zealotry on the rebels' part may well have ended up alienating the more responsible elements in their own camp. Phocion, no doubt speaking for Marivaux, ends the novel with a plea that the amnesty offered the Camisards in 1705 not be followed by excessive repression.

The tragic circumstances of the revolt in the Cévennes which served as a central theme in *Le Télémaque travesti* may also have helped Fénelon, creator of the original *Télémaque*, to experience a change of heart towards the Revocation policy. In any event, the archbishop revealed a new concern for the rights of conscience in a letter to the chevalier de St. Georges, son of James II:

> No earthly power can break into the redoubt within which the heart remains its own master. Force can never persuade men but only make hypocrites of them. When kings interfere with religion, they subjugate it rather than protect it. Grant civil tolerance to all your subjects, then, not by sanctioning all their beliefs as equally valid but by suffering patiently what God himself suffers and by trying to bring men toward the true faith by gentle persuasion.[7]

Two years later, while orchestrating plans for the dauphin's succession with the duc de Chevreuse, Fénelon confirmed this new orientation. With regard to the spiritual well-being of his subjects, he now argued, the King "ought to support and facilitate, not frustrate and subject."[8] Secular and spiritual authorities must of course remain in close interdependence, Fénelon continued; the crown had an obligation to suppress dangerous sectarian innovations while the clergy should continue to excommunicate rebels against the monarchy; but in matters of faith, the monarch must never command with words such as "we will, we enjoin, we ordain" which were only appropriate to the secular domain.[9]

While Fénelon had been reconsidering his opinions about the rights of religious non-conformists, France and the Protestant coalition against which she had been fighting during the War of the Spanish Succession were taking steps to end that conflict. During the negotiations which led to the peace at Utrecht in 1714 (as, earlier, during the preliminary discussions leading to the Treaty of Ryswick in 1697 and, later, the Treaty of Aix-la-Chapelle in 1748), the Huguenots succeeded in persuading the Protestant powers to place the question of their civil and religious rights on the agenda.[10] However, even with fairly intense lobbying on their behalf, the Reformed discovered in each of these instances that realpolitik prevailed over concern for their fate; neither England nor Holland nor Prussia was prepared to make an improvement in the condition of France's minority a precondition for signing the peace.[11]

Meanwhile the choice of the Jesuit Le Tellier as the King's confessor in 1709 helped set the stage for the Edict of March 8, 1715, which declared that those of His Majesty's subjects who had remained in France in 1685 had thereby given proof of their conversion: former Huguenots were henceforth categorized as 'new Catholics' or 'new converts'; those who continued to profess the "so-called Reformed religion" would be treated as relapsed heretics. In the funeral oration which he pronounced over the body of the dead Louis XIV, Jean-Baptiste Massillon, Bishop of Clermont, hailed what he saw to be the effective extinction of French Calvinism:

> Time, God's grace and sound teaching are slowly perfecting a change which brute force could only superficially effect. If fear made hypocrites in the early stages of this process, instruction in the faith has since made true believers of those whose conversion had followed.[12]

As though to mock the bishop's words, the Reformed were about to transform what had been mere spiritual survival into something approaching a full-scale restoration of their churches. Most of the credit for this goes to Antoine Court, a young lay preacher who in 1713 toured the area affected by the Camisard insurrection.[13] Court was appalled at the extent to which Calvinist orthodoxy as well as the the Huguenot tradition of loyalty to the crown had been undermined during this uprising and decided to commit his life to re-establishing theological as well as political conformity among his co-religionists. In August 1715, at a clandestine national synod, Court proposed a series of measures to effect this restructuring. These measures included the replacement of adolescent Cévenol preachers with a corps of properly trained pastors, the holding of open-air services of worship, and the reinstitution of conventional church structures (consistories, *colloques*, and synods), by means of which the faith and morals of the flock might be effectively policed. Then, in 1726, aided by Dutch and English subsidies, Court opened a seminary at Lausanne, where candidates for the underground church he was inaugurating would study under such eminent scholars as Alphonse Turrettini, friend of Newton, and Antoine-Noë Polier de Bottens, a future contributor to the *Encyclopédie*. Between 1726 and 1753, some ninety pastors were prepared at Lausanne for the hazardous career of preaching and ministering to the *Eglises du Désert* ; many would be arrested and executed. But while Court asked his fellow Huguenots to challenge French law by marrying, baptizing, and worshipping under the guidance of these underground pastors, he just as insistently demanded that they profess an unconditional devotion to the crown.

Throughout the eighteenth century, there would be a running debate within the Huguenot community over Court's view that participation in acts of public worship was an essential part of the Reformed creed. Some Calvinist theologians, with understandable encouragement from Versailles, argued that domestic worship (in which the whole family gathered together for Bible reading and prayer) could be seen as adequate, especially in times of oppression. This view was forcefully expressed by Pastor Jacques Basnage, whose *Instruction et lettre pastorale aux réformés de France*, composed in 1719 at the instigation of the Regent and distributed by the authorities throughout the sometimes turbulent south, urged Calvinists to avoid the large open-air religious assemblies which provoked the government and which were, in any event, not an absolute spiritual obligation.[14]

The spiritual reconstruction of the Reformed went ahead apace during the early years of the Regent, Philippe d'Orléans, a skeptic with a tolerant disposition who was disinclined to transform the Edict of 1715 into a measure of outright repression or forcible conversion. In fact, in June 1716, the Regent listened sympathetically to a proposal that a group of Huguenot emigrés be allowed to settle in Douai. He was, however, dissuaded from endorsing this project by his friend the duc de Saint-Simon who, while conceding that the Revocation had led to depopulation and commercial decline, noted that ever since the reign of Henri II the Calvinists had been fomenters of civil discord and that after the Edict of Nantes they had established "a separate, well organized republican government...in a word, a state within a state."[15]

The relatively indulgent policy of Philippe d'Orléans ended in 1724 when the duc de Bourbon, named first minister by the young Louis XV, decided to begin his administration with a dramatic reassertion of the Revocation system. The result was the Edict of 1724. Heavily influenced by a report which had been drawn up earlier by the *procureur général* of the Paris parlement, Guillaume-François Joly de Fleury, the Edict codified in harsh new language all existing statutes against the Huguenots. This legislation was intimidating enough by itself; but when Louis Phelypeaux, comte de Saint-Florentin, was made Minister of "the so-called Reformed Religion" in 1725, the Protestants had added cause to be alarmed. During the half century which followed, while he remained in charge of government policy towards the Reformed, Saint-Florentin was to treat them with unrelenting severity.

Fortunately for the Huguenots, Cardinal Fleury (who presided over French policy between 1726 and 1743) as well as Louis XV (who assumed personal control of the administration following the cardinal's death) were both so preoccupied with the increasing politicization of the Jansenist heresy that they were unable to devote their full attention to the difficulties posed to Versailles by the Calvinist resurgence.

In one respect, however, the passage of the Edict of 1724 brought new distress to the Huguenots. Taking their cue from the new law, priests began demanding tests of orthodoxy, including participation in the eucharist, from suspected 'new Catholic' couples presenting themselves for marriage. The difficulties for all parties concerned were obvious. The Reformed had no other means of legalizing their marital bonds and of guaranteeing the inheritance of their children, yet they were loath to take communion in the Roman rite. Priests were equally determined not to consecrate marriages of men and women whose faithless acceptance of the eucharist would be blasphemous. For their part, magistrates, caught in the middle, felt obliged under the new law to compel 'new Catholics' to present themselves to the local priest, who was bound to marry them as members in good standing of the Roman communion.

The middle years of the eighteenth century were filled with vain but well-intentioned efforts to devise a marriage ceremony which would accommodate the scruples of all parties. The first of these proposals, submitted to Cardinal Fleury in November 1726 by the abbé Robert, provost of the Nîmes cathedral chapter, urged that Protestants come before the local priest, who would offer them his blessing (but not the sacrament) and who would in fact act on such occasions as an agent of the secular authority, sanctioning a purely civil contract.[16] Fleury was impressed; but opposition among his colleagues in the First Estate made the implementation of such a formula unthinkable.

Given the impasse which they faced, more and more of the Reformed began having their marriages blessed by underground pastors at 'Desert' assemblies, even though the certificates which they received following such ceremonies were, of course, worthless in court. No tragic consequences issued from these arrangements until 1739, when the *présidial* at Nîmes declared a number of 'Desert' marriages null and void and ordered the couples involved to separate. The parlements at Grenoble, Toulouse, and Bordeaux followed suit, creating what was to become a serious social problem by mid-century. Not surprisingly, disgruntled spouses seeking separation or collateral Catholic relatives seeking inheritances presented the courts, and ultimately public opinion, with anguishing cases of Calvinist distress.[17]

During the War of the Austrian Succession in the 1740s, when the military forces which had helped patrol the countryside were off at the front, the Calvinists professed their faith more openly and defiantly than before; they met for worship by daylight and in large numbers; they began keeping a registry of births and marriages; most provocatively, they convened a national synod in August 1744.

The First Estate, which up to this point had trusted Versailles to police the Revocation system, expressed its alarm at the Calvinist revival during the Assembly of the Clergy held in the spring of 1745. The religious policy of Louis XIV had collapsed, Bishop Guénet of Pons announced to his colleagues; even the normally law-abiding propertied classes among the Huguenots were starting to show up at illegal outdoor services; the insolent heretics had even begun hiring their own schoolmasters to train children outside the faith.[18] This admonition was no doubt rendered all the more effective by the administration's dependence on the willingness of the clergy to vote a generous *don gratuit* to the nation. Last, but not least, disturbing reports of Huguenot activity near the coast, where the Protestant enemies of France might consider a landing, triggered a new wave of official repression against the Reformed in the late 1740s.

The pause between the peace at Aix-la-Chapelle in 1748 and the opening of the Seven Years' War offered another chance for a compromise settlement involving Versailles, the Reformed, and the First Estate. The vicomte de Saint-Priest (who became intendant of Languedoc in February 1751) tried to discover early in his mandate whether the southern episcopate would accept what seemed to him a reasonable solution in their dealings with 'new Catholics': priests would stop demanding written abjurations from suspected heretics asking for marriage; in return, the Huguenots would be obliged to have their children baptized by the curé, who would, however, no longer characterize such infants as *naturels*.[19] The bishops rejected the intendant's proposal out of hand; they were no more accommodating when sounded out a year later by Voltaire's protector, the duc de Richelieu, newly appointed governor of the southern province. Finding the clergy intractable, Richelieu ended by recommending that Versailles either enforce Huguenot submission to the existing law or compel the bishops to be more flexible in their dealings with 'new Catholics.' The administration responded by commissioning the distinguished magistrate, Omer-Louis-François Joly de Fleury, to conduct a thorough inquiry into the Protestant question. The proposal Joly de Fleury came up with was a variant on that advanced earlier by the abbé Robert: 'new Catholic' couples must continue to present themselves before the local priest who, acting as an agent of the civil authority, would authenticate the marriage without conferring the sacrament; should the priest refuse, the couple would be allowed to go before the *juge royal* and even, if necessary, before the regional parlement to have their marital bond solemnized.[20]

The efforts by agents of Louis XV's government to produce a compromise solution to the Protestant marriage issue ended in predictable failure, given the unwillingness of the First Estate to relinquish its monopolistic control of civil status. Meanwhile, as war threatened in 1755, the King's ambitious cousin, the prince de Conti, living in semi-exile outside Paris, undertook a secret but spectacular resolution of the Protestant question with Paul Rabaut of Nîmes, the dean of the underground pastors, and Antoine's Court's foremost disciple. In private conversations with Conti, Rabaut spoke of the main concern of the militant southern Huguenots whom he represented—they would not be content unless, among other things, they were allowed to worship publicly in their own rite. The prince responded by suggesting that a national synod of the Reformed churches be summoned to consider (and potentially to ratify) the terms by which Protestants would be fully reintegrated with the nation, adding that it would be helpful to have a full census of Calvinist males of arms-bearing age. At the synod which followed in May 1756, where the conservative urban Calvinists of the centre and north were well represented, Conti's proposals, especially the request for a census, were seen as an attempt to recruit a disgruntled minority for potentially subversive activity against Louis XV; as a result, the delegates voted to sever all ties with their dangerous would-be protector. [21]

The political reliability of the King's Protestant subjects was in fact a major issue at Versailles in the months preceding the opening of the Seven Years' War. The duc de Mirepoix, chosen governor of Languedoc at the end of 1755, was persuaded by local subordinates that the preventive arrest of a few Huguenot notables might be used to blackmail the underground pastors (including their leader, Paul Rabaut) into leaving the country. Without ministers to lead them, it was suggested, the Reformed would be docile in the event war did break out. As a result, at the beginning of January 1756, a few eminent Calvinists were arrested attending an illegal assembly for worship; paradoxically, however, Rabaut's refusal to go into exile in exchange for their release so impressed Mirepoix that he entered into an informal pact with the dean of the southern pastors. By the terms of this accord, up to 300 Huguenots would be allowed to worship at night in local barns. Although this arrangement was later repudiated at Versailles, it was soon adopted in somewhat modified form by Intendant Saint-Priest. As a result, a policy of de facto toleration was adhered to (with some exceptions) until the promulgation of the Edict of 1787.[22]

Following the opening of hostilities between France, England, and Prussia in 1756, one of Madame de Pompadour's agents, the ex-Calvinist Herrenschwand, came up with an idea designed to transform the administration's suspicions of the Reformed into benevolent protection. Why not have the Protestants rival their Catholic fellow citizens in patriotism, Herrenschwand suggested, by allowing them to make a *don gratuit* to the nation—a free will offering, to help meet the wartime crisis?

A variation on this scheme—the establishment of a bank based on funds deposited by Huguenots living abroad as well as in France and lending the government money at a modest rate of interest for the duration of the war—was endorsed by Lieutenant of Police René Berryer, Minister of War Bell'Isle, and Controller-General Etienne de Silhouette. However, rumours began to circulate that France's Protestants were about to use this banking scheme to purchase administration support for their right to marry in their own faith. In the end, the project was scuttled after being denounced to the redoutable Saint-Florentin by Intendant Saint-Priest. Needless to say, the First Estate thundered against a scheme by which toleration was to be obtained in return for monetary consideration. Meanwhile, some Protestants were beginning to have second thoughts about an arrangement which might conceivably be exploited by their enemies to milk them dry.[23] Yet, the boldness shown by the Reformed in proffering financial aid to a government which was still formally committed to their elimination reflects a radical shift of attitude on their part, a new sense of civic confidence.

The resilience of the Huguenots, the intractability of the Catholic establishment, and the wavering policies of the administration in the years following the Revocation produced a complex crisis, with social and political as well as religious ramifications. This crisis was bound to attract the attention of the philosophes, whose opposition to clericalism as well as to intolerance inevitably turned them into critics of the Revocation system.

---

1. The best overall analysis of the relationship between the Huguenots and the administration during the eighteenth century remains J. Dedieu, *Histoire politique des Protestants français, 1715-1794* (2 vols.; Paris, 1925).

2. D. Ligou, *Le Protestantisme en France de 1598 à 1715* (Paris, 1968), p. 253.

3. E.-G. Léonard, *Histoire générale du protestantisme* (3 vols.; Paris, 1961) III, p. 11. Historians have long debated whether French Calvinism was dealt an almost mortal

blow by the Revocation or whether the sufferings to which the Huguenots were subjected after 1685 produced a spiritual resilience which compensated for the obvious losses incurred through conversion and emigration. Philippe Joutard has examined the pros and cons of this debate and concludes that "but for the Revocation, the Protestant minority would have been slowly and progressively absorbed into the Catholic majority, with the exception of some groups who would have become the equivalent of sects. The minority which survived the reign of Louis XIV was smaller than it had been at the time of the Edict of Nantes, but it had been tempered by war. It had endowed itself with arms to maintain itself as a community, and had acquired a folk-memory." Philippe Joutard, "The Revocation of the Edict of Nantes: End or Renewal of French Protestantism?", Prestwick, *International Calvinism*, p. 367.

4. Ligou insists that the Camisards were motivated above all by religious conviction but adds that there was clearly a Freudian aspect to the revolt. "Les prophètes appartiennent à la jeune génération, qui n'a pas connu la dragonnade de 1684-1685, ou qui ne l'a connue que par récits et ils n'hésitent pas à se poser en défenseurs des fils trahis contre les pères coupables ou rénégats...Psychologie de déculturation qui entraîne un conflit oedipien violent." V. Le Roy Ladurie, *Les paysans de Languedoc* (Paris, 1969), p. 343; "Les villageois Huguenots écoutent les prophètes, mais ils n'oublient pas la capitation...le soulèvement camisard se révèle donc...comme un mélange détonant de névrose prophétique et d'agitation fiscale." Ibid., p. 266

5. An exhaustive historiographical study of the Camisard rebellion is offered in Philippe Joutard, *La légende des Camisards. Une sensibilité au passé* (Paris, 1977). The myth of the Camisards as prototypical freedom-fighters, resembling the World War II partisans in southern France who struggled against Vichy and the Nazis, is present in post-1945 literature: v. J.-P. Chabrol, *Les Fous de Dieu* (Paris, 1961), A. Chamson, *La Superbe* (Paris, 1967), M. Olivier-Lacamp, *Les Feux de la colère* (Paris, 1969), as well as in film: R. Allio, "*Les Camisards*" (1972).

6. Pierre de Marivaux, *Le Télémaque travesti, contenant les treize derniers livres retournés et réimprimés pour la première fois* (1714), F. Deloffre, ed. (Geneva, 1956).

7. Fénelon, *Supplément à l'Examen de conscience, II: Principes fondamentaux d'un sage gouvernement* (1709) in *Ecrits et lettres politiques*, ed. Urbain (Paris, 1920), pp. 90-91.

8. Fénelon, *Plans de gouvernement concertés avec le duc de Chevreuse pour être proposés au duc de Bourgogne* (novembre 1711), ibid., p. 106.

9. In a marginal note to Fénelon's comment, the duc de Chevreuse observed that interference in the spiritual domain was not typical of French monarchical policy but had been introduced by François I when legislating against sixteenth-century heretics. While acknowledging that the state had an obligation to employ "dramatic remedies" as a last resort against dangerous non-conformists, Chevreuse proposed the recall of France's exiled Calvinists, to be accompanied by a grant of limited freedom of conscience but without any right to public worship. Ibid., p.109

10. Lobbying on behalf of the Huguenots prior to the Treaty of Ryswick is recapitulated in Anon., *Relation de tout ce qui s'est fait dans les affaires de la*

religion réformée et pour ses intérêts depuis le commencement des négociations de la paix de Ryswick, (Rotterdam, 1698). An account of the interventions on behalf of the French Reformed before the signing of the peace at Utrecht is included in F.H. Gagnebin, "Gabriel Mathurin," *BSHPF*, XXVI (1877), p. 519. Antoine Court's powerful but unheeded appeal to the Protestant delegates assembled to sign the peace at Aix-la- Chapelle in 1748 is found in A. Court, *Mémoire en faveur des protestants de France, destiné pour les ministres des puissances protestantes députés au congrès d'Aix-la-Chapelle* cited in A. Coquerel, *Histoire des églises du désert* (2 vols.; Paris 1841), I, pp. 446-50.

11. Requests to England's Queen Anne to intervene on behalf of Huguenot galley slaves were more effective, however. V. F. Fonbrune-Berbinau, "La libération des forçats pour la foi en 1713 et 1714," *BSHPF*, XXXVIII (1889), p. 237. One of the galley slaves then released, Jean Marteilhe, was to turn the account of his own experience into a much-read book in the 1750s. V. *Mémoires d'un protestant condamné aux galères pour cause religion; écrits par lui-même* (Rotterdam, 1757).

12. J.-B. Massillon, *Oraison funèbre de Louis-le-Grand, le 9 septembre, 1715, Oeuvres complètes* (Paris, 1825), IX, pp. 252-54.

13. A full account of the career of Antoine Court is furnished by E. Hugues, *Antoine Court. Histoire de la restauration du protestantisme en France au XVIIIe siècle* (2 vols.; Paris, 1872).

14. Jacques Basnage, *Instruction et lettre pastorale aux réformés de France sur la persévérance dans la foi et la fidélité pour le souverain* (Rotterdam, 1719). This injunction to caution was re-published by the administration during the War of the Austrian Succession when the French authorities were again concerned about the possibility of internal subversion by the Huguenots. The result was another bitter debate within the French Reformed community. Pastor François-Louis Allamand, living in Switzerland, wrote a *Lettre sur les assemblées des religionnaires en Languedoc* (Paris, 1745), reiterating Basnage's message and downplaying the importance of public worship. This provoked two replies: A. Court, *Réponse à la lettre sur les assemblées* (Geneva, 1745) and Armand de la Chapelle, *La nécessité du culte public* (The Hague, 1746), each of which put the strongest possible case for public celebration of the Reformed cult.

15. Duc de Saint-Simon, *Mémoires* ed. G. Truc (6 vols.; Paris, 1947-61), V, p. 310. A comprehensive analysis of Saint-Simon's views concerning the Huguenots is offered in H. Himelfarb, "Saint-Simon face aux Protestants: contradictions et arrière-pensées d'un 'Bon François'" in Ph. Joutard, *Historiographie de la Réforme* (Paris, 1977), pp. 127-147.

16. Abbé Robert, "Mémoire sur les moyens que l'on doit mettre en usage pour convertir les protestants," B.N., Ms. 7046, fol. 58. In another key area related to their civil status— their right to a suitable burial— the Huguenots fared better during the Fleury regime. On April 9, 1736, a royal declaration stipulated that those Frenchmen for whom burial in consecrated ground was out of the question might be separately interred following a special investigation and the grant of a special burial permit by the local procurator.

17.   For an analysis of the sociological as well as the legal aspects of the Protestant marriage question in the eighteenth century, v. Emile-G. Léonard, "Le problème du mariage civil et les protestants français au XVIIIe siècle," *Revue de théologie et d'action évangéliques* (Aix-en-Provence, July 1942), pp. 241-299. For an examination of the role of French magistrates during the period, v. David Bien, "Catholic Magistrates and Protestant Marriages in the French Enlightenment," *French Historical Studies*, 2 (1961-62), pp. 408-428. Older but still useful studies include: E.C.F. Bonifas, *Le mariage des protestants depuis la Réforme jusqu'à 1789* (Paris, 1901); H. Anger, *De la condition juridique des protestants après la révocation de l'edit de Nantes* (Paris, 1903); F. Bessière, *Le mariage des protestants au désert de France au XVIIIe siècle* (Cahors, 1899); and E. Stocquart, *Le mariage des protestants de France* (Brussels, 1903).

18.   Minutes of the Assembly of the Clergy for April 7, 1745, in *Collection des Procès-verbaux des Assemblées-générales du Clergé de France, depuis l'année 1560 jusqu'à présent, rédigés par ordre de matières, et réduits à ce qu'ils ont d'essentiel* (9 vols.; Paris, 1772), VII, p. 2021.

19.   Memorandum of Intendant Saint-Priest to Minister Saint-Florentin on the marriage question, April 30, 1751, A.N., TT 325, fol. 46.

20.   Memorandum of M. Joly de Fleury, cited in C.G. de Lamoignon de Malesherbes, *Mémoire sur le mariage des protestants, en 1785* (n.p., n.d.), pp. 133-91.

21.   A full account of the Rabaut-Conti exchange is given in J. Woodbridge, "'The inviolable secret' of French Reformed Protestants: The Prince of Conti's Conspiracy against Louis XV (1755-1757)," *Dix-huitième siècle*, 17 (1985).

22.   "Mémoire lu et approuvé en conseil, pour servir d'instruction à M. le maréchal de Thomond, dans la conduite qu'il doit tenir à l'égard des Protestants du Languedoc, le 7 janvier 1758," cited in *BSHPF*, XVIII (1869), p. 431. The last signifjicant emigration of Calvinists from France took place in 1760, when Jean-Louis Gibert led a number of militant and potentially rebellious Huguenots into exile in Ireland. This emigration probably helped set the stage for the accommodation between the regime and the Huguenots which was beginning to take shape at the end of the 1750s. V. D. Robert, "La fin du 'Désert héroique.' Pourquoi Jean-Louis Gibert a-t-il émigré?,"*BSHPF*, 6th series, XVIII (1951), p. 247.

23.   A full account of the Protestant banking scheme is to be found in E. Hugues, "Un épisode de l'histoire du protestantisme au XVIIIe siècle," *BSHPF*, XXVI (1877), pp. 340-49.

PART TWO

THE REVOCATION ATTACKED, 1715-1760

LA
H E · N · R · I · A · D · E ·

SECOND CHANT.

REINE, l'excès des maux où la France est livrée,
Est d'autant plus affreux, que leur source est sacrée.
C'est la Religion dont le zele inhumain
Met à tous les François les armes à la main.
Je ne decide point entre Geneve & Rome.
De quelque nom divin que leur parti les nomme,

Canto II of *La Henriade:* Voltaire's indictment of Catholic intolerance.

CHAPTER IV

An Abstract Combat:
Voltaire's First Battles Against Intolerance,
1713-1750

The reconstruction of French Calvinism which began in earnest during the Regency period coincided with the advent of a generation of writers intent upon subjecting the inheritance of Louis XIV to an exhaustive critique. One of the major items in the lengthy indictment which they subsequently produced was, predictably, a condemnation of the dead monarch's repressive and counter-productive religious policy. Yet while these intellectuals were unanimous in deploring the wave of intolerance and fanaticism which had swept over France in the last decades of the seventeenth century, they were not always free of the anti-Calvinist prejudice which had helped to furnish Louis XIV with a rationale for the Revocation.

The most notorious, and no doubt the most brilliant, of this new generation of writers, Voltaire, is rightly celebrated for having made a more articulate, persistent, and effective effort in behalf of religious toleration than any of his intellectual contemporaries.[1] It has been suggested that his motives in battling intolerance were less than pure, that he intervened in the Calas case, for instance, chiefly out of a yearning for self-advertisement or from a perverse desire to bring organized Christianity of all kinds into disrepute;[2] but the real interest which he showed in the Huguenot condition, beginning in the 1760s, undoubtedly helped persuade a generation of Frenchmen to demand an end to the persecution of Calvinists.

Whatever the significance of this later involvement, Voltaire showed only an oblique interest in the situation of his Protestant fellow countrymen between his literary debut and the decision which he made in the spring of 1762 to defend the memory of Calas. A number of factors help explain this relative indifference. To begin with, except for a brief liaison with the young Calvinist refugee, Olympe Du Noyer, while he was secretary to the French ambassador at The Hague in 1713,[3] Voltaire knew very little about the Huguenot community living inside France. Lacking this awareness, the philosophe perceived French Calvinist society mainly through the scholarly sources, many of them biased against the Huguenots, which he consulted while writing works such as *La Henriade*.

Both his political and his philosophical convictions strongly influenced Voltaire's attitude towards the Calvinists. As a supporter of the *thèse royale*,[4] he could never forget or forgive the Camisard rebels who had challenged the authority of that most civilizing of monarchs, Louis XIV. His deism[5] made Voltaire feel as spiritually distant from orthodox Calvinists as he did from conventional Catholics, except for those moments when he sensed an inclination towards natural religion among the more radical pastors. He associated dogmatic religion of all kinds with rabies theologica, the carrier of superstition and intolerance. The toleration which he advocated was designed as a palliative to arrest this religious rage rather than as a device by which men of deep conviction would come to respect the spiritual integrity of those holding opposing views.

Although he knew little of the Huguenot condition and although he was in many ways predisposed against French Calvinism, Voltaire wrote a number of works during the first part of his career which directly served the cause of toleration. These include not only *La Henriade* (1723) and the *Lettres philosophiques* (1733) but a number of lesser works, some of them not intended for publication and, therefore, all the more likely to relay his true feelings.

Voltaire's views about French Calvinism as well as about toleration were given their first public expression in *La Henriade*.[6] In the course of researching the historical context for this poem, Voltaire consulted the standard sixteenth-century chroniclers, most of whom blamed the outbreak of the French religious wars of the sixteenth century on the Huguenots.[7] In the end, however, the single most important source for the underlying theme of *La Henriade* was neither a Catholic nor a Calvinist apologist, but François de Mézeray, one of the *Politiques* who had urged the monarchy to restore its authority by detaching itself from both Catholic and Protestant sectarianism.[8] For Mézeray as for Voltaire, the conversion of Henri IV to Catholicism, like the concession of toleration to the Huguenots which followed it, was designed above all to consolidate monarchical authority. By his magnanimity in victory to partisans of both factions, by his opportune conversion to the faith of the majority, the founder of the Bourbon dynasty is seen by the playwright as re-establishing civic peace and releasing the monarchy from religious and social factionalism. The toleration practised by Henri and applauded at great length throughout the poem is presented to the reader as a tactical ploy in the overall campaign to achieve French political unity rather than as an end in itself.

It is clear from the original title, *La Ligue*, which Voltaire selected for his poem that he regarded the Catholic Guise family and their priestly counsellors as having posed a greater threat to French unity than their Protestant counterparts. In the poet's view, Catholics had also outdone Calvinists in committing atrocities during the sixteenth century, however prone both might have been to do violence. In the preface, Voltaire warns his readers that he intends to dwell at some length on the Saint Bartholomew's Day Massacre of 1572. Although Frenchmen might shudder when they read his account of this carnage, it was salutary that they be reminded how their ancestors, misled by superstition and fanaticism, had butchered some 100 000 of their non-conforming neighbours. True, a more 'philosophic' frame of mind had been asserting itself since the age of Louis XIV, but aberrant religious ideas could easily overwhelm the public mind again if the civil authorities were not vigilant.[9]

Voltaire's epic opens with an impassioned request from the wounded Henri III to his brother-in-law, the Protestant Henri of Navarre, that he try to obtain support against the Catholic Ligue from England's Queen Elizabeth. Navarre embarks on the mission with his trusted advisor, the Protestant Duplessis-Mornay; stopping off on the isle of Jersey, they encounter a venerable Catholic who prophesies the conversion of Navarre to the Roman communion and thereafter the rapid decline of French Calvinism. The account of the rise and fall of French Protestantism which Voltaire puts in the old man's mouth reads like a synopsis of the anti-Calvinist polemic of Bossuet:

> J'ai vu naître autrefois le calvinisme en France;
> Faible, marchant dans l'ombre, humble dans sa naissance,
> Je l'ai vu sans support exilé dans nos murs,
> S'avancer à pas lents par cent détours obscurs.
> Enfin mes yeux ont vu du sein de la poussière
> Ce fantôme effrayant lever sa tête altière,
> Se placer sur le trône, insulter aux mortels,
> Et d'un pied dédaigneux renverser nos autels...
> Un culte si nouveau ne peut durer toujours.
> Des caprices de l'homme il a tiré son être:
> On le verra périr ainsi qu'on l'a vu naître.[10]

Upon his arrival at the English court, Henri makes a profession of neutrality vis-à-vis Protestant as well as Catholic Christianity which clearly reflects Voltaire's own position.

> Je ne décide point entre Genève et Rome.
> De quelque nom divin que leur parti les nomme,
> J'ai vu des deux côtés la tourbe et la fureur.[11]

However, in the long and impassioned account of the Saint Bartholomew's Day Massacre which he had Henri relay to Elizabeth, Voltaire is at his most potent and dramatic, sustained by a rising wave of inspired outrage as he describes the tragic sequence of events concerning the hatching of the perverse mass murder by Catherine de Medici: the surge of panic which sweeps through the Huguenot community in Paris when the curfew signalling the surprise attack is sounded; the gratuitous brutality of the Catholic mob whose cruelty is fuelled by mindless religious zeal; and finally the voyeur's pleasure which Charles IX displays as he watches the murder of his loyal and innocent Huguenot subjects. The lesson of this appalling day has not been lost on him, Henri concludes, adding that if he should one day come to power, he will end forever the policy by which the French monarchy had tried to effect conversions by force:

> Et périsse à jamais l'affreuse politique,
> Qui prétend sur les cœurs un pouvoir despotique,
> Qui veut le fer en main convertir les mortels,
> Qui du sang hérétique arrose les autels,
> Et, suivant un faux zèle, ou l'intérêt pour guides,
> Ne sert un Dieu de paix que par des homicides.[12]

Having heard Henri out, Elizabeth proposes a treaty of reciprocity by which England will concede toleration to Catholics while France grants freedom of worship to Calvinists, much as the Regent and George I were rumoured to be ready to do during the peace negotiations at Utrecht.

His English visit a success, Henri returns to France, where Discord reigns supreme and Fanaticism has armed the witless monk, Jacques Clément, to murder the King. In the interregnum which follows, Navarre assures Catholics and Calvinists alike that, for the sake of national unity, he will tolerate not only their different forms of worship but even some of their abuses, which God alone can forgive.[13]

France's patron, Saint Louis, descends from the heavens to bless Henri's Huguenot legions, then guides the Calvinist hero on a privileged tour of the future during which he observes and admires such Protestant patriots as Turenne and Condé as well as the Catholic, but tolerant, Vauban. Inspired by this anticipatory vision, Henri leads his troops to victory over the Ligue and becomes effective master of France. Saint Louis then intercedes with the Almighty so that Henri may be redeemed from heresy. Truth is commissioned to visit the conquering hero, whose subsequent conversion, as Voltaire sees it, is more bedazzlement than genuine illumination.[14]

Given the provocative attacks on the French ecclesiastical establishment which were scattered throughout *La Henriade*, getting the work published in France was no mean challenge. Voltaire was understandably bitter at the efforts made to prevent his poem from appearing: "I put the case for a spirit of peace and tolerance in religious matters too strongly, I spoke out too candidly for the taste of the Curia and I discharged too little venom against the Protestants to hope that I might be allowed to publish a poem composed in honour of my nation's greatest king."[15] By mid-December 1723, a somewhat modified version of the poem, published in Rouen, began arriving in Paris, the authorities having indicated that they would look the other way.

Despite the death of the Regent (in whom Voltaire had placed high hopes as a sponsor and protector) before the text began to circulate, *La*

Henriade became an instant success. From the first through the sixteenth, definitive, edition of 1768, the poem was one of the genuine 'best sellers' of the Enlightenment. The influential *Mercure de France* helped create this success with two very favourable reviews in its March and May 1724, issues, drawing the attention of the public to the moving description of the massacre of 1572.[16] Daniel Mornet uncovered copies of *La Henriade* in 181 of the 500 libraries which he examined—a very high score.[17] Writing at the end of the eighteenth century, Condorcet paid tribute to the way in which the poem had broadcast the message of "tolerance, love and humanity" throughout the Enlightenment.[18]

Predictably, orthodox Catholic critics did not share the general enthusiasm for *La Henriade*. For one thing, they expressed grave reservations about the characterization of the founder of the Bourbon dynasty as skeptical and tolerant, qualities singularly inappropriate in a Catholic sovereign. In addition, they charged that it was unconscionable in Voltaire to picture Catholics as propagators of discord and fanaticism while applauding the acts of the Huguenots, who had been notorious rebels as well as heretics.[19]

Although Protestant critics were understandably more enthusiastic about *La Henriade* than their Catholic counterparts, they were far from uncritical. Members of the refugee community in London were especially reserved about the English edition of the poem, for which Voltaire wrote a separately published introduction, issued late in 1727 after he had spent a year and a half in England. In this essay, the poet allowed that the superstitious and monastic sides of the pre-Reformed church and the pretensions of Rome to European domination had been cause enough for outrage. Man's passion for novelty and the personal ambition of Luther and Calvin had "then taken over, transforming indignation into insurrection." Unfortunately, protest against superstition and priestly tyranny had tended to degenerate into anarchy. French champions of the Reformed cause such as Condé and Coligny had "brought their griefs, their vengeance and their interests together so that a revolution both in the state and in religion was at hand."[20]

Huguenot exiles in London were quick to reply. One of their number, Faget, appended his *Pensées sur La Henriade* to an English edition of the epic which he published without Voltaire's knowledge. Certain passages of the epic were admirable, Faget conceded; everyone would benefit from learning by heart the verses dramatizing the Saint Bartholomew's Day Massacre, and the exposé of papal corruption could not be improved upon. Yet the poem as a whole clearly reflected the anti-Protestant prejudices which its author had absorbed as part of his Catholic upbringing.[21]

Moving from the general to the particular, Faget cited two cases of bias in *La Henriade* for which the poet deserved special censure. The passage in which the Jersey islander predicts the imminent collapse of Calvinism was manifestly absurd, given the forward-looking nature of Protestant culture in general. Even more outrageous was the exalted poetry which Voltaire had lavished on the 'low' theme of Navarre's conversion. Had there been in fact anything more deplorable in the career of Henri IV than his readiness to adjust his religious conviction to his ambition?[22]

Outraged by the criticisms of Faget whom he denounced as "a refugee enthusiast who knows neither English nor French,"[23] Voltaire wrote to Chancellor Chauvelin in an effort to prevent the importation of the offending edition into France;[24] and, for his own satisfaction, he jotted down responses to the refugee's remarks in the margin of the text. Despite what he might have implied in the speech of the elderly Catholic Jersey, Voltaire observed in one of these notes, he felt no horror, but quite the contrary, at the comment made by Faget that the Catholic faith might die out sooner than the Calvinist.[25]

While the Huguenots had their doubts about the spiritual perspective of *La Henriade*, Lord Stair, England's ambassador at Versailles, who had been shown the poem in manuscript form,[26] detected at once that it might serve as propaganda for the entente between his government and that of the Regent and pushed subscriptions to the first English edition. At Stair's suggestion, Voltaire wrote to George I in October 1725,[27] requesting royal patronage for a new edition of his epic, pointing out that he had praised both the Protestant faith and the virtues of the King's illustrious ancestor, Elizabeth, in his work.

Preceded by a considerable degree of literary notoriety and looking forward with some reason to a warm reception at the court of George I, Voltaire arrived in England in May 1726. Although the death of his royal patron in April 1727 and the succession of the francophobe George II somewhat dampened the poet's expectations, the tributes paid to English liberty and toleration in the 1728 edition of *La Henriade* helped win him the sympathy of his Protestant hosts.

At the beginning of his English visit, Voltaire lived at Wandsworth in Surrey where a number of Huguenot refugees had settled in 1685; later, in London, he met several distinguished Huguenot exiles, including Pierre Desmaizeaux, the editor of Bayle, and Jean Cavalier, the Camisard veteran.

Coming from a society where "one faith, one king, one law" had become a maxim of state, Voltaire was much impressed by the multiplicity of religions which enjoyed freedom of expression and organization in England. During a visit to Holland in 1722, the poet had already sensed the advantages of the policy of religious co-existence sponsored by the Dutch: "I see Calvinist, Arminian, and Socinian ministers, rabbis and Anabaptists, all of whom speak admirably in defence of their sect, and all of whom are right."[28] In England, this enthusiasm for religious pluralism was radically reinforced, as Voltaire made clear in the *Lettres anglaises* or *Lettres philosophiques*, the first edition of which was published in London in 1733. "This is a nation of sects," the French visitor noted: "As a free soul, an Englishman goes to heaven by whatever route he chooses."[29] Consciously or unconsciously, the English had discovered that the toleration of rival sects was the best guarantee that none of them would subvert public order: "If there were but one religion in England, despotism would become a threat; if there were two, they would cut each other's throats; but there are in fact thirty-odd and they live in peace and harmony together."[30]

This happy co-existence had not always been the rule, Voltaire pursued. The multifarious religious sects which had developed since the Reformation had once been inspired by the same fanatical spirit, the same claim to be exclusively possessed of the truth. This early zeal, however, had been spent in Cromwell's time, and subsequent administrations, awarding the spoils of office only to those who conformed at least outwardly to the Anglican creed, had reduced the devotees of heterodoxy to a marginal one-twentieth of the population. (Transferred to France, this comment might be read as a defence of the policy pursued in Cardinal Richelieu's time, when a number of Huguenot notables were in effect seduced into conversion by court appointments.)

In the course of examining the various denominations which made up the mosaic of English religious life, Voltaire expressed some patronizing interest in the Church of England but showed little sympathy for the spiritual cousins of the Huguenots, the Presbyterians, whose pastors he ridiculed for the ostentatious way in which they advertized their poverty, adding: "They walk about with an affected gravity and a dour expression on their faces and preach through their noses."[31] While damning wealthier denominations as decadent, these latter-day Puritans made English Sundays bleak with their self-conscious asceticism.

Soon after the appearance of the London edition of the *Lettres philosophiques*, Voltaire wrote to Jacob Vernet about the problem of getting a French edition past the censor:

> These letters seemed indeed philosophical to London readers but in Paris they are being denounced as impious by people who have not even read them. The man who passes for tolerant here will soon be regarded as an atheist there....The fact that a man has made a joke at the expense of the Quakers has led our Catholic friends to believe that he no longer believes in God.[32]

When Voltaire's tribute to English society appeared in France early in 1734, the Paris parlement condemned the work as "scandalous and anti-religious" and ordered copies of it burned by the public hangman on January 10, 1734. Voltaire suddenly found himself forced to choose between staying in Paris and facing the prospect of paying an even heavier penalty for praising English toleration or taking flight. He opted for the latter, finding asylum on the estate of his friend, Madame du Châtelet, at Cirey.

Undeterred by his scraps with French officialdom, Voltaire resolved to resume the battle against intolerance from the stage, as we shall see in a later chapter;[33] but the case for religious freedom which Voltaire presented to the theatre-going public in *Alzire* and *Mahomet* was also made in a number of lesser, more intimate, works written during the same period.

In the *Ode sur le Fanatisme* or *Ode sur la Superstition*, addressed to Madame Du Châtelet in 1732, the poet returned to the leitmotiv of *La Henriade*, namely, that fanaticism is an even greater threat to civic peace than atheism because it inspires citizens to commit acts of murderous violence against their neighbours. France had come to know what disorders theological controversy could engender during the sixteenth century, most dramatically in the nightmare of the Saint Bartholomew's Day Massacre. Only by exposing the scourge of fanaticism could the nation hope to achieve stability and peace:

> ...l'esprit humain qui dispute,
> Qui condamne, qui persécute,
> N'est qu'un détestable imposteur.[34]

In the *Discours en vers sur l'homme*, composed between 1734 and 1737, partially published in 1738 and 1745 but not appearing in its entirety until 1752, Voltaire makes yet another impassioned plea for the adoption of a simple deist creed and a tolerant outlook. Those whose capacity for tolerance had been strained should find consolation and encouragement in the sequel to the persecution of the noble Bayle by his bilious colleague Jurieu; Bayle was still universally respected for his scholarly detachment while the name of his tormentor had fallen into total oblivion.[35]

In the *Traité de Métaphysique*, a series of reflective essays written in 1734 but not intended for publication, Voltaire again asserted his belief in a Supreme Being and in toleration. Given the radical variations in religious belief and practice within most societies, he argued, a measure of mutual respect between men of differing faiths was a prerequisite for civil order.

In a mischievous mood, Voltaire cited the case of the Jews of Metz: the French monarchy which allowed these non-conformists to live out their lives in peace would commit them to the galleys were they to take two wives; on the other hand, were they to marry four women, they would gain instant acceptance in the Ottoman world.[36]

Of the many preoccupations which Voltaire shared with his readers during his early career, none was more persistently present than a warning against fanaticism and intolerance. As poet and essayist, he denounced these corrupt expressions of religion whether they were found in Catholic or

Calvinist culture; the persecution of Servet and the violent rebellion of the Camisards were indicted as severely as the fanaticism which had led to the Saint Bartholomew's Day Massacre. Although Voltaire wrote nothing during these years directly about the plight of the Huguenots living in eighteenth-century France, he must surely have conditioned those who read his early works to share his hatred of all forms of spiritual tyranny.

1.   G. Gargett, *Voltaire and Protestantism, SVEC*, vol.188 (1980), offers an exhaustive and, one is tempted to think, definitive analysis of the attitude of Voltaire towards Protestant culture in general and the Huguenots in particular; it clearly supplants L. Robért, *Voltaire et l'intolérance religieuse* (Lausanne, 1904) and E. Champendal, *Voltaire et les protestants de France* (Geneva, 1919).

2.   V. M. Chassaigne, *L'Affaire Calas* (Paris, 1929), p.292.

3.   Olympe's mother, an upper-middle-class Huguenot, fled France in 1685, then returned in 1687 and entered the *Institut des Nouvelles Catholiques* in order to conform (superficially at least) to the laws affecting suspected Protestant women. After resisting efforts at conversion, she fled, only to be captured and reconfined. Marriage to the 'new Catholic' Du Noyer whom she met in prison, offered freedom at a price: at the wedding which followed her release, she abjured, secretly vowing that she would raise any children born of the marriage in the Reformed faith. When Olympe was born, she was baptized in the Roman faith as the law prescribed; but when the marriage broke down, Madame Du Noyer fled to The Hague, taking her daughter with her. Voltaire fell in love with Olympe following his arrival in the Dutch capital as secretary to the French ambassador to the Low Countries. Madame Du Noyer disapproved of what she saw to be a socially disadvantageous liaison and demanded that Versailles recall the young secretary. In an effort to persuade Olympe to follow him back to France, Voltaire asked his old teacher, Père Tournemine, to intercede with Olympe's cousin, the Bishop of Evreux, so that she might return without running afoul of the laws governing 'new Catholics.' Having made these arrangements, Voltaire wrote Olympe indicating that all she needed to do in order to re-enter France was to respond favourably to a paternal summons. Upon her return, she would be placed in a Paris convent set aside for 'new Catholic' women— in fact, the same institution from which her mother had fled years earlier! As it turned out, Olympe resisted her lover's skillfully orchestrated plans. Had she accepted them, she would have become a virtual prisoner in an institution devoted to the spiritual re-education of young Calvinist women, and Voltaire would have become the accomplice of those whose chief function in life was to secure conversion under pressure. For a full account of the romance between Olympe Du Noyer and Voltaire, v. M. Fabre, *Voltaire et Pimpette de Nîmes* (Nîmes, 1936).

4.   The *thèse royale* would be most effectively articulated by the abbé Dubos in his *Histoire critique de l'établissement de la monarchie française dans les Gaules* (3 vols.; Paris, 1734).

5.   In *La Religion de Voltaire* (Paris, 1969), p. 80, René Pomeau contends that Voltaire's deist inclinations were already apparent in the satirical *Le Vrai Dieu*, published anonymously in 1715.

6.   Professor O.R. Taylor argues that the idea of writing an epic poem dedicated to
      Henri IV occurred to Voltaire in 1716 or 1717. V. *La Henriade*, ed. Taylor, in *The
      Complete Works of Voltaire* (Geneva, 1970), II, p. 20.

7.   E.C Davila, *Historia delle guerre civili di Francia* (Venice, 1630); L. Maimbourg,
      S.J., *Histoire du calvinisme* (Paris, 1682); Abbé L. Legendre, *Nouvelle histoire du
      France, depuis le commencement de la monarchie jusqu'à la mort de Louis XIII* (3
      vols. ; Paris, 1718).

8.   François de Mézeray, *Abrégé chronologique de l'histoire de France* (6 vols.;
      Amsterdam, 1712), v. esp. VI, pp. 6, 91, pp. 106-07, pp. 125-26.

9.   Part of Voltaire's intention in depicting the ravages of religious extremism in the
      sixteenth century was to point a warning and a lesson to the French leadership of
      his own day. The poet detected in Regency France a disquieting resemblance to the
      disorders he was portraying in *La Henriade*. Like the last of the Valois, Louis XIV
      had allowed himself to become enmeshed in partisan religious squabbles. His
      nephew, Orléans, whose skepticism in matters spiritual was notorious, should be
      encouraged to stay out of such nettlesome theological controversies and to show the
      same sense of secular priorities which had guided Henri IV and the Politiques. That
      Philippe d'Orléans fancied himself to be cast in the same psychological as well as
      physical mould as the first Bourbon would make this lesson all the easier to
      deliver. Preface to *La Henriade*, ed. Taylor, II, p. 360.

10.   Ibid., p. 378.

11.   Ibid., p. 391.

12.   Ibid., p.392.

13.   Ibid., p.496.

14.   Ibid., pp. 616-17.

15.   Voltaire to Isaac Cambiague, c. December 1725, Best. D. 259.

16.   *Mercure de France*, March 1724, pp. 583-84; May, 1725, p. 948.

17.   Daniel Mornet, "Les enseignements des bibliothèques privées 1750-1780," *Revue
      d'histoire littéraire de la France, XVII* (1910), pp. 460, 490.

18.   Condorcet, *Vie de Voltaire* (n.p., 1781), pp. 199-200.

19.   René de Bonneval, *Réflexions critiques sur un poème intitulé 'La Ligue,' imprimé
      à Genève et attribué à M. de Voltaire* (n.p., 1724), pp. 7-8; A. Poubeau de
      Bellechaume, *Lettre critique, ou Parallele des trois poëmes épiques anciens...avec
      La Ligue ou Henri le Grand de Voltaire* (Paris, 1724), p. 11.

20.   Voltaire, *An Essay upon the Civil Wars of France, extracted from various
      manuscripts and also upon the epic poetry of the European Nations from Homer to
      Milton* (London, 1727), p. 7.

21.   Faget went on to observe that the authorities in France, not satisfied with the pro-
      Catholic tenor of *La Henriade*, had criticized the poet for not scourging the
      Calvinists more, thereby proving that in Catholic states "it was not enough to be a
      papist, one had to be a furious partisan of popery" in order to gain recognition.
      Faget, *Pensées sur La Henriade*, in Voltaire, *La Henriade* (2nd ed.; London, 1728),
      p. iv.

22. Ibid., p. xx. A second refugee writer, Themiseul de Saint- Hyacinthe, echoed Faget in a series of *Lettres critiques* which were also appended to the Coderc edition of *La Henriade*.
23. Voltaire to Thieriot, May 2, 1728, Best. D. 333.
24. Voltaire to Chancellor Germain Louis Chauvelin, April 1728, Best. D. 331.
25. Voltaire, *Réponse à la critique de 'La Henriade,'* *Oeuvres* (Moland) VIII, p. 365, n.p. 9.
26. Voltaire to the earl of Stair June 20, 1719, Best. D.80.
27. Voltaire to King George I, October 6, 1725, Best. D. 250
28. Voltaire to the marquise de Bernières, October 7, 1722, Best. D. 128.
29. Voltaire, *Lettres philosophiques*, ed. R. Pomeau (Paris, 1964), p. 42.
30. Ibid., p. 47.
31. Ibid., p. 46.
32. Voltaire to Jean Jacob Vernet, September 14, 1733, Best. D. 653. At the beginning of this letter, Voltaire ventured to suggest that Vernet shared his own tolerant outlook: "I believe that you and I both believe in tolerance as far as religion is concerned, because in this area men can never be forced to change their convictions. I accept all men, provided they are not persecuters. I would even love Calvin if he had not had Servet burned."

    This was not the first reference by Voltaire to Calvin's complicity in the death of Servet for which the poet had already indicted the founder of the French Reformed churches in *La Henriade*. With the passage of time, Voltaire continued to press eighteenth-century Calvinists to join him in damning the founder of their faith for his intolerance and to repudiate once and for all the rationalization upon which Servet had been sent to the stake. The Servet issue would form a key element in the bitter polemical debate between Voltaire and Vernet which took place following their rupture in the late 1750s.
33. V. Chapter XII, pp.167-72.
34. Voltaire, *Ode sur le fanatisme*, in *Oeuvres* (Moland), VIII, p. 430.
35. Voltaire, *Discours en vers sur l'homme*, ibid., IX, p. 423.
36. Voltaire, *Traité de Métaphysique*, ibid., XXII.

Les Réfugiés François establissent des fabriques
dans le Brandebourg
Mem. pour servir à l'histoire du Refuge T.IV p.24

The high cost of the Revocation: Huguenot refugees prospering in
Brandenburg.

CHAPTER V

Montesquieu and the Huguenots:
A Conservative's View of Minority Rights

As the most conservative of the major thinkers of the French Enlightenment, Montesquieu might seem at first glance an unlikely champion of civil rights for non-conformists. Indeed, in his widely read *L'Esprit des lois*, the scholarly magistrate added to the embarrassment of the Huguenots by reviving the old hypothesis that Protestantism and republicanism went hand in hand. Politics apart, Montesquieu tended to find Protestants morally prudish and culturally Philistine. Yet, whatever reservations he may have had concerning their world-view, neither his character nor his circumstances would allow Montesquieu to remain indifferent to the sufferings of his Protestant fellow countrymen.

Montesquieu had a more direct personal acquaintance with the French Protestant community than most philosophes. As the husband of a Huguenot, he was able to form close friendships with leading members of the Calvinist "internal emigration." As traveller and scholar, he met a number of Europe's most gifted Protestant thinkers and writers, men such as the Genevan theologian Vernet and the itinerant publicist La Beaumelle. His most celebrated works, the *Lettres persanes* and *L'Esprit des lois*, were edited and published by Calvinist refugees. Finally, his cosmopolitan and tolerant inclinations were broadened as a result of contact with members of a second disadvantaged minority, the descendants of the Sephardic Jews who had been expelled from the Spain during the Inquisition and had settled in the Bordeaux area.[1]

His early training in the law brought Montesquieu to understand and deplore the ways in which French justice had been modified to transform magistrates into monitors of conscience. The political philosophy which the mature Montesquieu evolved made him the champion of corporate rights against the ever-encroaching pretensions of the monarchy. As a defender of the *thèse nobiliaire*, he saw both the Revocation of the Edict of Nantes and the repression of the Jansenists as part of a despotical design by which the crown had set about eliminating all spiritual as well as secular restraints on absolute power.

During the Regency period, the passionate antipathy which he felt towards the despotism of Louis XIV led Montesquieu to encourage a policy of religious pluralism for France. In his later years, he became more cautious about the wisdom of promoting spiritual diversity and more respectful of the role performed by the Catholic church in reinforcing the monarchist inclinations of the French. Montesquieu was to remain, however, a passionate critic of intolerance until his death and a helpful mentor to Protestants whose lives and property remained in jeopardy in the France of Louis XV.

The intimate links which were to bind Montesquieu to the French Calvinist community were forged during the last weeks of the Sun King's reign when he married the Huguenot Jeanne de Lartigue. The father of the bride, a former colonel in the French army, had been made a member of the Order of Saint Louis, the highest honour available to soldiers of the crown, despite his open profession of the Reformed faith. The same indulgence prevailed at the altar rail; no attempt was made to compel the bride to abjure her Calvinism before her marriage to Montesquieu in Bordeaux on April 30, 1715. The baronne de Montesquieu would, in fact, remain a believing Calvinist until her death in 1768, apparently without suffering any overt discrimination as a consequence.[2]

Montesquieu received a handsome dowry from his wife's family. Calculation rather than passion appears to have been the basic foundation of the marriage. By all accounts, Jeanne de Lartigue was a rather plain woman whose puritanical education ill suited her to become the partner of a man with a well-developed taste for the sensuous. Quite possibly, the sexual reticence of his young bride helped provoke in Montesquieu that special interest in the erotic which would find fuller release in Paris.[3]

Whatever its private disappointments, his marriage brought Montesquieu into contact with the small circle of titled Huguenot families which had opted to stay in France following the Revocation. It was through his wife that the president met Louis, chevalier de Jaucourt, the chief Calvinist contributor to the *Encyclopédie* and its co-editor (with Diderot) after 1758. Some of the political ideas of Montesquieu would reach readers of the *Encyclopédie* in articles written by his admiring Calvinist friend. Personal affection in Jaucourt was as strong as intellectual devotion; together with another Protestant, the Swedish ambassador Ulrik Scheffer, he was present at the death agony of Montesquieu in 1755.[4]

Between the marriage which associated him so intimately with the French Calvinist community and his death forty years later, Montesquieu reflected and wrote at great length about the role of religion in the shaping of social and political institutions. One principle guided him consistently throughout these reflections—that religions should be judged not in theological but in strictly utilitarian terms. The young *président* made this view abundantly clear as early as June 1716 in an address to the Bordeaux Academy to which he had been admitted two months earlier. The rulers of pagan Rome had provided a model of statesmanship and enlightenment in their treatment of religion, Montesquieu told his fellow academicians. Their deist convictions had raised them above the many parochial cults which were a source of divisiveness in the empire and made them natural partisans of toleration. As a result, they had been able to devise a policy which reconciled spiritual freedom and the interest of the state. According to this policy, all citizens of the empire paid at least nominal respect to the Almighty in the Pantheon where all of his multifarious incarnations were represented, but thereafter, "each citizen was high priest within his own household."[5] This sensible arrangement had allowed countless sects to co-exist inside the empire for generations. Unfortunately, the theocratic pretensions of the Egyptian priesthood, which Montesquieu clearly saw as the predecessor of the Jewish and Christian clergy, had undermined this statesmanlike balance between the rights of private conscience and the requirements of public peace.

However provocative, an address before a provincial academy had, of course, a rather limited impact. The first major public comment of Montesquieu concerning the relationship between religious faith and public order appeared with the publication in 1721 of the anonymous but highly successful *Lettres persanes*. Rica and Usbek, the Persian travellers who serve as the author's spokesmen in this work, find much that is startling in Western civilization but nothing more surprising than the way in which Christendom has been weakened and divided by theological controversy. Before arriving in Paris, they had naively assumed that all mankind had been converted to the view that the highest form of worship which one might offer the Almighty was the practice of civic virtue. Their own Moslem faith propagated a creed so simple that men had no occasion to quarrel over its meaning. They were delighted to learn that Europeans were beginning to lose the passion for theological disputes which had made them persecute those not sharing their creed. Anti-Semitism appeared to be losing its appeal for the Spanish, while Frenchmen were clearly having second thoughts about the need to persecute Christian non-conformists.[6]

The Persians, Usbek recalled, had learned the high cost of intolerance long ago during the reign of the shah Suleiman. Some of the shah's ministers had urged him to undertake the wholesale conversion of his Christian Armenian subjects, by force if necessary, in order to purge his realm of spiritual impurity. Suleiman had rejected the proposed crusade, however, after learning that the Armenians, rather than abjure, were about to seek asylum with his Indian and Mogul enemies, taking with them their considerable artisanal and commercial wealth. It had been a narrow escape. Had the shah allowed religious zeal to dictate state policy, the result would have been an inevitable decline in Persia's greatness.[7] French readers of Montesquieu were no doubt expected to regret that Louis XIV had not shown the wisdom of Suleiman.

Having celebrated the statesmanship of Suleiman, Usbek asked whether it might not be in the interest of sovereigns everywhere to promote religious diversity rather than conformity. If tolerance were given to different religions within the state, it would stimulate friendly emulation rather than strife. The sanction of new sects would also prevent the spiritual and moral sclerosis which usually develops when one faith holds a monopoly. Of course, distinctions might be maintained between the privileges given to members of the established church and the rights granted minority sects, since the latter, if denied public offices and honours, would inevitably seek to compensate for this limitation by giving themselves wholeheartedly to commercial careers, thus enriching the state:

> It should be noted that members of sects which are merely tolerated tend to make themselves more useful to the nation than those who belong to the dominant faith because, being kept from public honours and unable to distinguish themselves except by their wealth, they are prompted to acquire greater fortunes through their own industry and to undertake the most thankless tasks in the process.[8]

No possible danger could arise from the adoption of such a policy, Usbek argued, since all the world's religions preached submission to the civil authorities. The religious wars which had plagued Europe in the past had been the product, not of rivalry between contending sects within the same state, but of "the spirit of intolerance which animated that faith which regarded itself as dominant."[9]

Moving from the general argument for toleration to specifics, Usbek proceeded to develop what was to become one of the standard arguments for Protestant emancipation in the eighteenth century. It was reasonable to assume, the Persian argued, that there was a clear and direct link between the cult of priestly celibacy and the alarming population decline in the Catholic states of Europe, just as it was obvious that the Protestant sexual ethic guaranteed a healthy demographic expansion: "In the Protestant faith which permits neither priests nor dervishes, everyone has the right to have children. I dare say that, if the present state of affairs continues in Europe, it is impossible that the Catholic church should last five hundred years."[10] With their superior population, Usbek concluded, the Protestant nations had a broader tax base, the land was better cultivated, and commerce flourished because, whatever their faith, men were free to pursue their fortunes in the marketplace.

Given the vigilance of the censors, the attack on the religious policy of Louis XIV made by Montesquieu in the *Lettres persanes* was of necessity oblique. In his uncertainty about the reception which even this indirect assault upon the Sun King's memory might encounter, Montesquieu entrusted the printing of his manuscript to Jacques Desbordes, a Protestant refugee from Bordeaux who had settled in Amsterdam. The result was that the *Lettres persanes*, like many key works of the Enlightenment, reached its French readers through the good offices of exiled Calvinists who were themselves victims of the Revocation.

The ideas about religious freedom which Montesquieu expressed in the *Lettres persanes* were based on the passionate revulsion which he felt early in life for the despotical system of Louis XIV; they were ideas developed in the abstract at a time when their author had little real knowledge of Protestant society. In the Grand Tour which Montesquieu began in the spring of 1728, he would gain impressions and gather empirical data which would make him both less sympathetic to Protestant culture and more appreciative of the role played by Catholicism in the evolution of French civilization.

The eleven months which he spent in Italy beginning in the summer of 1728, including a two-month sojourn in Rome in the company of the Swiss pastor Vernet, brought Montesquieu a new appreciation for the Catholic contribution to the arts: "I feel much more attached to my religion since seeing Rome and the artistic treasures in her churches....How many beautiful works of art would have been denied us if the Protestant faith had triumphed in Europe!"[11]

The German states through which Montesquieu travelled in the summer and fall of 1729 had been spared religious conflict since 1648, when the Treaty of Westphalia separated the Catholic and Protestant states which had striven for domination in the area and granted partisans of each faith their freedom on a regional basis. Although Montesquieu recognized that the treaty had brought stability to the Germanies, he was concerned that it had weakened the Catholic influence there by removing the political attractiveness to Protestant princes of a shift to the Roman communion. The interest of the philosophe in the relative strength of the Catholic element in the German states was directly linked to his concern for a sound French diplomatic policy in the area. He was sharply critical of the principle which had guided his nation's relations with the Germanies since the age of Richelieu—that is, that it was in France's best interest to promote the northern Protestant German states against the Habsburgs. Times had changed, Montesquieu insisted, and the old policy ought to be abandoned:

> As far as I am concerned, the policy of leaguing ourselves with the Protestant princes is an outdated policy which is no longer valid. France had and will always have no more mortal enemies than the Protestants, witness our past wars....Germany's Protestants will always be allied to the English and Dutch because religion makes an eternal bond between them.[12]

The implication in these remarks that there was a "Protestant Internationale" operating in eighteenth-century diplomacy would no doubt strike modern students of international relations as an anachronism. In any case, the suggestion that Huguenots would be drawn by a common religious bond to collaborate with France's Protestant enemies was scarcely calculated to enhance the case for their emancipation.

From the Germanies, Montesquieu travelled to England, where he arrived in October 1729. Like his contemporaries Voltaire and Prévost, the *président* was startled at the degree to which conventional Christian beliefs had been abandoned in the English circles in which he moved: "In France, I am considered to have too little religion, in England too much.... If people talk of religion here, everyone begins to laugh."[13] In fact, the broad degree of religious toleration which Voltaire found to be such a welcome element in English life disquieted Montesquieu, who felt that the indifference of the English in religious matters was as deplorable as its extreme opposite, Spanish intolerance. The cult which the English had made of religious liberty had drawbacks as well as advantages. It was clearly beneficial that the English clergy, lacking that special status and privilege which set the priesthood apart in other states, were integral members of society; without any claim on the secular arm in the fulfillment of their mission, they must win souls by peaceful methods alone; in fact, any sect which set out to establish spiritual domination over the population would be quickly and effectively repudiated both by law and by public opinion. On the other hand, there were clear signs that an excess of religious freedom had dissipated the overall spiritual vitality of the people. Englishmen who had earlier been sincerely committed members of various religious sects now tended to pursue their own private inclinations in matters of faith while paying only the nominal respect to the doctrines of the established church which was required of them by law.[14]

If the spiritual condition of the English troubled Montesquieu, he was even less taken with the political outlook of the French refugees whom he encountered in London. Those whom he met were respectable enough: Pierre Desmaizeaux, the editor of Bayle's correspondence, Jean Théophile Desaguliers, who had been made Grand Master of the Masons in 1719, Pierre Coste, the editor of Montaigne and translator of Locke, Georges Louis Tessier, a Camisard veteran who proposed Montesquieu for membership in the Royal Society, and the marquis Gabriel Duquesne, grandson of the famous Huguenot admiral. Yet, however congenial these men may have been socially, Montesquieu deplored what he felt to be a clearly republican bias in their politics: "Our refugees are all Whigs. If the throne of England is ever toppled, it will be by these men, as it was during the time of Charles I by the French refugees of that period."[15]

Finally, although it interested him somewhat less, Montesquieu was curious about the relationship between Protestantism and English economic life. As he saw it, the commercial life of France's great rival had been enormously stimulated by the Reformation, most particularly by the decision of Henri VIII to confiscate the wealth of those sanctuaries of sloth, the monasteries.[16]

Travel to England and the Germanies and reflection concerning the contribution of Protestantism to the political and cultural life of Europe led Montesquieu to a number of conclusions which found their way into the pages of *L'Esprit des lois*, published in November 1748. The most provocative of these conclusions, that the Protestant temper was more suited to the northerly parts of Europe where it had first found expression and that its natural political complement was republicanism, gave new credibility to old allegations circulated at the time of the Revocation. As Montesquieu saw it, the rift in sixteenth-century Christendom had revealed two societies as incompatible in their politics as in their theology:

> Northerly populations have and will always have a spirit of independence and freedom which southerly people do not possess. A religion which has no visible leader is better suited to a hardy climate.[17]

The political repercussions of this fundamental divergence had become quickly apparent:

> In countries where the Protestant faith established itself, revolutions followed on the political level....Calvin, having behind him either people who already lived in republics or obscure bourgeois living in monarchies, was easily able to do away with honours and dignities.[18]

Geography had conditioned the ethical and aesthetic as well as the political outlook of post-Reformation Europe, Montesquieu continued. In the warmer southern half of the continent, the proliferation of holy days was both natural and welcome, while the bracing climate of the north had produced a cult of work. Catholic southerners, drawn by a "natural taste for sensual objects,"[19] had clung to the use of elaborate imagery in their church architecture while the rugged environment of northern Europe inclined the Protestant population there to choose more austere settings for their worship. Montesquieu allowed that there were exceptions to his general hypothesis: priestly celibacy was rigidly enforced in those warm regions of Europe where its acceptance imposed an almost unbearable burden, yet, paradoxically, it was proscribed in the Protestant north, where man's passions were tempered by nature.[20]

The comments about Protestantism in *L'Esprit des lois* formed only a tiny portion of a vast text full of precocious and sometimes provocative 'sociology.' Concerned that some of his opinions might cause him problems with the French censors, Montesquieu sent the completed manuscript during the summer of 1747 to Pierre Mussard, state secretary of Geneva and a remote relative of Rousseau, asking about the possibility of Swiss publication. Mussard not only found a willing publisher, Barillot; he also suggested that Montesquieu ask Jacob Vernet to proofread and edit the manuscript. Montesquieu was delighted, and Vernet proved himself a most eager and effective collaborator. When the scholarly pastor had completed the editing of *L'Esprit des lois*, he made discreet inquiries of the French resident in Geneva, Lévesque de Champeaux, concerning the book's passage into France. The resident in turn got in touch with the intendant at Lyon to ensure that the printed volumes would go unchallenged at the border. As a result of these subtle negotiations, copies of the freshly printed text destined for Montesquieu via a discreet Bordeaux address passed the French customs uneventfully. The Calvinist friends and acquaintances of Montesquieu thus ensured the editing, publishing, and even the distribution of this critically important product of Enlightenment scholarship.[21]

Soon after the appearance of *L'Esprit des lois*, those opposed to any change in the Huguenots' status took to citing the passages of the work which linked Protestantism to republicanism,[22] while spokesmen of the French Calvinist community expressed their surprise and disappointment that Montesquieu had furnished new ammunition to their enemies.[23] At least one Calvinist, however, the publicist La Beaumelle, welcomed *L'Esprit des lois*, giving it a series of highly favourable reviews in the pages of *La Spectatrice danoise* which he was then editing in Copenhagen.[24] During a visit to Paris in July 1750, La Beaumelle met Montesquieu, who had been genuinely flattered by his young admirer's critique. French Catholic opinion had been far less indulgent concerning his book, the author informed his visitor, adding that he had been obliged to defend himself against charges levelled in *Les Nouvelles Ecclésiastiques* that *L'Esprit des lois* contained deist and even atheist ideas.[25]

Incensed at the hostile reception which *L'Esprit des lois* had encountered in his homeland, La Beaumelle published an anonymous *Suite de la Défense de L'Esprit des lois*, the text of which recklessly exposed his own Protestant bias. In the original work, Montesquieu had made some rather critical remarks about clerical celibacy. La Beaumelle was much more caustic; the decadence of Catholic as opposed to Protestant Germany, he wrote in the *Suite*, clearly derived from the enormous strain imposed on an otherwise healthy population by the extensive practice of priestly continence. The Calvinist pamphleteer expressed himself even more boldly when recapitulating the hypothesis put forward in *L'Esprit des lois* that there were natural affinities between Protestantism and republicanism: "Blind faith leads to passive obedience. The Protestant religion is better suited to a republic because its fundamental principles bear a direct relationship to the republican form of government. An enlightened faith is in perfect harmony with the spirit of independence and liberty."[26]

The gratuitous apologia which La Beaumelle penned on behalf of his idol created a considerable degree of embarrassment. *Les Nouvelles Ecclésiastiques* assumed that Montesquieu was the author of the *Suite* and rebuked him roundly for what was seen to be a serious spiritual lapse. The *président* felt disinclined to respond to this attack. Need he bother to deny having written the *Suite de la Défense*, he asked his friend l'abbé de Guasco, since it must be clear that no one with a Catholic education could have written such a text?[27] Turning directly to La Beaumelle, Montesquieu pleaded with his Protestant champion not to fire off any more anonymous salvoes in defence of *L'Esprit des lois*. He added with charming tact: "When you wrote that brochure, you never dreamed that people would attribute it to me. If you had thought that this might happen, you would not have written it. It is so full of wit that people believed the author to have been carried away in the defence of his own cause."[28]

The hypothesis advanced in *L'Esprit des lois* and seconded with embarrassing eagerness by La Beaumelle, that Protestants were latent republicans, was scarcely designed to win support for French Calvinist emancipation. Although Montesquieu had surely not intended to add to the discomfiture of the Huguenots, it is clear from the notes and comments which he committed to paper during his middle years, many of which were to remain unpublished, that as time passed, he came to view more sympathetically the role played by Catholicism in reinforcing what he felt were the naturally monarchist inclinations of his fellow Frenchmen. In one of his *Pensées*, he makes what is perhaps his most categorical case for the collective commitment of France to Catholicism, arguing that it is this commitment which guarantees France's primacy among the nations:

> France should support the Catholic religion, which is ill-suited to all other Catholic countries but does her no harm. By this support, she maintains her superiority over other Catholic nations. Were France to turn Protestant, all other states would follow suit.[29]

Quite apart from the peculiar suitability of Catholicism to France, Montesquieu came to believe that all nations ought to cherish and protect the traditional religions which formed part of their peculiar cultural inheritance. In general, a state which was satisfied with its established faith ought to ban new cults, although it was reasonable to tolerate sects which, having established themselves, posed no threat to public order, such as the Calvinists in seventeenth-century France.

If and when a state decided to grant freedom to a religious minority, Montesquieu argued, it had the right to demand that the newly tolerated sect pledge itself to be tolerant in turn, since the evidence of history was that religious communities which had undergone any form of persecution tended themselves to oppress if and when they managed to gain the upper hand.[30] Civil magistrates should, of course, discipline sects which disturbed the peace. But the state should refrain from penalizing purely theological errors, since most religious groups possessed spiritual sanctions quite intimidating enough to dissuade would-be heretics. In one particularly forceful passage, Montesquieu summed up his life long conviction about the proper role of the secular authority in dealing with spiritual non-conformity:

> Where no public act is involved, there can be no question of a crime having been committed. Whatever occurs in such cases is between man and God, who best knows the appropriate measure and timing of His vengeance. If the magistrate, confusing his role, joins in seeking out hidden cases of sacrilege, he opens up an inquiry into a type of activity where it is in no way required....Wrongs have arisen from this false notion that one must avenge the deity. One should honour the deity, and never avenge Him.[31]

Reinforcing this argument, Montesquieu pointed out that two of the greatest crimes committed by the French monarchy had been based on the contention that it was the duty of the crown to make France all Catholic. The Saint Bartholomew's Day Massacre, preceded by the circulation of trumped-up charges of an impending Calvinist plot, had been nothing more than an act of ruthless power politics for which religion merely served as the pretext.[32]

The Revocation, rationalized by religious argument, had been decided upon by three key figures at court, all of whom suffered from peculiar personality problems: Louis XIV, a pitiable victim of Jesuit intrigue "whose piety finished off the little intelligence which had been awarded him by nature,"[33] Madame de Maintenon, who steadily undermined the King's spirit in order to advance her own ambitions, and Chancellor Le Tellier, who had gone along with the repressive legislation at a time when his judgment had lapsed.

Montesquieu did not limit his criticism of past and present attacks on religious repression to abstract denunciations. On at least two occasions towards the end of his life, one in behalf of a relative, once in support of the brash La Beaumelle, he used his influence discreetly but effectively to relieve Protestants caught in the toils of the law.

Because his wife was a Calvinist and because he had received training in the law, Montesquieu was bound to receive pleas for advice and help from in-laws beset by legal problems. One of the most persistent of those to seek his counsel was the lawyer Daniel Grenoilleau who fled to Geneva with his widowed mother, Judith Lartigue, to escape the penal laws against Calvinists. Grenoilleau had not disposed of his considerable property in the Bordeaux area before his flight, although he had been fully aware that the real estate of refugees was subject to confiscation. As time passed and legislation concerning the Huguenots seemed to fall into disuse, he wrote to Montesquieu asking about the advisability of his returning to claim his property. The *président* advised extreme caution. As a respected lawyer, well known in his new Swiss milieu, Grenoilleau might precipitate an unwelcome general return of avowed Calvinists from exile if his case were treated indulgently. Montesquieu suggested instead that Grenoilleau write a letter to the marquis de Tourny, intendant at Bordeaux, explaining that he had never intended to leave France and that he had done so only out of panic.[34] After prolonged negotiations, the intendant, who was on good terms with Montesquieu, ruled in favour of Grenoilleau, whose property was restored.[35] Although Montesquieu had remained fairly circumspect during his correspondence with Grenoilleau, he had been both loyal and, given the delicacy of the refugee's legal position, effective.

The second case in which Montesquieu came to the rescue of a Calvinist involved the irrepressible La Beaumelle, who managed to get himself shut up in the Bastille in April 1753 as a result of having indiscreetly lampooned both Voltaire and Madame de Pompadour. Montesquieu used his influence with Berryer, the lieutenant of police, to secure the pamphleteer's release in October of the same year.[36] Typically, La Beaumelle could think of no more appropriate means of expressing his gratitude than by bringing out an edition of his protector's controversial *Lysimaque*. Thoroughly alarmed at this ill-considered generosity, Montesquieu persuaded La Beaumelle to suspend all thought of publication just in time.[37]

In the four decades between his marriage to Jeanne de Lartigue and his death, Montesquieu gave a great deal of thought to the role of religion in society. His initial inclination, based in large measure on a desire to see the despotism of Louis XIV undone, had been to champion a rather uninhibited policy of religious toleration. However, the one constant approach of Montesquieu to all religions was that they be judged in terms of their social utility; and, as his experience of Protestantism increased, so did his skepticism about the suitability of Protestant values to French politics and society. Similarly, a deepening awareness of Catholicism made him come to appreciate the ways in which the Roman faith sustained what he believed were the deep and abiding interests of France at home and abroad. Yet there remained in Montesquieu to the end a sense of utter revulsion at the persecution practised against the Calvinists by the French monarchy in the sixteenth and seventeenth centuries and a compassionate concern, reinforced by ties of blood, and friendship, for those individual Huguenots who were still suffering intolerable discrimination in the age of Louis XV.

---

1. Two recent scholarly studies have emphasized the contrast between the tolerance of Montesquieu towards the Jews, even his philosemitism, and the anti-Semitism of such key writers as Voltaire. V. Léon Poliakov, *Histoire de l'antisémitisme. De Voltaire à Wagner* (Paris, 1968), pp. 96-103; Arthur Hertzberg, *The French Enlightenment and the Jews* (New York, 1968), pp. 273-76, p. 287.
2. Pierre Barrière, *Un grand provincial: Charles-Louis de Secondat, baron de La Brède et de Montesquieu* (Bordeaux, 1946), p.452.

3.   Ibid., p. 84.

4.   R. Shackleton, *Montesquieu, A Critical Biography* (Oxford, 1961), p. 393.

5.   Montesquieu, "Dissertation sur la politique des Romains dans la Religion," June 16, 1716, *in Oeuvres complètes,* ed. A Masson (3 vols.; Paris, 1950-55), III, p. 45.

6.   Montesquieu, *Lettres persanes,* ibid., p. 121.

7.   Ibid., p.172.

8.   Ibid., p.173.

9.   Ibid., p.174.

10. Ibid., pp. 234-35.

11. Montesquieu, *Voyages, 1728-29,* ibid., II, p. 1293; "De la manière gothique," ibid, p. 280.

12. Montesquieu, *Voyages,* ibid., p. 1281.

13. Montesquieu, *Pensées,* ibid., p. 306; *Notes sur l'Angleterre,* ibid., III, p. 292.

14. Montesquieu, *L'Esprit des lois,* ibid., I, p. 440.

15. Montesquieu, *Pensées,* ibid., II, p. 49.

16. Montesquieu, *L'Esprit des lois,* ibid., p. 75.

17. Ibid., p. 86

18. Ibid., p. 116.

19. Ibid., p. 107.

20. Ibid., p. 112.

21. Jacob Vernet to Montesquieu, June 15, 1750, ibid., III, p. 1311. Montesquieu to Vernet, June 26, 1750, ibid., p.1314. In return for the editorial labours which he had devoted to *L'Esprit des lois,* Vernet had asked Montesquieu for scholarly advice about a work of his own, a new French version of the Bible. The Protestants, the pastor reminded his friend, had always used "tu" when translating passages in which God spoke or was spoken to, but there was some feeling among his colleagues at Geneva that a shift to "vous" might be more fitting. Vernet was not sympathetic to the suggested change and had taken comfort from the use of the familiar pronoun by Usbek and Rica when addressing the Supreme Being in the *Lettres persanes.* In his reply, Montesquieu urged Vernet to reject the mistaken delicacy of his colleagues. In their earlier translation of the Scriptures, the Protestants had always managed to preserve the strong poetic feeling of the original text. Vernet should stick to this excellent tradition and make his new rendering of Biblical prose "male and vigorous" after the manner of Michelangelo's sculpture.

22. Abbé Jean Novi de Caveirac, *Apologie de Louis XIV et de son Conseil, sur la Révocation de l'Edit de Nantes* (Paris, 1758), pp. 271, 386; Bouniol de Montégut, *La voix de vrai patriote catholique, opposée à celle des faux Patriotes tolérans* (Paris, 1756), pp. 54, 106.

23. Antoine Court, *Le Patriote Français et impartial, ou Réponse à la 'Lettre de M. l'évêque d'Agen à M. le Contrôlleur-général contre la tolérance des Huguenots'* (2 vols.; Villefranche, 1753), I, pp. 171-72.

24. A. Taphanel, *La Beaumelle et Saint-Cyr. D'après des correspondances inédites et des documents nouveaux* (Paris, 1898), p. 39.

25. Montesquieu, *Défense de 'L'Esprit des lois,'* Oeuvres, I, pp. 431-93.

26. L.-A. de La Beaumelle, *Suite de la 'Défense de L'Esprit des lois,' ou Examen de la Réponse du Gazetier Ecclésiastique à la 'Défense de L'Esprit des lois'* (Berlin, 1751), p. 44.

27. Montesquieu to the abbé de Guasco, October 4, 1752, *Oeuvres*, III, p. 1441.

28. Montesquieu to La Beaumelle, February 24, 1753, ibid., p. 1451.

29. Montesquieu, Pensées, *Oeuvres*, II, p. 558.

30. Montesquieu, *L'Esprit des lois*, ibid., p. 117.

31. Ibid., I, p. 254.

32. Montesquieu, *Pensées*, ibid., II, p. 81.

33. Ibid., p. 392.

34. Montesquieu to Daniel Grenoilleau, January 9, 1746, ibid., III, pp. 1064-65.

35. Same to same, January 16, 1751, ibid., p. 1359.

36. Montesquieu to La Beaumelle, November 8, 1753, cited in Taphanel, *La Beaumelle et Saint-Cyr*, p. 148.

37. Montesquieu to La Beaumelle, January 12, 1754, ibid., pp. 150-51.

Eh! Monsieur, ne pensez vous pas à votre vie?

Calvinist catacombs in Louis XV's Paris: A scene from Prévost's *Doyen de Killerine*.

CHAPTER VI

A Friend in the Enemy Camp:
The Abbé Prévost

In his understanding of the Protestant world, the abbé Prévost had one very real advantage over most French writers of his time, in that for six years, beginning in 1728, he abandoned his monastic vows and became, nominally at least, a convert to Calvinism. Prior to this, Prévost had developed a considerable knowledge of Protestant theology while he was a young Benedictine scholar. Both in his Catholic and in his Protestant phase, the abbé was convinced that Christians of all persuasions were moving towards unity of belief, a development which he felt should be doubly welcome: to begin with, the spiritual convergence of formerly divided Christians would end centuries of disputatiousness and intolerance; in addition, it might serve as a step on the way towards the profession of the purely natural religion which Prévost privately favoured.

Following his conversion when he lived in England, Prévost came to admire the wisdom of his hosts, who had learned that religious toleration brings its own rewards, material as well as spiritual. This admiration was transmitted to French readers in *Le Pour et contre*, a newsletter which he edited between 1733 and 1740. More effective with the general public were the stories and anecdotes about Huguenot suffering, some based on real life, which he introduced into his immensely popular novels.

Although towards the end of his life Prévost unwittingly added to the conservative case against Protestant toleration by translating David Hume's history of Stuart England in which Protestant sectarianism was seen as a source of civil strife, he can hardly be blamed for the uses to which his translation was put by reactionary pamphleteers. Overall, the scholarly abbé remains one of the most compassionate and understanding analysts of Huguenot suffering and one of the most forthright champions of religious freedom in the age of Louis XV.

The conversion of the abbé Prévost to Calvinism in the fall of 1728 was one in a long series of spiritual false starts. Beginning in 1713, he had twice entered and twice abandoned the Jesuit novitiate before committing himself to the Benedictines. Having taken his vows at Saint-Germain-des-Prés in 1726, the young abbé bridled at what he felt to be the excessive severity of the Benedictine rule and sought in vain to obtain permission from Rome to transfer to a less strict branch of the order. There was, however, one consolation for Prévost during those austere years at Saint-Germain; the local Benedictines were working on the *Gallia Christiana*, the scholarly chronicle of the French church begun by the distinguished Jean Mabillon in the late seventeenth century. Research connected with this work, especially an interest in the movement for Christian reunion, brought Prévost into contact with Gabriel Dumont, French-born pastor of the Dutch embassy chapel in Paris. A combination of genuine intellectual sympathy for Protestant theology and calculation that his own conversion would guarantee him a ready asylum in Protestant Europe seems to have been behind the decision of Prévost to declare himself a Calvinist in the fall of 1728. Pastor Dumont was understandably jubilant. In a letter to his Genevan colleague Turrettini, he stressed the sincerity of the man whose soul he had just redeemed:

> The disgust which (Prévost) felt at certain superstitious Catholic practices brought him to inform himself more fully concerning the Roman faith. Easy access to the best scholarly works soon revealed to him that he had been brought up in a communion full of errors. I can testify, however, that he only accepted conversion after a long struggle.[1]

Flight to England followed this dangerous profession of faith. Late in November 1728, Prévost was received by William Wake, the archbishop of Canterbury, a man whose ecumenical outlook he had come to admire as a result of reading about Wake's proposals for a union of the English and French national churches. The archbishop's patronage brought the abbé into contact with members of the Huguenot refugee community in London, men such as Pierre Desmaizeaux, the pastors Pierre Daudé and Charles-Etienne Jordan, the historian Rapin-Thoyras and the convert to Anglicanism Hippolyte Beauchâteau.

The most significant of these new acquaintances, at least in terms of Prévost's later literary career, was Penelope Aubin, who introduced the abbé to the work of the contemporary French author Robert Challes. Prévost was to be much influenced by both the style and thematic material of Challes's *Les Illustres Françoises*, a series of short stories, some of which dealt with contemporary Huguenot life. Challes's style is flippant and light-hearted; yet he exposes with admirable clarity the deviousness, hypocrisy and spiritual anguish which are the inevitable by-products of efforts to force consciences. Prévost was to find him a very useful source.[2]

In the fall of 1730, Prévost travelled to Holland in the company of the chevalier de Chavannes, another member of the refugee community whom he had met in London. It was in many ways to be a fateful trip. In The Hague, the vulnerable ex-monk met and fell in love with Lenki Eccart, a Swiss Calvinist with a penchant for high living who was to cause him both financial and social embarrassment. His return to England in the company of this compromising mistress brought on a crisis. Contrary to her lover's hopes, Lenki did not qualify to receive the pension awarded Huguenot refugees in England, and her extravagance brought Prévost to try passing a forged note, a venture which brought him five days in jail. These mishaps persuaded Prévost to end his flirtation with heresy and to seek his reintegration into the Benedictine order. Without making any reference to his six-year spiritual lapse, he addressed a request for readmission into his order to Pope Clement XII early in 1734. Thanks in part to the sympathetic intervention of the cardinal de Bissy and the prince de Conti, Prévost was pardoned and granted his request on June 5, 1734.

The return of the abbé to his order did not pass unnoticed. One critic in particular, Lenglet-Dufresnoy, who obviously had inside information, took malicious pleasure in exposing what he knew of the Benedictine's spiritual wanderings. Prévost had been a 'Protestant' or 'Anglican' and probably did not know himself. He was returning to the fold not out of passionate conviction but because he had found Protestant society boring. No doubt he was seeking to reconcile himself with the Benedictines simply as a prelude to undertaking some even more venturesome spiritual trip. He might well end up as a Moslem![3] Stung by this attack, Prévost made a rare declaration of faith in the June 1734 issue of *Le Pour et contre*. He had always been a Catholic, he insisted, but the Christianity which he professed "ordered the practice of sound morality as well as a belief in miracles, the love of one's neighbour as well as the love of God; and it especially condemned slander."[4]

After a brief return to the monastic life, Prévost accepted the post of chaplain to the prince de Conti in December 1735. Given the prince's indifference in matters of faith, the new post brought with it few spiritual obligations. The abbé was thus able to devote his full time to writings in which the related themes of Huguenot suffering and the advantages of toleration were regularly set forth.

Le Pour et contre which Prévost began to issue in 1733 included a good deal of comment, most of its sympathetic, about life and literature in Protestant Europe. In one particularly forceful passage, the abbé lets an imaginary Englishman argue that the island's present prosperity is due to the influx of Huguenots after 1685:

> Even if zeal for the faith had not led us to welcome the French refugees, self-interest would not have allowed us to let pass such a glorious opportunity to enrich ourselves at the expense of our neighbours. I will leave it to moralists to discover whether the refugees have not brought their vices as well as their virtues with them, but it would be graceless not to acknowledge that England has changed its whole aspect since their settlement here. The time of their arrival is truly the moment when our arts and manufacture took on a new lease of life. Our manners have become more polished and our social customs have lost their awkwardness.[5]

The English had clearly learned that religious toleration brought concrete as well as spiritual rewards; yet, paradoxically, they had not taken this lesson to heart in their treatment of their Catholic fellow countrymen, who were allowed only the most marginal freedom. The readers of *Le Pour et contre* were given a moving description of a funeral of London Catholics, permitted to bury their dead in an Anglican cemetery but obliged to behave with an almost furtive discretion during the ceremony in order not to offend the religious establishment.[6]

In several passages of his newsletter, the abbé suggested that the general orientation of Christian scholarship was towards a new era of understanding and tolerance. He clearly felt that a good deal of the bitter dissension which had plagued Christendom derived from the violent temper of some of the early Reformers, especially Calvin, whose ruthless suppression of Servet he condemned as severely as did Voltaire.[7] Fortunately, Protestant theology seemed to have lost its former virulence. It might be an appropriate moment for Anglicans and French Catholics to take up Archbishop Wake's proposal and initiate the process of restoring Christian unity by making a joint commitment to the basic doctrines of the pre-Reformation church. The long-term solution to the problem of continuing intolerance between Catholics and Protestants lay in the revival of the ecumenical movement of the seventeenth century, to which Prévost invited scholars of all persuasions to contribute. With a bit of good will, the few remaining sources of theological conflict between Christians could surely be dispelled.[8]

Much of the knowledge about the Protestant world which Prévost had gained from his readings and travels was woven into the novels and short stories which he wrote between 1727 and 1741. A number of scenes in these works recreate for the reader tribulations endured by the Huguenots before and after the Revocation. While the novelist's fictional spokesmen openly rejoice at the policy of religious toleration which allowed Protestant victims of French oppression to find refuge in England and Holland, they also attack the continuing discrimination which keeps Irish Catholics from living out full and free lives. The lesson which Prévost intends his readers to draw from his dramatization of religious persecution on both sides of the Channel is clear: oppression of conscience is a crime as well as a sin, whether it is rationalized by priests or pastors. This lesson is reinforced by the central figures in the novels, paragons of toleration and enlightenment who worship without temples and marry without sacraments and whose theology is neither Protestant nor Catholic, but deist.

In the first volume of his *Mémoires et aventures d'un homme de qualité qui s'est retiré du monde*, published in 1727, Prévost is clearly writing the scenario for his own impending conversion and flight. The central figure of the novel, the marquis de Renoncourt, is a well-born youth who has felt bound by honour and filial piety to join a religious order. His spirit rebels at the strict regime under which he is obliged to live; and he travels to Rome hoping to obtain a dispensation from some of his order's regulations. When this petition is denied him, Renoncourt repudiates his vows and flees to Holland in the company of a Roman girl with whom he has fallen in love. Holland offers a ready asylum to the runaway monk, who indicates a desire to espouse the Calvinist faith. His hosts are delighted and trumpet the news that they have won a prize convert from the enemy camp.

Renoncourt subsequently travels to England with a young travelling companion. They visit Stonehouse near Plymouth where a colony of French refugees has been sustained by the liberality of a local nobleman.[9] Throughout their tour, they are much impressed, not only by such specific cases of English generosity, but by the overall spiritual atmosphere which prevails in England. True, they concede, the Reformation had produced the spiritual rift which had helped bring on the civil war of the 1640s and the beheading of Charles I; and the inscription at the base of the monument commemorating the Great Fire of 1666 carried the improbable and tasteless charge that the catastrophe had been the result of a popish plot. But what of France, where similar religious schism had been the backdrop to the Saint Bartholomew's Day Massacre? England in any case had learned her lesson from the tragic religious strife of the seventeenth century. She had become a tolerant and generous nation where religious diversity was respected. The churchmen whom the visitors encountered were both virtuous and scholarly, qualities sadly lacking in other Christian states. The enthusiasm of the two French travellers about religious life in England was summed up by the companion of Renoncourt at the end of their trip:

> The English have understood that constraint is an offence against the spirit of the Gospel. They know that men's hearts are in God's keeping, that violence produces only external changes in belief and that forced worship is a cruel sacrilege which damns those who exact it quite as much as those who submit to it.[10]

Thanks to their understanding of the need to respect freedom of conscience, the English had opened wide their churches without becoming too exercised if people did not worship there in great numbers. The faith which had survived in this free climate was solid, modest, and unaffected. Scandal and vice were at a minimum, and the ethics of the Gospel were practised as well as preached. The English, it was true, had arbitrarily confiscated the great holdings of the monasteries during the Reformation period, but this was not, as Catholic critics maintained, in order to promote secular enrichment at the cost of abandoning spiritual priorities. The real purpose of this confiscation had been to subsidize hospitals, schools for the poor, and homes for the aged:

> What man in his senses would not prefer these wise and pious foundations to our convents and monasteries where, as is common knowledge, laziness

and uselessness pass themselves off as disdain for the world and contemplation of heavenly truths?[11]

Having listened to this rapturous tribute in silence, Renoncourt laughingly chided his companion for having made what amounted to an apologia for Reformed Christianity. His friend replied that his perspective was neither that of a Catholic nor of a Protestant but one which even the most corrupt Italian prelate would come to share if he were to visit England.

The boldly anglophile sentiments which Prévost had expressed in his *Homme de qualité* did not pass unremarked. The pro-Jansenist abbé Desfontaines paid special tribute to the "high courage" with which Prévost had Renoncourt celebrate English religious freedom at the end of his visit to the island kingdom.[12]

In *Le Philosophe anglais, ou Histoire de Monsieur Cleveland*, Prévost gave his readers glimpses of French Calvinist society on both sides of the Atlantic. The novel's central male characters, Cleveland and Bridge, bastard sons of Oliver Cromwell, visit a number of Huguenot communities in the course of a life spent wandering through Europe and America. Bridge, banished to the West Indies by his tyrannical father, is rescued en route by a benevolent protectress who takes him instead to the island of Eden, a colony founded in the 1620s by Huguenot survivors of the siege of La Rochelle.

Like many of the episodes in the novels of Prévost, the background to this story was real enough: Henri and Abraham Duquesne, sons of the famous Huguenot admiral, had founded a short-lived settlement on the island of Eden near Saint Helena in 1689.[13] As Prévost recounts their adventure, the original settlers first seek asylum in England following their defeat by Cardinal Richelieu at La Rochelle. But they find the High Church regime of Archbishop Laud as oppressive as that of his French Catholic counterpart and, joined by a band of disgruntled English Presbyterians, they set sail for Eden, behind whose rocky coastline lies a fertile hinterland. From the bounty afforded them by Providence, they create a kind of utopia. One anomalous development in the colony mars the otherwise serene and blissful life of the islanders: something in the climate has produced a disproportionate number of female births. The local pastor, a dour and repellent figure, steps in to resolve the resultant crisis by decreeing that marriage should henceforth be by lot. This arbitrary and ill-considered decision precipitates civil war, in the course of which the pastor is killed and the colony collapses.

While Bridge has been experiencing the mixed pleasures of life in a Huguenot Arcadia, his half-brother, Cleveland, has been travelling through the English colonies in North America, reinforcing his deist inclinations through a sympathetic study of Indian religious rites. The brief visit which he pays to a colony of Huguenot refugees in Virginia proves much less uplifting.[14]

Forsaking the New World for the Old, Cleveland decides to pursue a course of studies at the Saumur Academy, the centre of French Protestant humanism. The year is 1667 and the town's pastor quickly alerts the Englishman to the dangers which are already threatening France's Calvinists, asking Cleveland whether he would be willing to ask Charles II to help relocate the academy in England. The benefits of this cultural transplant ought to be obvious:

> The emigration of the many Frenchmen who would not hesitate to abandon their fatherland to follow us would bring a great increase in strength and wealth to England, not to mention the blessings from heaven which would doubtless descend upon an arrangement which zeal for the faith had engendered.[15]

Cleveland remains indifferent to the pastor's appeal. Despite his nationality, he is not a Protestant, he explains, but a partisan of natural religion. Any reasoning man such as he is finds it impossible to choose between so many Christian sects when, by their own logic, only one of them can possess the purity of doctrine which all of them claim. In any case, Cleveland adds, as though to forestall further appeals to his conscience, "without understanding in any detail all the tenets of the Protestant faith, I had understood that one of these was to use no constraint upon any man and to regard the most sincerely held faith as the best."[16]

The pastor is distressed at this show of spiritual neutrality and resolves to effect Cleveland's conversion. Meanwhile, his Catholic housekeeper, who has overheard all, rushes off to find a suitably persuasive Oratorian who will nullify the pastor's arguments and win Cleveland to Catholicism. Siege is then laid to Cleveland's soul form both flanks. The Englishman makes it clear that he finds little to choose between the theological arguments advanced by his would-be converters, and the discussion shifts to the political implications of Roman and Reformed Christianity. The Oratorian argues that French Calvinism had originated in the minds of "a few unknown persons risen from the mob," men who had been moved to adopt heresy out of crude self-interest or mere love of novelty, rebels and disturbers of the peace.[17] However, Prévost grants the last word in the discussion to the pastor, who insists that the Huguenots had always respected the arrangements set forth in the Edict of Nantes. The latest crisis was the result of the violation of that solemn covenant by the crown, not by the Calvinists. Frustrated at his inability to convert Cleveland by peaceful means, the Oratorian orders the Englishman's two sons and niece taken off to a convent, where they are to receive thorough Catholic indoctrination. Outraged, Cleveland travels to Versailles for an audience with the King, whom he perceives as possessing "a great store of humanity and goodness of heart."[18] Louis XIV grants the release of the children at once, confessing to his English visitor that he has yielded control of religious policy to his clergy.[19]

Assuming that the protection granted him by Louis XIV will assure him the right to remain unmolested in France, Cleveland settles in Saint Cloud. A Huguenot neighbour, however, soon renews his sense of alarm. Marshal Turenne, who had decided to abjure in order to ensure his future in the King's armies, writes to the neighbour urging that he follow suit or take flight. The first alternative is much to be preferred, Turenne suggests, because flight means the abandonment of all one's property rights. Cleveland heads for England, interrupting his journey to the coast near Rouen just long enough to witness Huguenots at worship in Quevilly, one of the few towns where their temples are still standing.

In *Le Doyen de Killerine*, published between 1733 and 1740, Prévost balanced sketches of the French Calvinist world in the post-Revocation period, with revelations of the sufferings of the Catholic majority in Ireland. The novel's central character, an Irishman who had become a priest in a nation dominated by English Protestant reaction, has reluctantly decided to abandon his homeland "where one's religion was an obstacle which personal merit could not overcome."[20] When the ship bearing him to France docks at Dieppe, the captain salutes a family of Huguenots who, like the dean, have chosen to leave their homeland rather than endure what has become unbearable religious oppression. They have abandoned their country house near Paris, aware that it will be seized once their illicit flight is uncovered and handed over to any relatives willing to abjure their faith. The Calvinists eagerly accept the dean's suggestion that he occupy their property and that they take up his Irish residence in exchange.

In Paris, the dean discovers that his neighbour is a French diplomat who, having secretly abjured Catholicism while on a mission in northern Germany, has become the spiritual guide to much of the underground Paris Protestant community. The dean's nephew is witness to a moving burial service conducted in an improvised chapel built in the cellar of the diplomat's house.

If there is one central theme running through *Le Doyen de Killerine*, it is that the parallel intolerance pursued by the English against Irish Catholics and by the French against the Huguenots have brought not only considerable suffering but have caused a great deal of needless social and political dislocation. The central characters in the novel seek relief from persecution in flight, but Prévost makes clear that this brings little solace to men and women who remain attached to their homelands. The dean declares towards the novel's end that the sacrifice involved in abandoning Ireland was both misguided and useless, yet through the novelist, he implies that staying on in a nation where one's faith is proscribed has grave disadvantages, because loyalty to one's own communion under such circumstances means resorting to devices which are devious and dangerous. Finally, the novelist notes, repression of the kind endured by the characters in *Le Doyen de Killérine* provokes the most ardent spirits to insurrection; the tragic risings of Camisards and Irish Jacobites testify to the lengths to which religious minorities will be driven if deprived of the right to worship their creator in their own way.

In 1741, Prévost produced a novel whose central characters were real-life members of the refugee milieu in England. *Les Campagnes Philosophiques de M. de Moncal* was a highly romanticized version of the adventures of the seigneur de Moncal, a man whom Prévost may have met in London and who fought for William III under the Protestant hero Schomberg. The Moncal of the novel emerges as a swashbuckling libertine so given to duelling and amorous dalliance that the reader hardly gets a chance to evaluate his prowess in the field. Moncal is no religious zealot; he makes it clear that his motives in joining the Protestant exodus from France are far less high minded than those of most refugees. He is in fact simply eager to evade the wrath of a cuckolded husband. Perhaps reflecting the real opinion of Prévost, Moncal finds the refugee community as a whole both puritanical and self-righteous:

> There are few people of a more critical outlook than the French Protestants living in England. The zeal for the faith which led them to abandon their homeland makes them pitiless concerning moral laxity of any kind.[21]

Moncal and Schomberg, as portrayed by Prévost, are neither spiritual nor moral paragons; but they emerge as essentially attractive rascals, and the Protestant cause for which they fight is presented more sympathetically than that of the Irish Jacobites against whom they campaign.

In addition to the many allusions to the Huguenots which he made in the course of his novels, Prévost inserted a number of short stories dealing with the problems of religious minorities in *Le Pour et contre*. In one of these, a young Fleming who is arrested while fleeing from the monastery where he has pledged his vows confesses that he is in fact a Calvinist and that he has embraced Catholicism only as a result of social pressure.[22] Released from captivity, the youth falls in love with a Dutch Catholic girl whose mother, accused of collaborating with the French during a recent invasion of her country, has found asylum in a convent on the frontier. Despite her mother's suspect status, the girl has been allowed a Catholic education by an enlightened Dutch official. The lovers, parallel victims of the religious intolerance practised in their respective homelands, are permitted a mixed marriage. When his bride dies in childbirth, the widower finds solace in the Catholic faith which he had earlier rejected and enters a religious order. Later, when he leaves the order, he does so with a sincere appreciation of the monastic vocation. The whole melodrama, in which profane and religious devotion triumph over prejudice and repression, contains an obvious plea for toleration.

In 1760, twenty years after the appearance of the last issue of *Le Pour et contre*, Prévost produced a translation of David Hume's history of Stuart England. Scattered throughout this study are criticisms of the subversive politics and intolerant theology of English and Scottish Calvinists.[23] These comments about a cousinly branch of the spiritual family to which the Huguenots belonged were bound to embarrass those who were seeking to argue the case for French Calvinist emancipation. The Genevan Jacob Vernet took issue with Hume for including what he felt were slanderous misrepresentations of the Presbyterian outlook in his history. Such misrepresentations, he pointed out, could provide new arguments for the continued denial of civil rights to the Huguenots.[24]

Apart from the unintended contribution which he may have made, in translating Hume, to the arguments advanced for limiting Huguenot rights, Prévost had devoted a large part of his literary career to the promotion of more liberal attitudes towards French and English non-conformists. The anglomania which he helped launch in *Le Pour et contre* and in his *Homme de qualité* was in large measure based on the admiration which he felt for the English cult of religious liberty. The touching vignettes of suffering Huguenots which he included in his novels were bound to move readers in an age which prided itself on its sensitivity. His fictional heroes, when confronted by priests or pastors intent upon securing their conversion by fair means or foul, kept their spiritual integrity and fought for the rights of free conscience.

---

1. Claire-Eliane Engel, "Le véritable abbé Prévost," *BSHPF*, CIV (octobre-décembre, 1958), pp. 255-56.

2. The central character in one of Challes's short stories, the comte de Tercy, keeps his Calvinist faith in post-Revocation France so that he may inherit from a stubbornly Protestant aunt. Skeptical of her nephew's sincerity, the aunt dies, leaving Tercy out of her will. In his frustration, the count abjures and joins the Roman communion. The results of this opportunistic conversion are mixed: Tercy's business prospers but his Huguenot relatives are appalled at his apostasy, and his confirmation in the Catholic faith precludes marriage with his 'new Catholic' fiancee (who has meanwhile been confined to a convent for spiritual reorientation!). Despondent about resolving his personal life in conformity with French law, Tercy abducts his beloved and settles for a civil marriage abroad. V. Robert Challes, *Les Illustres Françoises, histoires véritables* (4 vols.; The Hague, 1748), I, p. 253.

3. Nicolas Lenglet-Dufresnoy, *De l'usage des romans, où l'on fait voir leur utilité et leurs différens caractères avec une Bibliothèque des romans, accompagnée de remarques critiques sur leur choix et leurs Editions* (2 vols.; Amsterdam, 1734), II, p. 360.

4. Abbé Antoine-François Prévost, *Le Pour et contre, ouvrage périodique d'un goût nouveau...par l'auteur des 'Mémoires d'un homme de qualité'* (20 vols.; Paris, 1733-40), IV. pp. 45.

5. Ibid., IX, pp. 226-27.

6. Ibid., III, pp. 294-95.

7. Ibid., XV, pp. 179-80.

8. Ibid., III, p. 296.

9. Prévost, *Mémoires et aventures d'un homme de qualité qui s'est retiré du monde. Tome V (Séjour en Angleterre)*, ed. M. Robertson (Paris, 1927), p. 119.

10. Ibid., p. 135.

11. Ibid., p. 136.

12. Abbé Desfontaines, *Le Nouvelliste du Parnasse, ou Réflexions sur les ouvrages nouveaux* (4 vols.; Paris, 1731-32), III, p. 15.

13. Prévost undoubtedly came across the story of the Eden colony in François Leguat, *Voyage et avantures de François Leguat et de ses compagnons en deux îles désertes des Indes orientales* (2 vols.; Amsterdam, 1708).

14. Prévost, *Le Philosophe anglais, ou Histoire de Monsieur Cleveland* (5 vols.; Utrecht, 1736), III, p. 35.

15. Ibid., V, p. 72.

16. Ibid., pp. 73-74.

17. Ibid., p. 84.

18. Ibid., p. 116.

19. These passages in the novel, beginning with the dialogue between Cleveland and the Oratorian and ending with the Englishman's visit to Versailles, contain one of the most vigorous and explicit condemnations of the Revocation system written since 1685. Considered too provocative by the censor, they were deleted from the first (1732) French edition of *Cleveland*.

20. Prévost, *Le Doyen de Killérine* (6 vols.; Paris, 1733-41), I, p. 18.

21. Prévost, *Les Campagnes philosophiques, ou Mémoires de M. de Moncal, aide-de-camp de M. le maréchal de Schomberg, contenant l'histoire de la Guerre d'Irlande* (4 vols.; Amsterdam, 1741), pp. 41-42.

22. Prévost, *Le Pour et contre*, IX, p. 290.

23. David Hume, *Histoire de la Maison des Stuart, sur le trône d'Angleterre*, trans. abbé Prévost (3 vols.; London, 1760), II, p.107.

24. Jacob Vernet, *Lettres critiques d'un voyageur anglais sur l'article 'Genève' du Dictionnaire encyclopédique, et sur la Lettre de M. d'Alembert à M. Rousseau touchant les spectacles* (2 vols.; Copenhagen, 1766), II, p. 131.

Loménie de Brienne: Liberal theology student, future first minister.

CHAPTER VII

Controller-General Machault Provokes a Public Debate on Huguenot Rights, 1751-1760

Sometime during the spring of 1751, Controller-General of Finances Jean-Baptiste Machault, a protégé of Madame de Pompadour, concluded that the Huguenots of the diaspora, whose aptitude for commerce was well established, should be invited to help pull France out of the economic crisis brought on by the recently concluded War of the Austrian Succession. The minister's favourable prejudice towards the Reformed was reinforced by his anger at their bitterest enemies, the clergy, who had rejected his proposal that they submit to a universally applicable tax—the *vingtième*, to help the national debt.

The calculated indulgence of Machault towards the Calvinists was revealed in a letter of recommendation written to a man named Frontin, a Huguenot refugee living in England who had expressed a desire to do business in France following the signature of the peace of Aix-la-Chapelle. When the contents of the minister's letter became known, two members of the southern episcopate vented their outrage in open letters to the controller-general. The bishops' intervention in turn provoked a decade-long debate on the issue of Protestant toleration, during which spokesmen for the clerical establishment faced a massive counter-attack by members of the Huguenot community as well as by a number of philosophes, parlementaires, lawyers, and liberal members of the First Estate.

The protagonists in this debate ranged over every aspect of the toleration issue, from the most abstract to the most precise. They asked themselves to begin with whether the Calvinists were deserving of religious and civil rights; if so, whether any limit should be placed on the exercise of such rights; finally, what the benefits or disadvantages to French society would be if the Huguenots were readmitted to citizenship.

The controller-general's letter which precipitated the long debate over toleration included a request that Frontin de "so well treated that when knowledge of his reception in France reaches other such businessmen, they will be induced to return to the kingdom."[1] When news of this initiative reached Bishop Chabannes of Agen, he addressed an open letter to Machault early in May 1751, reminding the minister that the clergy had been waiting since the war's end, not for new expressions of indulgence towards the Huguenots, but for the suppression of their provocative open-air meetings. Memories of the Camisard rebellion were surely still fresh enough at Versailles to indicate where the tolerance of such illicit assemblies might lead. Did the government not realize that the special permission accorded to Huguenots such as Frontin to dispense with the sacraments would be taken advantage of by lukewarm Catholics as well, thus encouraging the current drift away from Christian commitment of any kind? If the Protestants still remaining in France in defiance of the law were not too numerous, they deserved no special consideration; if the contrary were the case, they posed a threat to national security. Louis XIV, fully aware that the Huguenots were "rebels out of principle and republicans out of habit,"[2] had enacted the Revocation just in time to save France from the equivalent of the English Revolution of 1688. Perhaps the best course of action available to the government was the expulsion of the remaining Huguenots from a monarchical society which they seemed indisposed to accept. In any case, Catholic priests could not excuse from the sacraments men such as Frontin, through whom the government was apparently trying to give oblique assurances to heretics at home and abroad.[3] In the immediate aftermath of the appearance of the bishop's letter, however, Machault felt obliged to put out a statement that "the Huguenots had exaggerated when they spread the rumour that the government intended to admit them back into the kingdom."[4]

The Protestants, meanwhile, made known their own reaction to the views expressed by the Bishop of Agen. Refugee pastor Samuel Formey suggested that the prelate was clearly out of touch with the prevailing climate of opinion in France, which was increasingly favourable to toleration,[5] while Melchior von Grimm detected in the bishop's letters a dark design "to destroy the reputation of the controller-general who had devised a project of benefit to the nation as a whole (the *vingtième*) whereby the clergy would have been deprived of some of its excessive wealth."[6] In a *Lettre du curé de L*** à Mgr. l'évêque d'Agen* dated June 1, 1751, published anonymously, Antoine Court put in the mouth of a 'parish priest' an effective rebuttal to the case made for religious repression by the prelate.[7]

Meanwhile, a second ecclesiastic, Bishop Vivet de Monclus of Alais, wrote to the intendant of Languedoc in October suggesting that the proper response to the insolence of the Huguenots lay not in expelling them (and thereby admitting the bankruptcy of the Revocation policy) but in vigorously applying existing law, which clearly decreed that 'new Catholics' should be compelled to submit to the Catholic sacraments or suffer punishment as relapsed heretics. However, Vivet de Monclus was skeptical of the willingness of local magistrates to continue enforcing this legislation and proposed that, in the future, intendants or military commanders be empowered to judge refractory heretics on the spot, without a trial.[8] If the government would take this firm line, the clergy might be prepared to abandon the *épreuves* to which suspected heretics had been subjected before receiving the sacrament; parish priests would be instructed to stop categorizing the children of Huguenots as bastards; and a clerical amnesty would be accorded to those who had been married in the 'Desert' during the war.[9]

During the pamphlet war which followed, the two southern bishops were supported by a small band of clerical pamphleteers, led by the abbé Jean Novi de Caveirac, prior of Cubiérètes.[10] Born at Nîmes in the heart of Huguenot France in 1713, Caveirac enjoyed the protection of some of the most influential members of the southern episcopate, for whom he acted as something of an éminence grise; he rightly considered his major publications of the 1750s, a *Mémoire Politico-critique* and an *Apologie de Louis XIV*, to be an 'arsenal' of argumentation in favour of the Revocation. Caveirac's readers took him to have tried to justify the Saint Bartholomew's Day Massacre as well, which outraged them. Grimm denounced the abbé as a man of loathsome character and appalling literary style whose works should be totally disregarded.[11] Diderot penned a special article for the *Encyclopédie* ("journéee de la Saint-Barthelemy") as a direct result of the rage he felt while reading the *Apologie*.[12] Appalled by Caveirac's text and convinced that it must be rebutted, Voltaire wrote Jacob Vernet inquiring about what he felt were the grossly misleading statistics used by the abbé to minimize the significance of the Huguenot exodus from France after 1685.[13] Even Voltaire's old foe, the conservative critic Fréron, was less than charitable towards Caveirac: "I know few who, claiming to defend the cause of religion, open themselves more to criticism by faulty reasoning and a fanatical tone, just what one might expect of a southern zealot ready to trouble the public peace."[14]

The ex-Jesuit Gabriel-François Goyer attacked Caveirac in a letter to Père Berthier, editor of the *Journal de Trévoux*: The apologist of the Revocation should be written off as an ally in the church's campaign against the current wave of philosophical radicalism, Coyer argued, because he had shown himself to be such an inept polemicist. Except for a few fanatics, Coyer concluded, Frenchmen wanted to see their Calvinist fellow citizens treated decently, even granted a legitimate form of marriage.[15]

In his combat for the spiritual status quo, Caveirac was not alone. Among those who supported him in his battle to maintain the Revocation system intact was the abbé Marc-Albert de Villiers, a priest possessed of 'Gothic piety',[16] to use Grimm's words, who was drawn into the debate out of concern that public opinion was increasingly favourable to the idea of granting the Huguenots a form of civil marriage. Perhaps the most virulent anti-Calvinist tract put out in the course of the decade came from the pen of abbé Bouniol de Montégut: but the perverse zeal with which this cleric had composed *La Voix du vrai patriote*, observed Fréron, "shows us to what excesses one may be carried when defending a good cause if one is not guided by a spirit of gentleness and moderation...."[17]

The Calvinists, who had since 1685 limited themselves to forwarding private supplications to the crown for a change in their status, responded to this clerical offensive against them with a public defence of their position and an explicit statement of their demands.[18] From his sanctuary at Lausanne, Antoine Court launched a series of broadsides which were widely circulated in France. The boldest of these, published in the summer of 1751 as the reflections of an impartial patriot, was quickly bought up. Court made sure that copies of the work were distributed at Versailles, addressing one of them directly to Machault. The success of his *Patriote* prompted Court to have it reissued in the fall of 1753.

Meanwhile, the normally timorous Paris Calvinists, emboldened by Court's sallies, commissioned one of their most distinguished members, the chevalier de Beaumont, an ex-cavalry officer from Normandy who had won the Cross of Saint Louis despite his open profession of heresy, to pen a modified version of the *Patriote* for the edification of the court. This publication was encouraged by Machault, who was anxious to keep the issue of Protestant emancipation before the public.[19] In *L'Accord Parfait de la Nature* which he wrote under these seemingly auspicious circumstances, the chevalier de Beaumont openly identified himself as a Huguenot, even remarking to his Catholic readers that what kept France's Protestants from joining them in ecumenical reunion was the Roman Church's predilection for such post-apostolic fancies as Mariolatry and the worship of relics. Despite this frankness, *L'Accord Parfait* enjoyed a sympathetic audience at court where it was applauded, even by members of the First Estate.[20] Antoine Court, however, was very unhappy with a work which, while in large measure derivative from his own, was so blatantly partisan: "I am not all pleased with *L'Accord Parfait*. The *Patriote* has been weakened in the course of being copied. The whole argument had more force in the mouth of an impartial writer than in that of a spokesman who is pleading his own cause."[21]

Ideological divergence within the Protestant camp surfaced again in 1760 with the publication of *L'Esprit de Jésus-Christ sur la tolérance* by Pastor Frédéric-Guillaume Delabroue, born to refugees living in Holland, who had come to Paris in 1752 as chaplain of the Dutch embassy. Like so many others, Delabroue had been provoked to intervene in the debate as a result of reading Caveirac. But his solution to the Calvinists' dilemma—a recommendation that the government permit private family worship by the Huguenots,[22] while acceptable to most of the rather timorous Protestants living in Paris, was bound to be rejected by militant southerners who had grown accustomed to their outdoor services.

Even more important to the cause of Calvinist emancipation than their own willingness to become their own advocates was the contribution made by two groups newly converted to the cause of toleration: members of the legal profession who deplored the way in which abuses of priestly power had led to the undermining of family life for hundreds of thousands of Frenchmen, and a new generation of priests and theologians who were convinced that the Revocation had led not to French spiritual unity but to serious moral corruption both within the clergy and among 'new Catholics.'[23]

In a meticulously argued *Traité sur le Mariage*, published in 1753 and frequently cited by proponents of a form of civil marriage for French Calvinists, Pierre Léridant, a lawyer attached to the Paris parlement, clearly established that, despite the pronouncements of the Council of Trent in the matter, the legitimacy of all marriages in France was a matter for the secular authority alone to regulate. The Catholic clergy might refuse to bless a marriage; they might impose spiritual penalties on one of the contracting partners; but the state alone gave the marital contract its validity.[24]

Maître Rouvière, a well-intentioned colleague of Léridant who had spent some time pondering the problems posed for the legal profession by the continuing presence of Huguenots in France, proposed what was on the surface the simplest of all solutions to such problems—the reintegration of the Calvinists into the national church. Addressing himself to the underground pastorate in an *Essai de Réunion des protestants aux Catholiques romains* published in 1756, Rouvière repeated the arguments put to the Huguenots by Bossuet during the 'ecumenical' dialogue which had preceded the Revocation. Since the Catholic church had retained all the essential Christian dogmas and since it did not practise idolatry despite the charges to this effect made by the early Reformers, Protestants were no longer justified in remaining schismatics.[25] The *Essai de Réunion* delighted Voltaire, who expressed his enthusiasm to the author: "I remarked in your book straightforward intentions sustained by a great deal of erudition. I hope that your work will achieve what the Revocation of the Edict of Nantes was unable to accomplish."[26]

Probably the single most effective essay in defence of toleration to appear during the decade was the *Mémoire théologique et politique au sujet des mariages clandestins des Protestants de France*, written by Karl Friedrich Baër, a Lutheran pastor who taught theology at Strasbourg and who may have been commissioned to write this text by members of the Huguenot community in Paris. Two editions of the *Mémoire théologique et politique*, the core of which was a reasoned plea to the King to establish a form of civil marriage for non-Catholic Christians, were rapidly exhausted. Baër also gave his readers what must have been for most of them a first glimpse of the overall condition in which France's Huguenots lived at mid-century; and those revelations caused "a deep emotional response" among contemporary readers. Fréron reported that the *Mémoire* was well received by the general public as well as by the ministry,[27] while Grimm suggested:

"It was the government itself which had this memorandum published in order to see what impression it would make on the public."[28] Writing a century later, the Protestant historian Edmond Hugues argued that it was as a result of the appearance of the Mémoire "that the Protestant question was finally put on the agenda of the eighteenth century and that it forced itself on the public mind."[29]

Another work favourable to toleration, this time jointly written by a lawyer and a priest, was the *Questions sur la tolérance*, which appeared in 1758. The legal opinion came from Gabriel-Nicolas Maultrot, a specialist in canon law who had made a considerable reputation as a defender of Jansenist parish priests. The ecclesiastical contribution was by the abbé Jacques Tailhé, a bitter critic of Jesuit ultramontanism. Grimm applauded the civic spirit of the authors while regretting that they lacked the eloquence required to win new converts to the cause of tolerance.[30] Placed on the Index in March 1759, the *Questions sur la tolérance* was republished the following year as an *Essai sur la tolérance chrétienne*.

The boldest support for the Protestant cause during the toleration question came from three fellow seminarians at the Sorbonne in the late 1740s. Two of them—André Morellet, who spent five years preparing a *licence* before going off to Italy as a private tutor in 1752, and the future first minister of the crown Loménie de Brienne, would go on to become priests (although their commitment to Catholic orthodoxy was to be a matter of some concern to their ecclesiastical superiors). The third, Anne-Robert-Jacques Turgot, a member of the provincial gentry who had entered upon studies for the priesthood out of filial piety, abandoned all thought of a clerical career at the beginning of 1751 and became a *maître des requêtes* in March 1753, in preparation for the distinguished government career which lay ahead of him.

Years later, Morellet recalled how the three students had discussed the problems created for French society by their church's continuing insistence on policing the beliefs of two groups of spiritual dissidents—the Jansensists and the Calvinists. Influenced by their reading of Montesquieu and the *Encyclopédie*, the young seminarians became converts to the idea of civil toleration, convinced that the secular sovereign should reject all requests from ecclesiastical bodies to regulate the religious belief of the community at large, even when such bodies clearly represented the faith of the majority.[31]

In the spring of 1754, after he had been made suffragan bishop of Rouen, Loménie de Brienne, in collaboration with Turgot, defended the idea of civil toleration in *Le Conciliateur ou Lettres d'un Ecclésiastique à un Magistrat sur les affaires actuelles*. Two years later, having read Caveirac, Morellet produced a satirical parody of the abbé's ideas in which he imagines that France, having wrested the New England colonies from her ancient rival, loses all hope of consolidating her position by inflicting upon the Protestant colonists there the full rigour of the laws which still apply against the Huguenots in France.[32]

During the decade-long debate on the subject of Huguenot rights, Caveirac and his colleagues focussed on what they saw to be the republican, subversive, and fanatical qualities of the Reformed.

Caveirac made his allegation of Huguenot republicanism bluntly and directly: "A sect which recognizes neither authority, hierarchy nor even the need for organic unity in the state has only to change its focus to become a society in which the people is sovereign."[33] Caveirac went on to make a candid defence of the way in which the priesthood conditioned Frenchmen to be monarchists: "The Catholic religion is a religion of submission. It silences all reason and charms the understanding."[34] Seconding Caveirac, Bouniol de Montégut charged the Huguenots with harbouring "a republican and factious outlook which runs directly counter to all subordination and engenders a revolt against all authority."[35]

Replying to these charges, the Calvinists and their champions professed their unconditional royalism. Antoine Court found it hard to understand how someone as perceptive as Montesquieu could conclude that Protestants were inclined towards republicanism in the face of overwhelming evidence to the contrary. The Danes and the Prussians, for instance, lived under an all but despotic monarchy.[36] Tailhé and Maultrot agreed, arguing that "the Protestant religion is better suited to monarchies for the very reason that it is itself without a visible head."[37] The chevalier de Beaumont insisted that the allegation of Protestant republicanism must be based on an analysis of the political behaviour of such unrepresentative sects as the Arminians, the Quakers, and the Independents.[38]

Charging the Huguenots with harbouring republican thoughts was one thing. Accusing them of armed insurrection was another. Caveirac put the case for the prosecution with his usual bluntness: The heretical sect had been "insolent at its birth, seditious during its growth, republican at its apogee and a menace even in its decline."[39] Only fear had kept the Protestants under control. Bouniol de Montégut remarked: the Calvinists' role in French history had been "a categorical and sustained felony."[40]

The Protestants and their supporters repudiated these charges of treasonous behaviour. Forty years of peaceful submission to royal authority followed the first conversions to Calvinism in the 1520s, they pointed out. No doubt ambitious grandees had tried to find in Calvin's *Institutes* some rationalization for revolt; but the Huguenot community as a whole had not been compromised in this subversive activity: it was Catholic *Ligueurs*, not Calvinist partisans, who had threatened the last Valois kings.[41] The wars of religion into which the Huguenots had been drawn were the product, not of their own subversive designs, but of the unbearable pressure brought against them by an intolerant clergy. Henri IV had granted rights to the

Protestants of his own free will, not as a result of threats of armed insurrection. Antoine Court and his son noted that during the recent crisis over the *vingtième* it had been the Catholic clergy not the Calvinist minority which had justified resistance to the crown in the name of conscience.[42] Beaumont expressed the hope that the valiant leadership given France's armies in the field by the Maréchal de Saxe had at last dispelled the myth that Protestants were by nature rebels.[43] Loménie de Brienne argued that the Calvinists, if allowed this freedom, would be as devoted to the crown as were the Lutherans of Strasbourg, whose religious freedom had been guaranteed by the monarchy since the signing of the Treaty of Westphalia in 1648.[44]

On the surface at least, the Camisard revolt provided the most damaging evidence of the Protestants' capacity for both subversive and fanatical activity. Antoine Court met these twin charges frontally in a three-volume *Histoire des troubles des Cévennes* published in 1760, the last act in a long career dedicated to the moral and intellectual rehabilitation of the French Calvinist community. His history of the Camisard revolt is remarkably objective, clearly designed to win the sympathy and understanding of 'philosophic' readers. Court made no effort to hide or even to play down the atrocities committed by the Protestant rebels, including the murder of a number of priests. The leitmotiv of his long, detailed chronicle is that simple Cévenol peasants and mountain folk had been driven to fanaticism and subversion by the repressive policies of the clergy and by a government policy which deprived them of wise and enlightened pastors. Once the rebellion had spent itself, Court pointed out, "a new generation of leaders surfaced who enjoyed the confidence of the Protestant masses but whose spirit and temper were diametrically opposed to that which had held sway there for so long."[45]

Having debated the case for and against Calvinist emancipation, the champions and adversaries of the Huguenots went on to recommend specific changes in the law in line with their proposals. Among their sympathizers, there was universal agreement that the Calvinists should be granted freedom of conscience; most also recommended the right to public worship under the guidance of properly trained pastors; some suggested that a specifically Calvinist form of baptism and marriage be recognized; a few went so far as to argue that all discriminatory legislation against the Huguenots be removed and that they be given access to public office.

Antoine Court urged the crown, in line with a policy which it had long since adopted towards the Jews, to issue an edict allowing Calvinists to worship and to marry in their own rite; in return for such a concession, the Huguenots might be prepared to forego demands for equal access to public appointments and honours.[46] The abbé Yvon put forward a similar proposal, suggesting that non-conforming Christians be granted religious liberty but that they be denied public office. Such an arrangement would reconcile the proper Protestant insistence on spiritual freedom with the reasonable demand of the Catholic majority for a guaranteed control of political power and thus of public order.[47] Loménie de Brienne rejected any such limitations: Protestants must be granted the same rights which all other Frenchmen enjoyed.[48]

As Court and Yvon had surmised, the major preoccupation of many French Calvinists at mid-century was not their right to freedom of worship or even the prospect of their reintegration into the mainstream of French political and economic life, but the validation of their births and marriages. In order to encourage decisive government action in an area of such immediate concern to thousands of their co-religionists, the Protestants and their defenders released data designed to cause alarm and concern at Versailles. The chevalier de Beaumont, for instance, suggested rather improbably that there might have been more than 150 000 illicit 'Desert' marriages since the Revocation.[49]

In this effort to secure the regularization of marriages entered into without benefit of Catholic clergy, the Calvinists were joined by jurists in the *civiliste* tradition, men who were by education and training opposed to the clerical control of civil status defended by their *canoniste* confréres. As the *civilistes* saw it, the secular sovereign was obligated to guarantee a secure family status to all of his subjects, non-conformist as well as orthodox. If the crown had surrendered its powers in this area since the Council of Trent, this was an historical lapse which could easily enough be nullified by a new royal initiative. Baër reminded France's ecclesiastical and political leaders that, even in the orthodox Catholic tradition, the wedding partners were the officiants in the marriage sacrament; the priest was present essentially as a witness. What could be more simple than that the King propose an alternative witness for the validation of Protestant marriages, as in fact Louis XIV had done a month before the Revocation when he decreed that local law officers play this role?[50]

Those who continued to insist that the marriage of all French citizens should conform to canon law were in effect arguing for the full implementation in France of the decisions of the Council of Trent at a time when the ultramontanist position was being subjected to increasing criticism. Some did not hesitate to run this risk: Bouniol de Montégut insisted that, since Christ had elevated marriage to the status of a sacrament, an orthodox prince could establish no other legitimate form of wedlock for Christians except with the explicit accord of the church.[51] Caveirac agreed: only the irresponsible leniency of France's magistrates, he charged, had permitted the gradual falling away from the marriage sacrament of 'new Catholics' who were legally bound to submit to it.[52]

The marriage question apart, the opponents of Calvinist toleration offered a broad spectrum of recommendations. One maverick defender of the Catholic church's spiritual monopoly even went so far as to propose that Protestant Frenchmen be awarded not only freedom of conscience but all other civic rights except the free and open celebration of their own religion.[53] Militant conservatives advocated a much more rigorous policy. In a reckless display of ultramontanist zeal, Caveirac admonished Louis XV that, as a devoutly orthodox prince, he was bound to harmonize his religious policy with that of the Curia: "Above all, let nothing be done by the prince which has not been agreed upon in advance by the pontiff."[54]

The advocates of toleration, like the champions of the status quo, argued that the emancipation of the Huguenots was not simply good or bad in itself but that it would bring with it concrete benefits or disadvantages to French society. The supporters of religious freedom cited the losses which France had sustained as a direct result of the Revocation and insisted that these losses could be more than made up if the government would promote some form of toleration. The chevalier de Beaumont estimated the population loss from the Revocation to be high as 2 000 000.[55] Antoine Court insisted that at least 800 000 Huguenots had left France but that the 2 000 000 who remained had already, through natural increase, made up for this loss; the promise of a legitimate Protestant form of marriage and the offer of freedom of conscience to those living abroad, nine-tenths of whom longed for the opportunity to return, would bring the nation 1 000 000 new citizens. Yet, realizing that there was some peril in overdoing this argument, the exiled leader of the Calvinists hastened to point out that the Huguenots, who constituted perhaps one-seventh of France's population, would never, even in the most favourable circumstances, come to exceed one-quarter of the total.[56] Baër and Delabroue meanwhile claimed that there were still 3 000 000 Calvinists inside France and suggested that this number would be substantially swollen by the granting of freedom of conscience, since many refugees would be induced to return by such a reversal in government policy.[57]

The defenders of the Revocation system dismissed the demographic argument as insignificant. The abbé Bouniol de Montégut insisted that the Huguenot population was now made up essentially of modest numbers of "obscure bourgeois" and "country bumpkins" living in the remote reaches of the Cévennes.[58] Caveirac calculated that there were at most 400 000 heretics still in France; the nation's demographic loss as a result of the Revocation had not surpassed two-and-a-half per cent of the overall 1685 population of some 20 000 000; by contrast, some 400 000 lives had been lost to famine in 1709 and the nation easily survived that sudden and dramatic population decline; wild guesswork and misguided emotionalism had led to an irrational statistical inflation; in any case, whatever the dimension of the Calvinist exodus, it had not reinforced any of France's enemies because the Huguenots who possessed "that mania to disperse themselves which they share with the Jews,"[59] had settled all over the globe.

Countering both Caveirac and the more zealous Protestant apologists, Tailhé and Maultrot argued for statistical sobriety. Perhaps 300 000 Calvinists in all had left France during and after 1685, they argued, coming up with a figure which modern scholars accept. What was surely more pertinent was the quality as opposed to the mere number of those who had left as a result of the Revocation.[60]

Closely related to the demographic issue was the debate over the benefits of a more tolerant policy to France's economic life. "Is there a group more able to make our commerce flourish than the Protestants?"[61] asked the chevalier de Beaumont, who argued that the peculiar Calvinist stress on sobriety and frugality would provide a much-needed stimulus to France's economic growth. Morellet traced a direct link between commercial and religious liberty,[62] as did Court, who cited the economic development of England and Holland as evidence that prosperity was the inevitable reward for societies which guarantee religious toleration. Court even suggested that the productivity of his fellow Calvinists would double if they were "deprived of all honours, excluded from public offices and responsibilities while being granted the simple status of citizens."[63] Beaumont argued that legislation which guaranteed the Huguenots their religious freedom while continuing to exclude them from public office would bring them to concentrate their energies in the commercial arena and would thereby make them "tremendously useful to the kingdom."[64]

Predictably, Caveirac ridiculed the argument that toleration would produce such economic benefits. The Revocation had cost France no more than two-and-half per cent of her wealth, he calculated, a small price to pay for the immeasurable boon of spiritual and political unity. In any event, French industry had been in its infancy in 1685; the economic decline of the late seventeenth century had been caused less by Protestant exodus than by war and natural calamity; and since the Revocation, France's economy had been booming, not declining.[65]

Some conservative pamphleteers, while conceding that the Huguenots were demographically and economically insignificant, argued that they posed a real threat to France's moral standards. Protestantism, they contended, weakened all those sound restraints on appetite without which the movement toward materialism and moral decadence was inevitable.[66] Champions of the status quo also argued that concessions made to the Huguenots were bound to lead in time to freedom for all forms of religious dissent and, ultimately, to *indifférentisme*. Those who sought freedom of conscience for Huguenots without explicitly demanding the presence of Calvinist pastors might try to pass themselves off as conciliators, respectful of the established church, remarked Bouriol de Montégut. In fact they were aiding and abetting the propagation of Socinianism, deism, and other aberrant cults which dispensed with priests and pastors alike.[67]

Responding to the argument that their toleration was undesirable because it would lead sooner or later to spiritual anarchy, moderate Calvinists adopted a conciliatory approach. The chevalier de Beaumont conceded in advance that any legislation granting freedom of conscience should clearly exclude skeptics, atheists, and deists, all of whom refused to recognize any fixed and permanent principles of faith and morals, and "fanatical sects," such as the Quakers, who spurned allegiance to secular authority, adding that those religious groups which the French state might decide to tolerate should abstain from advertising their services of worship: all external publicity in this area belonged exclusively to the established church.[68]

At the end of the debate inadvertently launched by Machault, the Huguenots had several reasons for rejoicing. The discrimination from which they still suffered had become widely publicized. They had spoken out publicly in their own defence for the first time since the Revocation and done so in a way which went far towards dispelling the myth that they were politically and spiritually irresponsible. They had discovered formidable allies outside their own communion, especially among the clergy and the parlementaires . Perhaps most important, their adversaries, led by abbé Caveirac, had outraged enlightened opinion by arguing that the rationale used to justify the Revocation was still valid and that France in consequence must continue to commit herself wholeheartedly to the view that the profession of the Catholic faith was an indispensable prerequisite to citizenship.

---

1. J.-B. de Machault to Frontin, in J.-C.-G. de Chabannes, *Lettre de M. l'évêque d'Agen à Monsieur le contrôlleur-général contre la tolérance des Huguenots dans le royaume* (n.p., 1751), p.4.

2. Ibid., p. 13.

3. A. Picheral-Dardier (ed.), *Paul Rabaut. Ses lettres à Antoine Court, 1739-1755* (2 vols.; Paris: Grassart, 1884), II, p. 173, n. Machault continued to show a sympathetic interest in the Protestant question as long as he remained Controller-General. Pressure from the episcopate brought the King to shift Machault from the financial portfolio to ·the Ministry of the Marine in July 1754, when the government also abandoned its efforts to subject the First Estate to the *vingtième*. Support for the Protestant cause at court dropped significantly following the reassignment of Machault.

4. *Lettre de M. l'évêque d'Agen*, p. 20.

5. *Bibliothèque impartiale*, May-June, 1752, V, pp. 418-19.

6. Grimm, *Correspondance littéraire*, May 17, 1751, II, p. 60.

7. Antoine Court, *Lettre du curé de L*** à M. l'évêque d'Agen, au sujet de celle que ce Prélat a écrite à M. le Contrôlleur-Général contre la Tolérance des Huguenots dans le royaume* (n.p., 1751).

8. Bishop of Alais to the Intendant Saint-Priest, October 6, 1751, L. Anquez, *De l'état civil des Réformés en France* (Paris, 1868), p. 132.

9. In sharp contrast to his colleagues at Agen and Alais, the conservative Jean-Georges Lefranc de Pompignan who had just been made Archbishop of Vienne, gently rebuked the 'new Catholics' of his diocese in an episcopal letter of January 24, 1751 for having violated an agreement to suspend their illegal services of worship in return for a relaxation of the local clergy's surveillance. The prelate assumed that the Huguenots' prejudices against the Catholic faith were based on a lack of clear information and proceeded to set forth Roman doctrine concerning such matters as the eucharist and purgatory in an effort to win them peaceably back to the national church. V. Jean-Georges Lefranc de Pompignan, *Instruction pastorale adressée aux nouveaux convertis de son diocèse* January 24, 1751, *Oeuvres complètes de Lefranc de Pompignon*, ed. Migne (2 vols.; Paris, 1885), II, pp. 622-44. Grimm described the archbishop's letter as moderate but lacking in logic and dignity. Grimm, *Correspondance littéraire*, September 6, 1751, II, p. 93.

10. Abbé Jean Novi de Caveirac, *Mémoire politico-critique, où l'on examine s'il est de l'intérêt de l'Eglise et de l'Etat d'établir pour les Calvinistes du royaume une nouvelle forme de se marier* (n.p., 1756); *Apologie de Louis XIV, et de son Conseil, sur la Révocation de l'Edit de Nantes* (n.p. 1758); Abbé Bouniol de Montégut, *La Voix du vrai patriote catholique, opposée à celle des faux patriotes tolérants* (Paris, 1756); Abbé Marc-Albert de Villiers, *Sentiments des catholiques de France sur le Mémoire au sujet des mariages clandestins des Protestants* (n.p., 1756); Anon., *Dissertation sur la tolérance des Protestants* (n.p., c. 1756).

11. Grimm, *Correspondance littéraire*, October 1, 1758, IV, p. 40.

12. J. Proust, *L'Encyclopédie* (Paris, 1965), p. 146.

13. Voltaire to Jacob Vernes, February, 1759, Best. D. 8119.

14. *Année littéraire*, December 1758, IV, p. 280-281.

15. Abbé G.-F. Coyer, *Lettre au R.P. Berthier sur le matérialisme* (Geneva, 1759), p. 52, p. 60.

16. Grimm, *Correspondance littéraire*, April 16, 1756, III, p. 211.

17. *Année littéraire*, October 12, 1756, VI, p. 192.

18. Antoine Court and Antoine Court de Gébelin, *Le Patriote français et impartial, ou Réponse à la Lettre de M. l'évêque d'Agen à M. le controlleur-général contre la tolérance des Huguenots* (2 vols.; Villefranche, 1753); Court, *Lettre d'un Patriote sur la tolérance civile des Protestants de France et sur les avantages qui en résulteraient pour le royaume* (n.p., 1756); Chevalier de Beaumont, *L'Accord Parfait de la Nature, de la Raison, de la Révélation, et de la Politique* (Cologne, 1753), and *La Vérité vengée: ou Réponse à la Dissertation sur la tolérance des Protestants* (n.p., 1756); F.G. Delabroue, *L'Esprit de Jésus-Christ sur la tolérance* (Paris, 1760).

19. Paul Bosc to Antoine Court, April 13, 1753, Rabaut, *Lettres à Court*, II, p. 369, n.

20. Delabroue, *L'Esprit de Jésus-Christ*, p. 195.
21. E. Hugues, *Antoine Court, Histoire de la restauration du protestantisme en France au XVIIIe siècle* (2 vols.; Paris, 1872), II, p. 338.
22. Delabroue, *L'Esprit de Jésus-Christ*, p. 28.
23. Pierre Léridant, *Traité sur le mariage* (N.p., 1753); Abbé C. Yvon, *Liberté de conscience resserrée dans des bornes légitimes* (3 vols.; London, 1754); Loménie de Brienne, *Le Conciliateur, ou Lettres d'un ecclésiastique à un magistrat sur les affaires présentes* (Rome, 1754); Karl Friedrich Baër, *Mémoire théologique et politique au sujet des mariages clandestins des Protestants de France* (n.p. 1755); P.D. Rouvière, *Essai de Réunion des protestants aux Catholiques romains* (Paris, 1756); Abbé J. Besoigne, *Réponse à une dissertation contre les mariages clandestins des Protestants en France* (n.p., 1756); *Seconde réponse à des dissertations contre la tolérance pour les mariages des Protestants;* Abbé A. Morellet, *Petit Ecrit sur une matière intéressante* (Toulouse, 1756); G.-N. Maultrot and Abbé Tailhé, *Questions sur la tolérance* (Geneva, 1758) reissued as *Essai sur la tolérance chrétienne* (2 vols.; 'En France,' 1760).
24. Léridant, *Traité sur le mariage*, p. 244.
25. Rouvière, *Essai de réunion*, p. 146.
26. Voltaire to P.D. Rouvière, September 24, 1756, Best. D. 7006.
27. *Année littéraire*, June 6, 1756, III, p. 210.
28. Grimm, *Correspondance littéraire*, March 15, 1756, II, p. 192.
29. Hugues, *Antoine Court*, II, p. 296.
30. Grimm, *Correspondance littéraire*, June 1, 1758, IV, p. 18.
31. Abbé André Morellet, *Mémoires de l'abbé Morellet sur le dix-huitième siècle et sur la Révolution* (2 vols.; Paris, 1821), I, pp. 31-32.
32. Morellet, *Petit Ecrit*, pp. iii-iv.
33. Caveirac, *Mémoire politico-critique*, p. 190.
34. Caveirac, *Apologie de Louis XIV*, p. 508.
35. Bouniol de Montégut, *La Voix du vrai patriote*, p. 199.
36. Court, *Lettre d'un Patriote*, p. 76.
37. Tailhé and Maultrot, *Essai sur la tolérance*, II, p. 76.
38. Beaumont, *La Vérité vengée*, p. 48.
39. Caveirac, *Apologie de Louis XIV*, p. 196.
40. Bouniol de Montégut, *La Voix du vrai patriote*, p. 39.
41. Yvon, *Liberté de conscience*, III, p. 40.
42. Court and Court de Gébelin, *Le Patriote français et impartial*, I, p. 218.
43. Beaumont, *L'Accord Parfait*, I, p. 364.
44. Loménie de Brienne, *Le Conciliateur*, pp. 35-36.
45. Court, *Histoire des Troubles des Cévennes* (3 vols.; Villefranche, 1760), III, pp. 400-01.
46. Court, *Lettre d'un Patriote*, p. 26.
47. Yvon, *Liberté de conscience*, II, p. 175.
48. Loménie de Brienne, *Le Conciliateur*, p. 38.
49. Beaumont, *L'Accord Parfait*, II, p. 125.
50. Baër, *Mémoire théologique et politique*, p. 108.

51. Bouniol de Montégut, *La Voix du vrai patriote*, p. 156.
52. Caveirac, *Apologie de Louis XIV*, p. 507.
53. Anon., *Dissertation sur la tolérance*, p. 114.
54. Caveirac, *Mémoire politico-critique*, p. 220.
55. Beaumont, *L'Accord Parfait*, II, p. 134.
56. Court, *Lettre d'un Patriote*, p. 12, p. 98.
57. Delabroue, *L'Esprit de Jésus-Christ*, p. 185; Baër, *Mémoire théologique et politique*, p. 3.
58. Bouniol de Montégut, *La Voix du vrai patriote*, p. 208.
59. Caveirac, *Apologie de Louis XIV*, p. 86.
60. Tailhé and Maultrot, *Essai sur la tolérance*, II, 69.
61. Beaumont, *L'Accord Parfait*, II, 94.
62. Morellet, *Petit Ecrit*, p. 22.
63. Court, *Lettre d'un Patriote*, p. 40, p. 57.
64. Beaumont, *L'Accord Parfait*, II, p. 175.
65. Caveirac, *Apologie de Louis XIV*, p. 96.
66. Anon., *Dissertation sur la tolérance*, p. 34.
67. Bouniol de Montégut, *La Voix du vrai patriote*, p. 86.
68. Beaumont, *L'Accord Parfait*, II, 218.

ARTICLE

GENEVE,

TIRÉ DU SEPTIEME VOLUME

DE L'ENCYCLOPÉDIE.

LA Ville de *Geneve* eſt ſituée ſur deux collines, à l'endroit où finit le Lac qui porte aujourd'hui ſon nom, & qu'on appelloit autrefois *Lac Leman*. La ſituation en eſt très-agréable ; on voit d'un côté le Lac, de l'autre le Rhône, aux environs une campagne riante, des côteaux couverts de maiſons de campagne le

A

'Genève': The opening salvo of d'Alembert's tribute to the 'Socinian' Swiss pastorate.

CHAPTER VIII

Encyclopedists and Calvinists: An Exercise in Mutual Aid

The first seven volumes of the *Encyclopédie*, containing the articles beginning with the letters A to G, appeared between June 1751 and November 1757, a period during which, as we have seen, the question of Huguenot rights was being publicly debated in France for the first time since the Revocation. This substantial publication, followed by the simultaneous appearance of the last ten volumes in 1765, helped the Protestant cause in a number of ways, some oblique, some direct.

To begin with, in preparing their own publication, Denis Diderot and his colleagues consulted earlier encyclopedias, the most impressive of which had been compiled by Protestants; they were thus both consciously influenced by and indebted to men of the Reformed faith.

Diderot and his two co-editors, Jean d'Alembert and the chevalier Louis de Jaucourt, possessed very different perceptions of eighteenth-century French Calvinist society. All three were, however, united in their determination to make the *Encyclopédie* a vehicle for the propagation of toleration. In this resolve, they were joined by a diverse band of collaborators—Catholic priests of varying degrees of orthodoxy and Calvinists of differing degrees of conviction, as well as by a large contingent of deists and skeptics.

In the assessment which they made of Protestant as opposed to Catholic theology, the Encyclopedists were rigorously impartial; not surprisingly, they found Martin Luther and John Calvin no more congenial than Duns Scotus and Thomas Aquinas. They tended, however, to feel that the Protestant ethic was more conducive to civic virtue than the teachings of the Catholic Fathers; and, more directly relevant to the cause of Huguenot emancipation, they openly condemned the rationale used by the French Catholic establishment to repress dissent. When Attorney-General Omar Joly de Fleury, speaking before the Paris parlement in January 1759, drew up the indictment of suspect literary works deserving of censure which was to lead to the suspension of Diderot's enterprise, he cited the defence of toleration in Jaucourt's article "Conscience" (which had appeared in Volume III of the *Encyclopédie*) as typifying the kind of writing which called for the severest penalty.

Inevitably, the Encyclopedists consulted the work of those who had gone before them, almost all of which was by Protestants.[1] Bayle was the pioneer, with his *Dictionnaire historique et critique* which began to appear in 1697;[2] and a number of articles in the *Encyclopédie* such as "Liberté," "Manichéisme," and "Providence," clearly bear his stamp. A second important Protestant source for Diderot and his associates was the *Cyclopaedia* of Ephraim Chambers, published in 1728.[3] Of some 300 articles in the later French work dealing with religious matters, almost one-third can be traced to this English compendium. The third, and in many ways the most critical, Protestant publication from which the Encyclopedists took inspiration was the *Historia critica philosophiae*, a five-volume study by the Lutheran pastor Johann Jacob Brucker, produced between 1742 and 1744.[4]

Bayle, Brucker, and Formey, like most Protestants,[5] believed that the Reformation had played a critical role in the intellectual as well as the spiritual emancipation of Europe. Although many French Encyclopedists did not agree with this view, they shared with their Protestant predecessors an anti-clerical and especially an anti-monastic bias, an aversion to excessive asceticism and fanaticism and, most important, a loathing for all forms of religious persecution.

Their general indebtedness to Protestant scholarship apart, the chief editors of the *Encyclopédie* diverged widely both in their familiarity with the Protestant intellectual tradition and in their understanding of the Huguenot society of their own period.

Diderot grew up in Langres, a citadel of Catholic orthodoxy where there were no known Huguenots. Paradoxically, his first impressions of the Protestant world were formed during his early years in Paris, when he took to reading the deist Shaftesbury. The Englishman's *Letter on Enthusiasm*, published in 1709, had been based in part on a study of the extravagant behaviour of Camisard refugees in London.[6] Diderot found striking parallels between Shaftesbury's description of Calvinist zealots and his own observations of Jansenist convulsionaries in the Saint Médard quarter in the early 1730s. The 'miracles' to which partisans of these curiously similar sects pointed as evidence of divine sanction for their theology appeared to Diderot to be orchestrated by scoundrels and accredited by simpletons.

In the *Pensées philosophiques* which he wrote in 1746 while still under Shaftesbury's influence, Diderot argued that none of the existing religions had any appeal for the uncommitted since their devotees seemed above all intent upon inciting hatred, prejudice, and intolerance against their rivals:

> The Christian is an infidel in Asia, the Moslem in Europe, the Papist in London, the Calvinist in Paris, the Jansenist at the top of the rue Saint Jacques, the Jesuit in the heart of the Faubourg Saint-Médard. Who then is an infidel? Everyone or no one?[7]

The Paris parlement condemned the work to be burned while the Jesuit parish priest of Saint Médard denounced its author to the police in June 1747. Polemical volleys were aimed at the *Pensées* by a number of Calvinist theologians as well, including Samuel Formey[8] and François Louis Allamand.[9]

In *La Promenade du sceptique*, composed in 1746 or 1747 and seized by the authorities in manuscript form, Diderot cavalierly dismissed the leading lights of the Reformation—Huss, Luther, Calvin, and Zwingli, as both unreadable and intellectually sterile.[10] Twenty years later, having meditated more fully on the impact of the Reformation on European culture, Diderot handed down a somewhat more charitable verdict. Although conventional Christianity remained for the Encyclopedist the most absurd, unintelligible, and metaphysical of religions, the most riven with schism, the most subversive of public order, the most puerile in terms of ethic, the most "gothic" in style, and the most intolerant in outlook, Diderot was now ready to give a preferential rating to the post-Reformation churches: "Lutheranism devoid of certain absurdities is preferable to Catholicism, Protestantism (Calvinism) to Lutheranism and deism, provided it be accompanied by temples and ceremonies, to socinianism."[11]

During the years when his views concerning the Protestants were becoming somewhat more sympathetic, Diderot consistently denounced the repressive measures used against dissenters by the Catholic church. In letters to his brother, the abbé Didier-Pierre Diderot, the Encyclopedist makes what is probably his most eloquent and sustained plea for freedom of conscience on behalf of the Huguenots. When he learned late in 1760 that his brother, whom he clearly regarded as a bigot, had been put in charge of religious education in the diocese of Langres, he felt impelled to write, urging the abbé to make the new assignment a purely pacific one:

> It is blasphemous to expose religion to the odious charges of tyranny, harshness, injustice and unsociability, even when the intent is to bring back those who have unfortunately strayed from the fold.... Teaching, persuasion and prayer are the only valid means of spreading the faith.[12]

The simple-minded intolerance of the age of Louis XIV had been proven both irrational and self-defeating, Diderot pursued. A prince and his subjects owed one another mutual support and trust, whether or not they shared the same faith. The ostracism to which the abbé Caveirac had been subjected following his defence of the Revocation made clear that the old attitudes towards non-conformists would no longer be countenanced in France.

The abbé seems to have turned a deaf ear to this counsel; in any event, in September 1771, the Encyclopedist repeated his plea, urging his brother to consult the article "Intolerance" in the *Encyclopédie* in which he would read that "an intolerant man is an abomination in the eyes of God and man."[13] Shortly afterwards, in a further appeal, Diderot exhorted Didier-Pierre to forswear repression and intolerance in dealing with dissenters:

> Do not turn to persecution, to dragonnades, prison or the stake. Such is
> surely the teaching of the Gospel which I have read more often and more
> fully than you, just as it is the doctrine of Fénelon, who refused to go to the
> Cévennes until (the policy of conversion by) the bayonet was suspended.[14]

The Encyclopedist ended his letter on a note which suggested that he
had little hope of softening his brother's heart:

> If you had your way, we would soon see all the old horrors used against the
> Protestants revived.... Believe me, my friend, it is too late to transform
> yourself into an accomplice of the abbé de Caveirac.[15]

The interest of Diderot in matters theological and in the toleration
question was far more developed than that of his chief collaborator,
d'Alembert. Apart from a few random comments such as the observation in
"Fratricelles" that the burning of the radical followers of Saint Francis was
both pathetic and absurd,[16] d'Alembert made no special effort to indict
religious intolerance in his own signed contributions to the *Encyclopédie*;
and, as we shall see, the embarrassingly positive impressions about
contemporary Swiss Calvinism which he conveyed to readers of the article
Genève in Volume VII were more a transmission of the ideas of Voltaire on
the subject than the product of his own reflection.

Early in 1758, d'Alembert was replaced as co-editor of the
Encyclopédie by the nominally Protestant chevalier Louis de Jaucourt. Born
in 1704, Jaucourt belonged to one of the few titled Calvinist families which
did not abandon their homeland at the time of the Revocation. The parents of
the chevalier submitted formally to the Catholic sacraments; but they retained
a strong awareness of their Huguenot heritage, married within their own
communion, and observed the austere moral code which continued to
distinguish French Calvinist society.

Like other children of the well-to-do members of the Huguenot
internal emigration, Jaucourt was sent abroad for an education. In 1719,
after seven years schooling in Geneva, he enrolled in the local university,
intending to prepare himself for the Calvinist ministry. The theology which
the young Frenchman studied in the Swiss city was liberal, while the
patrician circles in which he moved conditioned Jaucourt more for his future
career as an Encyclopedist than for the rigorous life which he would have
had to face as an underground pastor back in France. In the end, abandoning
all thought of the ministry, Jaucourt moved to Cambridge in 1727 and, then,
the following year to Leyden where, having studied medicine under the
eminent Hermann Boerhaave, he was admitted to the profession in August
1730. While in the Dutch city, Jaucourt wrote articles on medical subjects
for the *Bibliothèque raisonnée des ouvrages savants*, a work edited by

members of the Calvinist diaspora. By 1737, Jaucourt was back in France working on a six-volume medical lexicon, the manuscript of which was lost in a shipwreck off the Dutch coast; the involvement of the chevalier with the *Encyclopédie* began in the aftermath of this disaster, for which it no doubt afforded a measure of intellectual compensation.

Diderot introduced Jaucourt to readers of the *Encyclopédie* in the preface to Volume II. The contribution of the Calvinist nobleman to this volume was slight, amounting to only seven articles; but following his appointment as co-editor in 1758, Jaucourt radically intensified his support for the collective task. The written contribution of Jaucourt to the text of the *Encyclopédie* was staggering: he penned some 17 000 out of 60 660 articles.[17] Nor did he limit his involvement to writing and editing: at one point, when the costs of publishing got out of hand, the chevalier sold his house to help raise needed funds. When the last ten volumes appeared in 1765, Diderot offered his Protestant collaborator a well-earned tribute:

> If we have let go with the kind of shout a sailor makes when he sights land after a dark night in which he has been lost between the sea and the sky, it is to the chevalier de Jaucourt that we owe this celebration. What he has not done for us, especially during this last critical period! How loyally he has resisted the blandishments of those who tried to steal him from us![18]

With the help of his co-editors, Diderot recruited an intellectually diverse band of contributors to the *Encyclopédie*, including at least nine priests. The abbé Edmé Mallet, who wrote most of the articles dealing with theological issues in the first five volumes, was a traditionalist who nevertheless adopted a long-term ecumenical attitude vis-à-vis the Calvinists. His successor, the abbé Morellet, an intimate of d'Holbach, was understandably even more liberal.

Two nominally Catholic laymen helped the cause of religious freedom by their outspoken comments in the *Encyclopédie*: Joachim Faiguet de Villeneuve, a former government official at Chalons who had moved to Paris to become one of the founders of the science of political economy, and Alexandre Deleyre, whose career spanned much of the Enlightenment and who, like Diderot, abandoned childhood piety for an integrally atheist outlook.

Of the Protestant contributors to the *Encyclopédie*, Jaucourt was both the most prolific and the most clearly identified in the public mind with the Huguenot milieu; but he was only one of the many French Calvinists who were associated in the enterprise. There was the Berlin-based conservative pastor Samuel Formey, for instance, whose orthodox outlook was apparent in such articles as "Atomisme," "Création," and "Dieu"[19] and who became increasingly uneasy at what he felt was the opposition of his more secular-minded colleagues to the idea that faith and scholarly detachment could and should be reconciled. At the opposite end of the theological spectrum stood Pastor Antoine-Noé Polier de Bottens of Lausanne, whose scurrilously unorthodox articles "Liturgie" and "Mages" provided cynical amusement for Voltaire and d'Alembert.[20] Other Protestant contributors were less controversial: Louis Necker, brother of the future controller-general, who had studied mathematics under d'Alembert, submitted a number of articles on scientific themes;[21] Jean Romilly, the distinguished Genevan clockmaker, wrote articles about his own specialty[22] while his son, Jean-Edmé, provided a reasoned argument for religious freedom in "Tolérance" which appeared when the last ten volumes were published in 1765.[23] The scientific research of Charles Bonnet, a Calvinist cosmologist with a keen interest in the cellular structure of plants and insects, supplied the basis for "Feuille" by Jaucourt.[24] The most celebrated doctor of the age, Théodore Tronchin, furnished a long and sustained defence of the latest medical wisdom in "Inoculation."[25]

As we have seen, Diderot's enterprise offered the Huguenots a critical entrée into French cultural life at a time when they were still formally excluded from it. The *Encyclopédie* was, of course, in no way a Protestant enterprise, and in the treatment of theological issues which had traditionally divided Protestant and Catholic Christians, Diderot was determined that his publication remain severely objective. For one thing, prudence dictated that an occasional tribute, albeit sometimes ironical, should be paid to orthodox opinion in a work published in a nation which still punished theological dissent. In addition, Diderot and his associates were neither sufficiently familiar with nor respectful of the writings of the sixteenth-century Reformers to engage in a meaningful analysis of their worth. As a result, articles which deal with such issues as the value of the Bible as a source of faith or which examine the peculiarities of Calvinist as opposed to Catholic doctrine show no particular sympathy for the Protestant point of view.

Diderot himself scoffed at the idea that any a priori faith be placed in the Christian Scriptures[26] and he rejected out of hand the thesis of the Calvinist Grotius that discrepancies between Old Testament prophecies and New Testament realizations might be reconciled by allegorical interpretations.[27] The editor of the *Encyclopédie* found the Calvinist view of human nature particularly abhorrent, and in "Grâce," he noted with obvious delight that Calvin's grim views concerning predestination had been abandoned by most of his spiritual descendants.[28]

The abbé Mallet made a direct attack on the Protestant notion that divine truth may be transmitted to individual believers through an inspired reading of Scripture in "Esprit particulier:"

> Without mentioning the innumerable variations of doctrine which this opinion introduced among the so-called Reformed Christians, it gave birth

to Socinianism and to a number of equally dangerous sects to whom the Protestants provided arms against which they were themselves helpless.[29]

In "Calvinisme," Mallet managed to temper an equally harsh indictment with an expression of ecumenical hope. At its inception, Mallet argued, the Calvinist heresy had been a peculiar blend of residual Waldensianism and incipient Lutheranism. Fortunately, Bossuet and Nicole had shown that this mélange of aberrant doctrines was indefensible, and the majority of the Calvinists had as a result abandoned most of their heretical opinions; the continuing denial of the Real Presence in the eucharist was the sole error of substance preventing their return to the fold.[30]

Paradoxically, some sympathy for the Protestant emphasis on the Bible is evinced in "Citation," written by the nominally Catholic Faiguet. Unlike their Protestant counterparts, Faiguet argued, Catholic priests did not seek guidance from the simple word of Scripture but preferred to consult the Church Fathers, whose artful glosses on the original text tended to reinforce priestly authority.[31]

Thanks to Samuel Formey, even the fundamentalist Protestant position concerning the Scriptures found its way into the *Encyclopédie*. In "Conservation," the pastor defended the account given in Genesis of the separate creation of all species and their subsequent reliance upon God's constant intervention.[32] Diderot was so upset by the tenor of this article, however, that he found it necessary to add a footnote dismissing the metaphysical meditations of Formey as absurd.[33]

When writing articles for and against Protestant theology, then, the Encyclopedists tended to cancel themselves out; but they expressed a clear and consistent bias in favour of the application of the Protestant ethic to everyday life. In "Célibat," for instance, Diderot ridiculed the efforts of Catholic scholars to rationalize the case for priestly continence on the basis of the alleged sexual abstinence of Adam and Eve following the birth of their first son. Indeed, had there been no prohibition against ecclesiastical marriage, France's population would have been increased by some four million in the period since Francis I. The argument that the marriage of priests would bring with it a loss of pastoral dignity and competence was refuted by the experience of Holland and England whose married clergy were much respected for their sense of social responsibility.[34]

In "Epargne," Faiguet indicted the Catholic Church for its abandonment of the frugal ways of the early Christians. The faithful could easily dispense with the costly superfluities which the modern priesthood had added to the simple form of worship enjoined by Christ. The parasitical practice of monasticism, for instance, could be done away with, as could the imposition of special fees for baptism, marriages, and burials. In these, as in other matters, Faiguet argued: "The Protestants have given us an excellent example to follow if only we were reasonable enough and disinterested enough to learn from it."[35]

In "Fêtes des Chrétiens," Faiguet pursued the same line of argument: one of the first achievements of the Reformation, he pointed out, was to reduce the number of holy days which had proliferated with the growth of Christianity, many of which had become simple pretexts for debauchery. By doing away with most of these needless interruptions in the work-week, the English, Dutch, and Germans had substantially increased their national productivity. Faiguet went so far as to suggest that, if Catholic France would only follow suit and abandon some of the gratuitous religious rituals which made her the butt of ridicule by non-conformists, the Protestants might reciprocate by showing less aversion to basic Catholic doctrine: "If we came closer to them in matters of discipline, they might well come closer to us in matters of dogma."[36]

These articles by Faiguet were attacked by the abbé Saas on the ground that their author, consciously or not, had implicitly endorsed heretical teachings, thereby giving the *Encyclopédie* a dangerously Protestant slant.[37]

Of obvious interest to Protestant and liberal readers of the *Encyclopédie* were the articles which dealt directly with the question of toleration. Not surprisingly, those who wrote about the issue tended to take a positive view, although there were clear differences of opinion about how generous the freedom afforded non-conformists should be. In the Preface to Volume VIII, Diderot declared that one of the central purposes of the collective enterprise was to wage war on intolerance, "that giddy spirit so disruptive of social peace and so abominably unjust in the eyes of God and man."[38] In a letter to Sophie Volland, he expressed the conviction that the great work "will with time produce a psychological revolution from which I think we may expect tyrants, oppressors, fanatics and intolerant men will emerge the losers."[39]

Diderot defended toleration in a number of his own articles: in "Anubis," [40] he praised the Romans for allowing the peoples whom they vanquished to retain their traditional gods; in "Cotereaux," [41] he suggested that the Catholic church had all too often indicted as dangerous groups such as the Albigensians who seemed to impartial observers to be no more than mindless bandits; and in "Futurition," [42] he took malicious pleasure in reciting the many trivial theological controversies which had brought Christians to engage in bloody civil wars over the centuries.

In "Calvinisme," Mallet suggested that when the Huguenots bewailed their present condition, they ought to be reminded that they had obtained the right to worship from Henri IV by force of arms; but the abbé concluded his article rather prudently: "This is not the place to examine whether or not it is advantageous for a state to tolerate only one religion."[43] In the article

"Gomaristes," posthumously attributed to Mallet but which smacks more of Morellet (who may have revised or rewritten it), a much more generous attitude surfaces. Praising the Protestant Dutch for conceding religious freedom to the Arminians, the author is clearly preaching to the clerical establishment in France:

> Arminianism no longer causes any problems in Holland: civil toleration has undone the harm caused by persecution. Dutch magistrates finally understand that, for the sake of peace, they should refrain from getting involved in religious disputes, permit theologians to speak and write as they please, let them meet in congress if they wish and come to a decision for themselves in these matters and above all, that no one should be persecuted on religious grounds alone.[44]

Of the clerical contributors to the *Encyclopédie*, the abbé Yvon was probably the most liberal as far as the toleration issue was concerned. In "Athéisme," based in large measure on material gathered by the Calvinist Formey, Yvon urged that Europe's princes grant toleration to all those who acknowledge that the ultimate sanction for the civil order resides in the will of an all-powerful Supreme Being on the ground that the sanction of religion was an "even better support for kings than the sword which has been committed into their hand."[45]

In the eyes of contemporaries, the most provocative plea for tolerance in the early volumes of the *Encyclopédie* surfaced in "Fanatisme," written by Alexandre Deleyre. In pagan antiquity, men had fought grimly enough in defence of rival deities, Deleyre argued; unfortunately, Christianity had intensified this madness by adding irrational dogmas and perverse moral principles to the raw zeal of the pagan world. Even more important, by inventing the notion of heresy, Christians had devised a means whereby a pretext for persecution could always be justified.

In Deleyre's view, the only sure means out of this centuries old cycle of fanaticism was to educate people to respect one another's spiritual freedom. Deleyre enjoined his fellow citizens to overcome their natural inclination to persecute and "(Try) a bit of tolerance and moderation. Above all, do not confuse a simple misfortune such as unbelief with a crime which is always willed."[46] Honest doubters, the Encyclopedists added, should be treated compassionately and saved from the wrath of the pious but ignorant multitude. If Christian churches were no longer safe asylums for the persecuted, let civil courts provide them with such a refuge.

Not surprisingly, "Fanatisme" evoked a strong negative reaction in conservative circles. The abbé Giry de Saint Cyr included selections from La Mettrie and other philosophical radicals in his comment on Deleyre's text, clearly aiming to establish guilt by association.[47] Abraham Chaumeix, opening the clerical offensive which was to lead to the second suspension of the work of Diderot and his colleagues, singled out "Fanatisme" for lengthy and severe comment. Those who believed in nothing had lost all reason to be intolerant, he thundered, without the slightest hint at irony.[48]

Diderot's Protestant collaborator Jaucourt was, of course, only too willing to broadcast the case for toleration in the pages of the *Encyclopédie*. In "Liberté de Conscience," he took as his starting point the familiar argument for respect of erring conscience first made by Bayle. There were, no doubt, cases in which actions inspired by wrong-headed but sincere conscience should be punished—the Greek and Roman practice of exposing unwanted children to death, for instance—but apart from such egregious examples, in which the principles of natural law clearly dictated intervention, judgment was all but impossible. The conclusion reached by Jaucourt was bold and liberal:

> When a spiritual error inspires neither actions nor teachings which are manifestly contrary to the general laws of human society and especially to civil law, the most suitable action to adopt vis-à-vis the deviant is to take care that he be drawn back to the truth by peaceful and solid guidance.[49]

A second article by Jaucourt, "Cruauté," began as a subtle study of the affinity between cowardice and the urge to persecute and ended with a forthright assault on 'destructive zeal.' The tone of the article is disturbingly pessimistic: "I am beginning to believe that nature put in man some natural inclination towards inhumanity."[50] One of the remedies Jaucourt suggested to modify this inherent cruelty was the reduction of radical social and economic disparities.

In "Constance," Jaucourt reminded his readers that John Huss had been burned in that city despite a promise of safe conduct by the authorities and suggested that the subsequent lack of trust by Protestants in the word of Catholics went far towards explaining the absence of a Reformed delegation at the all-important Council of Trent;[51] and in "Francfort sur le Mein," he praised the Lutheran administration of that city for its toleration of Calvinists, Catholics, and Jews, a policy both admirable in itself and highly advantageous to the city's development.[52]

Although the article "Christianisme" is unsigned and its attribution remains a matter of scholarly controversy, there are solid reasons for arguing that it was written by Jaucourt. Montesquieu, whose political opinions the Protestant took every occasion to relay, is generously cited in "Christianisme:" and readers of the article are urged to consult "Liberté de Conscience" and "Tolération," in which Jaucourt made his most significant and pointed comments on the issue of religious freedom.

"Christianisme" begins in mischievous vein. The claims of Christianity to the exclusive possession of spiritual truth cannot be doubted, Jaucourt asserts: it is a religion which must by its very nature be dogmatic and intolerant. How could it be otherwise with a faith whose central ceremony, the eucharist, it was beyond the human reason to fathom? Intolerance in fact derived from the sublime perfection of such mysteries as the eucharist, while the spurious toleration of the pagan world was the natural consequence of its incapacity to cope with matters requiring subtle theological interpretation. But, if Christianity was intrinsically intolerant, this did not mean, as so many had supposed, that consciences were to be forced and that worshippers were to be compelled to respect sacraments which they abhorred. Christian intolerance was purely and simply a question of turning away from the church those who insisted on confusing the faithful with false doctrine.[53]

As though guessing that "Christianisme" and "Liberté de Conscience" had come from the same pen, the conservative critics Fruchet and Bonhomme subjected the two articles to simultaneous attack. The notion that spiritual penalties would suffice to deal with the problem of heresy was absurd, they argued. The state must sustain the church by imposing civil disabilities on non-conformists, including the denial of public office. If France were to abandon her policy of upholding orthodoxy, she would be filled not only with Protestant heretics but with atheists, deists, and skeptics, groups against whom the spiritual weapons of the church were impotent. Past experience proved their argument: "The Protestant faith owes its foundation and deism its progress to civil toleration alone."[54]

Despite the presence in the *Encyclopédie* of articles defending religious freedom and praising the Protestant ethic, the work of Diderot and his associates was given a very mixed reception by the Huguenots of the diaspora, some of whom were disturbed by the apparent indifference of the Encyclopedists to the growing influence of deism and skepticism. David Boullier, an Amsterdam pastor born to refugee parents, responded to the *Discours préliminaire de l'Encyclopédie* by cautioning potential readers of the work against support for the Lockian approach to knowledge which was bound to reinforce the fashionable tendency towards skepticism.[55] The editors of the most conservative of French Calvinist newsletters, *La Bigarure*, noting that a band of so-called philosophers based in England, Prussia, and Holland had been plotting for some time to undermine traditional Christianity and replace it with simple deism, approved the banning of the work in 1752 as a salutary step to arrest the further spread of such subversive ideas.[56]

Criticism of the direction being taken by the *Encyclopédie* was also expressed by some of its principal Protestant contributors. Samuel Formey deplored what he felt was the increasingly anti-Christian tone of the later volumes of the *Encyclopédie* and, in 1756, went so far as to sound out various European booksellers about the possibility of their joining him in putting out a less abrasively anti-Christian *Encyclopédie réduite*.[57]

The reaction to the *Encyclopédie* among French Calvinists abroad was by no means uniformly adverse, however. *Les Cinq Années littéraires* of Pierre Clément, published at The Hague, consistently supported the *Encyclopédie*. One might quibble with some of the theological and metaphysical opinions which had been expressed in its pages, Clément consented, but the work as a whole was full of solid material concerning natural history, science, and the practical arts and trades.[58] The *Bibliothèque impartiale* published by Elie Luzac in Leyden deplored the suspension of publication of the *Encyclopédie* early in 1752[59] and applauded the later volumes as they were allowed to appear, singling out Jaucourt as among those whose articles were particularly deserving of attention. In his *Correspondance littéraire*, Grimm particularly recommended such articles as "Dimanche" by Faiguet and "Eclectisme" by Diderot.[60]

The Catholic establishment, which had succeeded in interrupting the publication of the *Encyclopédie* following the appearance of Volume II, offered only intermittent criticism of the next four volumes. With the publication in November 1757, of Volume VII, however, one anonymous commentator declared: "The governing principle of the *Encyclopédie* is to exalt wrongdoers in proportion to their felony. Thus all other things being equal, the heretic is given preference over the Catholic and the deist over the heretic."[61] In *Querelles littéraires*, the abbé Irail singled out the presence of pastors on the masthead of the *Encyclopédie* as particularly offensive.[62]

The campaign against the work of Diderot and his collaborators reached its climax in France with the stinging attack delivered by the *avocat-général* Omer Joly de Fleury before the January 23, 1759, session of the Paris parlement. Endorsing the views of Chaumeix, Joly de Fleury singled out a number of articles in the *Encyclopédie* which deserved to be stigmatized, among them "Liberté de Conscience" by Jaucourt:

> Are they (the author of the article and his fellow Encyclopedists) speaking of conscience? They are demanding in any case its freest possible exercise and thus by logical extension they are asking for universal toleration.... To speak in this way is surely to ask for the overthrow of the law and to open the gate to all sorts of disorders.[63]

Responding to what had become a formidable barrage of criticism, the government withdrew the publication rights of the *Encyclopédie* by an *arrêt du conseil* of March 8, 1759.

As in 1752, when Diderot had considered the possibility of transferring the headquarters of the embattled encyclopedia to Prussia, so, following the suspension of 1759, there was talk among the Encyclopedists and their friends of seeking asylum in a Protestant nation in which they might be allowed to resume publication. Voltaire suggested Lausanne; the Genevan publisher Cramer showed some interest; and there were rumours of a Dutch-based continuation of the *Encyclopédie*. In the end, however, these proposals were shelved. Instead Malesherbes lobbied the government to grant tacit permission to the *Encyclopédie* to resume publication and the last ten volumes, after a considerable delay, appeared in 1765.

The notoriety achieved by the *Encyclopédie* in its first seven volumes was in large measure due to the persistent attacks made by its contributors upon France's religious establishment. By the late 1750s, some French Calvinists were even beginning to feel that these attacks were directed not just at Catholicism but at Christianity as a whole. Nevertheless, the Huguenots had every reason to rejoice at the blows struck by the Encyclopedists at those who were oppressing them; and their own presence at the heart of the vast project started by Diderot gave them an irresistible opportunity to help attenuate the prejudices against them which had held sway for so long in France.

1. The Encyclopedists also borrowed material, including some quite unflattering character studies of the Protestant Reformers, from the Jesuit *Dictionnaire de Trévoux*.
2. Bayle, *Dictionnaire historique et critique* (2 vols.; Rotterdam, 1697).
3. E. Chambers, *Cyclopaedia: or, an Universal dictionary of arts and sciences* (2 vols.; London, 1728).
4. J. Brucker, *Historia critica philosophiae a mundi incunabulis ad nostram usque aetatem deducta* (5 vols.; Leipsig, 1742-44).
5. Lesser Protestant influences upon the Encyclopedists included Jacques Abbadie, *Traité de la religion chrétienne* (2 vols.; Rotterdam, 1684); Jean Le Clerc, *Historia ecclesiastica duorum primorum a Christo nato seculorum, e veteribus monumentis deprompta a Ioanne Clerico* (Amsterdam, 1716); and J.-A Turrettini, *Cogitationes et Dissertationes theologicae* (Geneva, 1737).
6. Shaftesbury, *Lettres sur l'enthousiasme* (The Hague, 1709). The original English version was published in 1708.
7. Denis Diderot, *Pensées philosophiques* (1746), in *Oeuvres philosophiques*, ed. P. Vernière (Paris, 1956), p. 29.
8. Samuel Formey, *Pensées raisonnables, contre les 'Pensées philosophiques'* (Berlin, 1749).
9. F.-L. Allamand, *Pensées Anti-philosophiques* (The Hague, 1751), p. 74.
10. Diderot, *La Promenade du sceptique ou les allées, Oeuvres complètes* (Paris, 1969) I., p. 322.
11. Diderot to de Viallet, (?) July 1766, *Correspondance de Diderot*, ed. G. Roth (16 vols.; Paris, 1955-70), VI, p. 232.
12. Diderot to the abbé Didier-Pierre Diderot, December 29, 1760, ibid, III, p.283.
13. Same to same, September 25, 1772, ibid., XII, p. 135.
14. Same to same, November 13, 1772, ibid., p. 171.
15. Ibid., p. 174.
16. "Fratricelles," *Encyclopédie, ou Dictionnaire raisonné des sciences, des arts et des métiers, par une société de gens de lettres*, ed. D. Diderot, J. Le Rond d'Alembert et al. (35 vols.; Paris, 1751-80), VII, p. 291.
17. Richard N. Schwab, "Un Encyclopédiste Huguenot: Le chevalier de Jaucourt," *BSHPF*, CVIII, p. 46.

18. *Encyclopédie*, VIII, p. 1.
19. "Atomisme," *Encyclopédie*, I, pp. 822-23; "Création," ibid., IV, pp. 438-44; "Dieu," ibid., pp. 976-84.
20. V. especially the letters of Voltaire to d'Alembert of February 4 and February 19, 1957, Best. D. 6443 and D. 6469.
21. "Frottement," *Encyclopédie*, VII, pp. 341-45.
22. "Frottement (Horlogerie)" ibid., pp. 345-54.
23. "Tolérance," ibid., XVI, pp. 390-95.
24. "Feuille," ibid., VI, pp. 652-55.
25. "Inoculation," ibid., VIII, pp. 755-69.
26. "Eclectisme," ibid., V p. 270.
27. "Prophétie," ibid., XIII, p. 463.
28. "Grâce," ibid., VII, p. 802.
29. "Esprit particulier,",ibid, V, p. 973.
30. "Calvinisme," ibid., II, p. 566.
31. "Citation," ibid., III, pp. 482-83.
32. "Conservation," ibid., IV, pp. 38-39.
33. Ibid., p. 39.
34. "Célibat," ibid., II, p. 805.
35. "Epargne," ibid., V, p. 748.
36. "Fêtes des Chrétiens," ibid., VI, p. 869.
37. Abbé Jean Saas, *Lettres sur 'l'Encyclopédie' pour servir de Supplément aux sept volumes de ce dictionnaire* (Amsterdam (Rouen), 1764), p. 106, p. 135.
38. Encyclopédie, VIII, p. ii.
39. Diderot to Sophie Volland, September 26, 1762, *Correspondance*, IV, 172.
40. "Anubis," *Encyclopédie*, I, p. 519.
41. "Cotereaux," ibid., IV, p. 304.
42. "Futurition," ibid., VII, p. 405.
43. "Calvinisme," ibid., II, p. 566.
44. "Gomaristes," ibid., VII, p. 735.
45. "Athéisme," ibid., I, p. 816.
46. "Fanatisme," ibid., VI, p. 400.
47. Abbé Giry de Saint-Cyr, *Catéchisme et Décisions de cas de conscience, à l'usage des Cacouacs, avec un Discours du Patriarche des Cacouacs, pour la Réception d'un nouveau disciple* (n.p., 1758).
48. Abraham Chaumeix, *Préjugés légitimes contre 'l'Encyclopédie.' Essai de Réfutation de ce Dictionnaire* (8 vols.; Brussels and Paris, 1758-59), II, p. 160.
49. "Liberté de Conscience," *Encyclopédie*, III, 903. 50 "Cruauté," ibid., IV, p. 519.
50. "Cruauté," ibid., IV, p. 519.
51. "Constance," ibid., IV, p. 58.
52. "Francfort sur le Mein," ibid.,VII, pp. 282-83.
53. "Christianisme," ibid., III, p. 387.
54. Fruchet and Bonhomme, *Réflexions d'un Franciscain*, p. 121.
55. *Journal des Savants*, November, 1751, p. 425.
56. *La Bigarure, ou Gazette galante, historique, littéraire, critique, morale, satirique, sérieuse et badine* (The Hague, March 24, 1752), p. 69.
57. V. *Correspondance de Diderot* (Roth), I, p. 204, n. 6.
58. Pierre Clément(ed.), *Les Cinq Années littéraires* (4 vols.; The Hague, 1754), IV, p. 282.

59.　*La Bibliothèque impartiale*, March-April, 1752, p. 305.

60.　Grimm, *Correspondance littéraire*, V,298.

61.　[Anon.] *Lettres sur le VIIe volume de 'l'Encyclopédie''* (n.p., 1759), pp. 18-19.

62.　Abbé Simon-Augustin Irail, *Querelles littéraires, ou Mémoires pour servir à l'Histoire des Révolutions de la République des Lettres, depuis Homère jusqu'à nos jours* (4 vols.; Paris, 1761), IV, pp. 118-19.

63.　*Arrests de la Cour de Parlement, portant condamnation de plusieurs livres et autres ouvrages imprimés. Extrait des Registres du Parlement, du 23 janvier 1759* (Paris, 1759), p. 15.

Laurent-Angliviel de la Beaumelle: Protestant provocateur.

CHAPTER IX

A Case Study in Incompatibility:
The Philosophe Voltaire and the Calvinist
La Beaumelle, 1750-1756

During the six-year period beginning in July 1750 when he arrived at the court of Frederick of Prussia, Voltaire came to grips with the realities of the French Calvinist experience for the first time. To begin with, he met scholarly Calvinist pastors such as Samuel Formey and Charles Louis de Beausobre, descendants of Huguenot refugees who had been welcomed to Berlin following the Revocation. However implausibly, Voltaire treated these and other Protestant theologians as potential converts to his own deist creed, as he made clear in two short works read or published while he was in Berlin—the *Sermon des cinquante* and the *Défense de milord Bolingbroke*.

The main preoccupation of the philosophe during the early part of his Berlin stay was the completion and publication of *Le Siècle de Louis XIV*, the fruit of some twenty years of meditation and research. Two of the central theses of this work—the contention that the civilizing achievement of the Sun King far outweighed the damage done to French society by his arbitrariness, and the argument that the record of French Calvinism had been both subversive and fanatical—provoked strong reaction in Huguenot circles. Voltaire's views were in fact almost immediately challenged by the Calvinist pamphleteer Laurent Angliviel de La Beaumelle who turned up in Berlin soon after Voltaire's arrival hoping to find in the celebrated playwright a patron and protector. The two men had a falling out, however, and, to spite Voltaire, La Beaumelle publicly challenged the version of French Protestant history set forth in *Le Siècle*. For the next four years, the pamphleteer and the playwright engaged in a bitter polemical exchange in the course of which the Protestant brought off something of a literary coup by publishing fifteen volumes of memoirs and correspondence centred around the career of the 'new Catholic' Madame de Maintenon.

Voltaire's decision to settle in Berlin in the summer of 1750 was a natural one. Fourteen years earlier, Frederick, then Crown Prince of Prussia, had written to applaud the attack on religious zeal made in *Alzire* and the two men had subsequently been in close correspondence, each exhorting the other to greater effort in the battle against superstition and intolerance.[1] The knowledge that the philosophe was preparing a major work on the age of Louis XIV was, of course, also bound to excite the curiosity of the local French Calvinist community. To Pastor Formey, who had indicated such an interest, Voltaire forwarded several chapters of his forthcoming text in manuscript form. Years later, the cleric noted in his memoirs that he had been disturbed at the lack of religious and patriotic conviction which he found in the 'philosophic' history of Voltaire.[2]

The relationship between Voltaire and Pastor Beausobre developed even less auspiciously. In the spring of 1751, several months before the appearance of *Le Siècle de Louis XIV*, Beausobre had published *Le Triomphe de l'Innocence* in which the Sun King was presented as a monarch of "boundless ambition" and "mindless zeal" who had been seduced by the Catholic clergy into abolishing the rights of his faithful Calvinist subjects. The plague and famine which had descended upon France in 1709 were proof enough of Heaven's wrath at the King's depravity, the pastor argued.[3] Voltaire relayed his contempt for this tract in verse form to Frederick:

> Je renvoye au héros dont je suis enchanté
> Cet empoulé fatras d'un ministre entêté
> Triomphe du faux goût plus que l'innocence.[4]

Yet, for all their weaknesses, Voltaire was convinced that scholarly Protestant clergymen such as Formey and Beausobre were not an altogether hopeless band. In two short works conceived during his Berlin period, Voltaire urged contemporary Protestant theologians to join him in completing the spiritual liberation which had been begun during the Reformation by moving towards deism or at least by suspending their attacks on the champions of natural religion. The *Défense de milord Bolinbroke*, published anonymously in November 1752, was a reply to an article in the *Nouvelle Bibliothèque germanique* in which Formey had taken to task a number of prominent figures, including Frederick, for espousing Bolingbroke's deist creed. Pretending to speak as a moderate Protestant, Voltaire asked why deists should be treated more harshly than papists, especially when they were not idolaters and when they freely declared themselves to be closer to Reformed than to Catholic Christianity. Why should Protestant leaders not reciprocate this generosity since, as the progenitors of deism, they had every right to claim that the followers of natural religion were their natural descendants?[5]

In the *Sermon des cinquante* (which he read before members of Frederick's court sometime during the year 1751-52) Voltaire imagines members of a Quakerish sect being urged by one of their number to complete the emancipation which their predecessors had begun in the sixteenth century by making a forthright profession of Socinianism:

> It is true that our ancestors shook off a part of the awesome burden of the past and that they threw over a number of errors and superstitions. But, my God, how much they left undone...! Already a number of theologians are

embracing Socinianism which closely approximates the worship of a single God.[6]

The chances of a favourable response from the French Protestant community to the suggestion made in these two works that it move towards deism were certainly not enhanced with the appearance of *Le Siècle de Louis XIV*, first published in December 1751 and reprinted eight times within a year. In the course of this work, Voltaire managed to offend the Huguenots doubly, by attacking both their politics and their religion. At the time when the *Siècle* was written, its author subscribed wholeheartedly to the *thèse royale*, the view that the French monarchy enjoyed a monopoly of public power and was thus not susceptible to challenges from intermediary bodies such as the parlements. In line with this reasoning, the age of Louis XIV seemed to Voltaire the crowning moment of what had been an achievement of centuries. In this stable and civilized society, the Huguenots had constituted a disturbing element, less because of their peculiar theology than because of their resistance to hierarchical authority of all kinds. Like the early Christians who had troubled the civil peace of the Roman world, France's Calvinists had reintroduced "the basic conflict between the republican spirit which animated the early church and established authority which hates resistance of all kinds."[7] The sixteenth-century revolt of the Huguenots, coinciding with that of the feudal nobility, had shaken the monarchy to its foundations, forcing French kings to concede privileges under duress. Henri IV had granted the Edict of Nantes to subjects who had wrested rights from his predecessors "at gun-point;"[8] and, with the death of the Vert Galant, "it was inevitable that the republican spirit of the Protestants should bring them to make an abusive application of their principles."[9] The result had been the La Rochelle insurrection of the 1620s.

While the main target of criticism in his *Siècle* was French Protestant politics, Voltaire clearly intended to ridicule Calvinist theology as well. In letters written soon after the appearance of the *Siècle*, he remarked: "I felt that by damning fanaticism and ridiculing theological disputes, I was doing humanity a service.... My history, beginning with the chapter on Calvinism, is the story of madmen."[10]

Having indicted the Huguenots, Voltaire proceeded in the *Siècle* to applaud the methods by which Richelieu and Colbert had tried to incorporate these troublesome citizens into the mainstream of national life. As he saw it, these methods had been generously rewarded. Calvinism had been all but moribund in France at the accession of Louis XIV, whose taste for splendour rendered the stern teachings of Calvin less attractive than ever: "The magnificent ceremonies of that splendid court made the pedantic style of the Huguenots look ridiculous."[11] Sound political judgment should have dictated that the King harness what Calvinist strength remained in the battle against the Papacy which the Gallican church was about to wage. Instead,

Louis XIV had chosen to do battle with Rome and Geneva simultaneously. For this royal blunder, Voltaire blamed the Jesuits as well as Chancellor Le Tellier and his son Louvois, who had persecuted the Huguenots as rebels simply "because Colbert protected them as useful subjects."[12]

Although the case which he presented against the Huguenots in the *Siècle* provided a form of retrospective justification for the Revocation, Voltaire was particularly critical of the way in which the French government had acted against the Calvinists after 1685. It would seem, he wrote, that everything had been done to produce martyr complexes, fanaticism, and rebellion, especially in southern France, "a country eminently suited to preaching, peopled by ignoramuses and hotheads."[13] As a result, France had lost some 500 000 citizens, thousands of whom had helped transform the barren plains of northern Germany into centres of bustling industry.

Thanks to the good offices of Joseph du Fresne de Francheville, a member of the Calvinist refugee community in Berlin, *Le Siècle de Louis XIV* was published in the Prussian capital during the last month of 1751. The impact of the work on French Protestant readers was predictable. A member of the refugee community in Holland suggested that, if Voltaire had been serious in wanting to understand the fundamental principles which underlay Protestant thought, he should have consulted the *Avis aux Réfugiés*, written by Bayle at the time of the peace negotiations at Ryswick in 1697. The so-called republican spirit which Voltaire had attributed to the earliest Protestants was "a hazy notion at best in which he is always confusing freedom of conscience with the concept of absolute liberty."[14] The chevalier de Beaumont, whose own treatise on Protestant rights, *L'Accord Parfait*, would appear in 1753, took Voltaire severely to task for reviving the myth of Calvinist insurrection which had been used against the Huguenots at the time of the Revocation and suggested that the philosophe had added cheap sensationalism to his history simply to increase sales.[15] The dean of France's underground pastors, Paul Rabaut, made known his feelings in a letter to Pastor Paul Moultou of Geneva:

> You are familiar, sir, with *Le Siècle de Louis XIV* of the famous Voltaire. I do not know if the author's intent was to please the French court, but I note with regret that in his work, without regard for historical truthfulness, without paying any attention to what he himself had earlier said in the historical background which he placed at the beginning of *La Henriade* and without hesitating to call down new persecutions upon a people which has already suffered the greatest injustice, he has maligned us viciously. This is especially true of the chapter dealing with Calvinism. Given the distinguished reputation which the author enjoys and the wide public which this work is bound to reach, it is vitally important that he be refuted, and in no uncertain way.[16]

In October 1752, ten months after the appearance of *Le Siècle de Louis XIV*, the wish expressed by Rabaut was dramatically fulfilled when the Calvinist La Beaumelle brought out a pirated and richly annotated edition of Voltaire's history. An examination of the personal and philosophical background of this impudent Huguenot pamphleteer will help us to understand how and why he came to quarrel with the most celebrated historian of his age over the merits of the Sun King's reign as well as over the historical role of the Huguenots.

In a recent study, Claude Lauriol, who had access to the family archives, has pointed out that La Beaumelle's friendship with Montesquieu, together with his lively battles against Voltaire, make him a figure of considerable interest, not just to students of eighteenth-century French Protestantism, but to students of the Enlightenment as well.[17]

La Beaumelle was born at Valleraugue in the Cévennes in 1726 to a Catholic mother and a father who belonged to the old Huguenot gentry. Under the constraint of the laws governing 'new Catholics,' he was baptized in the Roman communion and in 1734 began his formal education at the Collège de l'Enfant-Jésus. By 1742, following a visit to Protestant relatives in Lyon, he shook off whatever spiritual influence the Jesuits had exercised upon his young mind and in September 1745, moved to Geneva intent on preparing for a career in the Calvinist pastorate.

During the year-and-a-half which he spent in the Swiss city, La Beaumelle got caught up in the ongoing debate within the Reformed camp about the obligation to worship God publicly, in defiance of the law, if necessary. In an anonymous *Lettre sur l'état présent de la religion protestante* published in the November 1745 issue of the *Journal helvétique*, and purporting to be the comment of an objective Catholic eyewitness, La Beaumelle described the innocent nature of these assemblies, noting that they had become commonplace in many parts of France since the war crisis of the 1740s. The pastors presiding over these services, he pointed out, taught obedience to the King and made a special effort to avoid giving offence to the established church.[18]

La Beaumelle's seminary studies led him in the end to the conclusion that a career in the underground pastorate back in France was not for him and when in March 1747 he learned that the comte de Gram, Grand Chamberlain of Denmark, was looking for a tutor for his son, the young Huguenot left Geneva for Copenhagen, armed with an honorable discharge from the Venerable Company of Pastors and Professors of Theology. Danish society being caught up in incipient gallomania, the self-confident Frenchman had little difficulty in obtaining a generous pension from King Frederick V.

La Beaumelle quickly took advantage of the financial independence and psychological security which he felt in Lutheran Denmark to launch himself on what was to be a recklessly bold literary career. He succeeded in deceiving the French censors of his first major work, *L'Asiatique tolérant* (published anonymously in Paris in 1748), by implying through his choice of subtitle that he had written a sequel to a novel by Crébillon fils—*Les Amours de Zéokinizul* (in effect a transparent and rather scurrilous chronicle of scandal and intrigue at the court of Louis XV) which had appeared in 1746. La Beaumelle kept the easily decipherable anagrams used by Crébillon to designate leading figures in French public life but radically altered the central focus of the earlier work. The key chapters of *L'Asiatique tolérant* are a chronicle, not of petty court intrigue, but of the tyranny established by Emor (Rome) over the empire founded by the gentle Ristkesusi (Jesus Christ) and of the nearly successful campaign of Kanvil (Calvin) to restore the kingdom of the Korifans (Français) to its original freedom following centuries of Emor's oppression.

It is hard to imagine that La Beaumelle seriously entertained hopes of swaying official French opinion with *L'Asiatique tolérant*, since so much of his text is taken up with tactless comments about the degeneration of the monarchy in the land of the "Kofirans." "All kings are subjects, all people sovereign,"[19] proclaims the author at one point before endorsing the contract theory and arguing the case for popular insurrection against tyrants.

The ideas concerning religious freedom put forward in *L'Asiatique tolérant* were as provocative as the book's political comment. La Beaumelle quoted pronouncements on toleration by Kiérfli (Fléchier, bishop of Nîmes in the early eighteenth century) and Nélefon (Fénelon) before adding an argument for French Calvinist relief which many Huguenots would find embarrassing. The ruthless implementation of the Revocation, he wrote, had produced a series a predictable conversions, but these conversions had been to agnosticism, not Catholicism: "The suppression of the Tsandenit (Edict de Nantes) induced spiritual apathy in a large number of Kanviliens who preferred not to believe in Ristkesusi rather to believe in Emor against their will."[20] In any case, the thousands of Catholic Frenchmen taught to practise moral indifference by the Jesuits were surely more suitable objects of concern to the authorities than the remaining devotees of the austere Calvin.

La Beaumelle was prepared to agree that atheists and those whose teachings threatened public order should not be tolerated but, citing the *Lettres persanes*, he insisted that spiritual diversity was in itself both healthy and creative. To abolish differences in belief in a nation so accustomed to it as France was to guarantee a decline in intellectual vitality. It was clear, for instance, that the persecution of the Huguenots had seriously retarded French science. A policy of toleration, on the other hand, brought economic as well as intellectual advantages to nations which welcomed religious refugees; it had, for example, transformed the coastal wastes of Holland into an area of high productivity.

Half-way through *L'Asiatique tolérant*, La Beaumelle confessed that toleration would have to come "from some kind of *coup d'état* which one should rather hope for than count upon."[21] But he obviously hoped to win converts to his views among members of the French government, to whom he sent copies of his work, and he reminded his readers that France's Calvinists had offered to raise 50 000 soldiers for Louis XV during the War of the Austrian Succession, thereby dispelling rumours of their disloyalty and confirming their worth as citizens.

Thanks to the clever dodge by which La Beaumelle had passed off his work as the follow-up to that of Crébillon fils, *L'Asiatique tolérant* slipped past the French censors. Huguenots inside France who managed to get hold of the text were rather disconcerted by its boldness: Antoine Court included a sharp attack on the novel in his *Patriote français et impartial*[22] while Paul Rabaut reported that publishers who might normally have been willing to handle manuscripts written by moderate Protestants had been frightened off by the appearance of La Beaumelle's work and were afraid to touch anything with such an obvious Huguenot flavour to it.[23]

La Beaumelle spent the summer of 1750 in Paris, where he met Montesquieu as well as a number of other prominent writers. As noted in an earlier chapter, he was encouraged by the author of *L'Esprit des lois* to compose and publish a defence of this text, which had come under heavy attack in the pages of the Jansenists' *Nouvelles ecclésiastiques.*[24]

Earlier during that same Paris visit, in mid-June, La Beaumelle had been introduced to Voltaire, with whom he discussed an edition of the French classics he had been planning to produce for the heir to the Danish throne. Voltaire showed interest and forwarded a copy of *La Henriade* for possible inclusion in the series. La Beaumelle responded with a tactless letter in which he criticized parts of the epic poem for both style and content.[25] Infinitely more provocative, however, and far more damaging to the Protestant's later relationship with Voltaire, was the nasty jibe about the leading light of French letters which La Beaumelle included in his *Qu'en dira-t-on. Mes Pensées,* a collection of epigrammatic comments about contemporary men of letters published following his return to Copenhagen in August:

> There have been greater poets than Voltaire, but none has been so generously rewarded. The King of Prussia showers honours on men of talent for the very same reasons which induce any German princeling to reward a buffoon or a dwarf.[26]

Meanwhile, the scathing comments which La Beaumelle had also made about his Danish hosts in *Mes Pensées,* together with reports of the unorthodox opinions which he was airing in lectures delivered at the University of Copenhagen, led to a request for his resignation in October

1751. Later that month, La Beaumelle moved to Berlin, where he hoped (despite the insolent comments he had made in *Mes Pensées*), to obtain the patronage of Voltaire, who was Frederick's guest at Potsdam.

At a dinner to which the historian of Louis XIV invited him in mid-November, the conversation between the Huguenot and the philosophe led in two unfortunate directions. Voltaire began by asking La Beaumelle point-blank whether or not he intended to seek the seat in Frederick's Academy left vacant by the death three days earlier of La Mettrie. The Huguenot and Voltaire then turned to discuss the scholarly enterprises upon which they were both then embarked. As vain as his host, La Beaumelle made clear that he regarded his investigation of the life and works of Madame de Maintenon as being of equal importance with Voltaire's forthcoming study of the age of Louis XIV; at the same time, he refused to surrender any of the Maintenon correspondence, which Voltaire expressed an understandable interest in examining.

Highly irritated by his guest's behaviour, Voltaire sent La Beaumelle a letter on December 1, requesting a copy of *Mes Pensées*. The incriminating volume, forwarded to the philosophe soon after, was returned three days later with clear markings opposite the passage in which Voltaire had been slighted. Relations between the two men quickly degenerated. Meanwhile, not surprisingly, given what had been written about him as well in *Mes Pensées*, the Prussian monarch gave La Beaumelle clear indication that he could expect no court patronage. A scandal involving the Huguenot and the wife of a prominent Prussian army officer added to the Calvinist's miseries, leading to a brief jail sentence in January 1752. The following month, during a meeting with Voltaire (who had begun to circulate rumours that La Beaumelle had behaved very little like a Catholic in France in spite of the law which required all of His Majesty's subjects to profess the faith of the majority), the Huguenot pamphleteer refused to accede to the older man's request that he insert a cancel in a forthcoming new edition of *Mes Pensées* in place of the passage in which he had mocked Voltaire, instead vowing to himself to take the literary offensive at the first opportunity.

By May 1752, Voltaire had made life in Berlin intolerable for La Beaumelle, who departed for Frankfurt-am-Main to contemplate revenge. The recent publishing success of *Le Siècle de Louis XIV* afforded the pamphleteer his opportunity. What, he must have asked himself, would be more damaging than a pirated version of Voltaire's history with all sorts of mordant editorial comment?

When rumours of what the Huguenot was planning reached Voltaire, the philosophe was seriously alarmed, partly because he believed that La Beaumelle was in possession of the Maintenon papers containing new information about the reign of Louis XIV and partly because the forthcoming unauthorized edition of his *Siècle* might drive the original off the market. In his distress, Voltaire appealed to La Beaumelle through a mutual friend to drop his plan; La Beaumelle refused and the pirated version of *Le Siècle de Louis XIV* appeared in late December 1752 or early January 1753.

The tone of the unauthorized version is apparent from the three letters which the Huguenot editor addresses to Voltaire in the introduction: "You subject all themes to your imagination just as you subordinate all facts to your peculiar reasoning."[27] It is in his extensive footnoting, however, that La Beaumelle gives a clearly Calvinist gloss to Voltaire's narrative. France's sixteenth-century wars, the Protestant comments, were the product, not of Calvinist factionalism as suggested by Voltaire, but of a denial of justice to peaceable subjects of the crown. The motives of Louis XIV in repressing the Calvinists had been religious, not political: "He did not persecute them for political reasons but out of piety, not out of *raison d'état* but out of *raison d'église*."[28] There had been 4 000 000 not 1 000 000 Huguenots in France at the time of the Revocation, of whom more than 1 000 000 not 400 000 (as Voltaire claimed), had remained in the country after the edict. The first victim of government repression after 1685, Pastor Claude Brousson, was not guilty of conspiracy with France's enemies, nor had there been any general Protestant involvement in the Camisard rebellion.

Although he had been unable to prevent the publication of the pirated edition of his history, Voltaire may well have found some solace in the action taken against La Beaumelle by Madame de Pompadour; bitterly resentful of the way in which she, too, had been caricatured in *Mes Pensées*, the marquise secured the author's incarceration in the Bastille in April 1753.

Scorning the advice of friends that it would be wiser not to prolong debate with such an aggressive polemicist, Voltaire published a *Supplément au Siècle de Louis XIV* late in April 1753. Determined to vindicate his scholarship, the philosophe in this bitter counter-attack charged that La Beaumelle had deliberately blinded himself to overwhelming evidence that France's civil conflict in the sixteenth and seventeenth centuries had been caused by religious fanaticism, much of it Calvinist. "You have laboured in vain to exonerate Pastor Brousson of the charge of conspiring with France's Protestants," Voltaire declared: "Preachers of your faith who came into France in violation of the law were hanged. Those who stirred up revolt were broken on the wheel. Such was the law which, however harsh, was executed impartially."[29] Finally, Voltaire dismissed as mere squeamishness the Calvinist's criticicism of the methods which had been used to subdue *Cévenol* firebrands.

The most ideologically revealing passages in the *Supplément* were those in which Voltaire defended both the personal qualities and political achievements of Louis XIV. La Beaumelle, like his mentor Montesquieu, had contended that the King's denial of basic civic and religious freedoms had corrupted French public life. Voltaire, on the other hand, was clearly prepared to forgive and forget this abuse of royal power in the light of the overall glory of the reign:

> I defy anyone to show me a monarchy on earth where the laws and the concern for distributive justice and the rights of humanity were less trampled on and where more was achieved for the public good than during the fifty-five years when Louis XIV reigned by himself.[30]

Voltaire concluded the *Suppément* with the observation that the critical reception given his history in Protestant as well as Catholic circles attested to the high level of objectivity which he had maintained while writing it.[31]

Meanwhile, the anger of La Beaumelle towards Voltaire had, if anything, intensified during his imprisonment and, following his release in October 1753, his first inclination was to make a definitive response to Voltaire by writing his own history of the age of Louis XIV. Instead, during May 1754 or shortly thereafter, he published a *Réponse au Supplément* in which he charged that Voltaire had presented a Hobbesian rationalization of despotism and again defended the memory of Brousson, whose life and works the philosophe had approached through the biased account written by the apostate Brueys. Even ignorant parish priests in the remotest reaches of Languedoc did not take the chronicle of Brueys seriously, La Beaumelle pointed out. In any case, it had been the policy of repression directed from Versailles, not the reasoned piety of men such as Brousson, which had touched off the tragic revolt of the Camisard peasantry:

> Brousson, an enlightened man, was aware that the *Lettres Pastorales et prophétiques* of Jurieu would excite the restive minds of those mountain folk whose brains had been enfeebled and souls hardened by persecution. He fought against the spread of disorder and offered these people immediate spiritual consolation so that they would not seek more radical remedies. His vigour won the day, and during his lifetime Jurieu prophesied in vain.[32]

The long polemical battle which had pitted Voltaire against an insolent Protestant pamphleteer had kept the philosophe in a state of high dudgeon. As the controversy became hotter, he damned La Beaumelle as a modern-day Erostratus who was making a fortune by debasing the scholarship of his betters.[33] However, when the last shot in this vigorous exchange had been fired, Formey, perhaps influenced by the enmity which he had come to feel for Voltaire as much as by objective judgment, was inclined to concede La Beaumelle the victory.[34]

In the fall of 1752, in the midst of his lengthy debate with Voltaire, La Beaumelle had published the first of the many volumes which he was to devote to the life and writings of Madame de Maintenon. The portrait of the marquise which the Huguenot sketched was that of "a compassionate rather than enlightened woman" who had challenged the right of the King to control private consciences. She had rejected the church's argument that those who had strayed from the fold might be brought back by any means, including the sword, La Beaumelle observed, adding: "This inclination towards tolerance was clearly a remnant of her Protestant upbringing."[35]

Protestant readers were none too pleased with this sympathetic treatment of a woman who was viewed as having been a vigorous advocate of the Revocation. Had she been as compassionate as La Beaumelle made her out to be, Formey wrote, she could surely have dissuaded Louis XIV from persecuting the Huguenots.[36] Voltaire took issue with this judgment, arguing that if the marquise had acquiesced in the Revocation policy (as she had acquiesced in the persecution of Racine and the Jansenists), it was simply because she had not dared challenge the royal will.[37]

Having perused the two volumes of correspondence by the marquise which were issued at the same time as the biography, Voltaire expressed outrage that a wastrel such as La Beaumelle should be in possession of this invaluable research material. In any case, what could one expect from a man whom Voltaire began at this point to characterize as a defrocked Protestant pastor?[38]

The first three volumes dealing with Madame de Maintenon were, in the end, superseded by a much longer and deeper study undertaken by La Beaumelle following his decision to settle in Paris in October 1752. A remarkable opportunity to study the confidential Maintenon papers housed in the convent founded at Saint-Cyr by the marquise presented itself when La Beaumelle met the convent's superior through her nephew, La Condamine. The obliging nun arranged for one of her subordinates, Madeleine-Charlotte Bouvet de Louvigny, to copy out much of this material, which was then transmitted to the Protestant author.

Madame de Louvigny, whom La Beaumelle was not to meet for some time and whom he identified for the moment simply as *L'Inconnue*, was fascinated by the enterprise into which she had been drawn. To atone for the thrill of guilt which she felt at this collaboration with a notorious heretic, she sometimes added coy invitations to conversion to the notes which she transmitted to La Beaumelle. The Calvinist jokingly protested at these tactics to his friend La Condamine: "I am told to believe in the pope. What terrible people you are! Always persecuting or corrupting!" La Condamine replied in kind: "My God, why not become a convert, then?"[39]

When rumours concerning the research being undertaken by La Beaumelle started to circulate at court, it was assumed that the brazen Calvinist was intent upon writing a work which would mock both throne and altar. On January 23, 1754, the police visited the writer's lodgings and confiscated much of the material which he had amassed. Thanks to the intervention of his powerful friends, this material was returned to the author in the early fall; however, the censor to whom his manuscript on the marquise was then submitted warned La Beaumelle that the anti-monarchical jibes, the satirical portraits of members of the court of Louis XIV, and the sarcastic comments about Quietism which he included in the work were bound to give offence.

Encouraged by the sympathetic curiosity which his impending work had aroused, but disheartened by indications of the government's concern about its contents, La Beaumelle decided to publish abroad, and moved to Amsterdam at the end of March 1755. Pondering whether to put pressure on the Dutch to forestall even this foreign publication, Louis XV asked to read the manuscript for himself. The King, who seems to have been more amused than offended by what he read, signalled that no effort should be made to hold up publication.[40]

The first volume of the *Mémoires pour servir à l'histoire de Madame de Maintenon et à celle du siècle passé* reached Paris in December 1755. The nuns of Saint-Cyr, who had warned La Beaumelle to be cautious, were distressed at the number of anti-monarchical and anti-Catholic comments which the author had inserted in his footnotes. By contrast, champions of toleration read with interest a memorandum titled *Rappel des Huguenots*, written by Madame de Maintenon in 1697, which La Beaumelle included in his text. Of even more interest was the editorial note which followed in which La Beaumelle made an explicit argument for Huguenot emancipation:

> The civil authority has no right whatsoever over the conscience of the people.... The King can only influence religious matters by his example.... Protected by their prince, France's heretics, like other loyal subjects, never engaged in activities directed against him. It was the tyranny of the dominant religion which produced in France and in England the civil wars which led Frenchmen to believe that Calvinism was in itself seditious and subversive.... Who is guiltier, the prince who tries to force his own views of religion on his people or his subjects who, obliged to choose between the prince's command and what they believe to be God's, prefer the second to the first?[41]

This bold passage almost brought Madame de Louvigny to break with the Protestant with whom she had been in such compromising collusion. Chastened, La Beaumelle agreed to delete from later volumes of his work passages which were bound to give offence in high places, such as the paragraph in which he damned French priests for trying to force deathbed professions of orthodoxy from Jansenists and Calvinists alike. [42]

Late in February 1756, La Beaumelle returned to Paris from Amsterdam. On March 22, he attended a performance of *Athalie* at Saint-Cyr to which only members of the court had been invited. That pillar of piety, Queen Maria Leczinska, had made his presence possible by consenting to the request of the nuns at Saint-Cyr that he be included in the guest list. The

Queen had read the Calvinist's study of Madame de Maintenon and praised it, noting that it was a pity such a gifted mind should remain blind to the true faith. During the course of a conversation with Madame de Louvigny, she remarked of La Beaumelle, whose conversion she ardently urged: "That is a Huguenot whom I love with all my heart."[43]

Voltaire was outraged at the way in which his impudent Calvinist challenger was being feted at court while he still languished in exile. By mid-June 1756, having read the fifteen volumes which La Beaumelle had devoted to the life and letters of Madame de Maintenon, he charged that the whole 'pseudoscholarly' enterprise had been designed to entrap an unsuspecting and gullible public.[44]

In the end, the success of La Beaumelle at court was short-lived, not because of the offence which he had given Voltaire, but because of passages in his work on Madame de Maintenon which were critical of the Habsburgs at a time when France and Austria were in the process of concluding a diplomatic alliance. In response to a protest from the court of the Empress Maria Theresa, La Beaumelle was committed to the Bastille early in August 1756. Happily, the Protestant's incarceration was made as bearable as possible, and a flood of appeals for his release, including petitions from the nuns of Saint-Cyr, descended upon Versailles. Maria Theresa ended up allowing that the Calvinist had been more rash than malevolent in his comments about her administration; and La Beaumelle was released at the beginning of September 1757 on the understanding that he would forthwith betake himself to his native Languedoc.

The removal of La Beaumelle from the centre of the French literary stage, where he had enjoyed a brief triumph, did not end his participation in the debate over the place of the Reformed in the nation's public life. In the summer of 1759, having sounded out Saint-Florentin in advance, he sent the minister in charge of 'new Catholic' affairs an analysis of the Protestant condition as it had evolved since 1685 and a passionate (as well as provocative) recommendation that the entire Revocation system be scrapped.[45] During the Calas affair, he helped prepare the defence of one of the accused, the 'new Catholic' Lavaysse; and he joined Paul Rabaut in putting together *La Calomnie confondue*, a refutation of the allegation made at the time of Jean Calas's arrest that Calvin had authorized the murder of rebellious children. Finally, towards the end of his life, La Beaumelle penned a *Préservatif contre le déisme* in which the fundamental teachings of Christianity were defended against the natural religion preached by Rousseau's Savoyard vicar as well as against the much more radical notions advanced by Helvétius in *De l'Esprit*.[46]

The personal and philosophical differences which separated Voltaire from La Beaumelle had become apparent soon after the Protestant's arrival in Berlin. Unlike most Huguenots who grew up in the France of Louis XV,

La Beaumelle was bold enough to suggest that the liberation of his fellow citizens lay in attacking monarchical as well as ecclesiastical tyranny, an opinion which could not have contrasted more with the sentiments expressed in the pages of *Le Siècle de Louis XIV*. Voltaire, who was prepared to be patronizing towards those 'progressive' Protestant theologians who seemed likely converts to his peculiar brand of natural religion, was equally ready to spread disparaging rumours about the spiritual integrity of a Huguenot pamphleteer who had crossed him. Both men were gifted polemicists; but the energy which they expended in mutual vilification did nothing to advance the cause of spiritual liberation in which each of them, in his own way, sincerely believed.

---

1.   When Frederick became King of Prussia at the beginning of June 1740, Voltaire applauded one of his first acts, the recall of a group of Anabaptists who had been chased from the kingdom. V. Voltaire to Frederick II, October 17, 1740, Best. D. 2341. At the beginning of November 1742, the philosophe wrote again, in similar vein, suggesting that if all kings were like the new ruler of Prussia, there would be no more wars of religion and no more funeral pyres would be erected upon which to burn to death the poor devils who could not properly decipher the mystery of the eucharist. V. Same to same, c. November 5, 1742, Best. D. 2681.

2 .   "An author who wants to write without passion or prejudice must (or so they say) have neither faith nor fatherland. Such is clearly the case with Voltaire." Samuel Formey, *Souvenirs d'un citoyen* (2 vols.; Berlin 1789), I, p. 329.

3.   Charles Louis de Beausobre, *Le Triomphe de l'Innocence, ou Particularités peu connues: aussi honorables aux Réformés qu'elles le sont peu à leurs adversaires* (Berlin, 1751), p. 124.

4.   Voltaire to Frederick, c. July 1, 1751, Best. D. 4513.

5.   Voltaire, *Défense de milord Bolingbroke*, in *Oeuvres* (Moland), XXIII, p. 553.

6.   Voltaire, *Sermon des Cinquante*, ibid., XXIV, p. 452.

7.   Voltaire, *Le Siècle de Louis XIV*, ed. A. Adam (2 vols.; Paris, 1966), II, p. 87.

8.   Ibid., p. 90.

9.   Ibid., p. 91.

10.   Voltaire to Charles Jean François Hénault, January 8, 1752, Best. D. 4761; Voltaire to the marquis d'Argens (?1752), Best. D. 4930.

11.   Voltaire, *Siècle*, p. 94.

12.   Ibid., p 95. In the later (1753) *Supplément au Siècle de Louis XIV*, Voltaire accepted the view relayed to him by Cardinal Fleury that it had been the pro-consular intendant of Languedoc, Bâville, who instigated the persecution of the Huguenots while Louis XIV, "utterly ignorant of their religious doctrine, regarded them, not without some cause, as former rebels who had submitted rather unwillingly." V. Voltaire, *Supplément au Siècle de Louis XIV, Le Siècle de Louis XIV*, ed. A. Adam (2 vols.; Paris, 1966), II, p. 324.

13.   Voltaire, *Siècle*, p. 49.

14.   R. Clément, *Les Cinq Années littéraires* (4 vols.; La Haye, 1754), IV, p. 58.

15.   Chevalier de Beaumont, *L'Accord Parfait de la Nature, de la Raison, de la la Révélation et de la Politique* (2 vols.; Cologne, 1753), I, p. 131.

16.   Paul Rabaut to Pastor Paul Moultou, October 24, 1755, Rabaut, *Lettres à divers*, II, pp.116-17.

17. Claude Lauriol, *La Beaumelle. Un Protestant cévenol entre Montesquieu et Voltaire* (Geneva, 1978). This study replaces A. Taphanel, *La Beaumelle et Saint Cyr. D'après des correspondances inédites et des documents nouveaux* (Paris, 1898).

18. *Journal helvétique*, November 1745, pp. 447-57.

19. La Beaumelle, *L'Asiatique tolérant. Traité à l'usage de Zéokinizul, roi des Kofirans, surnommé le chéri* (Paris, 1748), p. 105.

20. Ibid. p. 18.

21. Ibid. p. 61.

22. Antoine Court, *Le Patriote français et impartial* (2 vols.; Villefranche, 1753), I, p. 262.

23. Paul Rabaut to Antoine Court, October 11, 1751, Paul Rabaut, *Les Lettres à Antoine Court, 1739-1755*, ed. A. Picheral-Dardier (2 vols.; Paris, 1898), II, p. 168.

24. V. *supra*, p. 68.

25. La Beaumelle to Voltaire, June 22, 1751, Best. D. 4492.

26. La Beaumelle, *Qu'en dira-t-on: Mes Pensées* (Copenhagen, 1751), p. 70.

27. Voltaire, *Le Siècle de Louis XIV*, ed. L.-A. de La Beaumelle (3 vols.; Frankfurt, 1753), I, p. xii.

28. Ibid., I, p. 175, n.

29. Voltaire, *Supplément au Siècle de Louis XIV*, in *Siècle de Louis XIV*, ed. Adam, II, p. 330.

30. Ibid., p. 329.

31. Ibid., p. 360.

32. La Beaumelle, *Réponse au Supplément du Siècle de Louis XIV* (Colmar, 1754), p. 72

33. Voltaire to Thiériot, May 28, 1755, Best. D. 6285.

34. Formey, *Souvenirs d'un citoyen*, II, p. 221.

35. La Beaumelle, *Vie de Madame de Maintenon, pour servir de suite à ses lettres* (Cologne, 1753), p. 205.

36. *Nouvelle Bibliothèque germanique*, October-December, 1752, p. 425.

37. Voltaire to Formey, January 17, 1753, Best. D. 5162.

38. Voltaire to Jacques Emmanuel Roques, November 17, 1752, Best. D. 5077.

39. La Beaumelle to La Condamine, November 7, 1753 and reply of La Condamine, cited in Taphanel, pp. 180-81.

40. Ibid., p. 234.

41. La Beaumelle, *Mémoires pour servir à l'histoire de Madame de Maintenon et à celle du siècle passé* (6 vols.; Amsterdam, 1755-56), VI, pp. 98-9.

42. Taphanel, p. 268.

43. Ibid., p. 293.

44. Voltaire to Louis Eugene, prince of Wurtemburg, June 14, 1756, Best.D. 6887.

45. V. *infra*, pp. 198-99.

46. La Beaumelle's contribution to the Calas defence as well as his later writings are analyzed in Lauriol, pp. 538-47.

The call of conscience: Huguenot worship in the 'Desert.'

CHAPTER X

Mutual Disenchantment:
Voltaire and the Genevans, 1755-1762

During the years immediately preceding the Calas affair, Voltaire lived near Geneva and was thus able to observe Calvinist society at close range. In an effort to "civilize the natives," he presented plays on his property at Les Délices, defying the local taboo against the theatre. Even more provocatively, he made attacks on the character of Calvin and, together with d'Alembert, suggested that most Swiss pastors had become Socinians, thus obliging his hosts either to rebut him and profess a traditional faith which they no longer believed or remain silent and thereby implicitly accept his view that they had abandoned a number of vital Christian dogmas. These challenges produced shocks and misunderstandings, followed by a long and bitter polemical battle. Voltaire's attitude during this prolonged exchange moved from friendly condescension towards the Swiss Calvinists to outright contempt. From Ferney across the border in Burgundy where he settled in 1758, he directed a series of sustained attacks on Geneva until he learned the news of Jean Calas's execution in March 1762.

The friendships which Voltaire made or renewed at the beginning of his stay at Les Délices reinforced his most positive impressions about Calvinist society. Although his relations with more conventional Swiss Protestants, such as the naturalists Albrecht von Haller and Charles Bonnet, were distant to begin with and utimately quite hostile, he enjoyed the company of pastors whose Calvinism seemed only nominal, men such as François-Louis Allamand of Gex in the pays de Vaud, Elie Bertrand of Berne, Jacob Vernes of Geneva, and Antoine-Noé Polier de Bottens of Lausanne. The spiritually emancipated patricians whom Voltaire knew and cherished included the publishers Gabriel and Philibert Cramer as well as members of the powerful Tronchin clan: the city councillor François, the banker Jean-François, and Théodore, the distinguished physician.

The most critical of Voltaire's Calvinist associations in Geneva was with Jean Jacob Vernet, dean of the local pastorate. Vernet, whom the philosophe had met in Paris in the 1720s, was both scholarly and sophisticated (he had proofread Voltaire's *Histoire universelle* in 1754). However, as the major spokesman of Genevan Calvinism in the middle years of the Enlightenment, Vernet felt obligated to defend his city's commitment to the Reformed faith and soon after the philosophe's arrival, he sent Voltaire a polite but unambiguous warning that Genevans were not ready to accept visitors whose views were openly irreligious.[1]

The impetuous philosophe ignored this friendly warning. In March 1755, in defiance of local ordinances, he staged a production of *Zaïre* at Les

Délices before some of Geneva's most distinguished pastors and civic leaders, the kind of audience which he knew would find the play's message of religious toleration appealing.[2]

Having demonstrated the seductions of the stage to his hosts, Voltaire moved on to challenge them on higher ground. Early in 1756, he published his *Poème sur le Désastre de Lisbonne* in which his own non-Christian theology was subtly set forth. News of the earthquake at Lisbon had reached Voltaire late in November 1755; in the wake of the disaster, Voltaire urged that men cease adding to Nature's cruelty by ending their own intolerance because "while a few holy men are burning heretics, the earth is swallowing all of them up indiscriminately."[3]

Commenting on the *Poème*, Pastor Bertrand remarked that if, as a result of the earthquake, Voltaire was inspired to enlist Swiss Protestants in a campaign against superstition and intolerance, he could count on their support. But while they were ready to fight religious corruption, Genevans were not about to renounce their basic Christian commitment.[4]

Hard on the appearance of his reflections on the Lisbon disaster came the *Poème sur la loi naturelle*. Voltaire's intention to propagate deism and toleration among the Genevans now became quite explicit. Nature, the poet wrote, provides men with irrefutable evidence of the existence of a supreme legislator who has fashioned a universally valid moral law. Fully understanding this, the statesmen of pagan Rome had tolerated speculative debate concerning this supreme being so long as it did not produce views subversive of public order. By abandoning this enlightened policy and attempting to enforce conformity to their own peculiar version of universal religion, Christians had brought only bloodshed and persecution, horrors which reached their paroxysm during the religious wars of the sixteenth century:

> Calvin et ses suppôts, guettés par la justice,
> Dans Paris, en peinture, allèrent au supplice.
> Servet fut en personne immolé par Calvin.
> Si Servet dans Genève eût été souverain,
> Il eût, pour argument contre ses adversaires
> Fait serrer d'un lacet le cou des trinitaires.[5]

Voltaire felt confident, however, that a sea-change had occurred in the Genevan mentality since Calvin's time, as he noted in a letter to his friend Cideville:

> Geneva is no longer Calvin's city, not by a long shot. It is a society of true philosophers. The rational Christianity of Locke is the religion of almost all the ministers here, and the adoration of the Supreme Being together with the profession of sound morality is the creed of nearly all the local magistrates.[6]

Given this assessment, the bitter attack on Calvin which Voltaire included in the *Essai sur les Moeurs* (1756) was no doubt predictable. In this world-history survey, Voltaire paid generous enough tribute to the achievements of Luther, Calvin, and their companions, noting that they had restored moral standards in society, eliminated belief in diabolical possession and withchcraft, denounced the unnatural cult of celibacy, and provided a rationalization for the confiscation of church property. But, like all religious enthusiasts, the first Reformers had excited violent theological disputation; and their irresponsible trumpeting of spiritual liberation had been used to justify political and social subversion. In the long run, Voltaire argued, the balance sheet of the Reformation was thus negative rather than positive: "More blood was spilled because of it and theological squabbles degenerated into cannibalistic wars."[7]

When he turned to examine in detail the Genevan Reformation and Calvin's part in it, Voltaire openly expressed the revulsion which he had always felt for the founder of French Protestantism. Calvin, he observed, had arrogated to himself the powers of a Protestant pope. His decision alone had been responsible for the banning of stage performances in Geneva. Jealous rages had brought him to chase Castellio from the city and to permit the execution of Servet, whose theological opinions were inoffensive and who deserved special consideration because of his contribution to our knowledge of the blood's circulation. This persecuting tendency in Calvin was doubly repugnant, given the passionate plea for his own right to dissent which the Reformer had made while living in France.

Having delivered himself of this indictment, Voltaire went on to remark that the conversion of eighteenth-century Genevans to the kind of natural religion for which Servet had paid the supreme sacrifice constituted an act of collective penance for Calvin's sin.[8]

Voltaire's purpose in describing the spiritual conversion of the Swiss Calvinists was to flatter and encourage rather than embarrass his hosts. As their French visitor saw it, Genevans had become free and tolerant at a time when his own countrymen were still being challenged to produce *billets de confession* and when religious zealots were still driven to murder their rightful rulers. A week after the pious fanatic Pierre Damiens made his attempt on the life of Louis XV early in January 1757, Voltaire wrote to Jacob Vernet:

> You Genevans are not in the least Calvinist, you are fully human. In France...one can see that people are raving maniacs. Ravaillac has spawned a breed of bastard heirs.[9]

Two months later, crudely paraphrasing the comments he had made about Calvin in the *Essai sur les moeurs*, Voltaire boasted to his friend

Thieriot that Genevans were now sufficiently emancipated from their past to allow him to characterize their spiritual ancestor as "une âme atroce aussi bien qu'un esprit éclairé."[10] This provocative sally, which ended up in the May 1757 issue of the *Mercure de France*, touched off a furious exchange. The Venerable Company of Pastors and Professors requested that Geneva's magistrates censure Voltaire publicly for these remarks while Vernet published an anonymous letter justifying Calvin's condemnation of the 'Spinozist' Servet who had been given due process at a time when heresy and blasphemy were regularly pursued in the courts. Eighteenth-century Genevans were willing to concede that Calvin had a rather forbidding character and that he had not shaken off the intolerant spirit inherited from the papists; but Voltaire's portrait of the great Reformer had gone beyond reasoned analysis to distortion and caricature and he had clearly violated Swiss hospitality by preaching irreligion in their midst.[11]

Privately, Vernet sought a compromise with Voltaire, suggesting through their common friend Théodore Tronchin that the philosophe write a conciliatory letter to the Venerable Company.[12] But Voltaire was in no mood to retract: Calvin had been unambiguously culpable in the Servet case; as for the present, all the Genevans worth knowing had become converts to natural religion. Vernet tried yet again to bring about an accommodation, but Voltaire's ear had become deaf. He now dismissed the distinguished Genevan pastor as "a tartuffe, a little madman, an antitrinitarian who is ready in this day and age to rationalize the execution of Servet."[13]

While relations between Voltaire and Vernet continued to deteriorate, a new and greater source of friction between the philosophe and his hosts surfaced with the arrival in Geneva early in December 1757 of Volume VII of the *Encyclopédie*. The article "Genève" which was included in this volume and which touched off an immediate scandal had been researched and written by d'Alembert at Les Délices during the last three weeks of August 1756.

Since d'Alembert knew almost nothing of Protestant theology and since he seems to have attended only one service of worship while in Geneva, his opinion of the local religion was easily shaped. It may be an exaggeration to state that Voltaire orchestrated a series of impressions about Genevan society which his friend merely recorded, but both the tone and the critical comment in "Genève" are peculiarly Voltairean.

D'Alembert's text includes high praise for Geneva's pastors, who impress the visitor by their tolerance; unlike their counterparts in all-Catholic France, they make no effort to persuade the civil authorities to enforce religious conformity. They are so tolerant in fact that they have become suspect in the eyes of Calvinists elsewhere in Europe. The fact that Voltaire has recently published in Geneva an open attack on Calvin for his role in the death of Servet and gone uncensored for it testifies to the degree of spiritual change which has occurred in the city since the middle of the sixteenth century.

It was the analysis which d'Alembert made of the theological outlook of the Genevan clergy which was to cause the greatest shock and embarrassment. The most distinguished of the city's pastors, wrote the Encyclopedist, openly voice their skepticism concerning the divinity of Christ, thereby implicitly endorsing the very doctrine which had brought Servet to the stake:

> Respect for Jesus Christ and for the Scriptures is perhaps the only thing which distinguishes the Christianity of Geneva from pure deism.[14]

Voltaire was delighted with d'Alembert's "Genève," which had forcefully taken up two of his favourite themes: the promotion of toleration and the indictment of Calvin for Servet's death. When he learned that Geneva's pastors were preparing to lodge a protest against the article, he wrote to d'Alembert, urging the Encyclopedist to stand firm against any effort to get him to retract. The Genevan clergy, it turned out, were no better than their Catholic counterparts:

> Fanatical Papists, fanatical Calvinists, they are all formed from the same shit moistened with putrid blood.[15]

On December 23, 1757, the Venerable Company of Pastors and Professors met to consider how best to react to "Genève." A committee of eleven, including Vernet and Théodore Tronchin, was mandated to uncover the names of those responsible for giving d'Alembert his information and to prepare a declaration reaffirming Geneva's commitment to orthodox Calvinism.

As Voltaire's closest friend on this committee, Tronchin did his best to forestall the open conflict between the Genevan establishment and the philosophes which now seemed inevitable. When both the chevalier de Jaucourt and Diderot declined to act as go-betweens for him in the matter, Tronchin appealed to d'Alembert directly, suggesting that the deletion of a few lines from a revised edition of "Genève" should suffice to defuse a potentially explosive situation.[16] D'Alembert's reply was blunt and unyielding;[17] and, in his irritation at a similar appeal for retraction from Vernet, the Encyclopedist brought out one of the most devastating arguments used by Bossuet against the Huguenots at the time of the Revocation—that the kind of Socinianism being practised in eighteenth-century Geneva was the logical and inevitable end-product of the theological revolution began by Luther and Calvin.[18]

Tronchin and Vernet had thus only made matters worse by their efforts at conciliation. In any event, early in 1758, insisting that the furore over

"Genève" was only one factor in his decision, d'Alembert resigned as co-editor of the *Encyclopédie*. Shortly afterwards, "Genève" appeared in unamended form in a four-volume edition of his works published in Amsterdam.[19] In this way, d'Alembert once and for all made clear his determination to stand by the verdict concerning Geneva's religious life which had touched off such a storm.

Meanwhile, the committee of which Vernet and Tronchin were members had drawn up the profession of faith required by the Venerable Company. Ironically, when the text was made public on February 10, 1758, it revealed the fundamental ambivalence of eighteenth-century Genevans about essential Christian doctrine as much as it affirmed their adherence to traditional Calvinism. Voltaire could not resist paying a mocking tribute to this aggiornamento prepared by Tronchin and his associates who "in a word...profess themselves to be Christian deists,"[20] thereby subscribing to a faith which Servet himself could have endorsed.

In the course of the lengthy polemic over "Genève," d'Alembert had made the case that Socinianism was a logical extension of the teachings of the early Reformers, an argument used by Bossuet against the Huguenots before and after the Revocation. This unhappy borrowing from the arsenal of clerical reaction infuriated those who were trying to persuade the government of Louis XV that France's Calvinists deserved to be freed. One of the few Protestant Frenchmen able to take d'Alembert to task for this was Frédéric-Charles Baër, a native of Strasbourg who had been appointed chaplain of the Swedish embassy at Versailles in 1742. In an open letter to d'Alembert, Baër deplored the cavalier way in which the Encyclopedist had revived the hypothesis of Bossuet without subjecting it to the kind of rigorous critique which he prided himself on using in other areas of knowledge. How would d'Alembert react were some enterprising Catholic pamphleteer to contend that his privately expressed opinions contained a latent atheism? D'Alembert was too good a Catholic, Baër noted sarcastically, not to appreciate the seriousness of the charge which he and others had levelled at the Genevans. By his careless syllogisms, the Encyclopedist had done a grave disservice to the Huguenots who had surely suffered enough from Catholic oppression since 1685:

> France's Protestants are already all too unjustly slandered in the minds of an ignorant population. What will become of them if men of genius as well as philosophes join forces with the apologist of the St. Bartholomew's Day Massacre (Caveirac) to oppress them?[21]

D'Alembert made no reply to this plea. Like Voltaire, the Encyclopedist had become thoroughly fed up with the Calvinist world. Even the most advanced minds in Geneva were, as Voltaire had begun to describe them in January 1758, no better than "shamefaced Socinians,"[22] unworthy of associating with real champions of spiritual and intellectual enlightenment.

By the end of 1758, Voltaire had decided to move across the border to Ferney in French Burgundy. In a parting shot, he suggested to Elie Bertrand that Protestant Europe had a long way to go before it could convince him of its devotion to religious freedom: "There is no way in which you can justify the discriminatory and penal laws of the English, Danes and Swedes against us (Catholics) without in turn justifying our laws against you. I agree that all these laws are equally absurd, inhuman and contrary to enlightened politics, but we have only imitated you in this area."[23]

However cynical he had become regarding Genevan society, Voltaire would soon enough be reminded that there was still religious oppression across the border in Catholic France. The area surrounding Ferney had been seriously depopulated as a result of the Revocation, he discovered, and soon after his arrival, his friend Pastor Allamand asked whether he would be willing to help redevelop the area by attempting a discreet revival of Calvinist worship on his new estate. Allamand had uncovered evidence that Protestant worship had been permitted at Ferney immediately preceding the Revocation at a time when it was banned in the surrounding area. Might this not serve as a pretext for inviting a pastor to Ferney as soon as Voltaire had settled in?[24] The whole idea was highly fanciful, Voltaire replied. The French authorities would be just as opposed to having a Calvinist preach at Ferney as the Genevans had been to having mass said at Les Délices. However, the philosophe added roguishly, if he were to be permitted un pasteur *à huis clos*, nothing would please him more than to nominate Allamand for the post, given his friend's congenially progressive theology.[25]

Despite his bitter disenchantment with the Genevans, Voltaire maintained a correspondence with a number of them after moving to Ferney. Inevitably in these letters he brought up the Servet affair. "In connection with the Servet business," he wrote Haller in March 1759, "I respect your judgment enough to believe that you find his death cruel and cannibalistic."[26] Haller replied rather angrily that one case of Calvinist persecution hardly counted against the thousands of victims of the Catholic Inquisition.[27] In a subsequent note to his colleague Bonnet, Haller suggested that a man such as Voltaire who was still a nominal Catholic, might remind himself that the laws of France still decreed the death penalty for those caught attending Calvinist services of worship.[28]

When Voltaire once again raised the Servet case, Haller could not contain himself. The Genevans of Calvin's time, he responded, had inherited their concept of penalizing religious non-conformists from their Catholic predecessors. The notion of freedom of conscience which they had subsequently developed had produced the intellectual freedom which

Voltaire was now able to enjoy. While philosophes such as Voltaire were exploiting this freedom to try to persuade eighteenth-century Calvinists that they were morally implicated in the condemnation of Servet, French magistrates were condemning pastors to a death at least as cruel as that suffered by Calvin's rival.[29]

It was, of course, Vernet rather than the conservative Haller who had shattered Voltaire's idealistic vision of the Genevan Calvinists. The philosophe let all the pent-up contempt which he felt for the pastor find expression in the *Dialogues chrétiens* which he published in the summer of 1760. In this savage satire, Voltaire introduces a reactionary Catholic priest in two separate conversations, one with a liberal layman, the second with a Protestant pastor, following the banning in March 1759 of the *Encyclopédie*. The priest asks both men whether they would be willing to sanction the suppression of all such subversive works in the future, by Inquisitorial means if necessary. The layman is appalled at the idea; but the pastor, a theologically ambivalent and morally warped creature whom Voltaire clearly intended his readers to identify as Vernet, listens sympathetically. And when the priest assures him that Rome is ready to offer forgiveness to Protestants for past lapses if they will help extirpate philosophes and Encyclopedists, the pastor cannot contain his enthusiasm. Citing the case of Servet as precedent, he is even prepared to sanction the burning of Encyclopedists at the stake! But, he adds, there may be a subtler way of punishing these advocates of eighteenth-century impiety. Having perused some of the key manuscripts of these reprobates—a clear enough reference to the editorial services provided Montesquieu and Voltaire by Vernet—the pastor reveals that he has come upon information capable of destroying their reputations. The priest is overwhelmed at this enthusiastic offer of collaboration. He offers the pastor a handsome subsidy and urges him "to undermine the enemy in subtle ways which I go forth with fire and sword to overthrow and burn everything which stands in my path."[30]

As though eager to play out the role assigned to the Calvinist pastorate in Voltaire's satire, the city council condemned the *Dialogues chrétiens* to be burned on September 8, 1760. Six years later, Vernet published the *Lettres critiques d'un voyageur anglais*, in which he took it upon himself to rebut all the allegations about Genevan faith and morals which had been advanced by Voltaire and d'Alembert in the 1750s.

Vernet is at his most effective in these *Lettres* when he questions the sincerity of philosophes such as Voltaire and d'Alembert who so loudly advertize their commitment to the cause of toleration. Towards the beginning of his career, Vernet concedes, in works such as *La Henriade*, Voltaire had made a passionate and moving plea for freedom of conscience. But with the passage of time it had become clear that the real aim of the sage of Ferney and his associates was the propagation, not of genuine religious freedom, but of spiritual indifference. Only when men had learned to practise the mutual love preached in the gospel would they understand the true meaning of toleration. Meanwhile, having perceived that the real motive of the 'philosophic' argument for religious freedom was the spread of deism, the Catholic states of Europe were bound to tighten rather than relax their repressive laws against dissenters. Thus Voltaire, who pretended a genuine concern for suffering religious minorities, was in fact doing them a grave disservice. The Huguenots living inside France, for instance, who were sincerely loyal both to their King and to their conscience, had been placed in new jeopardy by the self-serving arguments on behalf of toleration advanced by Voltaire and his friends.[31]

Voltaire had in fact paid scant attention to the plight of his Protestant compatriots during the period 1755-1761. Two pieces of news from southern France which reached him during the winter of 1761-1762 were to end this indifference and persuade the philosophe of the truth of what the Swiss Calvinists had been telling him all along, that the persecution of Huguenots in eighteenth-century France was every bit as real and far more general than the attacks on spiritual deviance in sixteenth-century Geneva.

The first piece of news concerned the arrest on September 14, 1761, of a 'Desert' pastor, François Rochette. A Huguenot businessman wrote Voltaire asking if he would use his good offices on behalf of Rochette with his influential friend the maréchal de Richelieu, governor of Guyenne. The philosophe was none too enthusiastic about intervening on behalf of a stubborn preacher who seemed intent on martyrdom. He wrote Richelieu nevertheless, suggesting that the marshal urge Louis XV to pardon the wilful Huguenot following what was bound to be a condemnation of Rochette by the parlement at Toulouse. Richelieu did nothing and Rochette was executed on February 18, 1762.

A month after the death of Rochette, Voltaire learned of the execution at Toulouse of the cloth merchant Jean Calas on a parricide charge. Despite his initial assumption of the Huguenot's guilt, Voltaire was quickly persuaded that there had been a monstrous miscarriage of justice. His involvement in the Calas case would transform Voltaire from a bitterly cynical critic of the Calvinist world into a crusader for French Protestant rights.

---

1.   Jean Jacob Vernet to Voltaire, February 8, 1755, Best. D. 6146.
2.   Following a successful first performance, Voltaire transmitted the news that he had begun to refine the manners of Calvin's Geneva: "I have never seen so many tears shed. The Calvinists have never been so moved...Calvin never dreamed that one day a Catholic would make Huguenots weep on Genevan soil" (Voltaire to the comte d'Argental and to Jean Robert Tronchin, April 2, 1755, Best. D. 6229 and 6231).
3.   Voltaire to Jean Robert Tronchin, November 24, 1755, Best. D. 6597.

Calvinist or Socinian?: The deathbed confession of Rousseau's Julie.

4. "Declare war on superstition, on fanaticism, on the intolerance which contradicts all the principles of Christianity....Make war on all corrupters of pure and simple Christianity and I will march under your banner....But let us respect and try to win respect for that holy faith which the divine teacher preached in his sermons and in which, condemning all abuses, he taught only unity, peace, love, humility and all the social virtues." Elie Bertrand to Voltaire, c. March 1756, Best. D. 6789.

5. Voltaire, *Poème sur la loi naturelle* (1752), *Oeuvres*, ed. Moland (52 vols.; Paris, 1877-85), IX, p. 453.

6. Voltaire to Pierre Robert Le Cornier de Cideville, April 12, 1756, Best. D. 6821.

7. Voltaire, *Essai sur les moeurs et l'esprit des nations et sur les principaux faits de l'histoire depuis Charlemagne jusqu'à Louis XIII* (2 vols., Paris, 1963), I, p. 218.

8. "Today it would appear that an act of contrition is being made over the ashes of Servet. The opinions of Servet as well as those of Socinus have been adopted by a number of scholarly Protestant pastors, including the finest minds among them. These men have gone even further: their religion has become the worship of a single God through the mediation of Christ" (ibid., p. 247).

9. Voltaire to Jacob Vernes, January 13, 1757, Best. D. 7119.

10. Voltaire to Nicolas Claude Thieriot, March 26, 1756, Best. D. 7213.

11. Anon., "Lettre à Mr. de Voltaire à Lausanne," *Journal helvétique* (Neuchâtel, juin 1757), pp. 611-27.

12. Vernet to Théodore Tronchin, July 19, 1757, Best. D. 7319.

13. Voltaire to François Tronchin, September 2, 1757, Best. D. 7364; Voltaire to Elie Bertrand, September 9, 1757, Best. D. 7371; Same to same, October 21, 1757, Best. D. 7428.

14. 'Genève,' in *Lettre de M. d'Alembert à M. J.J. Rousseau sur l'article 'Genève' du septième volume de 'l'Encyclopédie'* (Amsterdam, 1759), p. 35.

15. Voltaire to d'Alembert, December 12, 1757, Best. D. 7512.

16. Théodore Tronchin to d'Alembert, early January, 1758, *Oeuvres posthumes de M. d'Alembert* (2 vols., Paris, 1799), I, p. 416.

17. D'Alembert to Théodore Tronchin, January 6, 1758, cited in J. Vernes, *Lettres critiques d'un voyageur sur l'article 'Genève'* (3 vols., n.p., 1766), II, p. 272.

18. D'Alembert to Voltaire, January 11, 1758, Best. D. 7572.

19. D'Alembert, *Mélanges de littérature, d'histoire et de philosophie* (5 vols., Amsterdam, 1759), II, p. 359-86.

20. Voltaire to the comte d'Argental, February 25, 1758, Best. D. 7652.

21. Frédéric-Charles Baër, *Lettre d'un professeur en théologie protestante à M. d'Alembert* (Strasbourg, 1759), p. 20.

22. Voltaire to d'Alembert, January 19, 1758, Best. D. 7592.

23. Voltaire to Elie Bertrand, January 5, 1759, Best. D. 8092.

24. François-Louis Allamand to Voltaire, August 6, 1759, Best. D. 8421.

25. Voltaire to Allamand, August 16, 1759, Best. D. 8442.

26. Voltaire to baron Albrecht von Haller, March 24, 1759, Best. D. 8210.

27. Haller to Voltaire, April 11, 1759, Best. D. 8259.

28. Haller to Charles Bonnet, April 16, 1759, Best. D. 8263.

29. Haller to Voltaire, April/May 1759, Best. D. 8282.

30. Voltaire, *Dialogues chrétiens, ou Préservatif contre 'l'Encyclopédie,' Oeuvres* (M), XXIV, p. 139.

31. Vernet, *Lettres critiques d'un voyageur anglais sur l'article 'Genève' du Dictionnaire encyclopédique, et sur la lettre de M. d'Alembert à M. Rousseau touchant les spectacles* (2 vols.; Copenhagen, 1766), I, p. 60.

CHAPTER XI

Distant Cousins:
Rousseau and the French Calvinists

Of all the men of letters to whom the Huguenots turned for help in their struggle for civil rights in pre-Revolutionary France, none seemed a more plausible ally than Jean-Jacques Rousseau. To begin with, the Swiss writer was himself descended from a victim of French religious discrimination, Didier Rousseau, who had found asylum in Geneva in the 1550s. In the second place, the attenuated Calvinist doctrine which Jean-Jacques absorbed during his childhood closely resembled that being taught at nearby Lausanne to young Frenchmen who were preparing to preach the gospel to underground congregations back in their homeland.[1] Thirdly, although he was to abjure his childhood faith for Catholicism and, later, deism, Rousseau retained a lifelong respect for much in the Protestant tradition and, as eloquently as any writer of his time, he reasserted the revolutionary claims on behalf of the individual conscience made by the great sixteenth-century Reformers. Fourthly, given his concern about the progress of irreligion and his conviction that the spiritual foundations of the European social order needed shoring up, Rousseau, it was felt, would surely defend the thousands of French Calvinists who continued at great risk to come together for meetings of public worship during which they offered up prayers for the Catholic monarchy which oppressed them. Finally, it was taken for granted that a man of Rousseau's sensitivity would feel compassion for those who were still being persecuted, occasionally even martyred, for their faith as a result of the Revocation of the Edict of Nantes. Since he was an acknowledged master of the art of evoking sympathetic responses from his readers, it seemed only natural that he use this talent to dramatize the plight of the Huguenots and thereby to support the campaign for their emancipation.

Despite these factors which suggested that he would make an ideal champion of the Huguenots, Rousseau involved himself only marginally in their struggle for civil rights. He put the philosophical case for freedom of conscience strongly enough in his most significant writings, but in only one work, the *Lettre à Christophe de Beaumont*, did he explicitly plead the cause of Huguenot relief; and, following the denunciation of his political as well as his religious views by the Genevan establishment in 1764, even this short-lived interest in the French Calvinists faded away.

The bitterness which Rousseau felt towards Swiss Calvinist officialdom in the middle 1760s offers us only a partial explanation of his lack of commitment to the Huguenot cause. As the years passed, his increasing persecution mania and his alienation from former friends

147

undoubtedly made it more difficult for him to feel concern for others, even for those who were themselves being oppressed.[2] But, personal hurt apart, Rousseau felt that he could justify his refusal to join the campaign for Calvinist civil rights on solid moral and intellectual grounds. The author of *Emile* was convinced that the vexations still being inflicted upon one another by rival Christian sects were a minor problem compared to the threat posed to European civilization by skeptics and atheists. In addition, his early years in Geneva had conditioned him to believe that individual citizens should bring their public professions of religious belief into harmony with the established cult of the society in which they lived. Like most of his contemporaries, Rousseau did not accept the view that spiritual liberty was best secured by offering public recognition to a variety of contending sects; he was not a religious pluralist.

The conversion of Rousseau to Catholicism following his sortie from Geneva in 1728 is a familiar story, as is the influence upon him during this period of spiritual orientation of the priest of Confignon, the 'new Catholic' Madame de Warens, the catechists of Turin and the abbés Gaime and Gatier.[3] For our purposes, it is worth noting that between 1730 and the moment during 1747-1748 when he ceased to be a practising Catholic, Rousseau made a public profession of his adoptive faith wherever he found himself although he felt considerable embarrassment (especially in the upper reaches of French society) at the epithet 'Nouveau Catholique' which was attached to him following his abjuration.[4]

After his second conversion when, influenced by Diderot and Grimm, Rousseau became a deist, he showed a renewed interest in Calvinist ritual, turning up for services of worship at the Dutch embassy chapel in Paris during the early 1750s.[5] His readmission into the Reformed communion at Geneva on July 25, 1754, however, was the indispensable prelude to his resumption of citizenship rather than an act of spiritual reintegration.[6]

While remaining formally reconciled to Calvinist doctrine during the next decade, Rousseau attacked the political as well as the theological conventions upon which the patrician domination of Geneva was founded. Yet, despite the bitterness with which he made his definitive break with Calvinism in 1764, he remained deeply attached to much that was peculiar to Reformed Christianity: he continued to admire the architectural simplicity of the temples in which his former co-religionists worshipped and the unaffected manner in which they intoned the psalms; he cherished the habit of daily Bible reading; but by far the greatest influence on Rousseau the mature writer was his recollection of the sermons which he had heard during his youth (an influence which is clearly apparent in the long-winded moralizing speeches of so many of his fictional characters).

When he made his peace with the Reformed church in 1754, Rousseau could not, of course, have guessed that his erstwhile idol Voltaire, settled in at Les Délices nearby, would so soon be threatening to undermine the civic morality of the Genevans by offering stage performances on his estate, nor that d'Alembert would second this subversive enterprise in the article "Genève" written for Volume VII of the *Encyclopédie*.[7] The response which Rousseau made to this cultural assault in the *Lettre à d'Alembert sur les spectacles* brought him not only to inveigh against the insidious dangers of the theatre but also (albeit with much less conviction) to defend the city's pastors against the embarrassing suggestion made by the Encyclopedist that they had become converts to Socinianism.[8] D'Alembert's reply was to republish his provocative article in 1759. Assuming that Jean-Jacques shared his own indignation at the appearance of this offensive reprint, the Genevan Pastor Jean-Ami Martin wrote Rousseau, suggesting that the most effective riposte to d'Alembert might be a brilliant polemical tract in favour of the French Calvinist minority.[9] The novelist, however, showed no interest in such an exercise.

What was preoccupying Rousseau increasingly at this point was the spiritual crisis caused by the headlong conflict between conventional Christianity and militant atheism. This concern is apparent in *La Nouvelle Héloïse*, published in 1760. Since the solution to the struggle between faith and incredulity which Rousseau puts forward in the novel includes the concession of a limited degree of toleration to religious minorities, it may be argued that he was thereby making an oblique defence of Huguenot rights. In any event, the spiritual dialogue between the atheist Wolmar and his Calvinist wife Julie which *La Nouvelle Héloïse* part of its thematic unity leads both protagonists in the end to reject the dogmatic positions which they originally espouse. Julie moves from the rigid Calvinism in which she has been raised to a profession of crypto-Socinianism; Wolmar, whose exemplary conduct reflects an inner grace even as he clings to his unbelief, seems at the novel's end to be on the point of conversion to his wife's watered-down Protestantism;[10] while Saint-Preux, Julie's lover and Wolmar's friend, helps the couple to bridge the spiritual gulf which had earlier separated them, symbolizing Rousseau's hope for an end to the larger religious conflict of the age through reconciliation and synthesis.

In their discussions about matters theological, the three central figures of *La Nouvelle Héloïse* all defend the cause of spiritual freedom; Rousseau reinforces their argument in footnotes to the text. Below a comment by Wolmar denouncing the campaign to impose Catholicism on all Frenchmen following the Revocation, for instance, the novelist notes editorially: "No one whose faith is genuine can accept either intolerance or persecution," adding that, were he a magistrate in a nation which condemned atheists to die, "I would start out by sentencing to death anyone who came forward to denounce someone else as an atheist."[11]

During the lengthy correspondence which he exchanged with Malesherbes, then *directeur de la Librairie*, concerning the admission into France of *La Nouvelle Héloïse*, Rousseau was informed that there were two main objections to putting the novel in the hands of French readers. Versailles would have found it unexceptionable had Rousseau simply presented Julie as a Calvinist—after all, she lived in Geneva; but since she was presented as a model of enlightened piety, her deathbed profession of what amounted to Socinianism was contentious and should be deleted. In addition, Malesherbes insisted that the passages in which Julie and Saint-Preux argue the case for theological toleration had to be excised because such a notion was totally unacceptable in France.[12]

Predictably bitter at these proposed emendations, Rousseau reminded Malesherbes that the abbé Prévost's *Cleveland*, which had given readers an objective look at the Protestant world, had been allowed to circulate freely in France. In any case, his Julie pleased him infinitely more as a lovable dissenter than as the glum conformist Malesherbes would have her become.[13]

Although Malesherbes wrote back in a conciliatory tone, insisting that it was not a question of removing from the novel references to Julie's Protestantism but rather of deleting "ideas which are not accepted either in the Catholic or in the Reformed faith,"[14] Rousseau remained unconvinced. Since the persecution of non-conformists was clearly still inherent in Catholic dogma, he commented sarcastically, his Saint-Preux was no doubt bound to excite hostility whether he was presented as a Calvinist or as a Socinian.[15]

While his lengthy but ultimately fruitless negotiations with Malesherbes over the acceptability of *La Nouvelle Héloïse* were still in progress, Rousseau was hard at work on *Du Contrat social*, which appeared in April 1762. In the historical survey of the relationship between religion and society with which he prefaces his chapter on civil religion in this work, Rousseau comes down hard on the Jewish and Christian faiths for the exclusiveness, intolerance, and civil tension which they have brought into the world and proposes that such unhappy by-products of conventional religion be removed by getting the citizenry at large to subscribe to a simple deist creed, following which each individual would be free to cultivate the Supreme Being in his own manner (exception was made of those whose doctrines were themselves intolerant, who would be subject to banishment).[16]

This proposal for the tolerance of privately expressed dissent was scarcely calculated to satisfy the Huguenots, who were rarely disturbed during the 1760s so long as they contented themselves with domestic worship. Their energies at this point were being directed towards obtaining the right to public worship and to having their civil status regularized through an appropriate form of non-Catholic baptism and marriage.[17]

What would have pleased the French Calvinists more was the tribute to their faith which Rousseau included in the original draft of *Du Contrat social* but which he deleted from the published text:

> Experience teaches us that, of all the Christian sects, the Protestant is not only the wisest and gentlest but also the most pacific and sociable.... It is the only sect which recognizes the integrity of the laws and the authority of the prince.

Wilfully ignoring these admirable qualities, Rousseau remarked, Louis XIV had promulgated the Revocation; then, recognizing too late the damage done the state by the flight of these loyal and productive citizens, he had tried to retain them by force. The Huguenots had in consequence been reduced to the most nightmarish of dilemmas, unable either to stay inside their homeland or to flee:

> They are not permitted either to be foreigners or citizens or for that matter even human beings. The Protestant minority is at one and the same time tolerated and proscribed: the intention would seem to be to keep the Protestants alive, yet at the same time to ensure their death.... The situation seems without parallel; and, thinking about it, I hasten to put down my pen lest I let go with a cry of revolt against what nature has allowed to occur.[18]

In a further comment in this unpublished draft, Rousseau addressed himself to one of the Calvinists' main grievances, that they were obliged to wed in the Catholic rite or run the risk of having their children designated as bastards and even, on occasion, disinherited. As long as Catholic priests were allowed to determine the civil status of all Frenchmen in this way, they were the arbiters of citizenship itself and thus the ultimate masters of the state.[19]

While Rousseau was reading the proofs for *Du Contrat social*, news reached him of the execution at Toulouse on February 19, 1762 of the underground pastor François Rochette and of three Calvinist laymen who had tried to force his release following his arrest in October 1761. The outburst against the Revocation which he had inserted in the text had been motivated in part by indignation at these arrests; but, once the fate of the four Huguenots became known to him, Rousseau decided to remove these remarks since they could no longer influence the course of justice and since they might have the additional disadvantage of provoking the authorities into banning the entry of *Du Contrat social* into France. With the same end in mind, the novelist requested his publisher to substitute a more moderate comment about the Huguenots' marriage dilemma in the final version of the work.[20] (A number of copies had already gone to press, however, so that a few French readers at least were to read Rousseau's original remarks unamended.)[21]

In his *Emile*, published in May 1762, Rousseau reiterated the views about church-state relations which he had put forward in *Du Contrat social* and again made passing reference to the French Calvinist condition, albeit in a way which was scarcely designed to further the campaign for Huguenot rights. While counselling young Emile about the need to reinforce the spiritual foundations of society, the Savoyard vicar suggests that any of the religious cults which man had devised over the ages might offer such reinforcement, provided it were shorn of the dogma and ritual which had accrued to it through historical accident and provided it proscribed intolerance. In line with this reasoning, the vicar notes, he had, while remaining an ordained Catholic priest, transformed himself into a simple minister of good works, practising the precepts of sound morality which were common to all religions and enjoining his congregation to do likewise. If he were to discover Protestants among his flock, Emile's tutor declares:

> I would make no distinction between them and my regular parishioners in so far as Christian charity is concerned.... I believe that to urge someone to abandon the faith in which he was born is to urge that person to do wrong and thus to do wrong oneself. While waiting upon greater illumination to reach them, let us above all preserve public order. We should respect the laws of all countries and not disturb the public worship which those laws proscribe. Let us not incite citizens to disobedience because, while we cannot know for sure whether or not it is a benefit for them to abandon their religious convictions for new ones, we do know that it is wrong to disobey the laws.[22]

This last comment, enjoining citizens to put conformity to the law above the commands of conscience, was scarcely calculated to comfort those Protestants inside France who were defying the law in order to proclaim their faith; nor would they have been much mollified by the vicar's proposal that Emile return to France and re-enter the Calvinist communion on the ground that it approximated natural religion: "Of all the religions on earth, I believe it to be that which teaches the purest morality and that which our reason finds it easiest to accept."[23]

The response of French officialdom to the appearance of *Emile* was swift and furious: on June 9, 1762, the work was condemned by the Paris parlement and, on August 28, Archbishop Christophe de Beaumont fulminated against it in an impassioned pastoral letter. Rousseau's response, the *Lettre à Christophe de Beaumont*, appeared in March 1763. Given the unexpected vehemence with which his latest work had been denounced in France, the Swiss writer was more ready than might otherwise have been the case to reconcile himself to the Genevan establishment—which may help to explain why he made a more explicit defence of the French Calvinist community in the *Lettre* than in any other of his published works.

Rousseau begins by remarking how odd it is that a Swiss Calvinist like himself, whose comments about Catholicism had been published in Protestant Holland, should find his work condemned in France. He reminds the archbishop that Spinoza, who advertized his atheism openly, had been graciously received in His Most Christian Majesty's domain; but so, too, he added sarcastically, had the tracts celebrating the Saint Bartholomew's Day Massacre and the Revocation written by the abbé Caveirac.[24]

Having defended himself against the archbishop's allegation that he no longer believed in the divinity of Christ, Rousseau returns to one of the themes of his earlier works—that, since God has created us to live in harmony with or fellow creatures, we ought to seek out that religion most conducive to civil harmony. Religions such as Christianity (especially in its Catholic form) which based their ascendancy on the forcing of consciences, could only survive through the policing of a hypocritical conformity. It had once been accepted that such repression at least guaranteed civil peace and public morality; but this assumption had proven fallacious, removing the last rationalization for religious persecution. It remained for Europe's sovereigns to promulgate a new religion for their subjects, based upon but transcending the monotheistic Judaeo-Christian tradition, adding to it whatever national variants seemed appropriate. Had France adopted such a creed, much bloody civil conflict might have been averted "and, under our very eyes, the innocent Calas, after being tortured by his executioners, would not have perished on the wheel."[25]

As in his earlier writings, Rousseau proposes in his letter to Beaumont that a generous degree of theological toleration be granted to those who subscribe to his proposed national creed; he has reservations, however, about civil toleration, since it implies the formal recognition of separate religious corporations within the state. An already established religion should not be proscribed; but the sovereign is clearly justified in denying legal status to new and alien cults. Thus, when Calvin's partisans first made their presence felt in France, they had no claim to protection under the law. Once the Reformed faith had been embraced by a substantial minority, however, and especially once it had been accorded rights under the Edict of Nantes, it had achieved an undeniable legal status.

The treatment of the Huguenots at the time of the Revocation had been unconscionable, Rousseau continued. Had Louis XIV contented himself with eliminating the aristocratic leadership of the Calvinist minority which had occasionally engaged in subversion, he might have been justified; the rest of the Huguenot community clearly posed no political threat:

What intrigues and cabals are merchants and peasants able to hatch?...A
merchant proposing an armed rising may well make himself heard in
England, but he will always be a laughing-stock to the French.[26]

If some Calvinist plebeians had taken up arms during the Camisard
revolt, they had done so only when driven to despair by their persecutors. In
any case, the government of Louis XV had a clear and obvious means of
repairing the damage done his kingdom by the wrongheaded policy of the
Sun King:

Let us allow these poor folk to populate our empty provinces. Let them be
merchants, nothing but merchants; farmers, nothing but farmers. They will
bring new respect to commerce and agriculture which everything brings us
to neglect; they will feed our taste for luxury; in a word, they will toil and
we shall enjoy.[27]

Nowhere in his considerable writing about church-state relations had
Rousseau been so critical of Catholic intolerance against the Huguenots as in
the *Lettre à Christophe de Beaumont*: yet all that he had in the end
recommended on behalf of the Calvinists was second-class citizenship—
freedom of conscience and the right to participate in economic activity, rights
they in fact already enjoyed, albeit not formally.

The appearance of the *Lettre* triggered a debate within the French
Calvinist community which Rousseau was invited to join. Inspired by the
ideas which Rousseau had set forth in his *Lettre*, a little-known writer from
Soissons, Turmeau de La Morandière, published early in 1764 the *Principes
politiques sur le rappel des Protestants en France* in which he urged
Versailles to recall the Huguenots from their diaspora, but on very restrictive
terms: they should be granted access to the nation's guilds and corporations,
a civil form of marriage and burial and the right to bequeath property; but
they should be denied public worship, they should remain ineligible for
public office, and their children should continue to be baptized in the
Catholic rite.[28]

Late in March 1764, Pastor Gal-Pomaret of Ganges wrote to
Rousseau asking the Swiss writer to make it clear that he agreed with the
French Calvinist majority that the limited measure of toleration proposed by
Turmeau was totally unacceptable.[29] Rousseau replied that his letter to
Beaumont accurately reflected his views concerning the French Protestant
question; he considered these views generous, yet the Huguenots had
shown nothing but ingratitude for his kind words on their behalf; like their
Genevan cousins, they always whined when they were being repressed,
then turned vicious whenever they were themselves in power.[30] A further
plea for his intercession elicited even more bitter comment from Rousseau:

The Protestants of France are now enjoying a period of tranquility to which I may well have contributed, not through vainglorious declamation as is the case with so many others, but through sound political reasoning well set forth.... They admit to being left alone; but they wish to be even better off.[31]

When, following this refusal, Gal-Pomaret drafted his own reply to Turmeau and sent the manuscript along to the Swiss writer for comment, Rousseau advised him to delete or modify the passages in which the pastor had discussed Calvinist doctrine at length and even engaged in anti-Catholic polemic; if the Huguenots wished to bring about a change in their condition, Rousseau insisted, they must use tact and restraint, especially in their dealings with the French ecclesiastical establishment. They would not, of course, convert the First Estate to toleration by such an approach, but they might very well embarrass priests into silence and, more important, they would give encouragement to the liberal elements at Versailles which were trying to modify the Revocation system.[32]

The Genevan establishment, meanwhile, which Rousseau had hoped to propitiate with the publication of his letter to Beaumont, ended up attacking not only his spiritual non-conformity and his political opinions, but his personal life as well.[33] Outraged at this multifaceted assault, Rousseau responded with what was perhaps the most effective polemical writing of his career, the *Lettres écrites de la Montagne* which reached Geneva in December 1764. Reminding the spiritual leaders of his native city of the embarrassment which they had felt when d'Alembert exposed the ambivalence of their theological opinions in 1757, Rousseau pointed out that he had professed his Calvinism freely and openly while in Paris and that in his writings he had defended the principal tenets of the Reformed faith—the authority of reason, the inviolability of individual consciences, the need for evangelical tolerance, and the obligation to obey the civil authority even as regards public worship. He could only hope that the defenders of the Protestant faith in Switzerland (as well as in France) would not live to rue the day in which, persecuting such enlightened Christians as himself, they had given back to superstition the dagger he had struck from her hand.[34]

This telling sally helped to bring about the inevitable denouement: publicly denounced, then summonned to give an account of his religious views before the consistory of Môtiers, Rousseau fled his would-be Calvinist inquisitors for Paris; the decade of his formal reconciliation to the church of his homeland was over.

During the four years which preceded his break with the Genevan authorities, Rousseau had written clearly if conservatively both on the toleration issue in general and on the situation of the French Protestants in particular. His refusal to support the campaign for a full bill of rights for the Huguenots in his written work during this period was paralleled by his reluctance to join in the efforts being made by Voltaire and others to rescue individual Calvinists caught in the coils of French law.

The first appeal to Rousseau on behalf of a Huguenot in trouble reached him in September 1761; it came from Jean Ribotte, a Protestant merchant of Montauban who informed him about the arrest of the underground pastor François Rochette and of the three glassmakers who had tried to force his release. Surely Rousseau, creator of the divine Julie, would find it in his heart to intercede on behalf of these poor wretches who were clearly innocent of all criminal intent? A letter to the duc de Richelieu or to members of the ministry at Versailles might work wonders, Ribotte suggested, adding rather tactlessly that he had already solicited this kind of help from Voltaire.[35]

In his reply, Rousseau expressed concern for those arrested before commenting that the attempt to force the liberation from detention of fellow citizens, however unjustly apprehended, smacked of outright rebellion. While it was bitter for France's Protestants to have to endure adversity without the solace of hearing God's word publicly preached, the message of the gospel was explicit: Christians must obey the civil authority, even when that authority forbade their assembling to worship; in any case, they could in certain circumstances dispense with public services without betraying their faith. Rousseau added rather petulantly that any appeal which he might make to Richelieu was unlikely to be listened to; in any case, Voltaire was much better placed to influence the duke. The novelist went on to observe that he had put the case for toleration as best he could in his published works; it was not his fault if people had not been persuaded by reasoned argument.[36]

Undismayed by this response, Ribotte returned to the charge in December 1761, when the trial of Rochette and his would-be liberators was about to begin in Toulouse. Rumour had it, he informed Rousseau, that Chancellor Malesherbes had requested the parlement in the southern city to forward the dossier in these cases to Versailles; people were saying that the government did not want to see the full rigor of the law applied. Ribotte added that this slight ray of hope had been increased by the appeal on behalf of the accused which Voltaire had agreed to send to Richelieu, again apparently not guessing at the offence which indication of Voltaire's intervention in the case would cause Rousseau. As for Rousseau's comment that Rochette and his companions had transgressed the law, Ribotte argued that there were times when the claims of conscience overrode those of man-made statutes; after all, both Christ's apostles and the sixteenth-century Reformers had defied the secular princes of their day. Then, in a final effort to move the novelist, Ribotte appealed to him in the name of one of his most endearing fictional characters, Lord Edouard Bomston. Could the mind which had conceived such a sensitive personality be indifferent to the suffering, not just of Rochette and his friends, but of some one million

fellow Protestants? Surely Rousseau could at least take the time to compose
a petition for Rochette which Ribotte would be willing, if necessary, to copy
out in his own hand so that it would remain anonymous? Such an appeal
might work wonders if given to Choiseul or, better still, if it were
transmitted to Frederick of Prussia so that it might be put on the agenda of
the forthcoming peace conference.[37]

The novelist's reply closed off all hope that he might involve himself
in the case of the Calvinist prisoners:

> You are no doubt aware, sir, that the man from whom you are requesting
> well-phrased petitions and seductive letters is in such a state of weakness as
> to allow him barely to count on living through the day ahead.[38]

Quite apart from his serious physical indisposition, Rousseau added, a
properly prepared defence of the accused would require a full-scale inquiry
on the spot, something he was clearly not in a position to undertake.

In March 1762, his publisher, Marc-Michel Rey, wrote to inform
Rousseau of the execution of Rochette and the three glassmakers and
suggested that a narrative of the whole tragic affair written by a man of his
gifts might arouse the French public to feel a compassionate interest in the
semi-martyrdom still being endured by the Huguenots.[39] Rousseau
acknowleged that the subject lent itself to a treatise on human rights; were a
full documentation of the affair available, he might under normal
circumstances have been willing to write such a work; however his physical
condition was such that he was quite incapable of the sustained effort
required.[40]

The news of the execution of the cloth merchant Calas which Ribotte
conveyed to Rousseau later in March evoked no more concern in the novelist
than had the fate of Rochette and his companions. His *Emile* had just been
condemned by the Paris parlement, and Rousseau saw nothing
disproportionate in comparing the burning of his treatise on education by the
magistrates of Paris with the execution of a non-conformist businessman by
the judges of Toulouse.[41] When Geneva's attorney-general followed the
lead of Paris and publicly condemned both *Emile* and *Du Contrat social* on
June 19, 1762, Rousseau's disinclination to lend either his name or his pen
to the cause of Huguenot relief was reinforced.

Two months later, writing to Jean-Antoine Comparet, a fellow
Genevan who had just published a critical edition of his works, Rousseau
suggested that any champion of Calvinist orthodoxy who rejoiced (as
Comparet had) over the burning of his allegedly subversive writings should
weigh carefully the high cost of repression, whatever form it might take; to
cite one example, had Frenchmen been converted to the tolerant faith
preached by the Savoyard vicar, the life of Calas would have been spared.[42]

By Christmas time, when Voltaire's campaign on behalf of the Calas family was moving into high gear, one of the novelist's few remaining admirers encouraged Jean-Jacques's inclination to focus more than ever not on other men's woes but on his own persecution mania:

> Whenever I hear Voltaire's partisans in this part of the world boast of what he has done on behalf of the widow Calas, someone always replies: "Yes. But he is persecuting le 'Citoyen!'"[43]

When, in February 1763, Rousseau began to consider leaving Geneva for good, he pointedly referred to the martyrdom which, like Servet, he might undergo should he remain; the Swiss city was no better than Goa, where the Inquisition still held sway.[44]

Late in March the Genevan banker Toussaint-Pierre Lenieps, then living in exile in Paris, recounted to Rousseau how deeply Chaplain Duvoisin of the Dutch embassy had moved his congregation by offering thanks to God for the decision reached by the *conseil du roi* allowing the Calas appeal to go forward.[45] Rousseau remained untouched. When it was over, and the Calvinist cloth merchant was posthumously vindicated, Voltaire summarized his feelings about Rousseau's refusal to get involved:

> Jean-Jacques Rousseau would have done better, it seems to me, to use his time and talent in the defence of innocence rather than invent unfortunate sophisms and search out scurrilous ways of subverting his fatherland.[46]

The indifference shown by Rousseau towards the fate of Calas was again apparent when the novelist learned in July 1764, about the arbitrary cloistering of a young French Calvinist woman. Marc Favenc, a merchant from the Quercy region whom Rousseau had met through Chaplain Duvoisin in Paris, wrote to tell of the efforts he was making to secure the release of his daughter, who had been taken to a convent for indoctrination in the Catholic faith. He hoped that the novelist, to whom he forwarded the relevant documentation, would agree to write a petition on the girl's behalf for submission to the authorities in Versailles.[47] It would be hard to imagine a less sympathetic response than that given by Rousseau to this appeal:

> I am not a lawyer, sir. I have never written briefs for anyone and I neither can nor will begin to do so now. I haven't even the time to read through all these scribblings. Let me know, then, please, by what route you wish me to return them because they are perfectly useless in my hands.[48]

In December 1764, a lobbyist for the French Calvinists named Peyraube who had visited Rousseau at Môtiers earlier in the year wrote to ask the novelist for a letter of introduction to Chancellor Malesherbes.[49] The Frenchman had been commissioned to approach the ministry on behalf of some one hundred foreign Protestants living in Bordeaux who were requesting the right to worship publicly in their own communion. Friends of Choiseul, and of the duc de Richelieu, the military governor of Guyenne, were well-disposed to the petition, and Peyraube hoped that Rousseau would give it further support by writing an appropriate letter to Malesherbes.[50] Somewhat reluctantly, the novelist obliged, forwarding to Peyraube the desired letter to the chancellor in which he suggested that a positive response to the foreigners' petition would do the government honour and serve France's economic interest; but he went on to say that he would prefer that someone other than himself serve as intermediary in arranging the meeting between Peyraube and the minister.[51] In any case, late in April 1765, Peyraube reported from Paris that he had transmitted the Bordeaux petition without resorting to Rousseau's letter on the ground that it might have indisposed the ministry.[52] (In the end, the adminstration did nothing to accommodate the resident aliens; but Bordeaux being a city where the Huguenot community enjoyed a generous degree of de facto toleration, this negative response was far from tragic.)

A decade later, towards the end of the reign of Louis XV, Rousseau was for the last time approached on behalf of victims of the Revocation system. This time the supplicant was Claude Eymar, a young businessman from Marseille. Eymar had been deeply moved by the reading of *Emile* and hoped to interest its creator in the liberation of Antoine Riaille and Paul Achard, who had been condemned to life sentences in the King's galleys thirty-four years earlier by the parlement at Grenoble for attending an illegal Calvinist service of worship. Rousseau not having responded to a first impassioned appeal, Eymar asked friends of the family to arrange a meeting with the novelist on the pretext of a common interest in music. When the young Frenchman finally met the novelist on May 2, 1774, at Montmorency, he renewed his plea for the convicts, but to no avail. Undismayed, Eymar visited Rousseau several more times, bringing with him on one occasion a manuscript written by a Calvinist layman of Saint Jean du Gard in Languedoc in which a case was made for giving the French Calvinists a legal means of marrying and of ensuring the inheritance of their children. After some hesitation, based partly on his deteriorating physical condition, Rousseau agreed to read the manuscript (which was to remain unpublished); but he made it clear to his visitor that he saw the chief issue of the day to be the battle against irreligion, not the resolution of what he saw to be petty squabbles within the Christian world.[53]

The responses which Rousseau gave to those who sought his intervention on behalf of Huguenots executed or imprisoned for defying the Revocation system were consistent with his innermost convictions as well as with the view about church-state relations which he had set forth in his published works. Freedom of conscience he was prepared to defend; no citizen should be troubled for worshipping his creator as he saw fit; but such freedom required for its fulfilment neither the presence of pastors nor the erection of churches; and those who, like the Huguenots, insisted upon retaining these elements of organized religious life outside the national church ought to be reminded that they did so not by natural right but by sufferance of the civil sovereign. Thus, in revoking the Edict of Nantes, Louis XIV had rescinded a privilege, not an inherent right. The repression which had been visited upon the Huguenots since 1685 was to be deplored, and Rousseau regularly reminded his correspondents that he had done his best to educate humanity to a more tolerant and indulgent attitude towards religious dissenters. But he would not move beyond this abstract philosophical position, however much his sometime co-religionists might implore him.

---

1. An analysis of the theological outlook of the French underground pastorate during the eighteenth century and of the influence of the philosophes upon the evolution of their doctrinal viewpoint is offered in J. D. Woodbridge, "L'influence des philosophes français sur les pasteurs réformés du Languedoc pendant la seconde moitié du XVIIIe siècle"(unpublished thesis, Toulouse, 1969).

2. Lester Crocker, whose analysis of Rousseau's personality verges on the mean-minded, attributes Jean-Jacques's indifference to the suffering of his fellowmen in large part to a latent homosexuality which brought him to transform male friends into potentially conspiratorial enemies. V. Jean-Jacques Rousseau, *The Quest, 1712-1758* (New York, 1968), p. 235. More charitably, Jean Guéhenno sees Rousseau as constrained to solitude despite himself, trying to make a virtue out of his tragic isolation from his fellow humans. V. *Jean-Jacques. Histoire d'une conscience* (2 vols.; Paris, 1962), I, p. 347.

3. The most comprehensive examination of the spiritual evolution of Rousseau is to be found in P.-M. Masson, *La Religion de J.-J. Rousseau* (3 vols.; Paris, 1916). An excellent and far more succinct account is offered in R. Grimsley, *Rousseau and the Religious Quest* (Oxford, 1968).

4. Rousseau, *Les Confessions*, ed. L. Martin-Chauffier (Bruges, 1939), p. 246.

5. *Registres du Consistoire*, Geneva, July 25, 1754.

6. Rousseau, *Confessions*, p. 384.

7. Jean Le Rond d'Alembert, *"Genève," Encyclopédie ou Dictionnaire raisonné des sciences, des arts et des métiers par une Société des Gens de Lettres* (35 vols.; Paris, 1751-1780), VII, p. 578.

8. Rousseau, *J.-J. Rousseau, Citoyen de Genève, à M. d'Alembert, de l'Académie française, de l'Académie royale des sciences de Paris, etc.; sur son article 'Genève' dans le septième volume de l'Encyclopédie, et particulièrement sur le projet d'établir un théâtre de comédie en cette ville* (Geneva, 1758).

9. Minister Jean-Ami Martin to Rousseau, August 24, 1760, Leigh 1088.

10. Rousseau to Pastor Paul Moultou, June 24, 1761, Leigh 1436.

11. Rousseau, *Julie, ou la Nouvelle Hélöise*, ed. R. Pomeau (Paris, 1960), p. 576, n.

12. Chrétien-Guillaume de Lamoignon de Malesherbes to Rousseau, February 15, 1761, Leigh 1298.

13. Rousseau to Malesherbes (February 19, 1761), Leigh 1305.

14. Malesherbes to Rousseau, c. February 26, 1761, Leigh 1327.

15. Rousseau to Malesherbes, c. March 10, 1761, Leigh 1350.

16. Rousseau, *Du Contrat social; ou, Principes de Droit politique, Oeuvres complètes*, ed. Pléiade (4 vols.; Paris, 1959-69), III, p. 469.

17. Following the end of the Seven Years' War, the Huguenots began to enjoy a de facto toleration in many parts of France. V. B.C Poland, *French Protestantism and the French Revolution* (Princeton, 1957), p. 68.

18. Rousseau, *Du Contrat social ou Essai sur la forme de la république* (première version), *Oeuvres*, III, p. 344.

19. Ibid., p. 343.

20. Rousseau to Marc-Michel Rey, March 11, 1762, Leigh 1707.

21. Ibid., note b.

22. Rousseau, *Emile, ou de l'éducation*, ed. F. and P. Richard (Paris, 1964), p. 383.

23. Ibid., pp. 384-85.

24. Rousseau, *Jean-Jacques Rousseau, citoyen de Genève, à Christophe de Beaumont, archevêque de Paris, duc de St. Cloud, pair de France, commandeur de l'ordre du St Esprit, proviseur de Sorbonne, etc.* (Amsterdam, 1763), pp. 8 and 97. Rousseau's reference is to the *Apologie de Louis XIV et de son Conseil sur La Révocation de l'édit de Nantes*, published by the abbé Jean Novi de Caveirac in 1758.

25. Ibid., p. 98.

26. Ibid., pp. 88-89.

27. Ibid., p. 89.

28. Turmeau de la Morandière, *Principes politiques sur le rappel des Protestants en France* (2 vols.; Paris, 1764).

29. Pastor Jean Gal, called Gal-Pomaret or Jonval, to Pastor Antoine Gal, called Gal-Ladevèze, March 26, 1764, Leigh 3194.

30. Rousseau to Jerémie Pourtalès, May 26, 1764, Leigh 3293.

31. Rousseau to Pastor Henri-David Petitpierre of Neuchâtel, July 15, 1764, Leigh 3398. It is of some interest that Rousseau's arch-enemy Voltaire, writing to Pastor Moultou, felt that Turmeau would have done the Calvinists far more good had he set forth the conditions which would persuade those still in France to remain; as it was, the proposal to ban their public worship was an oblique recommendation to continue persecuting them. Voltaire to Moultou, March 11, 1764, Best. D. 11764.

32. Rousseau to Jean Foulquier, October 18, 1764, Leigh 3583. Gal-Pomaret did in fact revise his text, which appeared as a *Lettre à messieurs les évêques de France* (n.p., 1766).

33. Among the most powerful broadsides fired against Rousseau at this time were J. Vernes, *Lettres sur le christianisme de M. J.-J. Rousseau* (Amsterdam, 1764) and J.-R. Tronchin, *Lettres écrites de la campagne* (Geneva, 1765).

34. Rousseau, *Lettres écrites de la montagne* (1765), ed. H. Guillemin (Neuchatel, 1962), p. 101.

35. Jean Ribotte to Rousseau, September 30, 1761, Leigh 1498.

36. Rousseau to Ribotte, October 24, 1761, Leigh 1521.

37. Ribotte to Rousseau, December 9, 1761, , Leigh 1581.

38. Rousseau to Ribotte, December 28, 1761, Leigh 1615.

39. Marc-Michel Rey to Rousseau, March 17, 1762, , Leigh 1714.

40. Rousseau to Rey, March 25, 1762, Leigh 1719.

41. Rousseau to Minister Paul-Claude Moultou, June 7, 1762, Leigh 1835.

42.   Rousseau to Jean-Antoine Comparet, c. September 10, 1762, Leigh 2147. The
       essay in which Comparet attacked the novelist was *Lettre à monsieur J.-J.
       Rousseau, Citoyen de Genève* (Geneva, 1762).
43.   The marquise de Verdelin to Rousseau, December 24, 1762, Leigh 2403.
44.   Rousseau to Paul-Claude Moultou, February 17, 1763, Leigh 2489.
45.   Toussaint-Pierre Lenieps to Rousseau, March 24, 1763, Leigh 2562. Like many
       supporters of the Calas cause, Lenieps had been in close contact with the leading
       lawyer for the defence, Elie de Beaumont; when this eminent attorney set out for
       Switzerland following the vindication of Calas, he carried with him a letter of
       introduction to Rousseau written by the banker. Since Beaumont was a close friend
       of Geneva's attorney-general, Jean-Robert Tronchin, one of Rousseau's most severe
       critics, Lenieps warned Jean-Jacques to avoid too close an intimacy with this
       potential visitor. The two men appear not to have met, so that this advice proved
       unnecessary. In any event, Rousseau avoided even this most oblique contact with
       the Calas affair. Same to same, May 18, 1765, Leigh 4413.
46.   Voltaire to Charles Bordes, March 23, 1765, Best. D. 12497. This same reaction
       from Voltaire was apparent during the long battle to establish the innocence of
       Pierre-Paul Sirven and his family. Praising his friend Damilaville for the tireless
       efforts which he had made to organize the campaign for the Sirvens in Paris,
       Voltaire lamented the way in which the efforts of the philosophes to make the
       world more tolerant had been jeopardized by the mad antics of Rousseau. Voltaire to
       Damilaville, December 29, 1766, Best. D. 13778; and, writing to Pastor Jacob
       Vernes, he contrasted his own literary activism with the vain scribblings of
       Rousseau: "Jean-Jacques n'écrit que pour écrire et moi j'écris pour agir." Voltaire to
       Vernes, c. April 15, 1767, Best. D. 14117.
47.   Marc Favenc to Rousseau, July 25, 1764, Leigh 3426.
48.   Rousseau to Favenc, September 1, 1764, Leigh 3476.
49.   Peyraube to Rousseau, December 18, 1764, Leigh 3750.
50.   Same to same, January 7, 1765, Leigh 3847.
51.   Rousseau to Peyraube, January 20, 1765, Leigh 3907.
52.   Peyraube to Rousseau, April 26, 1765, Leigh 4342.
53.   Claude Eymar, "Mes visites à J.-J. Rousseau," in V.D. Musset-Pathay, *Oeuvres
       inédites de J.-J. Rousseau* (2 vols.; Paris, 1825), II, pp. 12-41.

JEAN HENNUYER

Mercier's *Jean Hennuyer*: Symbol of episcopal tolerance and ecumenism.

CHAPTER XII

The Stage in the Service of Huguenot Emancipation:
Volaire, Fenouillot de Falbaire, and Mercier

During the eighteenth-century debate over toleration, champions of the Calvinist cause usually put their argument in prose; but the case for religious freedom was sometimes made by playwrights, most of whom wrote in verse. Voltaire made his theatrical assault on intolerance with *Oedipe* (1718), *Zaïre* (1732), *Alzire* (1736), and *Mahomet* (1742); but his concern in these dramas was for religious freedom in the abstract; it would be difficult to discern any sympathy for the Huguenots in these early plays, which even include traces of anti-Calvinist feeling.

By the 1760s, the situation had changed radically; French writers for the stage began addressing themselves directly and compassionately to the Huguenot question. The reasons for this new involvement were partly aesthetic, partly political. Proponents of *le drame* had begun to urge playwrights to bring issues of civic interest before their audiences; happily for the Huguenots, this coincided with a growing public concern about the disabilities from which the Calvinist minority continued to suffer. Five plays resulted from this new sense of commitment: Voltaire's *Les Guèbres* (1768) and *Les Lois de Minos* (1772) and three plays by men of a younger generation: *L'Honnête Criminel* (1767) by Charles-Georges Fenouillot de Falbaire and *Jean Hennuyer* (1772) and *La Destruction de La Ligue* (1784) by Louis-Sebastien Mercier.

In his first play, *Oedipe*, presented to critical acclaim in November 1718, Voltaire transforms the Thebes of Sophocles' drama into a city dominated by the high priest, who exploits the fanaticism of the populace to promote his own theocratic ends. The play may be seen as the first salvo in Voltaire's long battle to rescue French consciences from priestly harassment. However if, as some critics have argued, Voltaire intended the tragedy of his central characters (Oedipus and Jocasta, predestined by a remorseless deity to suffer the double curse of incest and parricide), as an indictment of the Jansenist doctrine concerning grace, Huguenots could just as easily read the text as an assault on the equally rigorous teachings of their own church in the matter.[1]

Zaïre, the heroine of Voltaire's second play dealing with the toleration theme, is the grandchild of Lusignan, the last Christian King of Jerusalem. A prisoner of the Saracens since infancy, she has grown up a Moslem; only her cruciform pendant hints at her Christian background. Granted spiritual freedom by her abductors, Zaïre perceives that religious belief is the product not of innate truths, but rather of geographical and cultural influence. Her reason impels her to search out a universal creed which will unite all members of the human race. This enlightened outlook is shared by her captor and suitor, the Sultan Orosmane, who hopes to reach an understanding with his Christian adversary, the pious Louis IX.

Tragically, the 'ecumenical' disposition of Orosmane and Zaïre is subverted by the religious fanaticism of the young woman's grandfather, Lusignan, who makes a dying wish that she be baptized. When Zaïre indicates her consent to this request to her brother Nerestan (whom she identifies not as her blood relative but as a crusading knight), she is killed by Orosmane, who misconstrues her meeting with Nerestan as a love-tryst. When the sultan discovers his error, his first concern is to prevent this personal tragedy from touching off even more murderous conflict between Christians and Moslems; he releases his Christian captives and pleads with Nerestan to point out to his fellow Franks the grim consequences of the religious fanaticism which has brought them to the Holy Land in the first place.[2]

While the fervour of the Christian Lusignan makes him the unwitting villain of the piece, Voltaire is clearly trying through all his major characters to persuade his audience that the world's great monotheistic religions are compatible (if not interchangeable) and that some understanding of their essential convergence will lead humanity towards a deist conviction and a tolerant outlook.

Voltaire resumed the battle against intolerance in *Alzire*, first produced in 1736. One of the central themes in the play is the controversy within the camp of the Spanish conquerors of Peru about the methods by which the Indians are to be proselytized. Don Alvarez, the outgoing governor of Peru, has won many Incas to Catholicism by purely peaceable means; his son and successor, Don Gusman, is determined to effect the wholesale conversion of the natives by whatever methods prove necessary, including violence. Perceptive members of Voltaire's audience would have had little difficulty in identifying Gusman's techniques with those used by agents of Louis XIV against the Huguenots during the *grande dragonnade* of 1685. In fact, Voltaire puts words into Gusman's mouth which could easily be seen as a paraphrase of the rationale behind the Sun King's decision to revoke the Edict of Nantes:

> Je veux que ces mortels,
> Esclaves de ma loi,
> Tremblent sous un seul Dieu,
> Comme sous un seul roi.[3]

As the play moves towards its improbable but moving climax, Gusman, won over by his father, abandons his repressive attitude towards the Indians, embraces a policy of toleration, and proposes marriage to the

Inca princess Alzire, who has converted to Christianity because she has been persuaded of its moral and spiritual superiority. When Gusman is fatally wounded by the pagan Zamore, a rival suitor for the princess's hand, he offers his adversary both forgiveness and understanding. This demonstration of spiritual nobility even Zamore cannot resist; as the curtain falls, his own conversion is assured. Voltaire has demonstrated that tolerance brings not only reconciliation between people of differing creeds; it may bring an even nobler result—a deep sense of spiritual solidarity and communion.

The polemical intent of *Le Fanatisme, ou Mahomet le prophète* (1742) is, of course, evident from the play's title: Voltaire is bent on exposing the founder of one of the world's leading religions as a cynical imposter risen from the common herd who exploits the latent fanaticism of the masses to transform himself into an omnipotent priest-King. However, from a letter which Voltaire wrote to Frederick of Prussia at the end of 1740, it is clear that the dramatist saw a parallel between the partisans of Mohammed and the simple-minded Calvinist peasants and artisans who fell under the sway of self-appointed prophets during the Camisard revolt. Voltaire went on to remark that he would feel amply rewarded for the effort which he had invested in the composition of the play "if just one of those souls who are always ready to let themselves be swept away by religious fury could strengthen himself against such cruel temptation by reading this work."[4]

Fanaticism was the central leitmotiv of *Mahomet*, but Voltaire was anxious to drive home a second, related theme—the notion that founders of new religions pose a threat to the civil as well as to the religious order. In the play's opening scene, Sheriff Zopire tells us that he has banished Mahomet from Mecca because he is convinced that the self-styled prophet is intent upon inciting his followers to political as well as religious subversion. The thesis that the masses were given to following the propagators of radical new ideas, however extravagant, recurs regularly in Voltaire's writings; the deist philosophe agreed with the Catholic Bossuet that a mindless infatuation with intellectual novelty had been one of the central causes of the French Reformation and of the civil wars which had plagued the nation since the middle years of the sixteenth century.[5] The implications of such a view for the toleration debate were obvious; the civil authorities were well within their rights in denying freedom to embryonic religious sects. Toleration ought not, then, in Voltaire's view, to be granted in principle; it should be conceded only when it was clear that a substantial minority of the population had already espoused heterodox opinions or when those opinions were seen to pose no danger to civil order.

The exposure of Voltaire's play before the French public in 1742 was successful, if short-lived; the ecclesiastical establishment saw to it that *Mahomet* was withdrawn from the boards after only a few performances.

Voltaire's subsequent decision to dedicate the drama to Benedict XIV was both a brilliant tactical manoeuvre and a well-deserved tribute: the reigning pope was a sincere practitioner of toleration within his own domain where Jews as well as Protestants enjoyed more civil and religious freedom than was conceded them elsewhere in Catholic Europe.[6]

Composed in great haste in August 1768, more than a quarter of a century after *Mahomet, Les Guèbres* reveals Voltaire's powers as a dramatist in full decline; the play is too overcharged with polemical intent to make for good staging. However, its interest as a propaganda piece for Huguenot rights is clear. The setting is the Roman province of Syria during the reign of the emperor Gallienus. The area has become difficult to govern because its inhabitants are bitterly divided on religious grounds: the pagan majority has been persuaded by its tyrannous high priest to turn against the Guèbres, Zoroastrians of Persian origin whose peculiar rites include incestuous marriage. To ensure that matters do not get out of hand, Gallienus has appointed a veteran soldier, Iradan, to govern the province; but a crisis arises when the high priest decides to make an example of Arzame, a young Guèbre about to marry her brother, Césène. Iradan feels no antipathy towards the young Zoroastrians; their peculiar behaviour is clearly the product, not of inherent perversion, but of the persecution which they have endured at the hands of the Syrian priesthood. In fact, the governor's compassion is transformed into rapture when it is revealed that the betrothed are the children of marriages which he and his deputy had contracted years earlier while campaigning in Persia! This happy turn of events is not without its untoward side, however, for as Césène reminds Iradan, the marriages which they contracted in Persia have no validity in Roman law.

The parallel which Voltaire intended to draw here is clear: the marriages which many Huguenots were crossing into Switzerland or Holland to have celebrated in their own rite were not recognized by French courts, leaving wives to be denounced as concubines and children to be disinherited as illegitimate. To put it in Césène's words:

> Notre hymen malheureux, formé chez les Persans,
> Est déclaré coupable; on ôte à nos enfants
> Les droits de la nature et ceux de la patrie.[7]

Release from their predicament for the Roman officers (as for the Huguenots) would be possible only if the civil sovereign were to make birth, marriage, and death matters of civil record, not of sacramental sanction. But the hope that this might happen seems slight to Césène (as it did to Voltaire after the failure of Choiseul's initiative in favour of French Calvinist marriage in 1766):

> Que fait votre César, invisible aux humains?
> De quoi lui sert un sceptre oisif entre ses mains?
> Est-il, comme vos dieux, indifférent, tranquille,
> Des maux du monde entier spectateur inutile?[8]

While Iradan reflects on the implications of his newly discovered paternity, a report arrives that Arzane's brother has made an attempt on the high priest's life. Tragedy seems unavoidable except for the sudden arrival of the emperor, who has been kept informed of events and is intent upon ensuring that future developments in Syria will be determined by priorities of state not by the sectarian purposes of the local clergy. Henceforth, he insists, priests will function only as ministers of charity and compassion, never again as oppressors of conscience:

> Les persécutions
> Ont mal servi ma gloire et font trop de rebelles.
> Quant le prince est clément, les sujets sont fidèles.
> On m'a trompé longtemps: je ne veux désormais
> Dans les prêtres des dieux que des hommes de paix,
> Des ministres chéris, de bonté, de clémence,
> Jaloux de leurs devoirs, et non de leur puissance.[9]

At the play's end, Gallienus promulgates a limited bill of rights for the Guèbres: they may henceforth marry before the civil magistrate, possess property, and worship their god after their own fashion so long as they do not offend the official imperial cult.

In the preface to *Les Guèbres*, Voltaire declared that his original intention had been to write a tragedy based on the sufferings of the early Christians; but he had been warned to beware the misunderstandings which might follow were he to give his drama plausibility by presenting Christian and anti-Christian chararacters as dialectical equals. Heeding this advice, he substituted Zoroastrians for Christ's early followers. Readers should have no problem in grasping his original intentions, however; after all, the Guèbres were simple monotheists like the Christians who had been persecuted for their faith in Diocletian's time (and, Voltaire intended his readers to infer, like the Huguenots who were still being oppressed in Louis XV's France). Voltaire added that Gallienus's guarantee of religious freedom to the Guèbres at the play's end closely resembled the Edict of Milan granted to the Christians by Constantine.[10] In a separate letter to a friend, the playwright suggested that he had written the final scene with the intention of evoking in his readers an even more meaningful parallel—Henri IV's decision to grant the Edict of Nantes.[11]

In the *Discours historique et critique* which appeared with the third edition of his play (1769), Voltaire further explained the relevance of *Les Guèbres* to contemporary French religious life. Some ill-intentioned readers, he wrote, had suggested that his real target in attacking the Syrian priesthood had been the Jesuits because of the perverse counsel which they had offered Louis XIV at the time of the Revocation; in fact, his only purpose had been to help put to rest the bitter religious factionalism of the past; the resolve of Gallienus in the play's final scene to launch a new era of toleration and mutual respect among his spiritually divided subjects could not have been made more explicit. If his readers did not find the advocacy of such a policy attractive, let them be reminded that it was neither original nor provocative, since it closely resembled the view presented by the orthodox Corneille in *Polyeucte*:

> If the kind of toleration granted by a number of Roman emperors seems fraught with dangerous consequences to some of the inhabitants of Gaul in the eighteenth century; if they are ignorant of the fact that the United Provinces owe their wealth, England her power, Germany her domestic peace and Russia her greatness to just such humane tolerance; if these politically misguided souls have no regard for a virtue which nature herself would wish to imbue in all of us, let them at least recall that this (toleration) is recommended by Sévère in *Polyeucte*.[12]

However, Voltaire went on to reassure his readers, the degree of religious freedom which he had proposed in *Les Guèbres* was severely limited; the majority had ground for neither alarm nor offence:

> The emperor in my drama does not and cannot mean by the word 'tolerance' either the licensing of opinions which are contrary to sound morality, the sanctioning of disorderly assembly or the authorization of fanatical associations. He intends rather the indulgence which one owes all citizens who peacefully follow the dictates of their conscience and who worship the divinity without troubling civil society.[13]

From the first, Voltaire seemed to have been aware of the dramatic limitations of *Les Guèbres*. He conceded to his friend d'Argental that the play might well be more effective if read aloud rather than performed; but he persisted in the belief that its exposure in one form or the other would help generate a more compassionate attitude towards France's non-conformists.[14] He tried valiantly to convince the marquise du Deffand that performances of *Les Guèbres* before a well-chosen audience in Paris might persuade the administration to bring legislative relief to some 400 000 souls who were still without civil rights.[15] The reply of the marchioness was straightforward enough: there was no way in her view in which such a play could be staged until the changes in the law which it was designed to promote had been effected.[16] When, subsequently, a plan by the *prévôt des marchands* at Lyon to produce the play was cancelled out of fear of offending the local archbishop, Voltaire boiled over: "The large number of

Protestants living in Lyon, the natural relevance of *Les Guèbres* to their situation, in a word the prejudices which still govern the world, prevented the *prévôt des marchands* from risking the presentation."[17] Voltaire agreed with d'Alembert that the ideal site for a production of his drama would be the central square of Toulouse, where Calas had been broken on the wheel;[18] but despite the presence in Languedoc of a potential sponsor in the person of the liberal prince de Beauvau (then serving as governor), Voltaire knew that no one was likely to risk backing what would inevitably be seen as an affront to the ecclesiastical and judicial establishment of the city which had condoned the execution of Calas.

In *Les Lois de Minos*, written in 1772, Voltaire returned to some of the themes which he had treated in *Les Guèbres*; his ideas were becoming more and more obsessive as his dramaturgical powers declined. The setting of the play is Crete, whose founding father, Minos, son of Jupiter, has bequeathed to his people a number of customs, among them the obligation to put to death a prisoner-of-war every seventh year as a thank offering to the nation's legendary heroes. Minos's successor, Teucer, finds this custom abhorrent and determines to abrogate it, even if this means defying the high priest, the Cretan Senate, and the populace at large, always eager to indulge in cruel and fanatical exercises. Astérie, a young prisoner from the primitive Cydonian tribe which inhabits the northern rim of Crete, is slated to be the next ritual victim, but the King takes matters in hand, overturns the altar upon which she is to be sacrificed, abolishes the gruesome ceremony, and asserts his paramountcy in matters spiritual as well as temporal. Teucer's Erastian pronouncements at the end of the play ensure that Cretan society will henceforth be protected from theocratic priests, traditionalist senators, and fanatical mobs, all of whom had been ready to see murder committed in the name of religion.

Voltaire's preoccupation with human sacrifice in *Les Lois de Minos* came in part from his involvement with the Calas, Sirven, and La Barre cases in which French civil courts had rationalized their decision to impose the death penalty on the ground that they were defending the nation's established religion against insolent non-conformists. In a series of footnotes to his text, Voltaire reminds the reader that the sacrifice of human life in the name of religion has been both timeless and universal: the Jews of the Old Testament had willingly sacrificed their children to appease Jehovah; the Inquisition had sent thousands of heretics to the stake; just two centuries before the writing of his play, a large number of Huguenots had been massacred on Saint Bartholomew's Day; finally, the execution of the anti-Trinitarian Servet in Calvin's Geneva was testimony to the fact that Protestants, too, had succumbed to this religiously inspired bloodlust.[19]

In the sketch of Cydonian society which he offers us in *Les Lois de Minos*, Voltaire touches on yet another aspect of the campaign for Protestant toleration. As the playwright portrays them, the Cydonians sensed more clearly than their sophisticated neighbours that God could be fully and properly worshipped in simple ceremonies in the out-of-doors, without benefit of clergy or complex ritual. In a note below the text, Voltaire points out that the early Christians had worshipped in just such simple fashion as had, in more recent times, the Quakers, Anabaptists, Dunkards, Pietists, and Moravian Brethren.[20] This comment was hardly calculated to please France's Calvinists who, as Voltaire was by this time fully aware, had made clear to the authorities their unwillingness to accept such a radically reduced form of worship; their demands for the recognition of their temples and the free circulation of their pastors had become a source of continuing friction between them and Versailles.

L'Honnête Criminel, written by Fenouillot de Falbaire in 1767, was based on the real-life story of Jean Fabre, a young silk-stocking manufacturer at Nîmes who accompanied his father to an outdoor Calvinist religious service near the city's outskirts on New Year's Day, 1756. When this illegal assembly was raided by the militia and Fabre's father was arrested, Jean persuaded a compassionate sergeant to release the older man and surrendered in his father's place to face whatever penalty the courts might impose. Two months later, Fabre was sentenced to a life term rowing the King's galleys at Toulon. The story had a relatively happy end: thanks to a chance encounter on the quays at Toulon, the Calvinist *galérien* was able to recount his story to a sympathetic Frankfort businessman, who forwarded a petition on his behalf to Versailles; in May 1762, as a result of the intervention of Prime Minister Choiseul, Fabre was released. The original sentence remained on the books, however, and the Huguenot felt obliged to live obscurely, in semi-disgrace.

What transformed Jean Fabre into a touching symbol of France's loyal but long-suffering Calvinist minority was the dramatization of his sacrificial bondage by Fenouillot. In terms of the propaganda for Protestant toleration, the most effective scenes in *L'Honnête Criminel* begin at the end of Act 4, when the galley slave's father, close to death, arrives in Toulon to obtain his son's release by offering to serve out the remainder of what would have been his own sentence. The ship's captain, a stereotypically *sensible* and 'philosophic' figure, assures both father and son that the King will grant them their freedom once he learns of the circumstances of the case. In the captain's view, Louis XV is a paragon of enlightenment:

> Il prise la vertu, quelque part qu'elle brille;
> Et, demandant au ciel d'éclaircir les esprits
> Il vous traite en enfants égarés, mais chers,
> Qu'il se plaît à compter toujours dans sa famille.[21]

Overwhelmed by this assurance, the Fabres declare their devotion to King and country; the play ends on a note of civic reconciliation and reunion.

As the German pastor's son Melchior von Grimm noted, Fenouillot had nowhere in his text brought his characters to make an explicit profession of their Calvinism, so that it was difficult for audiences to understand why they had been ready to accept near-martyrdom in its defence.[22] The charge that Fenouillot had not made militant Protestants of his central characters was accurate enough. But, apart from the obvious difficulties which the playwright would have encountered had he tried to present them as the outspoken champions of a proscribed faith, he could not have written a play set in a convincing Calvinist milieu simply because, like most eighteenth-century French writers, he knew little or nothing of French Protestant society. The Calvinists, in any case, in their gratitude for a play which dealt so compassionately with their sufferings, did not quibble with Fenouillot's failure to focus accurately either on their theology or on their lifestyle. Paul Rabaut of Nîmes, who was much moved at reading the play, was convinced that its performance would increase the nation's interest in the plight of the Calvinists, especially in Paris, "where there is more humanity and enlightenment than in the rest of the kingdom."[23]

As it turned out, *L'Honnête Criminel* was to be denied a performance on the nation's public stage until the early years of the Revolution, when it ran for some time. Choiseul put the rationale for this prohibition candidly enough to the playwright: "If we were to permit a performance (of your play) to go forward, it would follow in logic that we should disallow the laws which condemn Protestants to the galleys."[24]

Meanwhile, an influential sponsor had been found in the person of the duchesse de Villeroi who volunteered to have *L'Honnête Criminel* performed on her private stage. Following the première early in February 1768, which was attended by a number of influential members of the court, the duchess submitted a formal petition for the full legal rehabilitation of Fabre to the administration. When the matter was raised in the *conseil du roi*, Choiseul and Intendant of Finances Trudaine de Montigny were sufficiently eloquent to carry the day; a writ for the annulment of the original sentence was issued in April. Commenting on this happy turn of events, Grimm noted, not without malice: "The author of this play may rightly claim to have been the direct force behind this tardy act of justice.... My word, at that rate, I would gladly consent to write a bad play every day of my life."[25]

Like Fenouillot, Louis-Sebastien Mercier was convinced that the stage was an appropriate vehicle for the propagation of civic virtue; in his anticipatory *L'An 2440*, for instance, he suggested that a dramatization of the Calas affair ought to become part of the national theatre repertory because it might serve to deter citizens from lapsing into the intolerance which had caused France such needless disorder in the past.[26] Mercier did not attempt such a dramatization himself, no doubt because he knew that it stood no chance of presentation in Louis XV's France. In 1772, however, Mercier did publish *Jean Hennuyer*, the central theme of which was the heroic refusal two centuries earlier of the bishop of Lisieux to join the rest of the French episcopate in sanctioning the Saint Bartholomew's Day Massacre.

The first scene of Mercier's play introduces us to the Arsenne family, middle-class Calvinists from Lisieux. It is the eve of Saint Bartholomew's Day; they are waiting for the head of the household, in effect their surrogate pastor, to return from Paris where he has gone to celebrate the marriage between Henri of Navarre and Marguérite de Valois, which is to herald the end to Calvinist-Catholic friction. However, when he appears, Arsenne *père* brings instead the tragic news that Charles IX, taking advantage of the presence in the capital of most of the Calvinist leadership, has ordered the wholesale extermination of France's Huguenots. Hearing this report, the Lisieux Protestants panic; Arsenne, who has spent much of his adult life fighting for freedom of conscience, longs above all else for the spiritual reunification of France; he would even sacrifice his Calvinist convictions in such a cause if he could do so without betraying his conscience:

> Appalled at the prospect of seeing our country again consumed by civil war, I would prefer that we could simply all become Catholic. But can one act against one's conscience? Is it in our power to embrace a faith which we reject in our hearts? We would then become deceitful and hypocritical and in such circumstances I would prefer to die.[27]

Arsenne, who is convinced (like Mercier) that the persecuting fury unleashed against the Huguenots has its origin in the Medici faction at the French court, not in the First Estate, dissuades his son from turning his wrath against the local Catholic clergy. In the end, father and son join in leading their co-religionists in a peaceful march on the episcopal palace, where Bishop Hennuyer has meanwhile been preaching a message of toleration and understanding to a potentially murderous Catholic crowd:

> Charged with the salvation of all those whom God's grace may reach, a pastor can only pray for the conversion of those who have not yet been called to salvation. It is only through example, gentleness and virtuous behaviour that it is given to us to convince those souls of the superiority of our belief.[28]

When the Protestant marchers arrive, the bishop reassures them that it is the secular authority, not the priesthood, which is intent upon their destruction; the local militia, touched by the bishop's message, resolves not to comply with the order to slaughter the Calvinist population and, in the closing scene of the drama, the Catholics of Lisieux join their Calvinist neighbours in a solemn parade of civic reconciliation and unity.

Published anonymously in Switzerland, Mercier's drama aroused the suspicion of the authorities as soon as it began to circulate in Paris. Grimm expressed the frustration of enlightened French society that *Jean Hennuyer* would not under the circumstances be given the public performance which it deserved:

> Such works would be of far greater benefit to the people than all the fancy rhetoric of Corneille's Romans and the florid heroics of Racine's Greeks, even though the author of *Jean Hennuyer* is not to be compared to Pierre Corneille or Jean Racine.... It would be extremely edifying if one could see on the stage of the Tuileries what one sees nowhere in France— a humane, gentle-hearted prelate whose natural enlightenment persuades him that it is hateful to draw others to our opinions by fire and blood. I am convinced that people would come from all corners of the kingdom to see such a rare bird. I hope that the theatres in the north of Europe will win the esteem of their public by having it per formed.[29]

In *La Destruction de la Ligue*, written twelve years after *Jean Hennuyer*, Mercier gave new expression to his thesis that the responsibility for the unleashing of anti-Calvinist passion in post-Reformation France lay with weak and misguided monarchs rather than with fanatical priests. More startlingly, Mercier adopted a candidly pro-Calvinist viewpoint in the play: Henri IV, founder of the Bourbon dynasty, is seen as having thrown away a glorious opportunity to liberate France once and for all from papal tyranny. On the eve of the decisive battle which would give him control of Paris, Henri asks his Huguenot advisor Sully whether "there would not be more heroism and firmness of purpose in my supporting the Protestant cause, in making its triumph coincide with my own enthronement and thus in giving to my subjects a simpler, purer religion, better suited to destroy the many abuses of priestly authority from which all Frenchmen suffer."[30] The Protestant Sully is, of course, all in favour of making the Reformed faith the state religion; but Henri hesitates, deciding in the end that political realism dictates that he embrace the faith of the majority. The two old comrades in arms end up consoling themselves with the hope that the generous measure of toleration which Henri plans to offer the Huguenots in the Edict of Nantes will be a first step towards the elimination of popery and the gradual enlightenment of their nation. Meanwhile, Mercier notes, the Protestant states of Europe—England, Holland, and Switzerland, had learned how to rise above divisive religious conflicts and to develop a strong sense of national solidarity.

It would no doubt be hazardous to try to elicit a clear formula for Protestant toleration from the text of these seven plays, especially since only three of them deal explicitly with Huguenots. However, several ideas surface in these dramas which together suggest a fairly coherent if rather conservative solution to the question of French Calvinist rights.

To begin with, Voltaire, Fenouillot, and Mercier categorically condemn the discriminatory legislation directed against the Huguenots as a result of the Revocation. Fenouillot does this most directly by bringing to his contemporaries a glimpse of the terrible penalties still being paid by the Calvinists in defence of freedom of worship; while Voltaire, especially in *Les Guèbres*, urges that the civil status of non-conformists be assured by taking it out of the hands of the Catholic priesthood. All three playwrights demand an end to the spiritual harassment of the Huguenots; their conversion, if it must be pursued, should be attempted through gentle persuasion and example, after the manner of Don Alvarez in *Alzire* and Bishop Hennuyer in Mercier's drama.

Each of these dramatists is anxious to see the curbing of popular fanaticism, whether Christian or Moslem, Catholic or Calvinist. Further, and even more important, they all feel the need to restrict the ecclesiastical establishment, whose tendency is always to exploit popular zeal in the pursuit of theocratic power. They all reject the "two-sword" theory of rule and insist that it is up to the civil sovereign to regulate the religious life of the nation.

Finally, there is in these playwrights an overriding desire to see their nation psychologically and spiritually one; the scene of 'ecumenical' reconciliation at the close of Mercier's *Jean Hennuyer* reflects a feeling which they all share. The unifying faith which these men have in mind for France may differ (Mercier in *La Destruction de la Lique* going so far as to declare a preference for Protestantism); but, like Bossuet before them and like the revolutionary generation which was to follow them, they are not religious pluralists. Vivid memories of the theologically inspired conflict of the sixteenth century (or, more recently, of the Camisard revolt) have convinced them that, as long as the spiritual allegiances of their fellow countrymen remain divided, the civic solidarity which they are so anxious to promote will prove impossible to achieve. Frenchmen who cannot subscribe to the national faith must be freed from efforts to force their consciences. They must be allowed to worship in their own fashion. Yet there were strict limits to this tolerance: non-conformists must not by their religious practices give offence to the devotees of the established faith; in practical terms, they ought to be content with domestic worship.

---

1.   R. Pomeau, *La religion de Voltaire* (Paris, 1969), pp. 87-88.
2.   Voltaire, *Zaïre, Oeuvres complètes*, ed. Moland (henceforth M), (52 vols; Paris, 1877-1882), II, p. 617, act V, scene 10. G.E. Lessing's *Nathan der Weise* (Berlin, 1779) would convey the same message of ecumenical reconciliation and toleration.
3.   Voltaire, *Alzire, ou Les Américains*, ibid., III, p. 389, act I, scene 1.

4. Voltaire to Frederick II, King of Prussia, December 1740, *Voltaire's Correspondence, The Complete Works*, ed. Besterman (Geneva, Toronto, Banbury, 1968-), Best. D. 2386.

5. V. Voltaire, *Le Siècle de Louis XIV* (1751), ed. A. Adam (2 vols.;Paris, 1966), II, pp. 87, 90, 91.

6. V. R. Haynes, *Philosopher King: The Humanist Pope Benedict XIV* (London, 1970), pp. 172-78.

7. Voltaire, *Les Guèbres, ou La Tolérance, Oeuvres* [M], VI, p. 559, act V, scene 2.

8. Ibid., p. 560.

9. Ibid., p. 455, scene 6.

10. Ibid., p. 489, "Préface."

11. Voltaire to the comte de Schomberg, August 16, 1769, Best. D. 15830.

12. Voltaire, *Discours historique et critique à l'occasion de la tragédie des Guèbres, Oeuvres* [M], VI, pp. 501-502.

13. Ibid., p. 502.

14. Voltaire to the Comte d'Argental, November 18, 1768, Best. D. 15321.

15. Voltaire to the marquise Du Deffand, July 24, 1769, Best. D. 15773.

16. Marquise Du Deffand to Voltaire, July 29, 1769, Best. D. 15782.

17. Voltaire to Madame Marie Louise Denis, September 11, 1769, Best. D. 15885.

18. Voltaire to Jean François Saint-Lambert, January 3, 1770, Best. D. 16072.

19. Voltaire, *Les Lois de Minos, Oeuvres* [M], IV, pp. 180-81, n. and p. 204, n.

20. Ibid., pp. 222-23, n.

21. C.-G. Fenouillot de Falbaire, *L'Honnête Criminel, ou l'Amour filial, drame en cinq actes et en vers* (Paris, 1768), p. 89, act V, scene 9.

22. Grimm et al., *Correspondance littéraire, philosophique et critique*, ed. Tourneux (16 vols; Paris, 1877-1882), VII, p. 485, November 15, 1767.

23. Paul Rabaut to Antoine Court de Gébelin, January 22, 1768. *Paul Rabaut. Ses lettres à divers, 1744-1794*, ed. C. Dardier(2 Vols. Paris, 1892), II, pp. 76-77.

24. Fenouillot de Falbaire, "Notes sur ce qui s'est passé à l'occasion de la pièce de 'L'Honnête Criminel' et relativement à l'état des Protestants de France, depuis 1756 jusqu'en 1770, signé le 1 mars 1788," B.N., Fonds français 7047, fol.549.

25. Grimm, *Correspondance littéraire*, VIII, p. 74, May 1, 1768.

26. L.-S. Mercier, *L'An 2440, Rêve s'il en fût jamais* (1770), ed. R. Troussson (Paris, 1971), pp. 227-28.

27. Mercier, *Jean Hennuyer, évêque de Lisieux, Théâtre complet*, (4 Vols.; Amsterdam, 1778-1784), II, p. 309, act I, scene 3.

28. Ibid., p. 358, act III, scene 3.

29. *Correspondance littéraire*, X, p. 54, September 1, 1772.

30. Mercier, *La Destruction de la Ligue, ou La Réduction de Paris, Théâtre complet*, IV, p. 45, act II, scene 1.

Ecce fpectaculum dignum, ad quod refpiciat
intentus operi fuo Deus: ecce par Deo dignum,
Vir fortis cum mala fortuna compofitus. *Senec.*

Marmontel's *Bélisaire*: An advocate of princely tolerance.

CHAPTER XIII

Reaction Put to Rout:
The *Dictionnaire Philosophique*, the Last of the *Encyclopédie* and the *Bélisaire* Affair, 1764-1767

During the middle 1760s, while Voltaire's interest in the Calas and Sirven cases was at its most intense, three bombshells burst on the French literary scene which, coming in rapid succession, decisively altered the balance in the long battle for toleration. It is true that apologists of the Revocation had been on the defensive since the late 1750s, when the effort of the abbé Caveirac to rationalize religious repression backfired; but they remained extremely powerful. During successive Assemblies of the Clergy, the First Estate reminded the King of his obligation to police existing anti-Calvinist legislation before yielding up the *don gratuit* upon which the government was increasingly dependent. Meanwhile, the threat of ecclesiastical censorship was enough to keep all but the boldest critics of 'fanaticism' and 'superstition' from joining the battle for toleration in the open field.

The new offensive against clerical reaction began in 1764 with Voltaire's *Dictionnaire philosophique*. A year later, the last ten volumes of the *Encyclopédie* were distributed. Then, early in 1767, the heretofore cautious Jean-François Marmontel joined the ranks of militant combatants for religious freedom with his novel *Bélisaire*, the fifteenth chapter of which caused something close to panic in the clerical camp. Rather unwisely, the ecclesiastical establishment sallied forth to teach Voltaire's new recruit a lesson, only to be ridiculed for the pathetic anachronism of its intellectual defences. The pamphlet war surrounding the *Bélisaire* incident offered Voltaire and his companions an irresistible opportunity to wing towards their adversaries a number of telling shafts: *L'Ingénu* and Marmontel's *Les Incas* contain parting shots against clerical oppression by warriors who have tasted blood.

The cumulative effect was devastating to the religious establishment. When the literary engagements of the 1760s were over, no detached observer could doubt that the champions of toleration had cleared the field.

The *Dictionnaire philosophique portatif*, first published in July 1764, continued to sell well through successive editions during the following decade; from 1770 on, its appearance was paralleled by that of the author's *Questions sur l'Encyclopédie*, containing much of the same or parallel material.[1]

In these, as in his earlier writings, Voltaire saw the urge to persecute as an essentially plebeian phenomenon. But while persecution had always been the product of mass frenzy, it had been given an added impetus with the advent of Christianity; Christ was the first inquisitor of the new order in which men were to be condemned merely for harbouring heterodox ideas.[2]

Although the Reformation had brought some spiritual relief to humanity, it had not eliminated the shameful record of Christian intolerance, as witness the fate of Ireland's Catholics and the murderous bigotry of two the chief figures of French Protestantism, Calvin and Jurieu. In "Catéchisme chinois," Calvin and his fellow Reformer, Luther, are characterized as spiritually hard and intellectually intransigent:[3] in "Dogmes," the founder of French Protestantism is pictured as having kicked and abused the idol of papistry only after it had been brought down off its pedestal by earlier Reformers; Voltaire imagines Calvin, standing beside the funeral pyre on which poor Servet is about to be burned, rejoicing that his own peculiar version of the gospel is now crowned with uncontested success: "I have denounced painting and sculpture; I have made abundantly clear that good works are of no avail and that it is diabolical to dance the minuet."[4]

Jurieu, of course, had always been one of Voltaire's *bêtes noires* because of his treatment of Pierre Bayle. Voltaire notes that, as a prophet in exile, the Calvinist theologian had evaded punishment, while the *Cevenol* zealots whom he incited to revolt were hanged or broken on the wheel.[5] But, while Voltaire was convinced that persecution in its Protestant as well as in its Catholic form was far from dead, he had by the end of the 1760s come to believe that its fury had somewhat abated. There were still no doubt a few monks and members of fanatical Protestant sects who were foolish and backward enough to be intolerant, but they would never confess this publicly. Thanks to the philosophes, France seemed to have effectively rescued herself from fanaticism.[6]

One source of Voltaire's optimism was his conviction that, as humanity moved inevitably towards the worship of a single divine being, it would at the same time be guided towards mutual love and tolerance. In Europe, the Quakers, whom the philosophe regarded as de facto deists, had shown the way.[7] There were signs of an increase in toleration in China,[8] in the Ottoman Empire,[9] in Russia,[10] and in the English-speaking North American colonies.[11]

While Voltaire clearly welcomed the gradual emergence of a more tolerant disposition in so many parts of the world, he was not (and would never become) a champion of unlimited religious freedom. In "Cathéchisme du Japonais," for instance, resorting to analogy, Voltaire imagines a dialogue concerning eating habits between an Indian sage and a Japanese intellectual. The Nipponese rejoices that, after a two-hundred-year-old squabble over dietary taboos, his compatriots have agreed to a policy of *laissez faire* in the matter. The Indian is impressed but wonders whether, in Japan as elsewhere, the regimen of the sovereign should not set the standard; to which the Japanese replies that all the king's subjects should be allowed to eat according to their own individual taste. The Indian then asks what would happen if a group of dissidents were to assemble in large numbers in front of the royal palace and proceed to cook food abhorrent to the emperor, thereby causing certain insult and offence? The answer given by the Japanese is that it would be necessary to punish the offenders, not because their culinary taste was different but because they had challenged civil order by their provocative public assembly. The best method of anticipating this type of problem was to reward with public offices and honours only those who patterned their culinary habits on those of the sovereign.

In "Christianisme," Voltaire put the case against public defiance of the king's will by a dissident minority less obliquely: the French monarchy, he reminded his readers, still forbade large-scale Calvinist assemblies in Languedoc and sometimes even hanged pastors who insisted on presiding at such meetings in defiance of the law.[12] In "Religion," Voltaire suggested that Europe's princes make a clear distinction between *religion de l'Etat*, which involved such matters as the registration of holidays and the propagation of good morals, and *religion théologique*, from which the state should disassociate itself entirely, since it was inevitably a source of disputatiousness and war.[13] Voltaire's preference is for a situation in which the authority of the secular magistrate is paramount and in which a salaried clergy functions along the lines proposed by the abbé de Saint-Pierre—praying, teaching and providing models of moral behaviour.[14] Ecclesiastical laws should be without effect unless sanctioned by the civil authority, he adds. Everything affecting marriage, for instance, should fall under the jurisdiction of the prince; the role of the priest should simply be to give his blessing to the wedding, not to pronounce on its validity.[15]

The views expressed in the *Dictionnaire philosophique* about the limits which should be set to toleration disappointed French Calvinist readers. They were far more alarmed by the outright attacks made upon the theological and moral foundations of Christianity throughout the work. Early in September 1764, soon after copies were available on an under-the-counter basis in Geneva, the Magnificent Council ordered them seized, because Voltaire's text directly challenged the authenticity of Revelation. In a letter to his fellow naturalist, Albrecht von Haller, the devout Charles Bonnet described the work as Voltaire's most detestable to date.[16] Even the theologically liberal Rabaut Saint-Etienne, while deploring the seizure of the *Dictionnaire*, felt that its contents were abhorrent enough to warrant refuting.[17] The Catholic Fréron took understandable delight at the Protestants' reception of Voltaire's anti-Christian sallies, noting that the *Dictionnaire* had been printed on Genevan presses. Calvinists were at last reaping the bitter harvest of their support for intellectual freedom.[18]

To his own delight, the appearance of Voltaire's *Dictionnaire philosophique* served as a smokescreen, distracting attention away from the appearance of the last ten volumes of the *Encyclopédie* which Diderot and the Protestant chevalier de Jaucourt had continued discreetly to edit since March 1759, when the government suspended publication. The final volumes were ready for distribution by the end of 1765. Shortly afterwards, copies were made available to the public, with the tacit permission of the government. However, because Versailles was concerned about the adverse reaction which the publication of Diderot's work was bound to elicit during the Assembly of the Clergy scheduled for later in the year, these volumes were sold under the counter.

Like most philosophes, the editor-in-chief of the *Encyclopédie* saw intolerance and fanaticism as Christian rather than exclusively Catholic phenomena. Diderot's sympathy for the Huguenots was balanced by a feeling that they should assume their share of responsibility for the persecution which Protestants elsewhere had inflicted on religious dissenters and that they should eschew the spiritual excesses in their own communion which had forced governments to take action against them. In "Persécution," which he farmed out to the liberal abbé Yvon, the repression of English Catholics by the Tudors is listed among twenty-six separate instances of religious persecution unleashed on the world since the triumph of Christianity.[19] And in "Martyrologe" and "Puritains," Diderot displayed what contemporary Huguenot readers must have thought was heartless irony: had England's Puritans not been bloodily repressed by Mary Tudor, he suggests, they would not have had their quota of martyrs. Without such victims, the Puritans would have failed to attract a following, since their support had come from the fanaticism which only persecution can produce.[20]

While anxious to point out that Protestants could be as intolerant as Catholics, Diderot set the record straight as far as France's treatment of the Huguenots was concerned. As we have seen, he wrote "Journée de la Saint-Barthélemy"[21] in reply to Caveirac's "Apologie de Louis XIV;" and in "Réfugiés," he reminded readers of the grim consequences of the Revocation:

> Since that time, France has seen herself deprived of a great many citizens who have transmitted to her enemies a number of arts, talents and resources which these enemies have used against her. In the years since, there has not been a loyal Frenchman who has not bemoaned the deep wounds caused the kingdom by the loss of so many faithful subjects.[22]

In "Pacification," Diderot outlined the policy by which the monarchy could have averted these tragic acts of repression. In a state where two religions are contending for supremacy, he argued, the proper course of action is not to guarantee the absolute ascendancy of one by eliminating its rival but rather to encourage the appearance of still more sects. Such a policy would discourage fanaticism, which usually accompanies the dominance in the state of a single faith.[23]

Close to Diderot in outlook was Voltaire's friend, Etienne-Noel Damilaville who argued in "Population" that the surest means to encourage the demographic growth which France required was to increase political and religious freedom: "The human species has multiplied much more under popular and tolerant governments in which the citizenry enjoys a greater degree of religious and civic freedom."[24]

The chevalier de Jaucourt, whose signature ('D.J.') was familiar to readers of the first seven volumes of the *Encyclopédie*, remarked in "Hérésie" that, since the Reformation, France's kings had been committed by their coronation oath to exterminate heresy; yet earlier in the same ceremony, Jaucourt noted, they had vowed to preserve the peace of the kingdom. The earlier pledge surely took precedence:

> The first oath governs all the rest and consequently carries with it a commitment to gentleness and tolerance. I believe it is relevant to repeat these truths often and to inculcate them with all due respect into the minds of the sons and grandsons of our kings who must one day mount the throne, in order to implant in their hearts from the tenderest infancy the seeds of a true and radiant piety.[25]

Jaucourt conceded that when religious sects create a public scandal or disturbance the state has an obligation to intervene. But it was important that any such cases be heard before civil and not ecclesiastical judges.[26]

In "Hollande," Jaucourt declared, perhaps a trifle over-generously, that "while the Protestant faith is dominant there, all the world's religions are tolerated."[27] In "Inquisition," he observed that Spain had lost the great wealth of the Netherlands because "that iniquitous tribunal created to extirpate heresy is precisely what most alienates Protestants from the Roman communion."[28]

Apart from Jaucourt's substantial contributions on the subject,[29] the most comprehensive comments on toleration by a Protestant in the *Encyclopédie* were those made by Pastor Jean-Edmé Romilly, son of one of Switzerland's best-known watchmakers. Experience, Romilly began, must surely sober those still intent upon bringing humanity to accept a universal religion. All the efforts which men had made to police conformity of faith had been accompanied by grave injustices and tragic consequences. Even at this high cost, they had all failed, for oppression tended always to confirm dissidents in their heresy.

In a world still plagued by intolerance and repression, the most immediate remedy was to distinguish between the power of state and church, priest and magistrate. Romilly was no partisan of separation of church and state, however. Instead, he advanced the formula which he had discovered while reading Rousseau—that all citizens be required to make a simple profession of one basic civil religion, after which they would be free to subscribe to their own private cult except those guilty of a "culpable indifference," atheists, and partisans of sects with pretensions to exercise a dominance within the state.[30]

Apart from Jaucourt and Romilly, several other Calvinists representing a wide-ranging spectrum of theological opinions contributed to the *Encyclopédie*. Samuel Formey put forward the orthodox view in "Trinité"[31] while Antoine-Noé Polier de Bottens, senior pastor at Lausanne, responded to an invitation from Voltaire by contributing a number of articles for Volume VII, each of which was enough by itself to scandalize Christian readers, however progressive their theology. In "Liturgie", for example, Polier argued that all the Reformers had achieved by their reforms in this area was the removal of some of the cultural richness and vitality which gave Catholic ceremonies a certain popular appeal.[32]

Of even greater significance in the battle for toleration than the *Encyclopédie* was, despite its modest literary worth, the novel *Bélisaire*, published by Jean-François Marmontel in 1767. Earlier in his career, Marmontel had been something of a 'closet' philosophe, sharing the view of liberal intellectuals that human beings were inherently virtuous, confidently assuming that his *contes moraux* would encourage a gradual improvement in human relations, but not participating in the open combat against reaction being waged by his more militant contemporaries.[33]

During the lengthy battle to rehabilitate the memory of Calas, Marmontel had remained on the sidelines. Yet his assumption about the inevitable triumph of virtue had clearly been shaken by the affair; the seriousness with which he viewed his role as moralist, together with his desire to gain the unconditional respect of his peers, did the rest, slowly transforming him into an intellectual activist.

The central characters of Marmontel's novel—the emperor Justinian and his blind commander-in-chief Belisarius—are stock-in-trade figures of didactic fiction, unrelievedly virtuous, debating high policy with arguments designed to flatter and confirm the convictions and prejudices of the liberal eighteenth-century reader, possessing none of the saltiness or wit which would have made them a delight to follow had their dialogue been rendered by Voltaire. As most critics remarked, *Bélisaire* was didactic without being diverting, second-rate *Télémaque*. If it became a best seller nevertheless, it was because the fifteenth chapter, which focussed on the issue of civil toleration, provoked the ecclesiastical establishment, thereby guaranteeing a *succès de scandale*.

The offending chapter finds Justinian engaged in a wide-ranging discussion of religion with Belisarius. The emperor not only defends orthodox doctrine but insists that the secular sword must police spiritual conformity throughout the empire. The general,flirting with the old Pelagian heresy, argues that, since God is just and since, as his creatures, we are imbued with his goodness, our human nature is essentially virtuous and our redemption probable. In any case, since Christian doctrine is basically a re-edition of natural religion and its teachings are endorsed by all the world's great faiths, why persecute those who dissent from the established church only over matters of speculative theology which are of secondary significance? If princes resort to violence against their subjects, Belisarius pursues, it must be because their own religion is barbarous or, if not, because they are unworthy of serving it. Justinian's reply is a declaration of caesaropapism, pure and simple: any monarch who has been mandated by the Almighty to ensure unity of faith and worship within his dominions must use the sword against rebellious non-conformists who threaten this unity.

Belisarius concedes that physical revolt, whether or not inspired by religious conviction, must be put down, but the punishment of those whose only offence is to dissent from the official view in matters relating to speculative theology ought to be left to the Almighty. As absolute theological truth is so difficult to determine, how could even the emperor be sure? Even those princes who were convinced that they had received the true faith (from whatever source) should ask themselves whether they were obliged to impose this belief upon their subjects. Belisarius enjoins Justinian to avoid conversion by force: "Let faith descend freely from the heavens, that way it is sure to make converts. With edicts, one will only create rebels or scoundrels. The heroic will become martyrs, the cowardly turn hypocrite, while fanatics from all parties will be transformed into tigers on the rampage."[34]

The emperor's response is to cite the kind of argument used by Bossuet with Louis XIV, that the peaceful governance of one's subjects depends on their spiritual unity; Belisarius counters that "kingdoms are never more pacific than when those who live within them are free to follow their consciences."[35] Every time a group of citizens suffers discrimination because of its religious beliefs, it comes to regard the state and its rulers as its enemies; envy and a desire for vengeance follow, threatening to rend the social fabric. Still unconvinced, Justinian insists that freedom of belief would lead inevitably to acceptance of unlimited freedom of action, even when this threatened state security. The general points out that existing civil law is there to put a stop to anti-social acts, whatever their inspiration. The most effective way of ending the cycle of disputes inspired by theological differences was simply to ignore them instead of fuelling them by constant intervention. Justinian's silence following this last sally clearly signals to the reader an implicit acceptance of the old warrior's plea for toleration.

Marmontel read the first draft of his novel to the members of the Académie française on May 24, 1766. The '*Bélisaire* affair' which followed brought the novelist into direct conflict with the French ecclesiastical establishment. Marmontel would be far from isolated during this battle. Voltaire for one came to the aid of the beleaguered novelist in March 1768. This support took the form of an *Anecdote sur Bélisaire*, the core of which was an imaginary discussion of the novel's contents by a simple-minded monk, Triboulet, and two philosophes, one of whom is clearly intended to be Marmontel. In his reply to the suggestion that the Church Fathers would have no difficulty with Belisarius's comments about the probable salvation of virtuous pagans and that they might even hold out hope for humanitarian philosophes and just Protestant princes, Triboulet trots out the conventional orthodox view that damnation is the fate of all non-conformists, whatever their merits.[36]

The eight-man committee of examiners named by the Sorbonne to draw up an *Indiculus* (or list of the heterodox propositions contained in *Bélisaire*), identified thirty-seven such expressions, twenty-one of which were specifically related to the issue of toleration. The singling out for condemnation of one phrase in particular ("The truth illumines with its own light; there is no need to enlighten men's minds with flames and burnings at the stake") was to provide the philosophes with irresistible material for satire.[37]

At this juncture, the Sorbonne might have thought twice about proceeding with the public censure of Marmontel except for the appearance on the scene of two provocative new pamphlets. The first of these was by Voltaire, who responded to an appeal for further help from Marmontel in early April by penning a *Seconde anecdote sur Bélisaire*.[38] In this brief but salty work, which reached the salon world by mid-June, Voltaire introduced the reader to a trio of theologically conventional but otherwise earthy members of the Catholic priesthood who had foregathered to pass judgment on *Bélisaire* in a seedy tavern. Predictably, they end up damning Marmontel and sanctioning every kind of repression in the interest of preserving the faith.

To add to the discomfiture of the authorities, Turgot now entered the battle with *Trente-sept vérités opposées aux trente-sept impiétés de Bélisaire*, a rather heavy-handed effort at irony in which a theology student lets himself be won over to the liberal notions contained in Marmontel's novel before recovering his senses and spouting the repressively orthodox line.[39]

Its judgment mocked and derided in advance, the Sorbonne proceeded on June 26 to promulgate the formal censuring of *Bélisaire*. Although only nineteen of the original thirty-seven offending propositions were cited in the final text, the decision to proceed with the open indictment of the novel was enough by itself to guarantee that the battle would continue.

By early August the text of the faculty's censure of *Bélisaire* was coming off the presses; the theologians decided to hold up its sale, however, until a *Mandement* attacking the novel, which Christophe de Beaumont was preparing, had appeared. During this pause, the administration (which had been deeply concerned at the public reaction to the prematurely distributed *Indiculus*) decided to intervene in order to prevent a situation from developing in which it would be obliged to choose between sanctioning or disavowing the clergy's view that civil intolerance was the necessary corollary of theological intolerance. Aware of this governmental concern, the clergy refrained from releasing its fulmination against *Bélisaire*. D'Alembert hastened to send this good news to Voltaire, adding that the court as well as the parlement seemed anxious to ensure that nothing was said either by the Sorbonne faculty or by the archbishop of Paris which would conflict with the government's current policy towards France's non-conformists.[40]

Early in September yet another shot was fired in the continuing controversy. The *Honnêteté théologique* (which J. Renwick suggests may be the work of Damilaville, refined by Voltaire) offers the reader a recapitulation of the arguments for civil toleration put forward in *Bélisaire*, and points out that, over the years, Catholics have been far more guilty of teaching subversive doctrine than the philosophes whom they now condemn.[41]

If Marmontel and his supporters had called a halt to their polemical offensive at this point, when the Catholic clergy was clearly on the defensive, it is possible that the *Bélisaire* affair might then have come to an end. Among the philosophes, however, the urge to demolish an adversary on the run had become too strong to resist. Late in October the *Pièces relatives à Bélisaire* appeared, containing all the material concerning the novel which had so far been published.[42]

On November 27, shortly after the appearance of a *Réponse catégorique au sieur Cogé*,[43] the Sorbonne theologians held a special meeting to which only a limited number of the faculty were invited. Those present were informed that Versailles, having reviewed the *Censure*, was ready to sanction its publication, except for the passages dealing with the issue of civil toleration. The modified version presented to those in attendance would clarify and define the differing roles of the civil and ecclesiastical arm in dealing with non-conformity: it would also be made abundantly clear that conversions should and would be attempted by spiritual means alone; physical repression by the secular arm would be undertaken only in cases where the activity of the citizens involved threatened the maintenance of public order. The revised text concluded rather defensively: "It is slanderous to blame the Christian religion for the persecutions, the violence and the massacres for which it was perhaps on occasion the pretext but to which its real spirit has always been opposed."[44]

Shortly afterwards, when the *Censure* made its appearance in this attenuated form, it caused considerable dismay in the ranks of the clergy at large, who felt betrayed. Needless to say, it caused great rejoicing in the camp of the philosophes, who rightly perceived it as an implicit vindication of the principle of civil toleration. Grimm reflected the general delight of the liberal intellectual fraternity when he observed that the conservatives in the First Estate would have preferred no *Censure* at all to the current text in which they were seen to be accommodating themselves to the increasingly tolerant policies of the regime.[45]

Early in January 1768, Louis XV issued a *lettre de cachet* forbidding any further discussion of the *Bélisaire* issue in the general assembly of the Sorbonne. At the end of the month, Beaumont at last read from the pulpit his *Mandement,* which reflected the same moderate view which had informed the modified version of the *Censure.*[46]

Although it was not to appear until 1777, Marmontel's *Les Incas* was written during his sojourn at Aix-la-Chapelle, and it is clear that both the theme of this new novel and its treatment were much influenced by the novelist's recent dealings with the ecclesiastical establishment. The polemical intent of *Les Incas* is established at the outset by the quote from Fénelon which Marmontel places at the beginning of the text: "Grant all your subjects civil toleration, not out of an indifferent approval of every kind of faith, but from patient sufferance of all that God Himself must suffer and out of an effort to bring men back to the true faith through gentle persuasion."[47]

In the preface, Marmontel argues that all nations have their share of fanaticism. In its Christian form, this attitude could be traced back to Christ's transmission of plenipotentiary power to Peter, an arrangement subsequently ratified by the church's learned doctors. The Spaniards had transported this presumptuous claim to the New World, where they had invoked it to oppress, even to exterminate, the Indians.

The novelist goes on to remark (in a comment which clearly separates his point of view from that of the militant Voltaire of the 1760s) that the fanaticism which he is intent upon excoriating is a perversion, not a corollary, of the true Christian faith. Set against portraits of zealots and persecutors in the novel are a number of 'true Christians' such as Fra Bartolomeo de las Casas, the monk who denounced the forced conversions and physical enslavement of the Indians as violating everything in the gospels.

While talking over the *Bélisaire* affair at Aix with the bishops of Noyon and Autun who were also staying at the spa, Marmontel offered them manuscript copies of *Les Incas,* telling us that he silenced them with the comment: "Here is a work which will oblige your theologians to choose between burning the gospel or respecting in Las Casas, the apostle of the Indies, the same sentiments and the same doctrine which they condemned in *Bélisaire*."[48]

A decade later, when *Les Incas* was published, it circulated without official hindrance, a sign of the changing times. Its celebration of what had become the moral clichés of the day did not, however, guarantee it much success with the critics.[49]

During the long evolution of the *Bélisaire* affair, Marmontel always insisted that he was a genuine Christian, appalled by his church's often corrupt practices, but a believer nevertheless in a simplified, morally revitalized version of the gospels.[50]

Like Marmontel, Voltaire continued to put the *Bélisaire* affair to polemical use; in May 1767, at the height of the dispute, he began writing *L'Ingénu*. Apart from diverting the public, the philosophe had several aims in mind while he was launching this witty conte on the Paris literary scene: first, in order to sustain the onslaught against *l'infâme* which he had begun in the *Dictionnaire philosophique*, he hoped to strike a crippling blow at the recently expelled Jesuits, whose formerly awesome powers had been at their apogee during the Revocation period, in which Voltaire sets his tale; second, in order to reinforce the influence in the ministry of the duc de Choiseul, whose liberal views on the religious question were the antithesis of those of Saint-Florentin, the most persistent opponent of relief for the Calvinists since his appointment in 1725. Voltaire introduced the reader to a perverse fictional character, Saint-Pouange, clearly intended to represent the reactionary interior minister.

The tribulations of the central figure in *L'Ingénu* provide the thread around which Voltaire weaves a bitterly satirical picture of religious and political corruption in late seventeenth-century France, contrasting it with the naive purity of the Amerindian world as well as with the sophisticated liberalism of England. Captured by the English while doing battle for the French in the colonies (where, he tells the reader, the Jesuits were unable to make converts among his people and where the English more wisely did not even try), the Huron hero of the tale is brought to England, where everyone he meets, including Huguenot refugees, respects his simple deist faith. Things change radically, however, when the young Indian arrives on the Breton coast in 1689. Adopted by a local abbé and his sister, the Ingénu yields to their entreaty that he turn Catholic. In the course of a subsequent visit to Saumur, which had been one of the leading social and intellectual centres of French Calvinism before the Revocation, the Huron is startled to discover that most of the townfolk have fled, unwilling to stay if the price of their remaining is to be submission to papal authority. Slowly the grim backdrop of the Revocation system is exposed to this novice Catholic from the New World, who gathers that a fundamentally magnanimous Louis XIV has been deceived by wily Jesuits into believing that he should compel all of his subjects to give spiritual obedience to Rome, even though, puzzlingly enough, he is at war with the pontiff himself!

Misfortune brings the Huron to spend time in the Bastille, where he engages in a deliciously absurd debate over the nature of grace with a Jansenist fellow convict. During his confinement, the Indian also manages to browse through a history of the reign of Justinian; not surprisingly, he comes upon one of the propositions, the endorsing of which had brought Marmontel to be condemned:"La vérité luit de sa propre lumière et on n'éclaire pas l'esprit avec les flammes des bûchers."[51] Further reflection on theological matters brings the prisoner to the disheartening conclusion that "all sects seem to be nothing more than rallying-points for error."[52]

The Indian's French fiancée, meanwhile, has been doing her best to secure his release by appealing to the redoubtable Saint-Pouange, who will consent to her request only after she joins him in bed. When the outraged woman protests, a Jesuit quickly surfaces to give her the appropriate casuistical encouragement: by sleeping with the minister, she will be serving God and country, since Saint-Pouange is dedicated to the good cause of the church. His release gained at this terrible price, the ingenuous Indian is at least purged of the perverse religious notions which had followed his conversion; he finds ultimate solace by joining the French army.

In the three years following the appearance of Voltaire's *Dictionnaire philosophique*, the French religious establishment had been subjected to a series of blows, some deliberate, some unintended. The furious polemic of the patriarch of Ferney was greeted with horror by Protestants and Catholics alike, who rightly judged him to be increasingly anti-Christian; the efforts of the Encyclopedists on behalf of religious liberty seemed mild by contrast. Meanwhile, unnerved by the intensity of the battle in which they found themselves engaged, the official representatives of French Catholicism made fools of themselves by confusing the plea for toleration of the neo-Christian Marmontel with the irreligion of their real enemy. Ecclesiastical officialdom had been so weakened during this uneven combat that Protestants might reasonably hope for positive action on their behalf from Versailles.

---

1.   Voltaire, *Dictionnaire philosophique portatif* (London [Geneva], 1764); *Questions sur l'Encyclopédie* (Geneva, 1770). The numerous editions of these two works collated in R. Naves (ed.), *Dictionnaire philosophique* (Paris, 1967). My notes 2-15 are taken from the Naves text.

2.   "Inquisition," Voltaire, *Dictionnaire philosophique*, ed. Etiemble (Paris, 1967), p. 253.

3.   "Catéchisme chinois," ibid., p. 75, n.

4.   "Dogmes," ibid., p. 173.

5.   "Persécution," ibid., p. 342; "Philosophe," ibid., p. 344.

6.   "Fanatisme," ibid., p. 92.

7.   "Catéchisme du Japonais," ibid., p. 92.

8.   "Chine, de la," ibid., p. 109.
9.   "Prêtres," ibid., p. 354.
10.   "Lois, des," ibid., p. 567; "Torture," ibid., p. 410.
11.   "Tolérance," ibid., p. 625.
12.   "Christianisme," ibid., p. 127.
13.   "Religion," ibid., p. 369.
14.   "Crédo," ibid., p. 154; "Prêtres," ibid., p. 354.
15.   "Lois civiles et ecclésiastiques," ibid., p. 290.
16.   Bonnet to Albrecht von Haller, Best D. 12090, n. 2.
17.   Rabaut Saint-Etienne to Etienne Chiron, September 30, 1764, B.P., Ms. Chiron
      358, I, fol. 21 v.
18.   *Année littéraire*, December 6, 1764. In self-defence, Voltaire pointed out that many
      of the articles singled out for criticism by Protestants were in fact written by
      distinguished Calvinist theologians such as Polier de Bottens and Firmin Abauzit.
      Voltaire to Alembert, October 12, 1764, Best. D. 12137.
19.   "Persécution," *Encyclopédie, ou Dictionnaire raisonné des sciences, des arts et des
      métiers, par une société de gens de lettres*, ed. Diderot, d'Alembert et al. (35 vols.;
      Paris, 1751-80), XII, p. 426.
20.   "Martyrologue," ibid., X, p. 170; "Puritains," ibid., XIII, p. 582.
21.   "Journée de la Saint-Barthélemy," ibid., VIII, p.898.
22.   "Réfugiés," ibid., XIII, p. 907.
23.   "Pacification," ibid., XI, p. 737.
24.   "Population," ibid., p. 94.
25.   "Hérésie," ibid., VIII, p. 158.
26.   "Hérésie (Jurisprudence)," ibid.
27.   "Holland," ibid., p. 246.
28.   "Inquisition," ibid., p. 776.
29.   The boldest passages of the Protestant's texts were blue-pencilled by Le Breton.
      Several of his key articles were entirely cut. In the course of one of these
      ("Religion protestante") Jaucourt had characterized Protestantism as "that reasonable
      as well as holy religion which, far from reducing man to ignorance, allows him to
      be at one and the same time learned and believing, pious and human."
          In "Sectes du christianisme," a second article cut by Le Breton, Jaucourt
      suggests that a scholarly effort to determine which of the many Christian sects was
      the purest would uncover flaws in them all. For the true Christian, all that was
      needed was to accept Christ's own words as final and to practise the morality of the
      apostles. With regard to the many articles of faith which had become a source of
      controversy among Christians, the wisest course was to follow the teachings of
      one's own communion: "But one must make sure that this does not lead to the
      destruction of social unity or peace and, more important, that it does not induce us
      to persecute those who are of a different conviction; because there is no greater
      evidence that a society is not part of the church of Jesus Christ than that it should
      practise cruelty and persecution."
          The title of yet another of Jaucourt's articles which was not allowed past the
      proof state ("Théologie.Scholastique. Théologie barbare")was no doubt in itself
      provocative enough to alarm Le Breton. Here again Jaucourt takes up the defence of
      evangelical Christianity against the over-refined, and sometimes perverted, doctrine
      developed by the Church Fathers.

Finally, Jaucourt's most pointed article on the toleration theme ("Tolérance, Religion, Morale politique") never got into print. It is a pity that this article did not reach the public, for it is a minor masterpiece of persuasive writing. Jaucourt begins by arguing that ecclesiastical toleration should be accorded all Christians who accept those articles of faith made clear in the Scriptures. Persons failing to acknowledge such elemental truths should be excluded from the church, but pitied for their blindness rather than persecuted. Civil toleration, on the other hand, should be considered in the light of the purposes for which men first joined themselves together in organized society. These purposes clearly could not have included the preservation of any common beliefs; nor, in this primitive period, could men have alienated their consciences to the civil sovereign even had they wished to do so. The later corruption of the original social contract by the introduction of legislation against religious dissenters had led to nothing but misery in the form of declining population and decreasing prosperity; while the tolerance of religious diversity had been a boon in those societies which had encouraged it. In recent times, the Dutch had taught the English that tolerance and prosperity go hand and hand. In general, the Protestant world which had once been as culpable as the Catholic, was now converted to the need for toleration: "Today, all Protestants condemn the ideas of Beza and the conduct of Calvin; thus, the responsibility for the execution of Servet, among other vile acts, should be blamed on the   Reformer himself and not on the Christian religion itself   which condemns him as it does the Inquisitors."

Jaucourt concludes the article with a tribute to John Locke, who "converted his nation to the view that the greatest of all Christian heresies is intolerance."

Although most of the baron's "Mennonite" was passed by Le Breton, the officious printer took it upon himself to remove the following paragraph condemning intolerance before sending the article to press: "The misfortune of the Mennonites was such that in certain places they still suffered persecution at the hands of other Protestants who, at the beginning, when they thought themselves fully purged of papist errors, still retained this most gross and dangerous error, that which holds that the civil magistrate should punish religious opinions as he would a crime."

Finally, Le Breton radically altered articles by Jaucourt which attacked Catholic dogma or practice in too forthright a manner. Subtle changes in phrasing are made in "Morale", for instance, in which the heretical Encyclopedist is not permitted to say that Protestant thinkers, unlike their Catholic predecessors, had succeeded in evolving a sound system of Christian ethics. D.H. Gordon and N.L. Torrey, *The Censorship of Diderot's 'Encyclopédie' and the Re-established Text* (New York, 1947), pp. 78, 82, 87, 104, 701-71.

30.   "Tolérance," *Encyclopédie*, XVI, 395. Although Romilly was a tougher and more radical believer in the principle of toleration than his readers were led to understand, he was also, like many of his fellow-Calvinists, far from being unconditionally committed to the world view of the *Encyclopédie*. Though the critical middle decades of the century, he maintained a close personal as well as literary friendship with two of the leading conservative critics of the philosophes, Elie Fréron and Charles Palissot. The latter made explicit his appreciation of Romilly's uncompromising Christianity in an eloquent posthumous tribute. V. "Jean-Edmé Romilly," *Biographie universelle*, ed. Michaud, XXXVI, p. 412.

31.   "Trinité," *Encyclopédie*, XVI, pp. 645-47.

32. "Liturgie," ibid., IX, p. 597. Further evidence of Polier's capacity to shock Christian readers can be found in "Mages," IX, pp. 847-48 and in "Messie," X, p. 403.

33. V. J. Renwick, "Marmontel, Voltaire and the 'Bélisaire' affaire," *Studies on Voltaire and the Eighteenth Century*, CXXI (1974), p. 47. Much of what follows is taken from this comprehensive examination of the Bélisaire affair, and from the same scholar's earlier interpretation of the genesis of the 'Bélisaire' crisis in *SVEC*, LIII (1967), pp. 172-222.

34. Marmontel, *Bélisaire* (Paris, 1767), p. 247.

35. Ibid., p. 248.

36. Voltaire, *Anecdote sur Bélisaire* (c. end March, 1767), *Oeuvres* (M), XXVI, p. 113.

37. Grimm, *Correspondance littéraire*, VII, p. 338.

38. Voltaire, *Seconde anecdote sur Bélisaire* (May 1767), *Oeuvres* [M], pp. 169-72.

39. Anne Robert Jacques Turgot, *Les [37] vérités opposées aux erreurs de Bélisaire* (1767), J. Tissot, *Turgot, sa vie, son administration, ses ouvrages* (Paris, 1862), pp. 461-75.

40. Alembert to Voltaire, September 22, 1767, Best. D. 14436.

41. [Damilaville and Voltaire?], *Honnêteté théologique* (Paris, 1767).

42. *Pièces Relatives à Bélisaire* ([Geneva and Paris], 1767).

43. Voltaire, *Réponse catégorique au sieur Cogé* (late November/early December 1767).

44. *Registre des délibérations des assemblées particulières de la Sorbonne*, November 27, 1767, cited in J. Renwick, "Marmontel, Voltaire and the 'Bélisaire' affair," p. 291.

45. Grimm, *Correspondance littéraire*, VII, p. 501.

46. Christophe de Beaumont, *Mandement de monseigneur l'Archêveque de Paris, portant condamnation d'un livre qui a pour titre: 'Bélisaire' par M. Marmontel, de l'Académie française* (Paris, 1767).

47. Marmontel, *Las Incas, ou la destruction de l'Empire de Pérou* (1777), *Oeuvres complètes*, repr. Slatkine (7 vols.; Geneva, 1968), III, p. 323.

48. Marmontel, *Mémoires d'un père pour servir à l'instruction de son fils* (4 vols.; Paris, 1804); ibid, I, pp. 272-73.

49. J. F. de La Harpe, *Correspondance littéraire adressée à son Altesse impériale Mgr le grand-duc, aujourd'hui empereur de Russie, et à m. le comte André Schowalow, chambellan de l'impératrice Catherine II, depuis 1774 jusqu'à 1789* (5 vols.; Paris, 1801-07), II, 60-61; p. 75.

50. The genuineness of Marmontel's effort to reconcile his philosophical liberalism with his neo-Christian faith would be established years later, during the Directory, in the *Opinion sur le libre exercice des cultes* which he drew up for the Council of Ancients. The Council was contemplating legislation to ban any public advertising of conventional religion, a measure clearly aimed at the Catholic church. True to what he had argued in *Bélisaire*, Marmontel insisted that all expressions of opinion, including religious opinion, ought to be free except when they threatened public order. The proposed new law clearly discriminated against Catholicism, since the Roman communion had always been associated with external symbols. The novelist suggested that pressure for the legislation in question might have come from ex-Catholics with a guilty conscience who wished to suppress all visible reminders of their former faith. V. Marmontel, *Oeuvres*, repr. Slatkine, I, pp. 473-86.

51. Voltaire, *L'Ingénu*, ed. W.R. Jones (Geneva and Paris, 1957), p. 285.

52. Ibid., p. 293.

PART THREE

THE REVOCATION UNDONE,
1760-1787

PAUL RABAUT

Paul Rabaut, dean of the underground pastorate.

CHAPTER XIV

The 1760s: From Words to Deeds

By the beginning of the 1760s, what remained of the negative image of the French Reformed was beginning to fade, and an increasingly sensitive public was being made aware of the very real sufferings still being endured by the Huguenots. The Calas affair would do much to replace old myths of Protestant fanaticism and subversion with a positive picture of men and women who were sober, patriotic, and prosperous. This last factor, the contribution of religious minorities to national wealth, had been noted at the time of the Revocation by Vauban, observed first-hand by Montesquieu and Voltaire in England, and commented upon in the *Encyclopédie*. In a generation when physiocracy was the dominant economic creed and when men such as Turgot and Dupont de Nemours would help shape government policy, it was bound to have even greater impact.

While their view of the Calvinists was changing for the better, the philosophes' devotion to the general principle of toleration (and thus to the reintegration of the Huguenots into the national community) also continued to develop. During the minority of Louis XV, Montesquieu and Voltaire had celebrated the advantages of religious pluralism in the Protestant 'North.' Subsequently, they found evidence that the rest of Europe was following suit. Writing to Helvétius in the summer of 1765, Voltaire remarked:

> All the North is with us...Russia, Poland, Austria and Prussia have raised the banners of toleration and philosophy...We French are obviously not destined to be first in these matters; truths reach us from abroad; but even if such truths come to us from outside, it is, of course, excellent that we should adopt them.[1]

Wherever toleration was promoted, those who granted it were praised. Catherine II of Russia received the blessing of Voltaire when she sent troops into Catholic Poland on the pretext of guaranteeing freedom to religious minorities there.[2] To the delight of the philosophes, Joseph II of Austria adopted much of their religious agenda—shutting down monasteries, radically reducing papal authority inside his empire, and granting toleration to his Protestant subjects in 1781.[3] Even the papacy had undergone a spiritual *aggiornamento* when both Jews and Protestants were given a measure of religious freedom by Benedict XIV.[4] In Europe, only Spain remained as a symbol of the 'medieval' past, a world where state and church conspired to crush the spirit. Thinkers of Voltaire's generation were distressed that France might be seen in such dismaying company.

The American colonies, especially Pennsylvania, had long attracted the attention and applause of French liberal thinkers for their promotion of religious freedom.[5] After 1776, the United States offered the most radical formula imaginable for the resolution of the long spiritual crisis which had preoccupied European civilization since Constantine, by separating church from state.[6] It was, not surprisingly, during his service in the American cause that the young marquis de Lafayette became a convert to the campaign for Huguenot relief; his admiration for Washington played no small part in his decision to join the lobby working to achieve in France the kind of religious freedom the Americans had fought to confirm.

While the philosophes committed themselves more and more openly to the cause of Calvinist emancipation, the Reformed were gaining more self-confidence; their spiritual recovery gained momentum as the administration ended its policy of active repression. The last exodus of Huguenots on religious grounds took place in 1760.[7] The overwhelming majority of France's Protestants waited, albeit with rising impatience, for the nation's intellectual and political elites to find a formula which would release them from political and religious discrimination.

Two Huguenot writers—Voltaire's bitter adversary Laurent-Angliviel de La Beaumelle and Antoine Court, the organizer of the Protestant revival, symbolize this new self-confidence among the French Reformed.

In the summer of 1759, La Beaumelle put the case for Huguenot emancipation in a brief addressed to that intractable defender of the Revocation system, the comte de Saint-Florentin.[8] The Revocation had from the beginning been based on an illusion, the Calvinist pamphleteer began: the seemingly spontaneous conversion of the Huguenot minority in 1685 had been quickly belied, thanks to the resolve of refugee pastors and their Dutch protectors to turn all of France into mission territory. This defiance of the law had brought repression, and repression had produced revolt; but what was important for the administration to realize was that the Edict of Fontainebleau had been in the end effectively nullified. Rural Huguenots had taken advantage of the war crisis of the 1740s to rediscover their faith; nowadays, they even impressed their Catholic neighbours with the sweet simplicity of their worship. Urban Calvinists, meanwhile, who had revived their non-conformist beliefs quietly during the permissive years of the Regency, were drawing inspiration from the reasoned theology of Tillotson, Ostervald, and Saurin. Perhaps even more significant, the slow dissemination of the philosophic spirit had attenuated the once bitter animosities between Protestant and Catholic theologians.

Moving from the spiritual to the secular sphere, La Beaumelle estimated the French Calvinist population at 1 870 000, or more than one-tenth of the national total; he went on to note that this substantial minority which devoted its energy almost exclusively to farming and commerce had created more than its share of the nation's wealth. Then, shifting to the cocky tone which characterized so much of his prose, La Beaumelle warned that, if the Huguenots were now both prosperous and loyal, there was no guarantee that this would always be the case; if fact, they could not deny feeling a certain sense of divided loyalty when France was at war with Protestant Europe:

> The Calvinists cannot have the same feelings as the rest of the nation because they have other interests, other views, other laws, other experiences.... The discontented love their country conditionally while happy subjects give it their undivided love. That is the sole difference between Protestants and Catholics in France.[9]

La Beaumelle concluded his appeal to Saint-Florentin with a challenge. The Huguenots were sensitive to the changes in their condition brought about by Louis XV, whose regime had seen an end to the execution of non-conformists. They appreciated the initiatives taken on their behalf by such ministers as Machault, Bell'Isle, Silhouette, Berryer, and Choiseul. Might they not now reasonably look for their redemption from the man who had been in charge of 'new Catholic' affairs since 1725?

There is no record of any reply by Saint-Florentin to La Beaumelle's bold sally; in all probability, the Protestant pamphleteer's memorandum went unanswered. Meanwhile, (albeit posthumously) Antoine Court was reaching at least part of the reading public with a remarkably impartial study of the Camisard rebellion. This *Histoire des troubles des Cévennes* was in fact a sophisticated piece of historical scholarship, determinedly objective, based on an on-the-spot enquête, together with a close examination of all available sources, including the highly polemical material produced by Catholic as well as Protestant apologists during or immediately following the revolt.[10]

The central thesis of Court's work is summarized in the preface. As of 1685, Court insisted, most of the Reformed had accepted the Revocation passively, as unresisting victims. If some of them had ended up joining the Camisard rebellion, it was because they had discovered that peaceable response to repression brought them no special treatment from the authorities. The *petit peuple* among the rebels, lacking proper spiritual guidance and harried beyond endurance by local priests and civil officials, had put their trust in youthful self-deluded prophets. Their rebellion, in any event, had been directed solely against their immediate oppressors, not against the crown; they had never allowed their insurrection to be exploited by France's enemies. Once the revolt had begun, Protestant dignitaries had done their best to persuade their less sophisticated co-religionists to listen to reason and remain calm in the face of adversity; but mindless adventurers had exploited popular resentment to serve their own selfish ends. Court noted that there had been several attempts to unite Catholic and Calvinist *mécontents* in a common struggle for tax relief as well as freedom of conscience. Such an alliance had proven impossible to forge, however, and, instead, the local clergy, abetted by Rome, had excited the Catholic rabble to form a band of ruthless partisans—the *Cadets de la Croix*—who had turned out to be at least as violent and destructive as their Protestant counterparts.

The greatest irony about the Revocation, Court noted, was that the established church, in trying to convert others to its faith by force, had "instead of making Catholics, made libertines, faithless men, atheists and finally rebels."[11] The Protestant chronicler's attack on Catholic proselytizing is balanced, Voltairean fashion, by the satire which he directs at the simple-minded Calvinist peasants who had jointed the Camisard revolt. Court describes at some length an occasion when a band of Camisards breaks into a Protestant farmhouse and, too ignorant to recognize that the engravings on the walls are those of the sixteenth-century Reformers, tosses them into the flames as papist images.[12]

Court concludes his history by reassuring his readers that the fires of fanaticism which had stirred up such hatred and destruction on both sides of the Camisard conflict were now banked. Following the end of the rebellion, he writes:

> Men of a new type emerged in the Cévennes and in Languedoc, men who enjoyed the confidence of their people and whose thoughts and principles were quite the opposite of those held by their predecessors who had enjoyed support for such a long time in that part of the country. These new men transformed the situation totally, calmed the population and thereby spared France the uprisings and disorders which otherwise sooner or later would have had disastrous consequences.[13]

The *Histoire des troubles des Cévennes* may be regarded as Court's testament. It was history convincingly written, designed to establish that the Camisard rebellion, with its accompanying fanaticism and aberrant folk religion, had been a momentary lapse in the evolution of French Calvinism, a frantic insurrection supported at best by a tiny band of zealots. The new leadership which Court described (and of which he was, of course, the pre-eminent representative) was by implication ready to guarantee in the Reformed community at large the devotion to the monarchy and the peace-loving attitude which made its readmission into the national community an eminently rational policy.

The new assertivness of the Calvinists and of their leading spokesmen provoked an inevitable reaction from the Catholic priesthood. On June 7, 1760, delegates to the Assembly of the Clergy addressed a lengthy remonstrance to Louis XV, reminding him that the clear intention of the Sun King had been to extinguish heresy, and pointing out that this objective was now being openly flouted. Pastors who had been trained abroad were crossing the border to revive what had been a moribund sect; nothing was being done to put an end to illicit assemblies for worship during which the whole accursed liturgy of the Reformed faith was observed; non-Catholic baptisms were being celebrated and psalms chanted in bad French. But even more scandalous was the complicity of certain persons at court who had sponsored the publication and circulation inside France of such subversive works as the *Mémoire politique et théologique* which advocated the civil marriage of Protestants and the *Esprit de Jésus-Christ sur la tolérance* in which Catholic doctrine was openly attacked.[14]

This unrelenting hostility of the Catholic establishment was to remain the single greatest obstacle in the way of Protestant emancipation until the eve of the Revolution. Fortunately for the Calvinists, a substantial group of Jansenist priests and magistrates (whose constituency had suffered parallel if much less violent forms of persecution and discrimination throughout the eighteenth century) were to join the battle for Protestant toleration in its last phase, a phase in which members of the administration were also to play a more and more active role.

Beginning in the early 1760s, Versailles effectively changed its Protestant policy. Physical repression of the Huguenots all but stopped, giving way to a form of de facto toleration; and the King's ministers began to play a more active role in matters affecting the Reformed. Many of these men were supporters or colleagues of the philosophes; they tended to share Voltaire's antipathy towards the ecclesiastical establishment and his desire to promote a more spiritually open society. Beginning with Choiseul in the 1760s, and continuing until 1787, many key figures in the administration expressed sympathy for the Huguenots, and some were moved to urge legislative changes which would afford the Protestants relief from the Revocation system.

The initiatives on behalf of the Protestants taken or supported by Etienne-François, duc de Choiseul, in the 1760s represent a turning point in the government's handling of the Huguenot question, halfway between the tentative steps taken by Machault in the 1750s and the forthright placing of the toleration question on the administration's agenda by Turgot in 1775. The first of these initiatives, a plan to colonize Guyana with European settlers, was part of a general effort by the then navy minister to restore France's strategic position in the Atlantic following the disastrous Seven Years' War. Late in November 1763, Choiseul wrote Voltaire to announce that the expanded colony would have as its governor the liberal Etienne-François Turgot, brother of the physiocrat. He added that considerable interest in the scheme had already been elicited in the Germanies. There was just one hitch: the ecclesiastical establishment, which had got wind of the project, was determined that the venture should not include the granting of religious liberty to the Protestant Germans who had so far volunteered.[15]

Voltaire's sympathy was immediately aroused. Early in 1764, he wrote to Turgot expressing his excitement on behalf of those about to set sail for the new "El Dorado" under such an enlightened captain, adding the suggestion that the government make the project known to the nation's Protestant *galériens*, thereby at one and the same time recruiting additional hardy spirits for the enterprise and erasing a shameful chapter from France's religious policy.[16] Voltaire followed up his suggestion by writing to his contact with the Huguenot galley slaves, the Marseilles businessman Louis Necker, who informed him that the men were indeed interested, adding that their sponsors might even be able to raise some 20 000 livres to help subsidize the project. The philosophe was, of course, delighted but thought it necessary to warn would-be Protestant volunteers through Necker that they ought not to ask for a pastor or a house of worship in Guyana; the liberal governor under whom they were to serve would surely grant them freedom of conscience which was, at present, all they could hope for.[17]

As it turned out, the twenty-four *forçats pour la foi* who had shown an interest in the Guyana scheme lost heart. Voltaire was outraged and expressed his contempt for these would-be "companions of Ulysses" who had so timorously thrown away the chance to regain their manhood.[18]

The Guyana fiasco did not discourage Voltaire from promoting and Choiseul from seconding a somewhat parallel scheme a few years later, this time much closer to home. The origin of this second project lay in Voltaire's increasing preoccupation with the rising social and political tensions across the border in Geneva.[19] Although his sympathies had once been with the *Negatifs* (whose advanced aesthetic and theological views he had found so congenial in the mid-1750s), and although he had flirted briefly with the cause of the *Représentants* (Geneva's solid but politically impotent bourgeoisie), Voltaire ended up espousing the interests of the *Natifs*, the mainly artisanal group who made up three-quarters of the city's population but were totally excluded from civic affairs.

In 1768, the *Negatifs* appealed to France to mediate what was becoming open civil strife. Versailles made an unsuccessful attempt to arbitrate, then closed the border between Geneva and the *pays de Gex* and imposed a blockade on the Swiss city. Charles Leopold Chazel, the chevalier de Jaucourt, who arrived with troops to police this blockade, suggested that France take advantage of the crisis by creating a port facility at Versoix near the border, thus giving Geneva some serious economic competition. Voltaire seconded the idea: the public investment required would help revitalize the *pays de Gex* which had gone into a decline since the Revocation; the proposed port would surely attract some of Geneva's disaffected *Natifs*, especially the artisans who could start up watchmaking and stocking manufacture; most of all, the admission into France of Genevan Calvinists would obviously have to include the granting of some form of toleration; it might even serve as a test case for religious co-existence for the nation at large.

Voltaire got support for the proposal from the French resident in Geneva, Pierre Michel Hennin, and, more important, from Choiseul. Although the idea of creating the new model city was viewed skeptically by some members of the cabinet (especially Controller-General Terray, who insisted that the state of the nations's finances made it impossible), Choiseul pressed ahead, promising that, if necessary, the cost would be paid out of the foreign affairs budget.

As the outlines of the new city began to take concrete form, Voltaire wrote confidently to Pastor Gal-Pomaret in January 1769:

> Agreement has finally been reached that a city will be built here on the frontier in which, by an exceptional arrangement, Protestants will be able to marry legally... There will certainly be established here as much toleration as politics and prudence allow.[20]

A new immediacy was given to the Versoix scheme in February 1770 when a number of *Natifs* were attacked by a pro-government mob. Some of the victims fled across the border seeking asylum; unfortunately, there was no housing awaiting them, and most ended up having to return to their homeland. Nevertheless, Choiseul felt able to send relatively reassuring news about the Versoix project to Voltaire:

> The Versoix business interests me greatly because I feel it to be good, humane and politically useful. It would be absurd to conceive of the project without freedom of religion; it is towards that end that I am working, but it is so hard to secure such a result easily; before long, we will know where we stand in the matter.[21]

While the ministry at Versailles continued to dilly-dally, Voltaire received enthusiastic support for the Versoix scheme from his neighbour, Charles de Brosses, who saw in it "the means so long sought and at last uncovered of giving a suitable status to such a large number of citizens who are still without it, and of bringing back many who wish to return to France and finally, of allowing toleration to be established in at least one small corner of the realm."[22] To the physiocrat Dupont de Nemours, Voltaire wrote enthusiastically that the Versoix project would, like his own little world at Ferney, provide convincing proof that "freedom of commerce and freedom of conscience are the two tenets upon which the prosperity of states both large and small is based."[23]

Unfortunately, as with the Guyana project, the hope for an experiment in religious toleration near the Swiss border was not to be fulfilled. Through their agent in Paris, the banker (and future French minister) Jacques Necker, Geneva's *Petit Conseil* encouraged resistance to the Versoix scheme inside the Choiseul ministry, while the bishop of Annecy (within whose spiritual jurisdiction the experiment would have been conducted) denounced the potentially dangerous presence of heresy in his diocese. Meanwhile, Choiseul found his political position seriously compromised; and when Louis XV and Vice-Chancellor Maupeou decided upon strong measures against the parlements, his fate was bound up with that shift in policy. Louis XV dismissed his first minister in December 1770, and the Versoix project suddenly ceased to have any priority on the administration's agenda.[24]

Although the notion of establishing zones of religious liberty on the outer edges of French society had in the end to be abandoned, the government gave tacit support during the Choiseul years to the efforts of Voltaire and other reform-minded Frenchmen to eliminate one of the most repressive elements in the Revocation system—the imprisonment of Calvinist laymen and women who had been caught attending outdoor services of worship. Few people at Versailles in the 1760s were aware that there were still some dozen men serving life sentences on the King's galleys in the Mediterranean for this offence, while eighteen of their sisters languished in a medieval fortress of Aigues-Mortes near the coast.

Voltaire's campaign to obtain the liberation of the remaining Calvinist galley slaves was prompted by Louis Necker, who urged him late in 1763 to intercede at court on behalf of Claude Chaumont, a cobbler who had been condemned in March 1751 for attending an illicit outdoor service. Half flippantly, Voltaire remarked that men foolish enough to sacrifice their freedom in the defence of religious dogma ought to be willing to undergo martyrdom; but, of course, he would write to Versailles, he added.[25] Choiseul lent a favourable ear to the petition for the convict's release, which was forwarded to him by Voltaire and somehow managed to outmanoeuvre Saint-Florentin. By mid-February 1764, Chaumont was free, on condition that he never again attend a 'Desert' service.[26]

Delighted at this first success, Voltaire wrote Necker asking for the names of the remaining Huguenot *galériens*, together with a summary of the charges against them.[27] The philosophe was fully aware that a successful follow-up to the Chaumont release would not be easy at a time when the administration was preoccupied with the crisis brought on by the expulsion of the Jesuits (and, perhaps just as important, when there was an almost total unawareness at court of the existence of Protestant galley slaves).[28] For a while, the Guyana venture promised a quick means of liberating the remaining *forçats pour la foi* but, as we have seen, the potential beneficiaries of this scheme refused in the end to commit themselves to it.[29]

Even less well known than the plight of the galley slaves was the sequestering inside the medieval fort at Aigues-Mortes (the *Tour de Constance* as the Huguenots called it) of Protestant women arrested at public services of worship. In 1768, when the liberal military commander in

Languedoc, the prince de Beauvau, first learned about the tower, there were still eighteen women inside. The commandant appealed at once to Saint-Florentin and was able as a result to secure the freedom of four of the most elderly prisoners. His concern for those who remained brought him to visit the scene of their captivity in the company of his nephew, the chevalier de Boufflers. More than a generation later, the chevalier recalled the feelings of horror and compassion which he and his uncle experienced as they confronted these victims of French intolerance face to face:

> We saw a large round room without air or daylight. Fourteen women languished there in misery and tears. The commandant had difficulty in restraining his emotion.... I can still see them, upon his sudden appearance, fall at his feet, then, emboldened by our expressions of sympathy, recount to us all at once their common sorrows. The youngest of these martyrs was more than fifty years old; she had been eight when they arrested her.[30]

Following his visit, Beauvau wrote to Versailles to request the immediate and unconditional release of the women. The results were dramatic: by December 15, 1768, only five of the prisoners remained inside the tower, two of whom were shortly to die: then, on the prince's initiative, these last detainees were set free before the year's end. In reporting his act of insubordination to Saint-Florentin, the commandant proudly declared:

> Since justice and humanity pleaded with equal vigor in favor of these unfortunate creatures, I had no choice in the matter. After the departure of the prisoners, I had the tower locked up in the hope that it would never again be opened for such a purpose.[31]

When the minister let it be known that Beauvau might be dismissed from his post unless he arranged for the recapture of the women, the proud nobleman replied that, while he clearly had the power to rescind his appointment, he could not prevent one of his servants from carrying out his functions according to his conscience and his honour. The dialogue ended there: a sensitive and tolerant agent of the crown had in effect unilaterally removed one of the most cruel elements of the Revocation system. Rejoicing at this act of administrative compassion, one of Paul Rabaut's colleagues wrote to suggest that the liberation of the prisoners at Aigues-Mortes went far towards justifying the policy of patient expectation which the Huguenots had long since determined to adopt.[32]

As it turned out, patience was a quality the Reformed would need to call upon more than once during the twenty years which separated the freeing of the Protestant prisoners of conscience and the granting of the Edict of Toleration in 1787.

---

1. Voltaire to Helvetius, June 26, 1765, Best. D. 12660.

2.   Following the Russian intervention in Poland, Voltaire wrote d'Alembert to report that Catherine "has sent 40 000 Russians to preach toleration with bayonets in hand." Voltaire to d'Alembert, May 3, 1767, Best. D. 14157. Voltaire published at least three tracts defending Catherine's action on the ground that it provided a guarantee of toleration for Poland's religious minorities in the face of Catholic repression. V. *Essai historique sur les dissensions des églises de Pologne* (1767); *Sermon prêché à Bâle, le premier jour de l'an 1768, par Josias Rossette* (1768); *Sermon du pape Nicolas Chariteski* (1771). For a full discussion of the tendency of French philosophes to defend Catherine II, v. A. Lortholary, *Les Philosophes du XVIIIe siècle et la Russie: Le mirage russe en France au XVIIIe siècle* (Paris, 1951), pp. 86-169.

3.   The Jansenist Adrien Le Paige, who became a vigorous advocate of Huguenot toleration early in the reign of Louis XVI, maintained a watching brief on the religious policies of all the European states. His library contained material in French and Latin relating to the edict of toleration which Joseph II of Austria awarded the Protestants in 1781. Société de Port Royal Fonds. Le Paige No. 827. "Tolérance religieuse. France. Allemagne. 1782-1784."

4.   Voltaire's dedication of his play *Mahomet* to Benedict XIV was part machiavellian ploy, part sincere tribute to a pontiff who had granted the Jews and Protestants living in the Papal States as much freedom as was being conceded them elsewhere in Catholic Europe at the time. V. R. Haynes, *Philosopher King: The Humanist Pope Benedict XIV* (London, 1970), pp. 172-78.

5.   Voltaire called attention to the religious pluralism of colonial Pennsylvania in his *Lettres philosophiques*; Jaucourt relayed this flattering view to readers of the *Encyclopédie* in "Pensylvanie" and "Quaker" V. *Encyclopédie*, XII, pp. 313-14; XIII, pp. 648-50.

6.   For an analysis of the ways in which French observers of the American scene evaluated the religious policy of the new United States, v. G. Adams, "Light from the West: American Influence on the Campaign for French Protestant Emancipation," *Proceedings of the Consortium on Revolutionary Europe* (Athens, Georgia, 1979), pp. 179-87.

7.   D. Ligou, *Le protestantisme en France de 1595 à 1715* (Paris, 1968), p. 253.

8.   La Beaumelle, "Mémoires d'état, le 19 août 1759," B.N., Ms Fonds Fr., Nouv. Acq. 7047, fols. p. 441-94.

9.   Ibid., fol. 491.

10.   Antoine Court, *Histoire des troubles des Cévennes, ou de la guerre des Camisars, sous le règne de Louis le Grand; tirée de manuscrits secrets et autentiques et des observations faites sur les lieux mêmes, avec une carte des Cévennes* (3 vols.; Villefranche, 1960).

11.   Ibid., II, p. 439.

12.   Ibid., I, p. 445.

13.   Ibid., III, p. 401.

14.   *Remonstrances de l'Assemblée du clergé au Roi, presentées le 7 juin 1760, Collection des Procès-verbaux des Assemblées-générales du Clergé de France* (9 vols. in 8; Paris, 1771), VIII, 1ère partie, pièces justificatives, p. 295.

15.   Choiseul to Voltaire, November 27, 1763, Best. D. 11518.

16.   Voltaire to Etienne-François Turgot, January 24, 1764, Best. D. 11659.

17.   Voltaire to Louis Necker, March 19, 1764, Best. D. 11785.

18. Voltaire to d'Argental, June 17, 1764, Best. D. 11930. As it turned out, the would-be Protestant colonists were lucky. Most of the men and women who sailed to Guyana died within two years and the venture ended in collapse.

19. For a full study of Voltaire's involvement in Genevan politics, v. Peter Gay, *Voltaire's Politics:The Poet as Realist* (New York, 1965), pp. 185-238. Voltaire's interest in the Versoix scheme is analyzed in depth in J.P. Kerrier, *Le Duc de Choiseul, Voltaire et la création de Versoix-la-ville* (Geneva, 1922).

20. Voltaire to Gal-Pomaret, January 15, 1769, Best. D. 15432.

21. Choiseul to Voltaire, March 2, 1770, Best. D. 16192.

22. Charles de Brosses, baron de Montfalcon, to Voltaire, March/April, 1770, Best. D. 16270.

23. Voltaire to Dupont de Nemours, July 16, 1770, Best. D. 16528.

24. Voltaire tried his best after the collapse of the Versoix project to find outlets for the artisans who had sought refuge in France. The new navy minister, Pierre-Etienne-François Bourgeois de Boynes (among others), agreed to purchase a few watches which might be used as diplomatic gifts. Bourgeois de Boynes to Voltaire, July 1, 1771, Best. D. 17280.

25. Louis Necker to Voltaire, January 11, 1764, Best. D. 11637.

26. Upon his release, Chaumont sought asylum in Switzerland. Pastor Etienne Chiron of Lausanne who welcomed him felt it appropriate that the cobbler be taken to see his benefactor at Ferney. Voltaire received the ex-convict with the charming condescension he tended to display in the presence of simple-minded plebeians. All of this was a bit much for poor Chaumont who remained speechless, and Voltaire ended up dismissing the pious artisan as an imbecile. Chiron felt embarrassed at the social ineptitude of his co-religionist which, together with his 'Lilliputian' physique, had made him an unprepossessing representative of his faith. Further public exposure of such near-martyrs for the faith, the pastor wrote to his colleague Rabaut, would clearly do the Calvinist cause little good. Etienne Chiron to Paul Rabaut, March 8, 1764, Best. D. 11731.

27. Voltaire to Louis Necker, February 15, 1764, Best. D. 11700.

28. Voltaire to Paul-Claude Moultou, c. February 15, 1764, Best. D. 11702.

29. Despite these frustrations, Voltaire was able to intercede successfully in 1766 on behalf of the *galérien* Jean-Pierre Espinas from Chateauneuf in the Vivarais country, who had been arrested in 1743 for harbouring an itinerant pastor. Voltaire drew up a *requête* in support of Espinas in September 1766 but the intense pressure being brought upon him at the time as a result of the publication of his *Dictionnaire philosophique* brought him to call upon third parties to transmit this appeal to the ministry. The philosophe asked madame de la Tour du Pin de Saint-Julien, the duchesse d'Anville, the duc de Richelieu, and the duc de Nivernais to do their best to persuade Saint-Florentin, "an atheist who tries to please fanatics," to release the Protestant galley-slave. In the end, it was thanks to Choiseul that Espinas gained his freedom early in 1767. V. Voltaire to Moultou, c. September 14, 1766, Best. D. 13557. As Voltaire noted in a letter to Necker, the administration was more likely to release the very elderly among the *galériens*. Voltaire to Necker, March 5, 1764, Best. D. 11750. In 1769, the military commandant in Languedoc, the prince de Beauvau, was able to obtain the freedom of Alexandre Cambon, an octogenarian who had spent twenty-seven years aboard the galleys.

30.   Report of the chevalier de Boufflers, cited in Coquerel, *Histoire des églises du désert*, I, p. 524.
31.   Princesse de Beauvau, *Souvenirs* (Paris, 1892), p. 18.
32.   Pastor Journet to Paul Rabaut, July 13, 1769, B.P., Papiers Rabaut, XIX, fol. 14.

Jean Calas bids farewell to his family: Chodowiecki's melodramatic rendering of a real-life *drame bourgeois*.

CHAPTER XV

The Calas Affair:
A Catalyst for the National Conscience,
1762-1765

Like Alfred Dreyfus more than a century later, Jean Calas, found guilty of a crime which posterity judges he did not commit, belonged to a minority whose ideas and customs were considered suspect, even threatening, by many French Catholics. But, while anti-Semitic prejudice predisposed much of the nation's social and intellectual establishment to assume that a Jewish artillery officer was capable of treason merely on the basis of his ethnic background, France's elites in the 1760s rejected in the end the notion that a Protestant cloth merchant was capable of murder in order to prevent his son's conversion to the Roman communion.

A generation ago, the American scholar David Bien argued that the wave of intolerance which led so many citizens of Toulouse to believe Calas guilty of parricide was an anachronism, an aberration in an otherwise relatively tolerant urban environment.[1] The Huguenots were a tiny minority in the southern city, Bien notes (perhaps 200 out of some 50 000); relations between the two communities had for some time been based on mutual deference and respect; Calvinists entered the city's professions as well as its commercial life; furthermore the local parlement had ceased to police existing anti-Calvinist legislation. But the period 1759-1762 brought a sudden shift of mood. The war against Protestant England and Prussia was going badly and the local economy was in a state of recession. In these circumstances, old fears and prejudices were easily reactivated, not against the Huguenots as heretics, but as fomenters of civil discord. The arrest of a self-confessed underground pastor, François Rochette, in the fall of 1761 and the subsequent apprehension of three gentlement glassmakers who had tried to effect his release by force created a sense of imminent insurrection throughout the Toulouse area. The public execution of all four men helped to increase the overall feeling of alarm. Thus, Bien argues, the Calas tragedy and the furious anti-Protestant feeling surrounding it should be seen as simply part of a brief but intense revival of old fears. Bien reinforces his own case by noting that a more tolerant mood returned to Toulouse soon after the execution of Calas.

Lawyers for the defence of Jean Calas and his family, no doubt naturally enough, took a less serene view of their fellow citizens. *Toulousains*, they argued, were heirs to a tradition of mindless religious persecution which went back at least as far as the Albigensian period and which had found particularly violent expression during the massacre of the city's Huguenots in May 1572, the bicentennial of which was approaching at the time of Calas's trial; finally, they noted that this historic antipathy had been revived after 1685 as the local Calvinists tried to compensate for their political and religious ostracism by cultivating success in business, thereby arousing envy.

After the execution of Calas, the long struggle to vindicate his name and to annul the penalties imposed on members of his household for their complicity in the alleged parricide began when Voltaire, who at first took the guilt of the accused for granted, was persuaded that a tragic miscarriage of justice had occurred. For the defence, the philosophe mobilized the best available legal minds and appealed for moral and political support from France's social and intellectual elites.

As the battle to rehabilitate the good name of the cloth merchant intensified, Voltaire emphasized more and more the need to award some measure of toleration to the Calvinists, not only so that they might have the full protection of the law which Calas had been denied, but also so that the senseless prejudices which had brought so many of Calas's Catholic fellow citizens to presume his guilt might be dispelled.

To an objective observer, it would be hard to imagine less likely candidates for a conspiracy to commit ritual murder than Jean Calas, a successful cloth merchant, his wife, Anne-Rose, born in London to refugee parents and related to several noble families in Languedoc, their son Jean-Pierre, Gaubert Lavaysse, a 'new Catholic' acquaintance who was their guest on the night of the tragedy, and their pious Catholic servant Jeanne Viguère. The victim of the tragedy, the Calas's eldest son Marc-Antoine, had prepared for a career in the legal profession but was, of course, unable to practise law without abjuring; his resultant sense of frustration was no doubt enough to explain the symptoms of psychological withdrawal which he began to manifest in the fall of 1761 and which ultimately led to his suicide.

Between the arrest of the Calas family and the posthumous rehabilitation of Jean Calas in 1765, lawyers for the defence put forward two types of argument. They pointed out that the accused were eminently respectable citizens; the notion that they had conspired together to murder one of their own was patently absurd. They added that the procedures followed by those who had condemned the Calas household were seriously flawed. The presence on the scene soon after the tragedy of the notoriously anti-Calvinist *capitoul* David had prejudiced the case from the beginning; the tendentious questioning of the neighbours had been wrong-headed; the preventative arrest of the five suspects and their separate interrogation without benefit of legal counsel was outrageous; the decision of Archbishop Dillon to have the city's parish priests read out a *Monitoire* to their congregations, in effect inviting the faithful to come forward and testify, but only if they had evidence against the accused, was monstrous; the decision by the *capitouls* to order a Catholic burial for Marc-Antoine, thereby prejudging the verdict by implying that at the time of his death he was a virtual convert to Catholicism and not a despondent Calvinist, was totally out of order; finally, the transformation of the funeral procession of the victim into a triumphant celebration of a Catholic martyr was a blasphemy to all parties concerned.

Those intent upon a conviction in the Calas case argued not only that the cloth merchant and his family had plotted the murder of Marc-Antoine but that justification for such an act could be found in Calvinist doctrine. Indignation at this charge brought Voltaire's old adversary, La Beaumelle, to compose a lengthy letter on behalf of his co-religionists in which he heaped ridicule on the notion that members of the Reformed were enjoined to punish rebellious children severely, even to the point of death. The text of this letter was given to Pastor Rabaut, who drastically reduced its length and decided that it should be sent to Riquet de Bonrepos, attorney-general of the Toulouse parlement. In its revised form, the letter was published in January, 1762, as *La Calomnie confondue*.[2]

In their passionate apologia, Rabaut and La Beaumelle remind their readers that the case being made against the Calvinists is in no way novel; after all, the first Christians were charged by pagan society with committing all manner of monstrous acts. What was particularly lamentable in the present circumstances, however, was the way in which magistrates had joined priests in branding Calvinists as unnatural parents, thus exposing them to the fury of the credulous mob. The allegation that the death of Marc-Antoine Calas had been planned at a Huguenot meeting for worship and that it might even have been sanctioned by the synod of Nîmes, was too outlandish to be given credence even for a moment. Louis XV, whose ancestor Henri IV had been nurtured in the Reformed faith, must know that child-slaying was not part of Calvin's creed. In fact, His Majesty's Protestant subjects were not only loyal but totally pacific; they were, however, intent upon obtaining at least that freedom of conscience which Europe's Protestant states had long since accorded to their Catholic minorities.

Predictably, the boldness of *La Calomnie confondue* aroused the fury of those whom it specifically indicted, the judicial and ecclesiastical authorities at Toulouse. On behalf of the Catholic clergy, the abbé de Montezat published a brief rejoinder in which, having cited Voltaire's celebrated comments about the *âme atroce* of Calvin and about the role played by the French reformer in the execution of Servet, he argued that fanaticism was an inherent characteristic of Protestantism in both its Lutheran and Calvinist form.[3] The magistrates of Toulouse did not need convincing; they denounced *La Calomnie confondue* as seditious and the work was condemned to be burned on March 8. Two days later, Jean Calas was found guilty and executed.

What transformed this execution into a European *cause célèbre* was, of course, the involvement of Voltaire. In mid-March, when the philosophe learned the bare outlines of the story from his friend Dominique Audibert, a Calvinist businessman from Marseilles who was paying a visit to Ferney, Voltaire's initial reaction was to assume the guilt of Calas; after all, during the Camisard rising, southern French Calvinists had proven that they were as capable of extravagant behaviour as Jansenist convulsionaries in Paris.[4] Yet the enormity of the allegations levelled at Calas and his fellow accused deeply troubled Voltaire; on closer examination, he saw that there were disturbing elements in the prosecution's case; finally, he was persuaded not only that Jean Calas had been a solid citizen and a decent family man but that he had died nobly, preserving his spiritual integrity until the end.

Voltaire's doubts about Calas's innocence were dispelled in mid-April when he talked with the merchant's youngest son, Donat, who had fled Nîmes for Geneva.[5] The candour of the boy's language and his moving description of the Calas's family life were totally convincing. Voltaire's perception was further sharpened by a reading of the brief for the Calas family composed by Théodore Sudre, a Toulouse lawyer who had risked his reputation by coming to their aid.[6] Rallying a devoted band of supporters in France and Switzerland, Voltaire began to orchestrate a campaign for the posthumous redemption of the name of Jean Calas in the spring of 1762. One of the key elements in Voltaire's strategy was to give maximum public exposure to the surviving members of the Calas family, whose gentleness of character would clearly dispel any lingering assumption that they were murderous fanatics. The philosophe used the good office of friends to persuade Madame Calas to travel to Paris and make a direct appeal to members of the ministry. The widow's stay in the capital (where she remained incognito) was subsidized by Protestant banking families and by Voltaire himself.

Voltaire noted that there were well-disposed people at court such as Controller-General Bertin, Madame de Pompadour, and her friend Doctor Quesnay who could arrange for Madame Calas to meet some of the judges in the case in advance. Since she was not especially eloquent (at one point Voltaire referred to her as "that silly little Huguenot"),[7] there would be no advantage in getting her to discuss her case with potential protectors; the sight of her in mourning, preferably with one or two of her children, would be enough; the main point was to arouse compassion for the Calas family, not antipathy towards the magistrates of Toulouse. To further advance the cause, Voltaire composed a number of letters purporting to be written by the survivors among the accused in the hope that this might persuade public opinion of the innocence of Jean Calas and force the government to intervene in the case.

These allegedly personal testimonials were followed on July 7 by letters to Chancellor Guillaume de Lamoignon and to the *conseil du roi*,[8] written by Voltaire but signed by Donat Calas, in which the young man formally appealed for a review of the case against his father, claiming that all Europe joined him in this petition.

Late in July, Voltaire fired two further salvoes in his battle to arouse public sympathy and force the ministry to act. The *Mémoire de Donat Calas* bears Voltaire's unmistakeable imprint. We Protestants, he has the young Calvinist confess, may have erred, like the Albigensians and Lollards before us, in condemning the worship of images and in challenging the doctrine of transubstantiation; but at least we erred in good faith. More recently, the 'confession' proceeds, our parents, by becoming both fanatical and subversive, committed spiritual excesses into which the sixteenth-century Guises had also fallen. But all that was past history: "The horrors of the Cévennes, committed by maddened peasants provoked by the unrestrained licence of the King's dragoons, have been forgotten, like the horrors of the Fronde."[9] The Huguenots had become devoted subjects of the King, ready to join the administration in checking the ultramontanist tendencies in the First Estate.

His own family,'Donat' goes on to remark, had always been on good terms with non-Calvinists; his mother was linked to some of the nation's noble houses. Perhaps after all, it was this very respectability, together with the family's relative wealth, which now aroused prejudice against them:

> It may be that a few merchants, jealous of the prosperity of a business run by members of another faith, stirred up the populace against us; but our constantly moderate behaviour would seem calculated in time to soften this antipathy.[10]

Voltaire's final contribution at this stage of the legal battle was a *Déclaration de Pierre Calas* in which he had one of Calas's sons declare:

> Blind prejudice caused our downfall; enlightened reason sympathizes with us today; the public, the ultimate judge of honour and shame, is already rehabilitating my father's memory; the King's council will confirm the verdict of the public if only it deigns to examine the evidence.[11]

Having put the facts as he understood them before the public, Voltaire turned his full attention to the problem of getting the *conseil du roi* to intervene in the case. It was of paramount importance to get Chancellor Guillaume de Lamoignon to support such an initiative, and Voltaire enlisted the marquise de Pompadour as well as the chancellor's son-in-law, the marquis de Nicolai, in this endeavour. As it turned out, the highest court in the kingdom was not eager to challenge the judgment of one of the nation's parlements at a time when provincial magistrates were increasingly eager to establish their autonomy; but, quite apart from this problem, the *conseil du roi* was empowered to make such a challenge only when it was asked to do so by two lawyers from its own ranks. In order to set this process in motion, Voltaire recruited some of the nation's most renowned lawyers to whom he forwarded copies of all the documentation he had so far accumulated for the defence.

First in the field was Pierre Mariette, an *avocat au conseil du roi* who began his brief by asking the parlementaires at Toulouse to transmit to Paris the original trial proceedings in the Calas case so that a proper review could be conducted. In the course of his argument, Mariette went on to point out how remarkable it was that the alleged justification of parricide in Calvinist doctrine which had played such an important role in the prosecution's case had escaped the notice of Sorbonne theologians since the sixteenth century.[12]

Mariette's submission was supplemented in August 1762 by a memorandum prepared by the eminent Elie de Beaumont and counter-signed by fifteen of his colleagues, including the well-known Boucher d'Argis. In his summation, Elie de Beaumont urged those entrusted with the supervision of French justice to establish in this case "whether our separated brethren are citizens or hangmen."[13] Voltaire thought this brief superior to that of Mariette, calling it a "masterpiece of reason, jurisprudence and eloquence."[14]

A third brief, this time in the name of Donat, Pierre, and Louis Calas, was prepared by Alexandre-Jérôme Loyseau de Mauléon, an independently wealthy lawyer who knew both Grimm and Rousseau and who had won a reputation early in his career by defending Borach Lévi, a converted Jew abandoned by his wife who had petitioned for the right to remarry. Loyseau de Mauléon exploited the theatrical side of his profession, using histrionic effects which Elie de Beaumont had not been able to produce. The opening passage of his memorandum gives us some idea of his style:

> Overwhelmed by the burden of living, a young man does himself in in his father's house.... The cries of despair which the father utters at the sight of his son's corpse are taken to be the cries of resistance and struggle made by the son as he calls out against his father's barbarity and, as a result, we see the most tender-hearted of parents put to death on the wheel for the crime of parricide.... Yet the 2 000 who witnessed this death shuddered as they watched.... The sight of this sublimely heroic death began to clear away the cloud of doubt which had spread over Toulouse.[15]

By the late summer of 1762, there were welcome indications that the plight of the Calas family had begun to touch those in a position to have the case reviewed. Towards the end of August, the King's mistress reported that Louis XV had been deeply moved after hearing an account of the trial and execution of the Protestant cloth merchant.[16] A month later, there was more good news: the man named as *rapporteur* in the case, Louis Thiroux de Crosne, was known to be sympathetic to the appellants.

Two developments threatened to disrupt the orderly pursuit of a revision in the Calas case. There was an alarmingly similar case of alleged parricide in the small town of Mazamet, near Castres. In March 1762 the local court had found Pierre-Paul Sirven guilty of murdering his daughter to prevent her conversion to Catholicism. The rest of the family had been condemned as accomplices. Voltaire persuaded the attorneys for the Calas family to avoid making any reference to this new case in their briefs in order not to jeopardize delicate negotiations under way to secure vital documents concerning the Calas trial. More alarming, from the philosophe's point of view, was the decision of Antoine Court de Gébelin early in 1763 to rush into print with *Les Lettres toulousaines*, a highly partisan tract which assigned full responsibility for the execution of Pastor Rochette and Jean Calas (as well as for the condemnation of Pierre-Paul Sirven) to clerical reaction and popular Catholic fanaticism. Voltaire was furious at this untimely outburst and pleaded with Moultou to persuade the author to withdraw the work. By grouping together actions which the magistrates of Toulouse were already too prone to see as part of a campaign of Calvinist illegality, the Huguenot pamphleteer was playing into the hands of his enemies.[17] Equally alarmed, the authorities of Geneva banned the work. In the end, Gébelin agreed to withdraw it from circulation, at least until the parlement at Toulouse had furnished the required documents for the revision in the Calas case.

As Voltaire had foreseen, the *Lettres toulousaines* was scarcely calculated to appeal to moderate opinion, especially in the Catholic camp. Gébelin's argument was transparently polemical: the civilized world had made steady progress since the Reformation, he began, but France remained sadly out of step with this forward movement. Toulouse, in particular, retained the persecuting instinct which it had developed in the middle ages. Europe's Catholics continued to adhere to incomprehensible dogma and to repeat liturgical exercises in an unintelligible language; the Roman clergy remained basically ignorant and often, as in the case of the *Pénitents Blancs*, corrupt. By contrast, Protestants had moved well beyond the concepts advanced by Luther and Calvin; they were all believers in toleration; their pastors were men of moral principle and well-formed intellect (even when, as in France, they were denied formal theological training in their homeland). There was in fact, Gébelin proceeded even more provocatively, solid evidence that France's Calvinist population was on the rise and that, as its influence expanded, it might one day emancipate the whole nation. In fact, one of the chief causes of the popular prejudice against the Calas family was undoubtedly resentment at the way in which they and their Protestant neighbours had re-established their economic ascendancy in Toulouse since the Revocation.[18]

In May 1763, the Toulouse parlement yielded up the documentation in the Calas case which had been requested by the *Conseil des Dépêches*. The next stage in the battle was, of course, to ask the *conseil du roi* to set aside the original verdict on the basis of this newly available material. Voltaire helped set the stage for this new round late in October by issuing the *Traité sur la tolérance* which he had finished in manuscript form at the end of 1762 but which he had held back in order not to damage the judicial negotiations between Paris and Toulouse.

During his research for this treatise Voltaire examined the substantial body of polemical literature on the subject of toleration published during the 1750s. He knew about the *Apologie de Louis XIV* written by the abbé Caveirac in 1758, but he was unaware of the many pamphlets supporting toleration written during the previous decade by Calvinists and philosophes, many of which he was able to borrow from Moultou. Voltaire found several flaws in this propaganda for religious freedom: it was long winded, solemn, and for the most part, crudely partisan, Catholics being painted as monsters, Calvinists as martyrs. If the sophisticated men and women who established the standards of French behaviour were to be converted to the idea of toleration, Voltaire reasoned, they must be amused, not irritated along the way. In fact, the best way to win people to the cause was to induce an indifference towards religious prejudices of all kinds while trying not to offend those still foolish enough to retain them.

Moultou, to whom Voltaire submitted his manuscript, was rather unhappy about his friend's philosophical perspective. The marginally orthodox pastor wondered why his friend had not stated that, among other things, intolerance was against divine law. Voltaire replied that such an argument would be difficult to sustain in the light of the cruel punishments for religious deviation set forth in Deuteronomy. Moultou was on surer ground when he reproached the philosophe for including in his text the old chestnut that the Huguenots were inherently republican, thus rationalizing the French government's continuing denial of their most basic rights. Voltaire replied that he had never said "that the Huguenots are in principle enemies of kings;"[19] but, he added, he was convinced that there was a good deal of truth in this view.

From the beginning, Voltaire aimed the *Traité* at the social and intellectual elite which, he hoped, would bring France into line with her more tolerant neighbours; the plan was to keep the work out of the booksellers' hands and to distribute it directly to well-placed ministers and magistrates as well as to a few discreet friends.

In its final published form, the *Traité sur la tolérance* is the most comprehensive and persuasive statement made on the subject by Voltaire. The philosophe deals with the Calas affair itself in the first fifteen pages of the *Traité*, summing up rather simplistically the arguments made in the legal briefs for the defence. He then turns his attention to the two themes which form the core of the *Traité*—the impact of the Reformation on European society and the debate over toleration. In his earlier comments on the influence of the Protestant Reformers, Voltaire had mixed praise for the victories which they had achieved over ignorance and superstition with sharp criticism of their political radicalism and their intolerance. In the *Traité*, perhaps influenced by Moultou, the philosophe took a far more positive view. Not only had the Protestants played a vital role in the emancipation of the human spirit, they had been burned at the stake for denouncing the doctrine of purgatory, the worship of relics, and the tyranny of the papacy. While it was true that the first generation of Reformers had been fanatics like their Catholic contemporaries, present-day Calvinists were well-read, gentle folk. In Alsace, where Lutherans predominated, there was neither political nor religious disorder. There might still be a few zealots among France's Huguenots, but nothing to compare with Jansenist society, as witness the convulsionaries of Saint-Médard.[20]

Voltaire's second theme was that religious toleration was the best guarantee of social stability and prosperity. Why could the government not at least allow Calvin's disciples the same conditions which had been given Catholics in England—freedom of conscience and a valid form of legitimizing their family status, balanced if need be by a veto on public worship and a denial of public office.[21]

Apart from the pragmatic advantages of toleration, there were philosophical arguments in its favour. Freedom of conscience was one of the most fundamental principles of natural law; the ancients, all of whom worshipped a single supreme being, had regarded the diversity of religious cults as a source of strength, not weakness. The Jewish tradition in this area, from which Christians had derived their notions of religious freedom, was ambiguous: there had been brutal theocracy at the beginning, then gentle tolerance in the Essene communities in Christ's time. As for those who cited the words of Jesus ("Make them come in"), they had confused what was intended as an injunction to press home an argument with a licence to kill. However, contrary to what had been written by Catholic propagandists, Christians had been, at least since the time of Constantine, persecutors rather than victims. Recent French practice was in this tradition: since 1745, eight Calvinist pastors had been executed whose only crime had been to pray for their King in faulty French and to give bread and wine to a few empty-headed rustics!

Voltaire conceded that there were cases in which intolerance might be justified. Fanatics were not deserving of freedom, nor were those who preached homicide, and Versailles had been well within its rights in expelling the Jesuits, whose constitution clearly violated French law.

The government's reaction to the *Traité sur la tolérance* was hesitant; copies of the work were seized early in June 1764 and some distributors were briefly imprisoned. The fact that the author's much more provocative *Dictionnaire philosophique portatif* was being sold under the counter during this same period no doubt increased the administration's nervousness.

The Calvinists reacted unfavourably to the *Traité*. Paul Rabaut was deeply disturbed at reports about the passages in the work which charged Christians with initiating persecution against pagan society;[22] while Elie Bertrand felt that, since the spiritual freedom proposed by Voltaire was based on indifference, it ignored the deep passions latent in all men which, if unharnessed, were bound one day to flare up anew in partisan conflict.[23] Voltaire answered that the Christians, like the Jews before them, had always been furiously partisan, murdering those who did not share their view. Catholics at least were honest in this respect, since they insisted on total acceptance of dogma handed down from above; but Protestants violated their own teachings every time they persecuted dissidents, since they proclaimed themselves believers in freedom of conscience. Voltaire added that it was singularly graceless that the Calvinists, for whom he had written the *Traité*, should take offence at it.[24]

In a postscript to the *Traité*, Voltaire noted that, while he had been writing his apologia for religious freedom, the notorious abbé Caveirac had brought out *L'Accord de la Religion et de l'Humanité sur l'intolérance* which the *philosophe* denounced as "a holy libel, worthy of an Inquisitor."[25] A brief examination of this and other works dealing with religious freedom written by Catholics and published in 1762 reveals the confused state of mind regarding this issue in ecclesiastical circles at the time of the Calas affair.

In *L'Accord de la Religion*, Caveirac returned to the argument which he had developed four years earlier in the *Apologie de Louis XIV*: civil intolerance against heretics is not only sanctioned by the scriptures and therefore right in itself; it is also, despite arguments to the contrary, effective in the defence of the faith. The prejudiced views of the *philosophes* notwithstanding, the abbé argued, the Revocation had been "a violent operation to which it had been necessary to subject the nation."[26] The anti-Calvinist policies of Louis XIV had been remarkably successful, radically reducing the Calvinists' numbers and shoring up the security of the state. If only the German princes of the sixteenth century had acted with similar vigour, the scourge of Protestantism would never have materialized. The granting of religious freedom to the Calvinists along the lines suggested by the philosophes might conceivably increase the nation's prosperity and its population, but it would bring with it even greater disadvantages. While it was a matter of some distress that the many Huguenots born of 'Desert' marriages were illegitimate, the males among them did after all make good recruiting material for the King's armies!

By the 1760s, few representatives of the First Estate were ready to commit themselves publicly to the defence of intolerance which had made Caveirac notorious. In an essay published at about the time Calas was being executed, the abbé Fonbonne urged his fellow Catholics to treat Calvinists as good citizens possessed of a genuine if misguided faith, loyal subjects who had long since abandoned the extravagances of their sixteenth-century predecessors. The violence visited upon the Huguenots during the Revocation period had been utterly unjustified; the moderate policy which Louis XV had adopted towards his non-conforming subjects was sound and had already proven itself with the refusal of the Calvinists to collaborate with France's enemies in the recent wartime crisis. Only through patience and gentle persuasion would the work of religious reunion be resumed and completed.[27]

The abbé Fonbonne's approach was paralleled by that of the abbé Pluquet in the *Dictionnaire des Hérésies* published in the same year. In the comments which he made about Calvin, Pluquet was clearly influenced by Voltaire, as his portrait of the founder of the French Reformed church indicates:

> There emerged then a second Reformation which had as its leader a skilful theologian, an excellent writer, a clear logician, a witty mind and a clever sophist. To these qualities he brought imagination, an unshakeable conviction and all the feeling for power which fanaticism engenders, the love of dominating and the desire for fame.[28]

Recapitulating Bossuet, Pluquet went on to remark that the inevitable consequences of Calvin's invitation to seek all truth in scripture or in individual consciences had been spiritual chaos and, ultimately, the emergence of Socinianism. However, the furious passion with which the King's armies had attempted to extirpate heresy in the late seventeenth century had been tragically misspent. The Camisards had rebelled only when driven to do so by their tormentors. More recently, state and church had resorted to the more humane methods which alone stood some chance of producing the much-to-be-desired rallying of heretics to the faith.

Meanwhile, the parlement of Toulouse had furnished the *conseil du roi* with the full documentation from the original Calas trial. Armed with this, Mariette in January 1764 produced new *Observations pour la dame veuve Calas et sa famille* in which he argued that the case for the prosecution had in the last analysis rested on nothing more solid than the gossip of biased witnesses: "Enthusiasm and fanaticism ended up providing the court with nothing more than hearsay, suspicions and so-called probabilities."[29]

The arguments put forward by Mariette proved conclusive. On June 4, the supporters of the Calas family won a signal triumph: in the presence of a number of sympathizers, including ministers and intendants, the *conseil du roi* by unanimous vote threw out the earlier judgment on procedural grounds. The battle was, of course, only half won; full vindication of the Calas family depended on the willingness of the *Conseil des Requêtes* to re-try the case.

The most comprehensive of the briefs arguing the case for a revision of the original verdict was drawn up by Elie de Beaumont, who pointed to the overwhelming evidence of Marc-Antoine's persistent Calvinism. On behalf of the children, Elie de Beaumont prepared a separate memorandum which was countersigned by a number of his colleagues, including Loyseau de Mauléon and Mariette, before being presented to the forty-member *Conseil des Requêtes* in January 1765.

To supplement the arguments of the lawyers, Voltaire wrote an open letter to his friend Damilaville on March 1, 1765, in which he recapitulated the story of his own involvement in the case. He had told himself at the beginning, he reminded Damilaville, that acts of Calvinist fanaticism were believable, as had been evidenced in the Camisard revolt; but, on reflection, he had recalled that the Cevenol prophets were intoxicated adolescents; the notion that an elderly man of whatever creed would murder his son out of religious zeal had been too unnatural to be believed. Donat Calas had confirmed these second thoughts; what had then been unbelievably difficult was to persuade the world at large of the innocence of Jean Calas, especially the people of Languedoc, who seem to have been possessed of religious madness ever since the time of Simon de Montfort; just when wisdom seemed about to prevail over zealotry in the Calas business, the condemnation of Sirven suggested that this rage had still not abated.[30]

On March 9, 1765, the *Conseil des Requêtes* gave the Calas family entire satisfaction: all were fully discharged of responsibility for the death of Marc-Antoine Calas; their original interrogation and imprisonment were condemned as gratuitously harsh and injurious; they were awarded substantial damages; most important, Jean Calas was posthumously cleared of all guilt. On April 10, Madame Calas and her son Pierre were received by Vice-Chancellor Maupeou, through whom they transmitted their thanks to Louis XV for his sympathetic concern during the recent trial.

The judgment exonerating the Calas family was applauded and celebrated in a variety of ways. For Voltaire, it was not only the best fifth act to a tragedy ever written but, even more significantly, the first clear victory of sweet reason over superstition and fanaticism. Yet, in a letter to Elie Bertrand, the philosophe warned that the major breakthrough in the struggle for toleration (for which the vindication of Calas might normally have prepared the way) was not likely to occur. Voltaire went on to suggest (as had the authors of *Le Conciliateur* in 1754) that true religious freedom would not be achieved until church and state were separated:

> People are not yet mature enough (for toleration). They do not realize that one must separate all forms of religion from all forms of government and that religion ought no more to be a political matter than one's choice of cuisine. One ought to be allowed to worship God in one's own way, just as one would be permitted to eat according to one's own taste.[31]

Voltaire's comment about the significance of the verdict in the Calas case was echoed by the key supporter of the cause in the ministry, Choiseul, who wondered whether all the jubilation over the revised verdict was not disproportionate: "The original judgment in the Calas case was the product of human frailty which only brought suffering to one family; the *dragonnades* of M. de Louvois brought unhappiness to a whole century."[32] Impressed by these comments, Voltaire sent them along to a number of his Protestant correspondents who tended to assume that their general emancipation was now a foregone conclusion.

The lengthy struggle to restore the name of Jean Calas had been supported in a variety of ways by France's cultural community. One of the nation's most celebrated artists, Carmontelle, had painted a moving portrait of the widow Calas and her family as they awaited the verdict of the King's council in the *Conciergerie*. An engraving taken from this portrait was sold by subscription throughout Europe to help defray the family's legal costs. As a reminder of his own involvement in the case, Voltaire kept one of these engravings by his bedside at Ferney.

Following the verdict which posthumously exonerated Calas, three contemporary poets expressed the hope that spiritual understanding between Frenchmen would begin to replace the mindless prejudice and intolerance which had led to the tragic deaths of Marc-Antoine Calas and his father. Adrien Michel Hyacinthe Blin de Sainmore called the martyred father back to life, portraying him as a respectable businessman with an open-minded attitude towards his Catholic neighbours, eager for ecumenical reconciliation.[33] A second poet, Edouard Thomas Simon, summoned the shade of Marc-Antoine from hell (to which he had been assigned as a suicide) and had him plead for an end to the mix of religious exaltation and despair which had brought him to take his own life.[34] In like manner, Pierre Jean Baptiste Nougaret had Marc-Antoine surface briefly from the lower depths, confess to suicide, then condemn the Toulouse mob for relaying the monstrous notion that his father had been guilty of parricide.[35]

The Calas affair overshadowed but did not quite obscure a second, almost contemporaneous, case of alleged Protestant parricide. The central figure in this new drama was Elisabeth Sirven, the feeble-minded daughter of a Huguenot land steward (*feudiste*). Elisabeth disappeared from her home near Mazamet in Langedoc on March 6, 1760; shortly afterwards, the bishop of Castres, Jean Sebastien de Barral, informed the family that Elisabeth had applied for instruction in the Catholic faith and had been placed in a local convent. Pierre-Paul Sirven, Elisabeth's father, was convinced that any protest at his daughter's confinement would be futile. In any event evidence that his daughter was suffering grave mental and spiritual distress as a result of her confinement convinced the bishop to order her release. Back home, Elisabeth still seemed seriously disturbed; the family tried to restrict her movements, although her father made no objection to her daily attendance at mass. Then, during the night of December 15-16, 1760, Elisabeth disappeared. Early in the new year, her body was found at the bottom of a well.

The hypothesis of a religiously inspired parricide upon which the judges at Toulouse had built their case against the Calas family provided a suggestive precedent for the judges at Mazamet, who ordered the arrest of Pierre-Paul Sirven, his wife, and two surviving daughters. Happily, the accused were alerted to the proceedings against them and fled across the border to Lausanne. The verdict, following a trial in absentia, was handed down on March 24, 1762: all four accused were found guilty, the parents to be hanged, their daughters banished.[36]

When Voltaire learned of this new tragedy, his first instinct was to ensure that any efforts on behalf of this second Calvinist family in distress would not jeopardize the ongoing Calas campaign.[37] In any event, Voltaire noted, despite apparent parallels between the two cases, there were clear differences: on the positive side, there was not even any circumstantial evidence upon which to base a parricide charge against Sirven *père*; on the other hand, there was no Huguenot 'martyr' to redeem this time, not even the humiliation of a prison sentence to undo and, worse still, the accused had made themselves guilty of contempt of court by fleeing the King's justice.

The effort to reverse the verdict in the Sirven case began in earnest in January 1766, when Elie de Beaumont, with the aid of Voltaire, his friend Damilaville, and the lawyer Jean-Baptiste-Guy Target, drew up a brief aimed at persuading the *conseil du roi* to review the original judgment on procedural grounds.[38] A full two years later, the King's council ruled that it could not act in cases where contempt of court was at issue; it could only intervene following an appropriate trial in the original lower court. In line with this judgment, Sirven *père* was encouraged to travel to Toulouse, having been assured by Voltaire that the city where Calas had been condemned had cast off its reactionary image and was now a bastion of enlightenment.[39] Sirven was able to confirm this impression soon after his arrival in the southern city. He was invited to stay with the son of one of Toulouse's leading magistrates. He found an able defence attorney in Pierre Firmin de Lacroix, and Doctor Charles Le Roy of the medical faculty at Montpellier provided him with the written opinion that all the evidence pointed to suicide as the cause of his daughter's death.

Despite all these favourable developments, the Toulouse judges ruled that Sirven's request for a re-trial must be heard at Mazamet, where his ordeal had begun. The *feudiste* dutifully surrendered to the local authorities there. He was subsequently imprisoned, interrogated, then, after paying a fine for his original contempt of court, released, on November 16, 1769. At last the way lay open for a formal appeal to the Toulouse magistrates to have the original charges against him annulled. Firmin de Lacroix drew up a memorandum with this in mind;[40] Voltaire meanwhile speculated that it might help to get the support of the archbishop of Toulouse, Loménie de Brienne, whose radical views concerning toleration had been published (albeit anonymously) while he was a theology student in the 1750s. Unfortunately, the liberal but ambitious prelate was then lobbying to be made a member of the Académie française (he would be elected in the fall of 1770) as well as to be chosen archbishop of Paris, so that his inclination was to play down his 'philosophic' past.[41]

What finally turned the tide in Sirven's favour was the appointment in November 1770 of a new, liberal president of the Toulouse parlement, Antoine Joseph de Niquet. The Protestant's vindication followed a year later, on November 25, 1771, when the magistrates of Toulouse pronounced Sirven and his family innocent of the charges levelled against them and restored their good name as well as the property which had been confiscated from them following their condemnation.[42] Early in the next year, Pierre-Paul Sirven and his family gathered at Ferney to celebrate their vindication with the man who had done the most to achieve it.[43]

Six years earlier, in the heat of the battle he was waging to obtain justice for two Huguenot families charged with murdering their children, Voltaire had composed an *Avis public sur les parricides imputés aux Calas et aux Sirven*. This impassioned tract was specifically aimed at Europe's Protestant rulers rather than at the French public. Voltaire begins his argument in this text by noting that this most recent flare-up of religious fanaticism had been based on the deep-rooted conviction among Catholics in Languedoc that Protestants were in the habit of murdering their children to prevent them from abjuring heresy, at a time when somewhat more plausible notions such as the belief in the devil and in witchcraft had long since been laughed out of court everywhere in Europe. What was really alarming, Voltaire pursued, was the broadly based anti-Calvinist prejudice which had recently been fuelled by writers such as the abbé Caveirac. This popularly rooted antipathy had brought public support for the hanging of Protestant pastors and the condemnation to the galleys of Huguenot laymen.[44]

No doubt Calvinists and Lutherans could be as pitiless towards their adversaries as Catholics, Voltaire continued. Champions of the Roman communion were on solid ground when they indicted Calvin and his followers for criminal conduct in the Servet case or during the Camisard insurrection. The ideal solution would be a return to the situation which obtained before the reign of the Emperor Theodosius, when religious nonconformity was not a crime. In the meantime, the best one could hope for was that Europe's reigning monarchs continue to defend the cause of toleration, if need be in the face of the persecuting which still threatened innocent non-conformists such as the Calas and Sirven families.[45]

The long battle which had been fought on behalf of two Huguenot families falsely charged with parricide constitutes a key chapter in the history of Protestant emancipation. Those accused of conspiring to murder their children in order to prevent their conversion revealed themselves to be not religious zealots (as even Voltaire had at first assumed in the Calas case) but eminently respectable citizens as well as devoted subjects of the crown. The old myths about the Reformed—that they were not only fanatical but also republican and subversive, were now replaced by images of middle-class propriety. The Calas and Sirven families had lived out a real-life *drame bourgeois* for all to see and admire. The battle for Protestant toleration was far from over, but its chief protagonists had won new allies for the engagements which still lay ahead.

---

1. D. Bien, *The Calas Affair* (Princeton, 1960), sets the tragedy in its contemporary political and socio-economic context. E. Nixon, *Voltaire and the Calas Case* (London, 1961), offers a detailed analysis of Voltaire's involvement in the campaign to rehabilitate Calas's name. One of the best studies of the affair is still to be found in A. Coquerel, *Jean Calas et sa famille. Etude historique d'après les documents originaux* (Paris, 1875).

2. P. Rabaut and L.-A. de La Beaumelle, *La Calomnie confondue, ou Mémoire dans laquelle on réfute une nouvelle accusation intentée aux protestants de la province du Languedoc, à l'occasion de l'affaire du Sr Calas, détenu dans les prisons de Toulouse* ('Au desert,' 1762).

3. Abbé de Montezat, *Observations sur un mémoire qui paraît sous le nom de Paul Rabaut, intitulé 'La Calomnie confondue'* (n.p., 1762).

4. Voltaire to Antoine Jean Gabriel Le Bault, March 22, 1762, Best. D. 10382.

5. Voltaire to Damilaville, March 1, 1765, Best. D. 12425.

6. Th. Sudre, *Mémoire pour le sieur Jean Calas, négociant de cette ville; Dame Anne-Rose Cabibel son épouse; et le sieur Jean-Pierre Calas, un de leurs enfants* (Toulouse, 1762). Sudre was kept from practising law for a number of years as a result of his courageous defense of Calas, as Voltaire later learned. See Voltaire to D'Argental, December 10, 1766, Best. D. 13722. It is not clear whether Voltaire

knew of a second brief prepared for the defense. This was: J. M. de Lassalle, *Observations pour le sieur Jean Calas, la dame Cabibel, son épouse, et le sieur Pierre Calas, leur fils* (Toulouse, 1762).

7. Voltaire to the Argentals, September 14, 1762, Best. D. 10702.

8. "A Monsieur le chancelier,";" Requête au roi en son conseil," July 7, 1762, in Voltaire, *Oeuvres* [M] XXIV, pp. 379-82.

9. *Mémoire de Donat Calas pour son père, sa mère, et son frère*, July 22, 1762, ibid., p. 384.

10. Ibid., p. 386.

11. *Déclaration de Pierre Calas*, July 23, 1762, ibid., p. 397.

12. P. Mariette, *Mémoire pour Dame Anne-Rose Cabibel, veuve du sieur Jean Calas, marchand à Toulouse; Louis et Louis-Donat Calas, leur fils, et Anne-Rose et Anne Calas, leur filles, demandeurs en cassation d'un arrêt du parlement de Toulouse du 9 mars 1762* (Paris, 1762), p. 85.

13. J.-B.-J. Elie de Beaumont, *Mémoire à consulter et consultation pour la dame Anne-Rose Cabibel, veuve Calas, et pour ses enfants* (Paris, 1762), p. 42.

14. Voltaire to Bernard Louis Chauvelin, September 21, 1762, Best. D. 10702.

15. A.-J. Loyseau de Mauléon, *Mémoire pour Donat, Pierre et Louis Calas* (Paris, 1762), p. 1.

16. Madame de Pompadour to the duc de Fitz-James, August 27, 1762, Best. D. 10677.

17. Voltaire to Moultou, March 14, 1763, Best. D. 11096.

18. A. Court de Gébelin, *Les Toulousaines, ou Lettres historiques et apologétiques en faveur de la religion réformée et de divers protestants condamnés dans ces derniers temps par le parlement de Toulouse et dans le Haut Languedoc* ('Edinbourg,' 1763), p. 24. For a full account of Court de Gébelin's lobbying on behalf of the Protestant cause at court, see P. Schmidt, *Court de Gébelin à Paris 1763-84. Etude sur le protestantisme français pendant la seconde moitié du XVIIIe siècle* (St. Blaise, 1908).

19. Voltaire to Moultou, January 9, 1763, Best. D. 10897.

20. Voltaire, *Traité sur la tolerance, à l'occasion de la mort de Jean Calas* (1763) in *L'affaire Calas et autres affaires*, ed. J. Van den Heuvel (Paris, 1975), p. 111.

21. Ibid., p. 110.

22. Paul Rabaut to Moultou, October 24, 1755, Dardier, *Rabaut, Lettres à divers*, I, pp. 116-17.

23. Elie Bertrand to Voltaire, c. December 15, 1763, Best. D. 11562.

24. Voltaire to Elie Bertrand, December 30, 1763, Best. D. 11590.

25. Voltaire, *Traité*, p. 181.

26. Abbé J. Novi de Caveirac, *L'accord de la religion et de l'humanité sur l'intolérance* (n.p., 1762), p. 122.

27. Abbé Fonbonne, *Avis à messieurs les religionnaires de France, ouvrage propre à leur instruction, et à rappeller les Protestants à l'ancienne croyance* (Paris, 1762), pp. 9-10.

28. Abbé Pluquet, *Mémoires pour servir à l'histoire des Egaremens de l'esprit humain par rapport à la religion chrétienne: ou Dictionnaire des Hérésies, des Erreurs et des Schismes* (Paris, 1762), p. 270.

29. Mariette, *Obversations pour la dame veuve Calas et sa famille* (Paris, 1764), p. 3.

30.   Voltaire to Damilaville, March 1, 1765, Best. D. 12425.

31.   Voltaire to Elie Bertrand, March 19, 1765, Best. D. 12479.

32.   Choiseul to Voltaire, c. September 10, 1766, Best. D. 13549.

33.   Adrien Michel Hyacinthe Blin de Sainmore, *Jean Calas à sa femme et à ses enfants. Héroïde* (Paris, 1765).

34.   Edouard Thomas Simon, *Marc-Antoine Calas, le suicide, à l'univers, héroïde. Histoire des malheurs de la famille des Calas* (Paris, 1765).

35.   Pierre Jean Baptiste Nougaret, *L'ombre de Calas, le suicide, à sa famille et à son ami dans les fers, précédé d'une lettre à M. de Voltaire* (Paris, 1765). In a letter to Nougaret, Voltaire commented that the poet's work demonstrated the way in which creative art could change political attitudes: with men such as Nougaret, Parnassus had triumphed over the most reactionary of parlements. Voltaire to Nougaret, April 20, 1765. Best. D. 12562.

36.   An analysis of the Sirven case is offered in C. Rabaud, *Sirven, Etude historique sur l'avènement de la tolérance* (Paris, 1891) as well as in E. Galland, *L'Affaire Sirven, Etude historique d'après les documents originaux* (Mazamet, 1910).

37.   Voltaire to Debrus, November/December, 1762. Best. D. 10822.

38.   Elie de Beaumont, *Mémoire à consulter et consultation pour Pierre-Paul Sirven, commissaire à terrier dans le diocèse de Castres, présentement à Genève, accusé d'avoir fair mourir sa seconde fille pour l'empêcher de se faire catholique; et pour ses deux filles* (Paris, 1768).

39.   The impression that Toulouse had radically changed its outlook was conveyed to Voltaire by his friend the abbé Audra. V. Abbé Joseph Audra to Voltaire, November 2, 1768, Best. D. 15287. Voltaire relayed this impression to those involved in the defence of Sirven.

40.   Firmin de Lacroix, *Mémoire pour le sieur Pierre-Paul Sirven appellant contre les consuls et communauté de Mazamet* (Toulouse, 1770).

41.   When Voltaire indicated his surprise and irritation at the failure of the archbishop of Toulouse to get involved in the defense of Sirven, d'Alembert wrote to reassure him that Loménie de Brienne was indeed well disposed but that his position precluded his committing himself publicly. V. d'Alembert to Voltaire, July 25, 1770, Best. D. 16545 and same to same, December 4, 1770, Best. D. 16802.

42.   The *premier président* wrote the philosophe to give him the news directly. Antoine Joseph de Niquet to Voltaire, November 27, 1771, Best. D. 17478.

43.   Voltaire to Anne Duvoisin, January 13, 1772, Best. D. 17554.

44.   *Avis au public sur les parricides imputés aux Calas et au Sirven* (1766), *Oeuvres* [M], XXV, p. 524.

45.   Ibid., p. 537.

Controller-general Turgot: Would-be Protestant emancipator.

CHAPTER XVI

Large Expectations, Limited Gains: The Reform Efforts of Turgot and Malesherbes, 1774-1776

The character of the young prince who mounted the French throne in May 1774 was such that both pro- and anti-Calvinist groups rejoiced at the news of his accession. The Huguenots and their friends in the philosophe camp saw in the nineteen-year old Louis XVI a man of compassion, too sensitive to allow any of his subjects to suffer oppression or discrimination. Defenders of the status quo, on the other hand, were confident that the King's piety would preserve him from any inclination to rescind laws which had been drawn up to protect the nation from heresy. Both of these perceptions were to be proven accurate.[1]

By naming two reform-minded liberals, Turgot and Malesherbes, to his ministry early in his reign, Louis XVI raised high hopes among his Protestant subjects and their supporters. Yet the King in the end refused to accept the view of these ministers that the time had come to grant the Reformed the right to worship and to marry legally. Predictably, this royal diffidence was seconded by the clerical conservatives who dominated the Assembly of the Clergy which opened in July 1775. It is worth noting, however, that the First Estate was no longer unanimous in its support of repression: during the first years of Louis XVI's rule, an influential group of Jansenist magistrates and clerics repudiated the anti-Calvinist polemic which had been spouted by their spiritual forebears in the 1680s and committed themselves to the lobby for Calvinist relief. The Huguenots, meanwhile, did little to help the administration's limited efforts on their behalf by reviving the internal squabbling which had periodically plagued them since the Revocation.

When they received news of Louis XVI's accession, Calvinists from various parts of the nation forwarded to Versailles professions of royalism made more ardent by expectation.[2] At the same time, a group of Huguenots in the Auch area provoked the local archbishop by erecting a house of worship in his diocese. The King's first council meeting was in fact plagued by issues relating to the Protestant question: the prelate's protest, a counter-petition by the temple-builders and an enquiry from Calvinist refugees asking about the government's position if they returned to France.

Concerned but uninformed, Louis XVI asked his chief minister, the elderly Maurepas, for advice. Maurepas noted that the administration had for some years been following a policy of tacit toleration as far as Protestant public worship was concerned. Because the King was reluctant to offer any guidance in an area of policy which was so new to him, the council ended up complying with the archbishop's request that temple-building in his diocese be prohibited. Fortunately for those most directly affected, the Protestants' agent at court, Antoine Court de Gébelin, intervened with Maurepas to have this prohibition annulled.[3]

News of the archbishop's effort to subvert established government policy quickly spread. Voltaire, who was convinced that Louis XVI was by nature tolerant, remained optimistic. He wrote to Pastor Gal-Pomaret in September 1774, offering comfort and reassurance, and speculated that the administration was on the verge of conceding a legal form of marriage to the Reformed.[4]

Rumours about a favourable disposition by the government towards the Calvinists circulated throughout the winter. Late in March 1775, the Jansenist abbé Clément du Tremblai, having heard (perhaps through his friend the magistrate Robert de Saint-Vincent) that the Paris parlement was about to debate the issue of civil toleration for the Protestants, wrote the eminent Jansenist jurist Adrien Le Paige asking for the loan of scholarly works on the subject.[5]

Le Paige was the central figure in a small but influential coterie of Jansenist jurists and clerics who had come to feel both sympathy for and solidarity with the Huguenots. The spiritual predecessors of these eighteenth-century Jansenists, the theologians Arnauld and Nicole, had joined enthusiastically in the polemical assault against the Reformed during the Revocation era. Le Paige and his associates, however, had learned what policing of conscience could lead to when members of their own sect were obliged to present *billets de confession* before being admitted to the sacraments during the 1750s. The disciples of Jansenius had always stood for spiritual liberty and integrity. They now recognized that the Calvinists, who had suffered even more than they from would-be defenders of orthodoxy, must be released from civil and religious discrimination if they were ever to be won back to the true faith.

In answer to the inquiry which the abbé Clément had made of him in the spring of 1775, Le Paige confessed that he was unable to furnish any of the standard contemporary treatises on toleration. Instead, he suggested that Clément consult the reflections on the subject which he had published in the *Nouvelles ecclésiastiques* at the height of the *Bélisaire* affair. In that 1768 text, Le Paige had strongly defended the government's role in softening the Sorbonne's censure of Marmontel. He then went on to address the larger question of state intervention in matters of faith. Le Paige argued that France's kings had let themselves be persuaded by priestly counsellors, notably by Jesuits, into adopting a policy of persecuting religious groups which posed no threat to the state—the Revocation of the Edict of Nantes and the condemnation of Port-Royal were cases in point.

Having referred Clément to his earlier comments on the question, Le Paige conceded that there were times when religious non-conformity took on a subversive character, requiring vigorous action by the secular arm: the Albigensian and Camisard rebellions were cases in point. Le Paige concluded that what was needed was a flexible policy towards dissenters based on an evaluation of their threat to the social order. By implication, the jurist was saying, the Reformed were now clearly deserving of civil toleration.[6]

The convergence in views of philosophes such as Voltaire and Jansenists such as Le Paige that the government of Louis XVI would grant the Calvinists some change in status was based as much on the ministerial appointments made early in the reign as it was on an analysis of the King's inner disposition. On the surface, this optimism was well founded. The government's chief policy-makers in the first two years of the reign— Maurepas, Turgot, and Malesherbes—all supported toleration in principle, although their approach to the formulation of legislation in this delicate area varied substantially.

The elderly Maurepas was easily the most prudent in the matter. He was familiar with the Calvinists' situation as a result of having read the chevalier de Beaumont's *L'Accord parfait* and he shared the view held by many philosophes as well as by Huguenots that the Revocation was the result of a Jesuit plot upon the conscience of Louis XIV in which the turncoat Maintenon had been an eager accomplice.

Maurepas was initially inclined to recommend "a return to the period when the Protestants had privileges which have since been revoked."[7] Several factors brought the King's chief minister to change his mind. For one thing, the new King's reverence for Louis XIV made it unwise to recommend any sudden break with past policies. In the second place, there was always the possibility that the Calvinists, if granted civil marriage, would press for the right to hold public office and to have their own pastors.[8]

While Maurepas ended up a rather diffident partisan of toleration, the former intendant of Limoges, Turgot, who entered the ministry as secretary of state for the navy in July 1774 and succeeded to the vital post of controller-general on August 24, was a committed partisan. As we have seen, Turgot's views of state-church relations had been formed in the early 1750s during seminary discussions with Loménie de Brienne and Morellet. Concerned with the problems posed to the administration by the stubborn persistence of both Calvinist and Jansenist non-conformity, the young seminarian had ended up advocating what amounted to separation of church and state.[9]

In his career as a magistrate and later as intendant at Limoges, Turgot had demonstrated his tolerance in practice. He had argued passionately for the rehabilitation of Calas. Now, as controller-general, he chose as collaborators men known for their liberal religious views—Du Pont de Nemours, Condorcet, and the abbés Morellet and de Véri.

The third cabinet member from whom the Huguenots might expect to receive a sympathetic hearing was Malesherbes, who joined the ministry as secretary of state for the King's household on July 21, 1775. Malesherbes thereby took over the 'new Catholic' portfolio which, for an astonishing half-century, had been administered by the intractable comte de Saint-Florentin. In fact, just a few months earlier, Saint-Florentin had been forced to recognize that his attitude was anachronistic: in March, when he recommended the renewal of the ban on the free disposition of Calvinists' property which had been reconfirmed on a three-year basis since the Revocation, the ministry had taken no action in the matter, thus allowing the law to lapse and thereby releasing the Reformed from one of the key restrictions placed upon their economic activity since 1685.[10]

Malesherbes, Soulavie suggests, was motivated to do something for the Huguenots at least in part out of guilt feelings at the repressive role played by his ancestor Intendant Bâville of Languedoc on the eve of the Camisard rebellion.[11] In any event, he was no stranger to the legal and political complexities of the Calvinist question. In the process of examining the papers left by his father, Chancellor Lamoignon, he had run across the memorandum dealing with the Protestants submitted to the government in 1752 by Attorney-General Joly de Fleury. He was also familiar with at least one other important work on the toleration issue—the *Mémoire théologique et politique* of 1755.[12] The appointment of Malesherbes to the cabinet gave hope to knowledgeable Calvinists that a substantial improvement in their condition might soon be forthcoming. Appeals began to arrive on the minister's desk requesting intervention in favour of Huguenots whose marital status was being challenged or whose children had been abducted for Catholic schooling. At the same time, the clerical lobby, nervous about the new minister's liberalism, pressed him to deal with the distribution of heretical literature and the establishment of separate Protestant burial grounds. Caught in this vigorous crossfire, Malesherbes found equivocation to be the best means of protecting the Huguenots from priestly harassment.

The Protestants did not have too long to wait for evidence that there was a change in government policy in their regard. The *guerre des farines*, a series of urban riots resulting from grain scarcity and high bread prices which began in late April 1775, provided Turgot with an opportunity to bring the administration and the Calvinists into direct official contact for the first time since 1685. Early in May, in an effort to stop the spread of disorder, Turgot wrote to the nation's bishops asking them to use their influence in restoring calm, and then boldly addressed the same message to the pastors of Lower Languedoc. The pastors replied at the end of the month, reassuring the controller-general that the patriotism of France's Calvinists was ample guarantee against the kind of brigandage which had been afflicting certain parts of the nation. They added rather pointedly that they were prepared to wait upon the King's grace as far as the critical question of their toleration was concerned.[13]

Turgot showed this same boldness in behalf of the Huguenots as the arrangements got under way for the coronation of the King, which was to take place at Rheims in June. The controller-general thought that this would be an appropriate time for the King to delete the traditional pledge to extirpate heresy from his coronation oath. In an energetic letter to Louis XVI, the draft of which he had earlier submitted to Malesherbes, Turgot pointed out that Henri IV, Louis XIII, and Louis XIV had all omitted this pledge from the coronation ceremony.

On first reading, Louis XVI was impressed by the arguments advanced by Turgot and by the suggested modification in the wording of the coronation service during which, instead of vowing to extinguish non-conformity, he would have promised that "all the churches of my kingdom should depend on my protection and justice."[14] Yet in the end, he rejected his minister's advice.

Probably the most significant factor in the King's negative decision was the change of mind which had occurred in Maurepas. Vexed at the unilateral initiatives on behalf of the Protestants which Turgot had taken and jealous at the increasing influence in cabinet of the controller-general, especially during the *guerre des farines*, the King's chief minister counselled Louis against making any alteration in the coronation ceremony. Maurepas noted that the oath to eradicate heresy was in any case purely symbolic and in no way obligated the monarch to pursue a policy of active persecution.[15]

In the end, after consulting with close advisors, including Maurepas, the King turned down Turgot's suggestion that the coronation oath be modified. He explained his decision in a note to the minister, remarking that Turgot had acted as an *honnête homme*, using the kind of forthright language which responsible sovereigns preferred to hear; his letter would be kept confidential.[16]

Encouraged by this courteous response, Turgot drew up a general memorandum on the toleration question. Political as well as religious factors, he wrote, dictated that the King "allow each of his subjects freedom to follow and profess that religion which his conscience persuades him to be the true one." Surely the King recognized that his personal religious convictions had no necessary bearing on the salvation of his subjects? Court priests had created in the mind of the pious but unperceiving Louis XIV an unhappy confusion between the demands of his conscience and his responsibility as protector of the national church.[17]

We have no evidence that the King replied to this memorandum. In any event, the interest of the controller-general in the Calvinist cause was in no way diminished. Towards the end of 1775, Turgot made discreet enquiries as to the number of French citizens of Calvinist origin living in London who might return if a measure of toleration were to be granted them. Less discreet was the argument made by the minister in the King's council that the return of a substantial number of these exiles would check the inroads being made by irreligion. Others at court, Turgot remarked, were openly speculating about "the considerable capital which French refugees abroad would bring the state."[18]

Although he had been frustrated in his effort to raise the general issue of Protestant toleration, Turgot did what he could to help Calvinists caught in the toils of the law. In the fall of 1775, for instance, he played a useful role in helping free the last remaining *forçats pour la foi*, Paul Achard and Antoine Riaille.[19] And, in the early summer of 1775, the ministry took another significant step forward in its handling of the Protestant question by releasing a recently arrested underground pastor, Benjamin Armand, on whose behalf Voltaire had intervened. As a result of these two gestures, the *Eglises sous la Croix* were able to function without the threat of martyrdom through the remaining years of the Ancien Regime.[20]

Turgot, meanwhile, was still determined to improve the Protestants' status. This resolve gained momentum at a meeting of reform-minded men in and out of power which was held at Montigny, the estate of the intendant of finances, Trudaine, in mid-October, while the Assembly of the Clergy was in session. The purpose of this meeting, which included Turgot, Malesherbes, abbé Morellet, archbishop Loménie de Brienne of Toulouse, and Lieutenant of the Paris Police Albert (who also was a *conseiller* in the Paris parlement), was to discuss remedies for a number of problems, many of them economic, which needed the government's attention.[21] After three days of intensive talks, those present agreed that a new approach should be made to the complex question of normalizing Calvinist marriages.

The decision reached by the group meeting at Montigny coincided with a growing impatience on the part of the well-to-do urban Reformed about their marital status. Aware of the ministry's interest in their plight, representatives of the Huguenot community had begun lobbying Malesherbes during the summer of 1775. In August, Lecointe de Marcillac (who had acted as intermediary between the Protestants and the regime in the 1750s) had sent Malesherbes a memorandum indicating that he had found a means of settling the issue of Calvinist marriages acceptable not only to the administration but even to the First Estate![22] The minister's interest led Lecointe to submit a series of briefs dealing with aspects of the toleration issue well into 1776.

A second broker for the French Protestant community was Louis Dutens, a La Rochelle native who had emigrated to England early in life out of disgust at the forcible abduction of his sister for convent schooling and the recognition that there was no chance for him as a 'new Catholic' to pursue his chosen career in the army or the law.[23] During a series of visits to his homeland, Dutens had cultivated the friendship of influential liberals in or near the court, including the prince de Conti, Choiseul, and Trudaine.[24]

Thanks to intensive lobbying by Lecointe and Dutens, Malesherbes, Turgot, and the others meeting at Trudaine's property were fully aware of the mounting pressure in the Protestant community for government action on the marriage question. They were also aware that the most serious obstacle in the way of effecting any change in the laws affecting 'new Catholics' was opposition from the ecclesiastical establishment. On the other hand, there were clear indications that the First Estate was no longer monolithic in its hostility towards the Protestants. Seminary graduates of Turgot's generation, men who shared his tolerant disposition, had come to occupy key positions in the hierarchy; there was some hope that they would press liberal policies upon their colleagues in the Assembly of the Clergy which began meeting in Paris in July 1775.[25]

The abbé de Véri was convinced that his more judicious colleagues would see that the church would suffer less from the inevitable coming of toleration if it took the lead in conceding to the Protestants "all possible relief in the civil sphere in order to retain full control of purely spiritual matters." If the First Estate were to propose that Protestant marriages be allowed and the children of these marriages be given a decent status, Turgot's friend went on, its demand that no Calvinist temples be built and no Protestant public worship tolerated would be much easier to make.[26]

Abbé de Véri was fully aware of the reactionaries attending the Assembly of the Clergy, such as Archbishop Christophe de Beaumont, who opposed any concessions to the Protestants. Under the circumstances, any hope for a clerical initiative in favour of reform lay with the majority of the First Estate, who were neither repressive nor tolerant by conviction. Véri's optimism was not reinforced during the early stages of the Assembly of the Clergy. On July 9, the delegates notified Versailles of their continued hostility to any relaxation of the laws against non-conformists. Four days later, when Saint-Florentin appealed to the Assembly to approve a *don gratuit* of 16 000 000 livres to the crown, the clergy balked, insisting upon a prior guarantee that the administration suppress the heretical literature currently available in many parts of France. By late July, alarmed at reports of the government's increasing indulgence towards heretics, the Assembly urged a totally repressive policy, a reversion to the legislation of 1685-1724.[27]

In September, anticipating a government initiative on the marriage question, the Assembly requested a written opinion on the subject from the abbé Thierry, chancellor of the Paris archdiocese. The chancellor's verdict was categorical—civil marriage for Protestants was neither legitimate nor desirable. Armed with this expert opinion, the Assembly deputed Loménie de Brienne to relay it to the King on September 24.[28] Thus, ironically, the liberal archbishop was obliged to give Louis XVI views that were in conflict with his own. However, as we saw during the Calas affair, the prelate's devotion to career was far stronger than his commitment to principle. The King replied to the archbishop's submission with a vaguely worded undertaking to police the existing laws against heresy.[29]

It was at this point that the group which had been meeting at the Trudaine estate commissioned the abbé Louis Guidi to write a pamphlet aimed at winning the uncommitted among the delegates to the cause of Protestant relief. Guidi was an ex-Oratorian whose Jansenist sympathies had brought him to join the editorial board of the *Nouvelles ecclésiastiques*; more significantly, he was part of Adrien Le Paige's circle and in all likelihood sought the advice of this group while composing the *Dialogue entre un évêque et un curé sur les mariages des Protestants* which appeared while the Assembly was in mid-session.[30]

Guidi's *Dialogue* takes the form of a conversation between a conservative bishop on his way to the Assembly and a liberal priest set on lobbying for toleration there. The curé argues that, since it is the ecclesiastical establishment which Protestants have come most to abominate, it is up to the clergy to be conciliatory. This might best be achieved if the Assembly proposed the re-establishment of the Protestants in all rights and privileges compatible with the interest and dignity of the Catholic faith, that is, in all purely civil advantages, the most vital of which was the sorely contested right to marry.

The bishop yields to the logic of the curé's argument, but insists that if the right to a civil marriage were granted to the Huguenots, there must be a solemn understanding in return that the children of such marriages be baptized and educated as Catholics. The curé replies that such an arrangement would undermine basic natural and paternal rights. When the bishop expresses grave concern about the prospect of legalized Protestant worship, the curé remarks that, although the Catholic clergy should not solicit such a right, the government could hardly deny it once civil marriage had been conceded. As for the anxiety felt by some members of the First Estate that, with the coming of toleration, Catholics might be tempted to turn Calvinist, the solution was simple: certain dignities and public offices would be denied to avowed Protestants. What, the bishop finally asks, of Louis XVI's coronation oath to extirpate heresy? The curé observes that only their prior release from persecution will allow heretics to achieve true conversion through persuasion. Convinced at last, the bishop urges the curé to publish their dialogue so that the campaign for Protestant rights may gain ground at the Assembly.

Guidi's *Dialogue* enjoyed an immediate success with the lay public. Court de Gébelin warmly praised it[31] while the successors of Bachaumont noted that the Catholic clergy's apparent refusal to heed the prudent reasoning of their colleague and their efforts to suppress the work were destined to increase under-the-counter sales.[32] Grimm regarded Guidi's pamphlet as better calculated than any of its predecessors to dispel long-standing prejudices against the Calvinists.[33] La Harpe was impressed by the solid theological basis upon which Guidi had couched his case as well as by the genuine concern for the long-term well-being of his own communion which had clearly motivated him to write the *Dialogue*.[34] Finally, members of the Paris parlement, where the Jansenist interest was strong, appear to have applauded Guidi's tract.[35]

The response to the *Dialogue* among delegates to the Assembly of the Clergy was disappointing. On November 9, one of the bishops denounced the pamphlet, eliciting a solemn assurance by Loménie de Brienne that Chancellor Miromesnil had taken steps to prevent its further distribution.[36]

At this desperately late stage in the Assembly's proceedings, the Protestant deputy-general Court de Gébelin published an anonymous appeal to the delegates. This petition took the form of a letter purporting to be from the archbishop of Canterbury and designed, like Guidi's *Dialogue*, to win delegates to concede the need for a legalized form of Calvinist marriage. Dated October 31, 1775, *Le cri de la tolérance* urged the French Catholic clergy to heed the call of humanity and of natural rights and to reverse the repressive policy of their predecessors. As the 'Anglican' prelate saw it, France's Catholics were not justified in appealing to the secular sovereign to repress heresy, since kings had no authority in this area. As far as public worship was concerned, the state's interest required only that no assembly be permitted where conspiracies against the civil authority might be hatched. The King could control this by appointing a representative who could be present whenever these assemblies met.[37]

As the Assembly of the Clergy neared its end early in December, it was clear that France's ecclesiastical establishment remained opposed to any government initiative on the Protestant marriage issue.

In his diary for December 8, the abbé de Véri warned his clerical colleagues: "If you do nothing this year, something will be done ten years hence despite your prudence. The general cry for equity on behalf of the Protestants will force your hand."[38] Two days later, in the address to Louis XVI which officially closed the Assembly, the archbishop of Bourges insisted rather pharasaically that the First Estate had no intention of setting the King's heart against his non-conforming subjects; it had simply warned of the dangers inherent in allowing Protestants equal status in the eye of the law.[39]

The Dominican Charles-Louis Richard proved a worthy successor to the abbé Caveirac in rationalizing the Revocation system and rebutting the abbé Guidi. Late in 1775 he published *Les protestants déboutés de leurs prétensions*,[40]the tenor of which was simple and straightforward: worship in the Reformed rite remained a crime and those who committed it should be ordered to attend mass or pay a fine; their pastors should be confined to monastic houses for spiritual rehabilitation!

The editor of the *Mémoirs secrets* described Richard as a fanatic intent on making a career for himself by serving the interests of the most retrograde elements in the First Estate.[41] Duvoisin, the chaplain of the Dutch embassy in Paris, was so outraged at the "ignorance and fury" in the text that he volunteered to help the abbé Guidi prepare a rebuttal.[42] The result was a *Suite du Dialogue* signed on March 28, 1776, and published shortly afterwards, in which the co-authors suggest that Richard's outrageous polemical attack had probably done the Protestant cause even more good than Guidi's earlier pamphlet. In any event, it was high time that the administration recognize that "to be French, it is not necessary to be Catholic."[43] Religious non-conformists became full members of the body politic at birth when they came under the protection of the prince. In the present circumstances, the crown clearly ought to authorize Protestant marriage before the civil courts, thus fixing the status of the Reformed, recognizing their inherent integrity and promoting the general welfare. Guidi and Duvoisin concluded by arguing that the Calvinists ought to be awarded full freedom of expression and the right to assemble peacefully for worship.

Neither the Assembly of the Clergy's intractability on the marriage issue nor Richard's anti-Calvinist fulminations succeeded in discouraging the Huguenots and their friends at court from pursuing their efforts at reforming the law. In December 1775, Lecointe submitted to Malesherbes the draft of what amounted to a bill of Protestant rights. He reminded the minister that Maurepas had promised some action on the toleration issue early in the new reign.[44] Dutens meanwhile had turned up in Paris in November and submitted to Malesherbes a proposal that the government release the Reformed from the obligation to be baptized and married in the Roman rite. The minister was impressed and suggested that Dutens discuss the modalities of this proposal with Dionis Du Séjour, a *conseiller* in the *cour des aides*. After consulting with the jurist, Dutens submitted a formal brief to Malesherbes on November 28 in which he urged that the administration allow Protestants to be married before a notary after having their banns published by the clerk of the local court and to have their childrens' births similarly notarized and registered by a magistrate's clerk.[45]

Shortly afterwards, Malesherbes presented the Dutens proposal to the *conseil du roi*. Although no concrete legislative initiative resulted, Dutens's La Rochelle backers thought it warranted accrediting Dutens as Protestant agent at court, while the Nîmois maintained their rejection of any negotiations which might end up with halfway concessions, insisting that "the Protestants should seek to have the wall separating them from the rest of the nation broken down; they wish to see themselves treated like the King's other subjects as far as both their civil and religious status is concerned."[46] Dutens's sponsors persisted in pressing for his appointment, conceding that if he were supported by the entire Reformed constituency, they might be willing to commission him to argue the case for public worship as well as marriage. In the end, at the suggestion of the Bordeaux and La Rochelle communities, Dutens and Court de Gébelin met to concert their lobbying activity.

That this sometimes fractious Protestant lobbying was having some impact on the government became apparent in January 1776, when Albert, a *maître des requêtes* in the Paris parlement and lieutenant-general of the Paris police, made a report to the King's council on the toleration issue. The failure of the 1685-1724 legislation was complete, he argued: there remained in France a large community of Protestants peaceably devoted to commerce and agriculture whom it had proven impossible to convert. Although rich Calvinists frequently had their children baptized as Catholics (and even feigned membership in the Roman communion in order to have their marriages legalized), the Reformed remained generally loyal to their own baptismal and marital rites. What the *conseil du roi* might do, Albert suggested, was to encourage a more general acceptance of Catholic baptism on the part of the Reformed by making sure that priests did not define the status of children at will but acted as purely civil officers in the matter.

Although the cabinet did not act on Albert's proposal, Malesherbes (who had been receiving intermittent pleas for action from Dutens) gave it practical effect just before his resignation from the government in May 1776. The immediate circumstance which prodded the minister into action was a crisis in the diocese of La Rochelle, whose bishop had written to Malesherbes complaining about the refusal of a 'new Catholic' to have his child baptized by the parish priest. Reporting to cabinet, Malesherbes explained that the Huguenots' resistance must be seen in context: on the one hand, the Reformed had expected a measure of toleration upon the accession of Louis XVI; on the other, priests were still acting provocatively by designating children brought to them by Protestant parents as illegitimate. What was needed was for the government to spell out its policy once and for all: in baptizing those brought before him for the sacrament, including suspected Calvinists, the priest must act only as a witness, recording the status of the child as defined by the parents. The ministry having approved this recommendation, Malesherbes directed both the archbishop and the intendant at La Rochelle to see to its implementation.[47] Although a formal declaration of this new policy was not issued at the national level until 1782, Malesherbes's intervention in the La Rochelle case (followed by similar directives to other local authorities), guaranteed the Reformed against further challenges to the status of their children throughout France.

On the day following the cabinet meeting at which he obtained cabinet approval for his letter to the bishop of La Rochelle, Malesherbes was asked to resign, as was his fellow reformer, Turgot. The joint efforts of these two men to improve the lot of the Calvinists, like their even more ambitious efforts to reform the socio-economic and legal structures of France, had provoked the privileged to form a coalition against them which only the will of the King might have undone. Their departure caused understandable sadness in the Protestant community[48] and a sense of bitter regret in liberal intellectual circles. Voltaire reported to his friend Gal-Pomaret that the Calvinist marriage issue had been indefinitely shelved and that it would be politic to wait in patience for some new initiative in the area at a later time.[49] Paul Rabaut found consolation in the thought that the granting of unlimited toleration to the Huguenots might have caused more spiritual harm than good.[50] Court de Gébelin was convinced that, whatever else might have been obtained from the recently aborted campaign to improve their lot, the Protestants had stood no chance of obtaining the freedom of worship, which they should rate above all other rights.[51] That other proponent of the Calvinist cause, Louis Dutens, left France soon after the departure of Turgot and Malesherbes from the ministry, remarking: "I have done my best to be French. It was not in my power to acquire that honour."[52]

In the first two years of his reign, Louis XVI and the liberals in whom he confided vital cabinet portfolios had aroused the hopes of the French Protestant community that their physical persecution was soon to end and that their marginal status in the nation would be replaced by something approaching full citizenship. By the spring of 1776, the first of these hopes had been realized: the apparatus created by Louis XIV to effect the forcible conversion of his Protestant subjects was now totally dismantled. The second hope of the Huguenots, however, had been dashed: for another twelve years they were to remain without a secure civil status, subjects without being citizens, husbands and wives whose relationship to one another and to the society around them was constantly subject to challenge in the courts or to repudiation by the Catholic priesthood, which had still not abandoned its pretension to direct the conscience of the nation.

---

1.   For a study of Louis XVI's intellectual and psychological makeup, v. B. Fay, *Louis XVI ou la fin d'un monde* (Paris, 1955), pp. 1-56. Fay notes that the future Louis

XVI was brought up by his tutors to admire the ideal prince of Fenelon's *Télémaque*, but also that, like his brothers, he was revolted by Marmontel's *Bélisaire!*

2. V. Rabaut Saint-Etienne, *Discours sur la mort de Louis XV et sur le règne de Louis XVI, prononcé dans le Bas-Dauphiné par un ministre du désert* (Lausanne, 1774); Gal-Pomaret to Olivier-Desmont, June 1774, Arch. Cons. Nîmes, Reg L9, fol.26; Colloque général des églises réformées du Haut-Languedoc, August 4, 1774, Hugues, III, p. 104.

3. Olivier-Desmont to Etienne Gibert, September 17, 1783, Arch. Cons. Nîmes, Reg. B 29.

4. Voltaire to Gal-Pomaret, September 18, 1774, Best. D. 19120.

5. Abbé Clément du Tremblai to Adrien Le Paige, March 24, 1775, Paris, Société de Port-Royal, Collection Le Paige 579, fol. 1.

6. Le Paige to the abbé Clément, March 26, 1775, ibid.

7. *Journal de l'abbé de Véri*, ed. J. de Witte (2 vols.; Paris, 1928), I, p. 254.

8. Ibid., p. 385.

9. Turgot reasoned that one religion in the state might be accorded special privileges such as having its clergy subsidized by the public purse but that other religions ought to be tolerated provided they financed their own operations.

10 Paul Rabaut expressed his delight at this shift in government policy in a letter to Etienne Chiron on April 5, 1775. V. Paul Rabaut, *Ses lettres à divers, 1744-94*, ed. C. Dardier (2 vols; Paris, 1892), II, p. 184.

11. Jean-Louis Soulavie, *Mémoires historiques et politiques du règne de Louis XVI, depuis son mariage jusqu'à sa mort* (6 vols.; Paris, 1801), II, pp. 318-20.

12. A comprehensive examination of Malesherbes's involvement with the Calvinists' struggle for civil rights during these years is offered in P. Grosclaude, *Malesherbes, témoin et interprète de son temps* (Paris, 1961), pp. 355-385.

13. Manuscript copy of a letter from the Bas-Languedoc pastors to Turgot, May 29, 1775, B.P., Coll. Coquerel, Ms 339, fol. 125.

14. Turgot, *Formules de serment à substituer aux formules en usage, Oeuvres*, ed. Dupont de Nemours (9 vols.; Paris, 1808-11), VII, p. 314.

15. Pierre-Samuel Dupont de Nemours, *Mémoires sur la vie et les ouvrages de M. Turgot, ministre d'état* ("Philadelphie," 1782), p. 194.

16. Louis XVI to Turgot, Reims, June 10, 1775, in Turgot, *Oeuvres*, ed. G. Schelle (5 vols.; Paris, 1913-23), IV, p. 554. Dupont de Nemours reports that the king mumbled the critical oath almost inaudibly, as though embarrassed. *Mémoires*, p. 194

17. Turgot, "Project de mémoire au roi," ibid, pp. 558-67.

18. Dupont de Nemours, *Mémoires*, p. 221.

19. Court de Gébelin, the Protestants' deputy in the capital, brought the case of these two aging *galériens* to the attention of Turgot who referred the matter to Chancellor Hue de Miromesnil. The chancellor signed the order for their release in September 1775, thus ending one of the longest and most terrifying chapters in the Calvinists' book of suffering.

20. François Rochette, executed at Toulouse in 1762, was the last underground pastor to suffer martyrdom for his faith. Benjamin Armand, arrested for presiding over illegal

religious assemblies, was imprisoned at Briançon in Dauphiny in June 1775. Pastor Gal-Pomaret informed Voltaire who interceded with his friend the marquise de Clermont-Tonnerre, wife of the provincial governor. Armand's release followed shortly, confirming the government's desire that its policy of de facto toleration be maintained.

21. Metra, Imbert et al., *Correspondance secrète, politique et littéraire* (18 vols.; London, 1787), II, p. 216, October 24, 1775; Bachaumont, *Mémoires secrets*, October 22, 1775.

22. Lecointe de Marcillac to Malesherbes, August 21, 1775,, Archives de Tocqueville L 123, cited in Grosclaude, *Malesherbes*, pp. 377-78. Grosclaude has uncovered seven letters addressed by Lecointe to Malesherbes between August and May 30, 1776, when the would-be Protestant agent expresses his regret at the minister's resignation.

23. Louis Dutens gives a full account of his life, including his lobbying in the Calvinist cause, in his *Mémoires d'un voyageur qui se repose, contenant des anecdotes historiques, politiques et littéraires, relatives à plusieurs des principaux personnages de ce siècle* (3 vols.; Paris, 1806).

24. During a visit to La Rochelle in 1775, Dutens had been approached by a group of local notables who thought that he might be the right person to negotiate a regularization of their marital status. Jean Bétrine, the city's underground pastor, drew up a letter soliciting a mandate for Dutens to begin discussions with the government and circulated it throughout the Reformed communities. Predictably, the southern congregations were opposed to any arrangement with Versailles that did not explicitly permit public worship; and Court de Gébelin resented this effort by the Rochellois not only to undermine his own position at court but also to pre-empt the agenda for a dialogue with the regime. V. Court de Gébelin to Abraham Chiron, Papiers Chiron, III, fol. 223.

25. Soulavie lists the following prelates as naturally inclined to support some measure of relief for the Protestants: Dillon (Narbonne), Loménie de Brienne (Toulouse), Boisgelin (Aix), Cicé (Bordeaux), La Luzerne (Langres) and Colbert (Rodez). *Mémoires historiques*, III, p. 4.

26. Abbé de Véri, *Journal*, I, p. 383.

27. Bachaumont, *Mémoires secrets*, July 29-30, 1775.

28. "Rémontrances sur les entreprises des Protestants," September 24, 1775, *Collection des Procès-verbaux des Assemblées-générales du Clergé de France, depuis l'année 1560 jusqu'à présent* (8 vols. in 9; Paris, 1778), VIII, 2e partie, pièces justificatives, pp. 711-14; Bachaumont, November 21, 1775.

29. Ibid., p. 714.

30. Abbé Louis Guidi, *Dialogue entre un évêque et un curé sur le mariage des Protestants* (n.p., 1775). Guidi had made known his own views on the toleration issue a decade earlier during a pamphlet debate with d'Alembert, when he defended the Jansenists' stress on purely spiritual methods of conversion and blamed the persecuting attitude of the contemporary Catholic church on the Jesuits; he had even gone so far as to suggest that, because they posed far less a threat to the social order than philosophes such as d'Alembert, the Reformed ought to be given full freedom of expression. V. Guidi, *Lettre à un ami* (n.p., 1765), p.17.

31. Court de Gébelin to Etienne Chiron, 1775, Papiers Chiron, II, fol. 128.

32. Bachaumont, *Mémoires secrets*, October 22, 1775.

33. Grimm et al., *Correspondance littéraire, philosophique et critique*, October 1775.

34. Jean-François La Harpe, *Correspondance littéraire, adressée à Son Altesse Impériale, Mgr le grand-duc, aujourd'hui empereur de Russie, et à M. le Comte André Schowalow, chambellan de l'impératrice Catherine II, depuis 1774 jusqu'à 1789* (5 vols.; Paris, 1801), I, pp. 283-84.

35. Pierre Duplain to Société Typographique de Neuchatel, April 30, 1788, cited in R.Darnton, *The World of the Underground Book-sellers in the Old Regime*, pp. 453-54.

36. *Procès-verbaux des Assemblées-générales du Clergé*. VIII, 2e partie, pp. 2238-39.

37. Court de Gébelin, *Le cri de la tolérance, ou Lettres du lord Archevêque de Cantorbéry, primat et premier pair de la Grande-Bretagne, aux archevêques, évêques et autres gens du clergé de France* ("Londres," 1776).

38. Abbé de Véri, *Journal*, I, p. 385.

39. *Procès-verbaux des Assemblées-générales du Clergé*, p. 2609.

40. Abbé Charles-Louis Richard, *Les protestants déboutés de leurs prétentions par les principes et les paroles même du curé, leur apologiste dans son "Dialogue avec un évêque sur leurs mariages"* (Brussels, 1776).

41. Bachaumont, *Mémoires secrets*, May 24, 1776.

42. Duvoisin to Chiron, December 26, 1775, *Papiers Chiron*, III, fol.221.

43. Abbé Guidi, *Suite du Dialogue sur les mariages des Protestants; ou réponse de M. le curé de...à l'auteur d'une brochure intitulé: "Les Protestants déboutés de leurs prétention"* (n.p., 1776), p.27.

44. V. Grosclaude, *Malesherbes*, pp. 381-83.

45. "Mémoire en faveur des Protestants de France, rédigé par M. Dutens en 1775, et adressé par la chevalière d'Eon au baron de Breteuil, le 10 janvier, 1787," A.N., TT 335, fols. 17-22. This memorandum accompanied a letter from Dutens to Malesherbes dated November 29, 1775, and uncovered by Grosclaude in the Arch. de Tocqueville, L 123.

46. Letter of the Nîmes Protestants to Dutens, January 8, 1776, Papiers Chiron, III, fol. 232. 47.

47. Copy of the letter of Malesherbes to the intendant at La Rochelle, Papiers Gébelin, II, fol. 131.

48. Court de Gébelin to Turgot, May 1776, ibid., IV, fol.53.

49. Voltaire to Gal-Pomaret, April 8, 1776, Best. D. 18914.

50. Paul Rabaut to Chiron, March 13, 1776, *Lettres à divers*, II, pp. 214-15.

51. Court de Gébelin to Abraham Chiron, August 28, 1776, Papiers Gébelin, II, fol. 131.

52. Dutens, *Mémoires*, II, p. 216.

Jacques Necker: Proponent of appeasement.

CHAPTER XVII

Conservatives and Pragmatists Try Their Hand: Necker, Armand, and the Parlementaires, 1776-1784

The resignations of Turgot and Malesherbes in the spring of 1776 removed from the administration its only outspoken supporters of the Huguenots' cause. In the months that followed, government policy towards the Calvinists toughened, especially in areas where the Protestant revival was recent and perceived to be provocative. Antoine-Jean Amelot, who succeeded Malesherbes as minister in charge of 'new Catholic' Affairs, was a nephew of Maurepas and shared his uncle's cautious (although not actively hostile) approach to the Huguenots. Meanwhile, the pamphlet debate on the merits of toleration continued, much of it between liberal and conservative priests.

In the spring of 1777, the French Protestant community took new heart with the appointment of their Swiss co-religionist, Jacques Necker, as director general of finances. However, within two years the Genevan banker had compromised himself with all but the most timorous of the Huguenots by seconding the efforts of the Dutch embassy chaplain, Jacques Armand, to negotiate a settlement of their status which would have left them without freedom of worship. Meanwhile, early in 1778, a group of liberals in the Paris parlement pressed the King to revise the laws against heretics; they were ordered to suspend these solicitations, however, at the end of the year. Shortly afterwards, nevertheless, the administration sanctioned baptismal and burial arrangements which awarded the Calvinists a more secure social status without forcing their consciences.

Although the main battle over Protestant rights in this period was fought on the domestic front, the alliance between France and England's rebellious colonies provided an additional occasion for champions of toleration on both sides of the Atlantic to promote the cause of Calvinist relief.

The Reformed, meanwhile, were still unable to articulate their grievances with a single voice. Their three champions during this period—Lecointe, chaplain Jacques Armand, and Court de Gébelin, were all men of good will; yet none was able to gain the support of the Huguenot community at large.

A new severity in government policy towards the Protestants became apparent immediately after the resignation of Turgot and Malesherbes. In the face of this reaction, Paul Rabaut (who was convinced that it simply reflected the administration's need to offer at least token satisfaction to the First Estate), urged his colleagues to avoid needless provocation.[1] Violent repression occurred in areas such as Bearn and Picardy, where the Calvinist resurgence was recent and thus seen to be more alarming. Where tacit toleration had been the order of the day, the authorities tended to support discreet Calvinist gains.[2]

Meanwhile, the debate over the toleration issue within the First Estate which had been launched by the abbé Guidi in 1775 resumed two years later with the publication of *L'Intolérance éclairée* by the abbé Benant of Saint-Cyr. Benant argued that it was perfectly logical to combine ecclesiastical intolerance—the church's condemnation of heretical doctrine—with civil toleration, the protection which the state owed those living in spiritual error. This formula had clearly proven itself in Holland, England and, parts of Switzerland, not to mention Alsace. By contrast, the government's present policy vis-à-vis the Huguenots placed the Reformed in double jeopardy: on the one hand, it subjected them to priestly harassment since it characterized them as 'new Catholics;' on the other, it discriminated against them in the civil sphere whenever their continuing commitment to a prescribed religion was brought to light.

Benant further observed that the partisan religious fury which had produced such grave disorders in the sixteenth century was a thing of the past, on the Reformed side at least. The Paris bankers, Bordeaux businessmen, and prosperous Normandy farmers who made up the current French Calvinist population were clearly neither "democratic" nor "subversive."[3] In any case, to make the legal status of these respectable subjects dependent on their willingness to submit to the Catholic sacraments was a clear derogation of the King's authority. To relieve his Protestant subjects, Louis XVI should simply declare that the taking of vows before a civil magistrate was sufficient to validate a Calvinist marriage. If the King were worried that such an arrangement might facilitate divorce, he could rule that such marriages were indissoluble.

On the opposite side in this ecclesiastical debate was the abbé Pey, whose *La tolérance chrétienne opposée au tolérantisme philosophique* was intended as a diatribe against his colleague Guidi.[4] Pey insisted that the campaign to convert France's heretics must be pursued without let-up. The intrigues of the Reformed with France's enemies, their defence of the pernicious notion of popular sovereignty, together with their own record of intolerance, proved that the Protestants would be a menace if given a bill of rights. The recent opening of separate Calvinist schools had been an outrage; in contrast, the well-established practice of abducting Protestant children for religious reorientation should be maintained since it "enlightened and directed" rather than contradicted parental authority. The offer of a Protestant loan to the nation during the Seven Years' War in exchange for a government promise of freedom of worship had undoubtedly been inspired abroad and had quite properly been rejected. Only when they had given up their temples, their public meetings for worship and their pastors should Louis XVI negotiate with his Protestant subjects, perhaps conceding them some form of civil marriage in return for such an abandonment. In the meantime, the maximum one might grant would be to leave Calvinist property rights untouched.

The abbé Pey's defence of the existing state of affairs—halfway between repression and toleration—was hardly calculated to win sympathy from the Protestants. Nor, paradoxically, did the Calvinists give much support to the efforts of the nominally Christian abbé Guillaume-Thomas-François Raynal to come to their aid. The author of the highly successful *Histoire philosophique et politique des deux Indes* vowed in the preface to the 1780 edition of this work that "the little energy which remains in me shall be devoted to the history of the revocation of the Edict of Nantes."[5] To obtain documentation for this text, Raynal wrote to pastors living inside as well as outside France asking specific questions concerning the numbers, property, and social status of the Protestants who had remained in France since 1685 as well as of those who had sought refuge abroad.

Replies to this questionnaire began to reach Raynal in 1782. The author of one memorandum from inside France recommended that the government recognize the eighty-nine pastors serving the underground churches as *maîtres d'instruction* and allow them to preside over meetings for worship in private homes under the surveillance of a commissioner named by the local intendant. This same correspondent went on to suggest that, since any relaxation of the laws against the Reformed was bound to affect the nation's economy, it would seem appropriate to entrust the controller-general of finances with the supervision of Protestant affairs. Huguenots seeking marriage might declare themselves before the intendant or before a local magistrate, who could also deliver an act legitimizing any children which such marriages produced. The memorandum also included the suggestion that all Calvinists held in custody for religious reasons be released, that refugees be permitted to return, that the Calvinists be given the free disposition of their property, and that the government take a serious and complete census of their number in France.[6]

From pastors serving the communities of the Calvinist diaspora, Raynal received rather more cautious responses. From Berne and Lausanne came news of the prosperity which the refugees had found there and of the sacrifices which they had made to promote the Calvinist revival inside France.[7] Those living in Frankfurt-am-Main worried that any disclosure of the privileges which they had been granted in their adoptive homeland might jeopardize their status; in addition, they argued that it would be wrong to inspire a revulsion against France in the minds of their children by exaggerating the evils of the present French laws against heresy.[8] Some pastors living in the diaspora believed that Raynal's proposed history might be seen as doing a disservice to the states which had harboured the refugees, and so discouraged its publication.[9] When the liberal-minded abbé went ahead with the first part of his work despite these reservations, he found that no publisher inside or outside France would handle it and in the end, despite the encouragement of Frederick of Prussia,[10] he abandoned the project altogether.[11]

While the knowledge that liberal priests such as Raynal were ready to do literary battle on their behalf was no doubt welcome, news that there was someone at court who might be ready to take up the unfinished work of Turgot and Malesherbes was even more gratifying to the Protestants. Such good news seemed to be in the wind with the announcement late in June 1777 that the Swiss Calvinist Jacques Necker had been appointed to the administration at Versailles.[12] Yet when the moment of his appointment arrived, the would-be minister discovered that his foreign citizenship and, even more, his religious non-conformity, precluded his being named controller-general. Instead, a special post, that of director (later director-general) of the treasury was created for Necker, while the much less gifted Taboureau des Reaux, controller-general since October 1776, retained the official title and with it membership in the *conseil du roi*.

Liberal intellectuals had mixed feelings about the self-serving Genevan who had promoted himself into power by attacking their friend Turgot;[13] and, not surprisingly, the French ecclesiastical establishment observed the growing influence at court of an apparent heretic with anger and alarm.[14] Necker was, however, little attached to conventional Calvinist doctrine.[15] Early in life, he had adopted the deist outlook which was common in the upper reaches of Genevan society. At the same time, however, like his compatriot Rousseau, he was convinced that the sharing of a common faith was the best foundation for any political community. Thus Necker accepted the importance of the coronation ceremony at Rheims which had bound Louis XVI to his subjects in mystical union and, by contrast with Turgot, was hostile to the idea of a separation between church and state. Confessional pluralism, Necker believed, was likely sooner later to be socially divisive. In fact, everything short of coercion ought to be used to reintegrate minorities which had strayed from the fold of the national church.[16]

This appreciation of the social role played by national churches brought Necker to feel a certain affinity with members of the French Catholic hierarchy. Since he also hoped to find supporters for his financial policies in the First Estate, Necker cultivated a number of these prelates assiduously, even the most conservative among them.[17]

The calculated sympathies which drew Necker towards the defenders of conventional religion in Paris were complemented by the reserve which he showed towards militant members of the Huguenot community. Soon after taking office, Necker turned down an appeal from Court de Gébelin that he promote the cause of Protestant emancipation within the administration.[18] Instead, for advice on matters relating to the Calvinist question, the prudent Genevan turned to the chevalier de Beaumont and the conservative Paris committee.[19]

The deep-rooted conservatism of the director-general was made even more apparent by the support which he gave to the efforts of the Dutch embassy chaplain Jacques Armand to solve the Calvinist question single-handedly and in a manner which aimed at satisfying Versailles as well as the moderates in the Huguenot community. Armand, the grandson of French refugees, enjoyed the confidence of well-to-do Calvinists who turned up on Sundays for his embassy services; he was also known to and trusted by the foremost traditionalist in the cabinet, Foreign Minister Vergennes.

Armand's scheme, first broached during the spring of 1779, was that the French government offer a limited civil status to the Huguenots while maintaining a strict control over their religious activities. A few pastors would be allowed to circulate throughout the French countryside. Public worship would be tolerated in the northern parts of the nation on the understanding that it would not be accompanied by the psalm-singing which offended the established clergy. In the south, however, the assemblies for worship which had become part of the spiritual life of the Huguenots would henceforth be banned. To compensate for these limitations, Armand offered to make a twice-yearly round of the French Reformed churches during which he would baptize, marry, and administer holy communion. Those resisting his decisions would be dealt with by *lettres de cachet*.[20]

Having received the blessing of Necker and Vergennes,[21] Armand set out in June 1779 on a tour of the Calvinist communities in the north of France where he found a fair measure of support for his plans. In his incursions into the south, however, the chaplain encountered strenuous opposition, both locally and from Court de Gébelin in Paris, who warned the administration in 1781 that the Calvinists would never accept family services as a substitute for public worship, adding that the government's seeming support for the Armand mission was undermining the Protestants' confidence in its judgment.[22] The would-be broker between Versailles and the Huguenots was undeterred, however, which brought Pastor Olivier-Desmont to appeal to the playwright Beaumarchais to intercede with Maurepas in the matter.[23] In October 1781, Court de Gébelin suggested to Vergennes that the embassy chaplain was creating such distress in some areas that a new exodus of Protestants might occur, something which could only benefit France's enemies.[24] In the end, Armand remained in the field despite all these protests until the summer of 1783 when the administration discovered that he had been charging exorbitant fees for the marriages he had been celebrating during his circuit-riding and abandoned all support for his scheme.[25]

Ironically, although Necker's support for the Armand scheme thoroughly alienated him from the French Protestant community, it also offered his opponents within the administration a chance to accuse him of promoting the Huguenots' interests at court, even to charge that he was the willing agent of Protestant England and Geneva. In the summer of 1780, in an open letter to the director-general bearing the purported signature of his predecessor Turgot (but in fact written by the financial advisors of the King's brothers) Necker was charged not only with attempting to make himself the liberator of his co-religionists but also with placing France's credit in the hands of foreign Protestant banks.[26]

This outrageous broadside elicited a vigorous *replique*: the *Réponse à la lettre de M. Turgot*, unsigned but quite possibly the work of Necker's wife, challenged the director-general's critics to explain why France would suffer if the Reformed were given a measure of toleration. Surely the vicious campaign being waged against England's Catholics by Lord Gordon was evidence enough that religious intolerance bred riot and disorder rather than peace and prosperity.[27] Necker's critics replied by charging that the Genevan was set upon restoring the Edict of Nantes in collaboration with such notorious figures as the abbé Raynal (whose proposed work on the Revocation had become public knowledge).[28]

The publication in January 1781 of Necker's *Compte rendu au roi* produced more pamphlet-writing. It also prompted the director-general's colleague Vergennes to write two confidential memoranda to the King in which he pointed out the problems which had been created for the monarchy by the presence at court of a foreigner who was also both a republican and a heretic. The first of these memoranda, transmitted to Louis XVI on May 3, included a comment worthy of Bossuet: the French people, Vergennes remarked, were notoriously susceptible to new ideas, whatever their source or merit, a weakness which had brought them all too often to trust the direction of their affairs to foreign adventurers, each time with disastrous results. The current director-general of finances fitted this disturbing pattern: "Monsieur Necker, full of Protestant and Swiss schemes, is quite prepared to establish in France a new system of finances, a league inside the state and a fronde against the established administration."[29]

Placed on the defensive by this barrage of hostility, Necker demanded that he be elevated to full cabinet rank with the formal title of controller-general of finances. In response, Maurepas made it clear that abjuration must precede such a promotion. Left with no effective choice, Necker tendered his resignation on May 19.

The Catholic establishment which Necker and his protégé Armand had done their best to propitiate had in no way modified its opposition to the idea of Protestant emancipation. During the Assembly of the Clergy which met in the summer of 1780, the *rapporteur* for the committee dealing with the 'new Catholic' question, the archbishop of Arles, voiced his colleagues' ritual lament: Protestants were more and more present in the legal profession and in local government. Calvinist religious meetings were becoming more frequent and more provocative. Pastors were issuing certificates of baptism and marriage which looked deceptively authentic, and Protestant thinkers and writers were printing and distributing comments on all manner of public issues. What was more serious in the long run, the prelate continued, was the link between the tolerance of Protestant heresies and the spread of agnosticism, a link made clearer than ever by the spurious theology currently taught in Geneva in which even the divinity of Christ was called into question. Finally, given recent developments in America, the administration needed to be reminded of that other subversive influence which always accompanied the acceptance of Protestantism—the emergence of republican opinions. What Versailles should do in the face of these very real threats was to sanction and subsidize the peaceful proselytization of the Reformed, especially in such critical regions as Languedoc, Dauphiny, and Guyenne.[30]

Having adopted the archbishop's report, the Assembly commissioned the cardinal de La Rochefoucauld to press the King to police the laws affecting 'new Catholics' in order to disabuse them of false hope and to end their spiritual insubordination. Early in September, through the chancellor, Louis XVI promised to support the peaceful conversion of the Reformed, whose public worship he pledged himself never to authorize.[31]

If the accommodating approach of Necker had proven unproductive, it is not surprising that the bolder efforts on behalf of the Protestants made by the Paris parlement during this same period were even less successful. Because of its involvement in cases of contested Protestant marriages during the 1760s and 1770s, the parlement had been in continuous touch with the problems faced by the Reformed.

In April 1778, the parlementaires commissioned their colleague Achille-Pierre Dionis Du Séjour, an appeal judge, to prepare a report on the Protestant question. Du Séjour was a friend of Malesherbes and, like the former minister, a strong champion of toleration; the liberal abbé "Gaçon de Louancy" (perhaps a pseudonym for the abbé Guidi) described him to Paul Rabaut as "at the head of your party (in the parlement).[32]" In any event, Du Séjour began his enquête by examining in manuscript form the *Lettres de deux curés des Cévennes* which "Gaçon de Louancy" was to publish at the end of the year. The text took up the themes advanced in Guidi's *Dialogues*: it was up to the Catholic priesthood, which had urged the Revocation upon Louis XIV, to request its annulment; it was up to the Crown to issue arrangements for Protestant births and marriages as well as to decide whether the Reformed ought to be allowed a legal form of worship which, after all, had been granted to the Jews at Metz, Bayonne, and Bordeaux, and to Moslems at Marseilles. "Gaçon de Louancy" conceded that the Reformed might be excluded from key public offices; but they were owed protection of person and property because "they enter the body politic by right of birth and belong to the state."[33]

Meanwhile, that indefatigable champion of the Protestant cause, Lecointe, who had got wind of the Du Séjour enquête, approached the judge with the suggestion that the simplest solution to the marriage question would be to act on the unfulfilled pledge to deal with the issue contained in various *arrêts* and *déclarations* of the Sun King himself.[34]

Early in July, reinforced by what he had read and heard, Du Séjour made an impassioned appeal for Protestant relief before a committee of his colleagues. A series of further deliberations followed at the home of the parlement's *premier président*, Etienne-François d'Aligre, a defender of the status quo.[35] During these frank and informal sessions, Du Séjour, a normally rather remote and philosophical speaker, surprised his colleagues by his ardour for the Protestant cause; his well-known agnosticism, however, made him suspect to the substantial Jansenist element among the parlementaires.[36]

While these discussions, which lasted until August, continued, the magistrates were able to read two pamphlets written expressly to influence their judgment. The first of these was a new *Dialogue sur l'état civil des Protestants* written by the abbé Guidi.[37] The participants in what Guidi presented as a three-way conversation about the Protestant question are easily identifiable: a conservative magistrate who is dubious about proposed new legislation to emancipate the Protestants (d'Aligre) and two supporters of the Reformed: a curé (Guidi) and a *conseiller* (Du Séjour).

Guidi's arguments were challenged by the conservative Emilien Petit, who pointed out in a *Dissertation sur la tolérance civile et religieuse en Angleterre et en France* that France's Protestants had been given full scope for their activities in the economic and financial sphere while England's dissenters were still obliged (among other things) to pay special taxes.[38]

At the conclusion of the deliberations which Pey and Guidi had done their best to influence, the magistrates returned to Paris. The inevitable Lecointe surfaced at this point, determined to play middleman again, this time between the Paris magistrates and the Reformed. The southern Huguenots bridled at this: through Paul Rabaut's son, the future revolutionary Rabaut Saint-Etienne, they let it be known that, since they were not a political body, they were not in position to open formal negotiations with the regime or with any of its agents.[39] Happily, the administration decided early in November 1778 to exile Lecointe from the capital, thus effectively ending his career as self-appointed broker for the Calvinist constituency.[40]

Late in November, having been given encouragement by Necker and by Benjamin Franklin, the Paris parlement appealed to Louis XVI to grant the Reformed a measure of relief.[41] The magistrates were aware that the ministry preferred they take no action in their own in this delicate business so they were determined to be circumspect. However, the number of Protestant marriage cases coming before the nation's courts made the need for some action in this area imperative. One solution included the implementation of the *arrêt* of September 15, 1685, authorizing *juges royaux* to marry Calvinists. Such a procedure, the magistrates added, would leave it up to the Reformed to decide whether or not their weddings ought subsequently to be blessed by their pastors (who seemed in the main to be men of substance and who had in event become de facto custodians of the Protestants' civil status). Catholic baptism, the magistrates went on to say, should still be insisted upon, although royal judges instead of priests might register non-Catholic births. Burial of Protestants should be ordered in accordance with the declaration of December 11, 1685. The magistrates reassured Louis XVI that they were recommending nothing beyond the granting of civil status for the Reformed, but they reminded the King that great hopes for toleration had been aroused with his accession and expressed concern that the Assembly of the Clergy, by its intransigence, might end up creating bitterness and disillusionment.

Rabaut Saint-Etienne warned his colleagues against expecting too much from the parlementaires' initiative.[42] This pessimism was justified: the conservative clergy, led by the Archbishop of Paris, campaigned furiously against the magistrates' proposals.[43] In the end, early in December, Louis XVI heeded the counsel of the clergy (upon whom his government was depending for a generous *don gratuit* to help pay the cost of France's commitment to the American revolutionary cause) and ordered the parlement to suspend all discussion of the Protestant question until further notice.[44]

Despite this official discouragement, Bretignères made a final plea on behalf of Protestant toleration during the December 15 session of the parlement. It was not a question, the magistrate argued, of permitting Protestant worship or of admitting Calvinists to public office; what was at issue was the need to assure the status of the Huguenots' children. Thousands of marriages in the desert had produced "a prolific source of scandalous trials...and our tribunals, caught between natural law and the letter of positive law, are obliged to steer clear of both."[45] Two million Protestants looked to the parlement for a solution, failing which America beckoned as a land where they might live free.

The parlementaires meanwhile heeded the injunction to stop discussing the Protestant question, for the time being at least; however, to keep public interest in the issue alive, the liberals among them encouraged the marquis de Condorcet to rush into print with the treatise on the Protestant question which he had been preparing.[46] In the *Réflexions d'un citoyen catholique sur les lois de France relatives aux Protestants* which appeared in December, Condorcet spoke (like Guidi) of the revolution which had transformed once fanatical Huguenots into peaceful and productive citizens and (like Lecointe) recommended that the laws of 1685 and 1698 governing marriage serve as precedents for new legislation. Condorcet skirted around the delicate question of religious freedom: "We do not ask that Protestants have public worship; we ask only that they may have children."[47] As far as public office was concerned, Calvinists should have access to those posts which carried with them honour but not privilege; professional and military careers should be open to non-conformists, as should enrolment in the nation's academic institutions. Unless the government conceded some measure of relief, Concorcet concluded, Protestants might emigrate to the United States where they were sure to receive generous asylum.[48]

Encouraged by Condorcet's intervention, the parlement agreed early in 1779 to consider a revised version of the recommendations made by Bretignères.[49] The author of this new set of proposals suggested that Calvinists be allowed to have their marriages blessed by a pastor and then registered by the local magistrate; meanwhile mixed marriages, which should be encouraged because they so often led to the conversion of the non-conforming spouse, might be permitted according to the arrangements which obtained in Alsace. Whether baptism was in the Catholic or the Calvinist rite should be a matter of indifference; but a single local registry of births, marriages, and deaths had obvious advantages. Calvinist pastors should be allowed to preside over family worship although the government might find it advisable to keep them under some kind of surveillance. Protestants should be allowed to study in the nation's universities, to enter the medical profession and to publish; and the King should be ready to grant letters patent to those of them who were inventive. In all of this, the sponsor of these proposals noted, there was no question of granting France's Calvinists full toleration on the Prussian or Pennsylvanian model, even though Anabaptist farmers were living freely and happily in Alsace and steps had been taken to permit Jewish landowning in other parts of France.

In the end, this second effort by the parlementaires to persuade the King to regularize the civil status of his Calvinist subjects proved as unavailing as the first, largely because Louis XVI and his counsellors were convinced that such a reform, however desirable in itself, would alienate the Catholic hierarchy upon which the crown was increasingly dependent for funds. Nevertheless, in a series of piecemeal decisions made at the beginning of the 1780s, Versailles did help to stabilize the civil status of the Protestants, thus satisfying at least some of their grievances.

The first of these decisions was a royal declaration issued on May 12, 1782, and registered two days later by the Paris parlement.[50] This decree made into formal law the directive concerning the baptism of suspected Calvinist children which Malesherbes had addressed to the authorities at La Rochelle six years earlier. Article Four stipulated that, in recording baptisms, the priest should enter in a special register set aside for the purpose the date of birth, the name of the child and of the parents and godparents strictly in accordance with the statements of those who presented the infant for baptism and that he should abstain from adding any written comments of his own.

The *Mémoirs secrets* not only welcomed the new declaration but expressed the view that it would soon be followed by similar legislation governing Calvinist marriages.[51] Rabaut Saint-Etienne, on the other hand, was unimpressed: as long as priests saw themselves as agents of the Catholic sacraments and not as public servants, Protestants could not accept their offices.[52]

If the reaction of Rabaut Saint-Etienne to the declaration of May 1782 was skepticism, that of the Catholic hierarchy was outrage. The First Estate made these feelings known during a special Assembly of the Clergy summoned in the fall of 1782 to help cope with the deteriorating financial problems created by France's involvement in the War of American Independence. On November 20, the archbishop of Arles expressed the indignation of many of his colleagues when he declared that the new ruling transformed parish priests into blind instruments of state policy, passive recorders of statements which they were not even allowed to challenge.[53]

As was noted earlier, the circumstances created by the Franco-American alliance of 1778 helped to motivate both Condorcet and Franklin to lobby Versailles in favour of Protestant emancipation. These same circumstances offered the playwright Pierre-Augustin Caron de Beaumarchais an opportunity to promote the Huguenot cause at court. Interest in the situation came naturally to the celebrated dramatist; his father André-Charles Caron had been born to a Protestant couple married in a 'Desert' ceremony near Meaux in 1698.[54] During his long and brilliant career, Beaumarchais never forgot his 'new Catholic' background.

A first opportunity to show his concern for the Huguenots arose in February 1779, a year after France formally committed herself to the American cause, when Foreign Minister Vergennes and Navy Minister Sartine asked the playwright to draw up a brief on the state of the national economy. In the *Observation* which he submitted to the ministry later that month, Beaumarchais pointed out that French maritime interests had suffered from the policy of neutrality pursued during the early phases of the War of American Independence. At Bordeaux, he added, many of these enterprises (in which, the dramatist might have noted, he had invested substantial sums) were in the hands of Protestants. Surely it made sense to grant a voice in the making of national economic policy to men whose contributions to France's welfare were so substantial? Beaumarchais went on to recommend that Calvinists be admitted to the chambers of commerce in the King's chief ports and allowed to circulate freely throughout France on business, arguing that such measures were dictated by common sense as well as by simple justice, "especially at a time when the King of France has deigned to confide the administration of his finances to a man of genius who is neither French nor of the King's religion!" Recently, the English, although still passionately anti-papist, had modified their discriminatory laws against Catholics out of enlightened self-interest; why should the French not follow suit? The modest concessions which he was advocating, Beaumarchais went on, were a far cry from somewhat bolder measures such as the regularization of the status of Protestant children which, when one paused to reflect on it, "no prince on earth has the right to deny his subjects." The dramatist concluded his submission with the comment that the slight changes in the law which he was proposing could easily be granted in writing by ministers acting in the King's name; he noted that he was on the point of travelling to Bordeaux and would be pleased to transmit such written authorization to representatives of the Reformed community there.[55]

Although his friends in the ministry did not act on the suggestions which he had forwarded to them in his *Observation*, Beaumarchais took it upon himself when visiting Bordeaux later that spring to sound out the local Huguenots about a possible solution to the problem of their children's status. The visitor's proposed formula—the by now familiar idea that the parish priest be authorized to function as an agent of the state when registering the birth of infant Calvinists—was rejected out of hand by Bordeaux's leading pastor, Olivier-Desmont. The minister relayed to Paul Rabaut the essence of the response which he had given the playwright:

> The important question of the status of Protestants in the kingdom should not be solved piecemeal but in its entirety. One must not place the laws of the land above the demands of conscience but the other way around. Given that you have done me the honour of informing me concerning your views in this matter the best you can do for the Protestants is to forget them, since you are likely to do them more harm than good.[56]

This rebuff by the Huguenots at Bordeaux did not discourage Beaumarchais from maintaining a concerned interest in the Calvinists' situation. In the spring of 1782, when reverses in the war at sea against the English brought Vice-Admiral Charles-Hector, comte d'Estaing, to visit France's key seaports to raise money for the outfitting of new ships, Beaumarchais joined him and took advantage of the occasion to urge that Calvinists be included in the subscription campaign. In Bordeaux, the admiral followed up the suggestion and, braving the opposition of the

Catholic members of the local chamber of commerce, selected three Protestants to sit on the six-man preparatory committee which was to work out the details of the fund-raising operation. Before leaving the city, the admiral entrusted Beaumarchais with the supervision of the committee's activities. The dramatist was soon to discover that, while the Protestants were understandably full of zeal for a project which would have clearly established their patriotic credentials, the Catholics on the committee (who regarded Beaumarchais not only as a court lackey but also as prejudiced in favour of the Reformed) refused to cooperate in the project, making its failure inevitable.[57]

Advocates of Protestant toleration such as Beaumarchais no doubt had cause for discouragement as they measured the degree of resistance to their lobbying. The man who had been chosen deputy-general of the Reformed churches at court, Antoine Court de Gébelin, had reason to be even more despondent. The constant bickering and quarrelling about his mandate within the Calvinist community and the challenge to his role by men such as Dutens, Lecointe, and Armand finally took their toll; in the end, encouraged by friends in the intellectual world such as the president de Brosses, the marquis de Mirabeau, and the baron d'Holbach, the Protestant agent decided to abandon his lobbying efforts in 1784 and commit himself full-time to the writing of *Le Monde primitif* which was to become a much-admired study of the origin of myth and language.

The public recognition of Court de Gébelin's work testifies to the full integration of France's non-conformists into the highest levels of pre-revolutionary French society. The Académie française rewarded his scholarly enterprise with a handsome prize in 1780; and early in the following year, he was named a *censeur royal* by Chancellor Hue de Miromesnil. (He was, it must be noted, hardly an orthodox Calvinist: he had disconcerted some of his co-religionists by joining the masonic Lodge of the Nine Sisters; and when he died in 1784, it was in the arms of Antonio Mesmer, the notorious practitioner of therapy through animal magnetism!)

At the time of Court de Gébelin's death, the campaign for French Calvinist relief seemed to have lost its momentum. Continuing opposition to Protestant emancipation on the part of the Catholic clergy, internal wrangling within the Reformed community, the cautious conservatism of Necker and his protégé Armand, and the deference of Paris magistrates to the King's wish that they cease to agitate the Huguenot question, had all contributed to slowing down the efforts of those who were anxious that the Reformed be given a real bill of rights. Within three years of Court de Gébelin's death, however, all this was to change, as we shall see.

---

1.   Paul Rabaut to Chiron fils, September 25, 1776, B.P., Papiers Chiron, I, fol. 200.

2. In 1799, Amelot and Hue de Miromesnil sanctioned the election of a Calvinist as consul in Nîmes over the objections of a Catholic who protested its illegality. V. Amelot to Hue de Miromesnil, March 20, 1779, A.N., O1 473, fol. 123; Versailles granted an award for the protection of a special vellum to two Calvinist brothers of Annonay who had returned from exile in Germany to set up their own papermaking plant. V. Feuillet de Conches, *Louis XVI, Marie-Antoinette et Mme Elisabeth, Lettres et documents inédits* (2 vol.; Paris, 1864), I, p. 149; and the Protestants of the Lower Cévennes eagerly responded when the comte de Périgord asked them to furnish a demographic and economic survey of their solution. V. "Mémoire sur la population et l'industrie des Protestants des Basses-Cévennes, 1778," B.P., Papiers Rabaut, I, E, fols. 78-79.

3. Abbé Benant, *L'intolérance éclairée ou Lettres critiques d'un vicaire à l'auteur de la brochure intitulé: "Les Protestants déboutés de leurs prétentions"* (n.p., 1777), pp. 139-40.

4. Abbé Pey, *La tolérance chrétienne opposée au tolérantisme philosophique, ou Lettres d'un patriote au soi-disant curé sur son "Dialogue au sujet des Protestants"* (Fribourg, 1784).

5. Abbé G.-T.-F. Raynal, *Histoire philosophique et politique des deux Indes* (4 vols.; Geneva, 1780), I, p. viii.

6. Anon., "Mémoire sur les protestants de France, 1782," B.N., Ms Fonds fr., 6432.

7. Anon., "Mémoire sur les réfugiés de France dans le canton de Berne, 1782," ibid.

8. Anon., "Réponse publique aux questions secrètes sur les réfugiés français," *BSHPF*, VII (1859), pp. 320-40.

9. Anon., "Lettres à M. L'abbé Raynal sur l'histoire de la révocation de l'edit de Nantes qu'il se propose de publier, 1782," ibid., pp. 232-36.

10. Frederick II to d'Alembert, October 30, 1782, Frederic II, *Oeuvres* (33 vols.; Berlin, 1846-57), XXV, p. 270.

11. J.-P. Erman and P.-C.-F. Reclam, *Mémoires pour servir à l'histoire des réfugiés français dans les Etats du roi* (8 vols.; Berlin, 1782-1794).

12. Necker had come to Paris thirty years earlier as a clerk in the prestigious Thelusson banking house. Successful speculation in the grain market had brought him a private fortune, the chance to found his own banking establishment and, in 1768, the prestige of being named Geneva's resident minister in the French capital. By the early 1770s when his ambitions began to focus on the French political scene, Necker set about cultivating those in a postion to help him achieve this career transition. Maurepas gave encouragement and support, as did the marquis de Pezay, whose father was Genevan. Necker gave his political prospects a further boost by joining in the pamphlet war against two successive controllers-general, Turgot and Bernard de Clugny. Then, in November 1776, to the amusement of Maurepas and the French court, the ambitious Swiss purchased a chancellorship in the Order of Military Merit, a corporation created by Louis XV to reward foreign Protestant officers who had distinguished themselves while serving in the French army.

13. Paul-Claude Moultou to Jakob Heinrich Meister, October 4, 1777, Best. D. 20824. Voltaire's attitude towards Necker became somewhat more sympathetic early in 1778.

14. During 1776, Christophe de Beaumont made a determined effort to win Necker to the Roman communion, leading Condorcet to denounce the Genevan's impending "vile abjuration." V. Condorcet to Voltaire, November 28, 1776, Best. D. 19284. In point of fact, the archbishop's proselytizing efforts were unavailing, whereupon the cardinal de La Roche-Aymon, with the text of the Revocation in hand, protested to Maurepas that the administration was violating its own statutes by naming a Calvinist to public office. Half in jest, the king's chief minister retorted that, if the First Estate was ready to pay off the national debt, Louis XVI would gladly give the clergy satisfaction by dismissing his new director-general of finances. V. J.-L. Soulavie, *Mémoires historiques et politiques du règne de Louis XVI* (6 vols.; Paris, 1801), IV, p. 17.

15. For a thorough analysis of the religious ideas of Necker, v. H. Grange, *Les Idées de Necker* (Paris, 1974), pp. 515-61.

16. In 1796, after witnessing the attempts of successive revolutionary governments to reorganize and even to destroy France's national church on what he regarded as the spurious ground that Catholic predominance was bound to carry with it intolerance and persecution, Necker expressed the hope that the French would find a way to restore their links with the Roman communion. V. Necker, *De la Révolution française* (1796), *Oeuvres complètes*, ed. baron de Stael (15 vols.; Paris, 1820-21), X, pp. 213-14.

17. This paradoxical collusion brought inevitable taunts, as witness the following jingle which made the rounds after Necker's appointment:

> Nous l'avons vu, scandale épouvantable!
> Necker assis avec Christophe à table
> Et dix prélats savourant à l'envi
> Et grande chère et nectar délectable;
> L'église en pleure, et satan est ravi.
> Mais en ce jour, d'une indulgence telle,
> Quelle serait donc le motif important?
> C'est que Necker le fait est très constant,
> N'est janséniste...il n'est que protestant.
> (V. Soulavie, *Mémoires*, IV, pp. 72-73.)

18. Court de Gébelin to Necker, June 1777, B.P., Papiers Gébelin, IV, fol. 62.

19. "Mémoire adressé à Court de Gébelin par les Eglises du Nord," B.P.U.G., AC2, fols. 438-40.

20. Court de Gébelin to Pastor Oliver-Desmont, September 5, 1781, Arch. Cons. Nîmes, L 12, fol. 8.

21. Duc de La Vauguyon to Vergennes, February 19, 1780, *Correspondance diplomatique, Hollande*, vol. 540, fols. 212-13.

22. Court de Gébelin to Pastor Olivier-Desmont, August 5, 1781, Arch. Cons. Nîmes, L 12, fol. 4.

23. Olivier-Desmont to Beaumarchais, September 1, 1781, ibid., fol. 17.

24. Court de Gébelin to Vergennes, October 1781, B.P., Papiers Gébelin, IV, fol. 85.

25. Court de Gébelin to Paul Rabaut, August 5, 1783, Papiers Rabaut, XVII, fol.55.

26. "Mémoire de Cromot et de Bourboulon aux comtes d'Artois et de Provence, août 1780," cited in Soulavie, *Mémoires*, IV, p. 97-100.

27. (Madame Necker), *Réponse à la lettre de M. Turgot à M.N...., Collection complète de tous les ouvrages pour et contre M. Necker* (3 vols.; Utrecht, 1781), I, p. 13.

28. Anon., *Seconde Suite des Observations du Citoyen d'un écrit ayant pour titre: "Réponse à la lettre de M. Turgot à M. N., ."* ibid., p.3.

29. (Vergennes), *"Observations remises à Louis XVI et par ses ordres, le 3 mai, sur l'esprit du compte rendu relativement à la constitution de l'état, et sur le caractère de son auteur, considéré comme étranger par sa naissance, par ses opinions et par ses moeurs, à l'administration des finances de la France,"* Soulavie, *Mémoires*, IV, 154. Vergennes added that a reaffirmation of France's purely Catholic character was one means by which this most recent attempt at subversion might be thwarted. ibid., p.209.

30. Minutes of the Assembly of the Clergy, July 4, 1780, *Procès-verbal de l'Assemblée Générale du Clergé de France, tenue à Paris, au couvent des Grands Augustins, en l'année mil sept cent quatre-vingt* (Paris, 1782), pp. 185-92.

31. "Réponse du Roi au Mémoire de l'Assemblée concernant les Protestants," ibid., p. 663.

32. Abbé Gaçon de Louancy to Paul Rabaut, April 30, 1778, Papiers Rabaut, XV, fol. 154.

33. Abbé Gacon de Louancy, *Lettres de deux curés des Cévennes sur la validité des mariages des Protestants, et sur leur existence légale in France* (2 vols.; London, 1779), I, p. 93.

34. Lecointe de Marcillac to Du Séjour, July 4, 1778, B.N., Ms 10628, fol. 71.

35. Bachaumont, *Mémoires secrets*, August 21, 1778, XII, pp. 107-108.

36. Paul Rabaut to Etienne Chiron, July 6, 1778, Papiers Chiron, I, fol. 168.

37. Abbé Guidi, *Dialogue sur l'état civil des Protestants ("En France,"* 1778).

38. Emilien Petit, *Dissertation sur la tolérance civile et religieuse en Angleterre et en France à l'égard des non-conformistes à la religion dominante* (Geneva, 1778).

39. "Délibérations du comité de Bas-Languedoc, le 18 août 1778," Papiers Rabaut, I, E, fol. 68.

40. Paul Rabaut to Etienne Chiron, November 11, 1778, *Lettres à divers*, II, p. 252.

41. "Mémoire sur la démarche que Mssrs de la troisième chambre des Enquêtes se proposent de faire au sujet des mariages des Protestants, 1778," B.N., Fonds fr., Ms 10624, fol. 1.

42. Rabaut Saint-Etienne to Chiron, September 21, 1778, Papiers Chiron, I, fol. 186.

43. Bachaumont, *Mémoires secrets*, November 25, 1778, XII, pp. 180-90.

44. Ibid., December 13, 1778, XII, p. 211.

45. Brétignères, *Récit de ce qui s'est passé le 15 décembre 1778, à l'assemblée des chambres du parlement de Paris, Recueil de pièces sur l'état des Protestants en France (London, 1781)*. The Calvinists were understandably delighted by this intervention which Rabaut Saint-Etienne described as "simple, strong and backed by all the arguments which any Protestant might have spelled out." Rabaut Saint-Etienne to Chiron, January 25, 1779, Papiers Chiron, I, fol. 239.

46. Bachaumont, *Mémoires secrets*, December 28, 1778, XII, p. 235.

47. Condorcet, *Réflexions d'un citoyen catholique sur les lois de France relatives aux Protestants* (n.p., 1778), p. 60.

48. The *Mémoires secrets*, which applauded the general drift of Condorcet's essay, took special note of this reference to the serious loss of population which might result from the government's failure to give the Calvinists at least some minimal satisfaction of their grievances. V. December 28, 31, 1778, XII, p. 235.

49. "Mémoire sur le mariage des Protestants fait en 1779," B.N. Fonds fr., Ms 10125, fols. 45-51. In a later submission, the magistrates suggested that, since much of the difficulty surrounding the new legislation under discussion lay in the use of the word "Protestant," the adoption of a less provocative term such as "not yet converted" would have the advantage of conforming to the letter of the Revocation which the present monarch was so clearly nervous about abandoning, partly because of the wrath which such an abandonment would generate in the First Estate. V. "Projet de déclaration sur le mariage des Protestants," B.N., Fonds fr., Ms 10626, fol. 25.

50. *Déclaration du Roi concernant les acts de baptême, sur les registres des paroisses, donnée à Versailles le 12 mai, 1782, registrée en Parlement le 14 mai, 1782.*

51. Bachaumont, *Mémoires secrets*, May 30, 1782, XX, pp. 275-76.

52. Rabaut Saint-Etienne, "Réflexions sur la déclaration du roi, registrée en Parlement en 1782," Papiers Rabaut, I, F, fol. 113.

53. *Procès-verbal de l'Assemblée-générale extraordinaire du clergé de France* (Paris, 1783), p. 189. The chancellor effectively stalled the clergy by indicating that the nation's highest courts had not yet formally received the offending declaration. In any event, the First Estate seemed more alarmed on this occasion by a new edition of Voltaire's works and the chancellor was able to give the clergy some satisfaction by shifting some of the budget allocated to New Catholic Affairs to the subsidizing of writers who were prepared to defend the cause of Catholic orthodoxy not against Protestant heresy but against what was belatedly being seen as the even greater menace of "philosophic" ideas. ibid., p. 260.

54. Louis de Loménie, *Beaumarchais et son temps. Etude sur la société en France au XVIIIe siècle d'après des documents inédits* (2 vols.; Paris, 1826), I, p. 23.

55. Beaumarchais, *Observation d'un Citoyen, adressée aux Ministres du Roi, remise le 29 janvier 1779 à chaque Ministre du Roi, Oeuvres complètes*, ed. P.-D. Gudin de La Brenellerie (7 vols.; Paris, 1809), IV, pp. 479-83.

56. Olivier-Desmont to Paul Rabaut, June 17, 1779, Coll. Coquerel, Corres. Rabaut, F, fols. 19-20.

57. Beaumarchais to the comte de Vergennes, November 19, 1782, *Oeuvres*, VI, p. 380.

Malesherbes, persistent liberal.

CHAPTER XVIII

Genteel Conspirators: Breteuil and Malesherbes Set the Stage for Reform, 1784-1787

In October 1783, when he put Louis-Auguste Le Tonnelier, the baron de Breteuil, in charge of 'new Catholic' affairs, Louis XVI inadvertently opened the penultimate chapter in the campaign for Protestant toleration. Although the new minister did not become personally committed to the Calvinist cause until the spring of 1786, he did, shortly after taking office, ask the historian Claude-Carloman de Rulhière to prepare a study of the Huguenot question with special attention to the complex problems surrounding Calvinist marriages. Rulhière in turn got in touch with Malesherbes, who had been keeping a watching brief on the Calvinist question since his resignation from office in 1776. The historian and the ex-minister were subsequently joined by the marquis de Lafayette, whose zeal for philanthropic ventures of various kinds had been stimulated by his experience in America, and by Jean-Paul Rabaut Saint-Etienne, the eldest son of France's most eminent underground pastor. Two other figures—the physicist Jacques Poitevin and the lawyer-turned-publicist Pierre-Louis de Lacretelle, played enthusiastic but less critical roles in what developed into a genteel conspiracy on behalf of the Calvinists. During the middle 1780s, this small band of public-spirited plotters completed the most comprehensive review of the history of France's policy towards the Protestants undertaken since 1685 and drew up a succinct and convincing set of proposals for the remedying of the many problems bequeathed France and her Calvinist population by the Revocation.

By the spring of 1786, the way seemed open for a concerted effort to achieve this end. Those presenting the case for Calvinist relief faced a difficult tactical problem, however. They might attempt to introduce the desired changes in the law through the Paris parlement, where such well-known supporters of the Protestant cause as Bretignères and Dionis du Séjour (together with a new convert to the cause, the Jansenist Robert de Saint-Vincent) were prepared to press the issue; they might appeal directly to the King's council, where Louis XVI would be obliged to make his views on the matter explicit; or, as of December 1786, they might raise the question before the Assembly of Notables which the King had summoned to deal with the grave financial crisis facing the state. The case for Protestant emancipation was in fact put vigorously before all of these bodies; but sufficient momentum had not yet been built up to carry the battle for toleration to a successful conclusion, especially in the face of a still intransigent Catholic clergy.

The baron de Breteuil was one of a small group of conservative reformers in the pre-revolutionary period who perceived the need to humanize the nation's institutions in order to save the monarchy from functional sclerosis. To inform himself about the Protestants (for whom he felt a vague sympathy but about whom he know next to nothing), he turned soon after his appointment to Claude-Carloman de Rulhière, whom he had engaged as secretary during a tour of duty as ambassador to Saint Petersburg in the early 1760s.[1] Rulhière began his inquiry by seeking the advice of Breteuil's predecessor in office, Malesherbes, who was in fact preparing his own study of the Protestant question at the time.[2] At their first meeting (in May 1784), the two men agreed to exchange all the data which they so far had separately amassed and to make their further work complementary.

The two-volume *Eclaircissements historiques sur les causes de la révocation de l'édit de Nantes* which Rulhière prepared and which he finished in outline form in the spring of 1785 was to be published early in 1788, just as the legislation giving France's 'non-Catholic' minority was being promulgated.[3] In this most comprehensive of the many studies devoted to the question during the eighteenth century, Rulhière offers the reader a critical analysis of government policy towards the Calvinists since the 1680s and proposes a new approach to the toleration question. As Rulhière points out, one of the major obstacles to giving the Calvinists a legal status was the reticence of Louis XVI to challenge any of the major policies of the Sun King. The historian's solution to this problem was to persuade the reigning King that the Revocation had been urged on Louis XIV by three members of his entourage whose anti-Calvinism was motivated by self-interest rather than piety: Père La Chaise, keen to outflank the Jansenists and assure a paramount role for the Jesuits in the campaign to defend orthodoxy, Louvois, anxious to restore his influence and prestige at court, and finally, Madame de Maintenon, forced to adopt an anti-Calvinist position in order to establish her credentials as a 'new Convert.' As presented by Rulhière, the Revocation decision was thus neither an act of piety, nor of high politics, and the current sovereign had therefore no reason to feel that its abrogation would challenge either the Catholic church or the Bourbon dynasty.

By mid-April 1785, meanwhile, Malesherbes's first *Mémoire sur le mariage des protestants* (the text of which had been modified at the suggestion of Rulhière) was finished and on the 21st of the month, the magistrate transmitted it to Breteuil. The analysis of the Revocation decision which Malesherbes offers in this memorandum accords with that furnished by Rulhière: Louis XIV had been seduced by his Jesuit counsellors into believing that the tiny minority of Frenchmen still outside the Roman communion could be converted by fiat; he had not, however, intended to ordain the 'civil death' of his Protestant subjects. In support of this view, Malesherbes noted that the King had drawn up two separate plans during the period of the Revocation, one presupposing the quick and total conversion of his Reformed subjects, the other anticipating a lengthy period of proselytizing during which the civil rights of the unconverted would be guaranteed. Malesherbes described the resultant situation for 'new Catholics' as tense but somehow tolerable until the issuance of the grim edict of 1724. Fortunately, the way out of this unhappy legal impasse was simple: the King could simply rescind all legislation dealing specifically with 'new Catholics' and reissue the decrees which had been promulgated in 1685 by Louis XIV to assure the Calvinists an appropriate form of baptism, marriage, and burial pending their conversion.

In counselling Breteuil (and through him the King) to give priority to the regularization of the Calvinists' civil status, Malesherbes was clearly urging the administration to attend to the grievances of the northern, urban Protestants, whom he described as "very little attached to their faith."[4] By implication, he was suggesting that the problem of satisfying the Huguenots of the south (whom he knew to be preoccupied with obtaining freedom of worship), was much more nettlesome and might be for the time being left alone.[5]

Meanwhile, the ex-minister started working on a second memorandum on the Protestant question. In the midst of this new effort, he received encouragement from the youthful marquis de Lafayette who had returned from his exploits on behalf of American liberation determined to give himself to various philanthropic causes, partly because of the sense of genuine idealism which such causes excited in him, partly out of the need to obtain the approbation of his idol, Washington.

When he crossed the Atlantic in 1777 to serve as a volunteer in the cause of American independence, Lafayette was, like any well-tutored son of the aristocracy, familiar enough with the role played by Calvinists in the political evolution of France. Like many of his contemporaries, he took a rather complacent view of France's attitude towards her non-conformists, believing that, whatever the faults of that policy, it was undoubtedly more generous than that which England offered her Catholic minority.[6]

Lafayette's sojourn in America exposed him to a society whose leaders tended to be both deist and tolerant. And, as it turned out, it was while he was in the rebellious colonies that Lafayette was first made aware of the kind of discrimination to which the Huguenots were still being exposed. Late in 1783, Benjamin Franklin enlisted his support in pressing the claim of an American woman married to a French volunteer in the Maryland artillery whose right to her husband's inheritance following his death in action had been challenged by the French authorities on the ground that her marriage had been performed by a Protestant minister.[7] A second case which came to the attention of the marquis was that of a Protestant American boy who arrived in France early in 1785 and who, under French law, would have been obliged to receive a Catholic education. Lafayette was able to find a boarding school where the child could register without being required to attend mass and where every effort would be made "to ensure his being able to persevere in the religion of his ancestors."[8]

On March 19, 1785, Lafayette wrote to Washington to say that the Huguenot question had become one of his chief concerns, adding that he felt there was some hope of a rational solution to the problem in the forseeable future.[9] Malesherbes, to whom the marquis turned for background information on the subject, supplied him with a number of key texts concerning the legal status of the Reformed. By May, having familiarized himself with the situation, Layfayette was even more resolved to join in the campaign for Protestant emancipation. Malesherbes, of course, supported this enthusiasm, as did Navy Minister Castries, and Lafayette began to speculate about the possibility of winning over other, more conservative, ministers such as Vergennes and Miromesnil as well as members of the Paris parlement with whom he was on good terms.[10] Then, with the backing of Malesherbes and Castries, Lafayette decided to visit some of the major centres of Calvinist strength in the south in order to get a first-hand view of how the Huguenots saw their situation and how they wanted it improved.

As a result, Lafayette spent two weeks in Nîmes, during which he had several lengthy conversations with Paul Rabaut.[11] The veteran of the American Revolution was more impressed, however, by Jean-Paul Rabaut Saint-Etienne to whom he confided that Malesherbes and others at Versailles were actively preparing the way for toleration. The marquis suggested that the young Rabaut ready himself for a secret trip to Paris should it be deemed useful that a Protestant spokesman make a direct plea for toleration at court.

Following his ordination at the Reformed seminary in Lausanne, Rabaut Saint-Etienne had served as pastor in the Nîmes area beginning in 1765. By the late 1770s, his interest had shifted to the writing of propaganda for the Protestant cause; early in 1779, he published the *Triomphe de l'intolérance, ou Anecdotes de la vie d'Ambroise Borély*, which purported to be the autobiography of a Huguenot found among the papers of the recently deceased Voltaire. The imaginary author of this chronicle is a victim of punitive legislation against Calvinists in the age of Louis XIV who, having suffered near-martyrdom for his faith, joins the Camisard rebels out of despair and ends his days in London as a refugee. Rabaut Saint-Etienne interrupts this fictional autobiography to give his readers a detailed analysis of the legislation of 1685-1724, often with effectively sarcastic comment. Noting that the worst of these grim laws has fallen into disuse, he suggests that they are "proscribed by the tolerance of the age and annulled by the silence of the benevolent monarch who now governs us."[12] This 'autobiography,' which enjoyed considerable success with the public, was reissued as *Le vieux cévenol* in 1784; then, in 1788, Condorcet helped Rabaut Saint-Etienne bring out a modified version under the title *Justice et necessité d'assurer en France un état légal aux Protestants.*[13]

In his published works as well as in the confidential memoranda which he wrote to advance the cause of Protestant toleration, the younger Rabaut invariably focussed on the need to break down the artificial wall separating Frenchmen of different religious belief whose natural sense of community should be reinforced both by Christian charity and by a shared patriotism. He felt that Nîmes, where he spent his childhood, had come to exemplify the promise of a renewed peaceful co-existence between Catholic and Calvinist French citizens and he gave much of the credit for this to Charles Prudent de Becdelièvre, bishop of the local diocese. When Becdelièvre died, Rabaut Saint-Etienne paid tribute to a man whose just and gentle administration had done much to reduce old sectarian barriers and who was as a result as much mourned by Calvinists as by Catholics.[14]

In a brochure published in 1784 and reissued a year later, Rabaut Saint-Etienne outlined what he saw to be the Calvinists' central grievances and demands, stressing public worship and civil marriage. He went on to suggest that the old myth that Calvinist assemblies were centres of republican agitation would be quickly dispelled once the administration allowed such meetings since, "as far as the Huguenot element among them is concerned, the French gentry, the Paris bankers, Nîmes manufacturers, Bordeaux businessmen and Normandy farmers are all in favour of a monarchical system and are very far removed from adopting either an aristocratic or democratic form of government."[15]

Early in February 1785, several months before meeting Lafayette, Rabaut Saint-Etienne had also discussed the Calvinists' demands with Jacques Poitevin, a wealthy physicist and astronomer of Protestant background whose scientific achievements had been rewarded by his election to the Royal Academy of Sciences in his native Montpellier when he was only twenty-five. During this exchange, Rabaut Saint-Etienne again traced the lines of what might become an acceptable bill of Huguenot rights.[16]

Following Lafayette's visit to Nîmes in June, Rabaut Saint-Etienne urged Poitevin to travel to Paris to represent the Calvinists there while the brief for their toleration was being prepared. Poitevin set out early in July for the capital where he met Lafayette and then Malesherbes, who was much impressed by his discernment. The scientist submitted a number of briefs to the magistrate and was given in return a manuscript copy of Malesherbes' first memorandum which he described as "full of powerful, luminous, even novel ideas."

As time passed, Poitevin grew increasingly frustrated at the failure of Lafayette and Malesherbes to exercise effective pressure on the administration. In August he wrote to Rabaut Saint-Etienne suggesting that "the zeal of a persuasive advocate is needed here to inspire our influential solicitors to fulfill all our hopes," adding that he thought his correspondent would be ideally suited to provide such winning advocacy[17]. Poitevin consulted Malesherbes in the matter. Malesherbes sounded out Lafayette and the liberal duc de La Rochefoucault, who both indicated their support. The ex-minister then wrote to Rabaut Saint-Etienne suggesting that he come to Paris where he might gain access to men and women of influence by presenting himself for election to the Académie des Inscriptions et Belles-Lettres on the basis of his scholarly work on ancient Greece.

Rabaut Saint-Etienne accepted the idea of the Paris trip, although he was keenly aware of the difficulties which it posed. To begin with, the Calvinist community had proven itself notoriously reticent about providing its representatives at court with a decent subsidy. In addition, the young pastor knew that his mission must remain both unofficial and secret because, once known, it was bound to arouse hostility among defenders of the Revocation.

In anticipation of his mission in the capital, Rabaut Saint-Etienne forwarded letters outlining his views on the toleration issue to Malesherbes and Breteuil on September 22, again emphasizing the critical importance of civil marriage, but putting less stress on the issue of public worship.[18] When rumours about the younger Rabaut's mission reached Versailles, Breteuil (who was not yet totally committed to the campaign for Protestant relief despite Rulhière's memorandum), tried his best to discourage the venture. Lafayette and others helped reassure the authorities about the presence of Rabaut Saint-Etienne in the capital by letting it be understood that the scholarly young pastor was coming to Paris to consult with prospective publishers about a manuscript which he had prepared on early Greek history (his *Lettres à Bailly sur l'histoire primitive de la Grèce* was in fact to appear in 1787).[19] The marquis added that the comte de Périgord, who was currently at court, could be counted on to provide protection should the need arise.

Rabaut Saint-Etienne spent much of the winter discussing strategy with Lafayette. Both men turned for advice to Malesherbes, whose confidence the pastor soon gained after disabusing him of some of the preconceptions which the magistrate still harboured about the Calvinist mentality. The marquis and the pastor ended up formulating two guiding principles which they felt should be incorporated in any forthcoming legislation: first, in order to forestall the argument that recognition of the

Calvinists might precipitate renewed civil conflict, the French nation should
be explicitly defined as made up of a single people, possessing the same
inherent qualities and character, if not the same faith; second, the desired
legislation should clearly state that the establishment of a state religion was a
matter for the civil authority alone to decide and that this decision should be
made solely on the basis of what was deemed to be in the nation's best
interest.[20]

     Bearing these principles in mind and keeping in close touch with his
two friends, Malesherbes returned to the writing of his second
memorandum. The ex-minister's intention was to hold this second treatise in
reserve, to be used to win the King around if clerical conservatives put the
campaign for toleration in jeopardy.[21] In anticipation of probable appeals to
the King by the *dévots*, Malesherbes stressed the obligation upon the
reigning monarch not to abandon the ultimate spiritual aim of Louis XIV,
which was to make France all-Catholic; however, he was determined that
Louis XVI fully appreciate the futility of the means with which his
predecessor had pursued that objective. Even non-violent conversions,
Malesherbes argued, should be regarded as suspect if motivated by political
ambition: the opportunistic apostasy of John Law had lowered the prestige
of the regent's counsellor in the eyes of his peers, while the refusal of the
Maréchal de Saxe and Jacques Necker to sacrifice their conscience to their
career has imposed respect, even admiration.[22]

     In dealing with the practical aspect of any new legislation,
Malesherbes suggested, the government should realize that the Huguenots
did not represent a homogeneous bloc: there was a wide gulf between the
views of most pastors, anxious for sweeping religious privileges, and the
majority of laymen, "who do not demand public worship, but content
themselves with asking for a secure status."[23] Another shift in perspective
proposed by Malesherbes was that new legislation concern itself not with the
Calvinists alone, lest they become a privileged minority, but with "all those
who may not be married within the Catholic church."[24] This meant that the
large Lutheran minority in Alsace as well as France's Jews and Anabaptists
would by implication be included in the settlement.

     Malesherbes continued to believe that the resolution of the marriage
issue should remain the paramount aim of French law-makers. Here the *arrêt*
of September 15, 1685, provided a clear and helpful precedent: a revised
version of this measure would allow the civil marriage of non-Catholics
before a judge—or before a priest who would be designated a civil officer
for the occasion.[25]

     The most difficult aspect of any new settlement, Malesherbes noted,
would be the state's relationship to Calvinist clergymen, whose presence in
France was neither explicitly sanctioned nor prohibited in the text of his
proposal. From the government's point of view, it was essential to prevent a

recurrence of the Camisard troubles. This could be done if it were firmly stipulated that any pastors in France were "like all citizens, under the rule of the laws."[26]

While conceding that Malesherbes's views fell short of satisfying Protestant desires on some points, Rabaut Saint-Etienne respected the reasons which dictated a moderate line to the magistrate: "He is a clever man who deflects the prejudices which he cannot destroy, a legislator who speaks with the phlegmatic and impassive tone of the law. A flood of rhetoric would have spoiled everything."[27] Rabaut *père* agreed that, despite small errors of fact, the memoranda of Malesherbes were sound, impartial, and convincing.[28] Grimm felt that the *président* had expressed himself too timorously on the toleration theme but concluded that this had been deliberate, given that he was aiming much of his argumentation at traditionalist magistrates who were bound to oppose radical legislative change of any kind.[29]

During July 1786, Malesherbes discussed the proposals which he had set forth in his memoranda with a group of close friends at his country property. Rabaut Saint-Etienne was a member of the party, as was Lafayette (who had been doing his best to persuade Suzanne Necker and her daughter Germaine to espouse the campaign for Protestant toleration and was also trying, through the good offices of the duc de Nivernais to whom he had given a copy of Condorcet's *Réflexions d'un citoyen catholique*, to win the wavering Chancellor Miromesnil to the cause.)[30] Malesherbes had also invited the Paris parlementaire Bretignères as well as a new recruit to the campaign for toleration, Pierre-Louis Lacretelle.

Lacretelle had begun his career as an attorney pleading cases before the parlement at Nancy, but, his rhetoric proving less effective in spoken than in written form, he abandoned court appearances and soon established a reputation as the author of eloquent and persuasive briefs.[31]

Although Malesherbes and his friends spent long hours together, they reached no clear decision about the steps that remained to be taken to advance the cause of toleration. This failure was particularly disappointing to Lacretelle, who had hoped that the presence of Lafayette and Rabaut Saint-Etienne during the discussions would "revive the waning enthusiasm of the wise and venerable Malesherbes;"[32] in fact, soon after these conferences ended, Breteuil elicited a promise from Malesherbes that he would not see Rabaut Saint-Etienne again because such contact was against government policy.[33]

Despite the lack of any concrete new initiative on their behalf, the Protestants and their supporters remained optimistic. At summer's end, Rabaut Saint-Etienne was convinced that the ministry would soon take up the toleration issue, an assumption reinforced by the rumour that Marie-Antoinette had become a convert to toleration and that she was whispering propaganda for the cause in the ear of a reportedly sympathetic Louis XVI.[34] By the fall, Lafayette, too, had regained confidence, partly because of the decision of the heretofore ambivalent Breteuil to shift from benevolent neutrality towards the Huguenots to an attitude of heartfelt support.

This change of heart on the part of the minister of 'new Catholic' affairs was a byproduct of Breteuil's concern for the marquise d'Anglure, the daughter of a mixed Calvinist-Catholic marriage who was engaged in a bitter court battle over her inheritance.[35] After reading the eloquent *Consultation* which Elie de Beaumont, the champion of the Calas family, had prepared for the marquise, Breteuil decided to undertake his own enquête into the status of mixed as well as of Calvinist marriages in France. He began his investigation by sending Elie de Beaumont's brief to a number of lay as well as ecclesiastical authorities, asking for their comment.[36]

Some officials replied that they were now prepared to recognize the inheritance rights of children born of 'Desert' marriages because it was the 'philosophic' thing to do, although strictly against the letter of the law. Other respondents agreed that French magistrates were increasingly inclined to accept possession of marital status in the eyes of the community as sufficient evidence of legitimacy.[37]

Generously informed by his own investigations as well as those of Rulhière and his collaborators, Breteuil drew up a report on the Calvinist marriage issue in October 1786, intending that it serve as basis for discussion in the King's council. Following the lead of Malesherbes, whose memoranda he generously cited, Breteuil began by arguing that the Revocation had been "not a political project at all but an act of piety,"[38] carried out by a King who wished the peaceful conversion, not the liquidation, of his Protestant subjects and who had in consequence made specific arrangements to guarantee their civil rights. The failure of the Sun King's proselytizing hopes and a change in his advisors had brought some modifications in the government's Calvinist policy by the 1690s; of far greater significance, however, was the Edict of 1724, which had so compounded an already confused situation that it had proven impossible to apply. Fortunately, the remedy to all this disorder was simple: without consulting the clergy, which was sure to prove uncooperative in the matter, the government should revive the edicts promulgated by Louis XIV in 1685 in order to guarantee the Calvinists their fundamental rights pending their conversion.

Having learned that Breteuil intended to raise the Protestant question in the King's concil, Robin de Mozan, an advocate in the Paris parlement, sent the minister a copy of a *requête* dealing with the matter which he had drawn up for the ministry in 1782 but had not in the end submitted.[39]

Most of those who had submitted their views to Breteuil agreed that it would be farcical to pass legislation enjoining Catholic priests to officiate at

Calvinist marriages; but because there were still arch-conservatives such as the Montauban magistrate Lefranc de Pompignan who put the contrary argument with great vehemence, Breteuil sought the advice of two prominent ecclesiatics known for their enlightened outlook—Cortois de Balore, bishop of Alais, and Loménie de Brienne, archbishop of Toulouse—before presenting his proposals to the council.

The response of the bishop of Alais, which Breteuil described as containing "political and moral ideas which ministers of the faith are not in the habit of avowing,"[40] was that, as human beings, the Protestants were entitled to all natural rights, and most especially to the right to marry, preferably before royal judges, and that as taxpaying citizens, they should be allowed to sit on municipal assemblies. The state's only legitimate reservation concerning the Protestants should be to ensure that they did not form a separate religious or political corporation apart from the nation at large.

Again somewhat surprisingly, the response given Breteuil by Loménie de Brienne was far less liberal than that of his confrere from Alais: the archbishop of Toulouse insisted that Catholic priests continue to be the officiants at sacraments such as marriage, even when they involved non-Catholics.[41]

The opinion of the archbishop of Toulouse notwithstanding, Breteuil was determined to put legislation permitting Protestant marriage on the government's agenda. A suitable occasion seemed to present itself at the end of December 1786, when Louis XVI announced the convening of an Assembly of Notables for January 29 of the new year. Although the real reason for convoking this ad hoc conference was the government's desire to gain support for the floating of a much-needed loan, rumours quickly spread that the issue of Protestant toleration would be raised during the Assembly's proceedings.

In order to ensure that the toleration issue would be discussed by the Notables, the Jansenist Robert de Saint-Vincent, a *conseiller* in the Paris parlement, addressed his colleagues on the subject on February 9, 1787. The appeal judge began by recalling that delegates to an Assembly of Notables meeting in 1626 had agreed that unity of faith among Frenchmen could only be achieved peacefully, adding that legislation passed during the years 1697-1698 clearly indicated that the King and his council had planned to guarantee the Calvinists' civil status, especially their marriages and "it is the execution of this royal promise which Protestants living in the kingdom are today demanding."[42] The palliative measures adopted by the courts had given only a conditional status to the heretics, who might be tempted to emigrate if action were not soon taken to stabilize their situation.

Having listened sympathetically to their colleague, the parlementaires mandated their president, d'Aligre "to beseech the said lord our King to weigh in his wisdom the surest means of giving a civil status to the Protestants."[43] This resolution brought no immediate reaction either from the King or the ministry, however; in fact, the parallels which Saint-Vincent had drawn between Jansenism and Calvinism during his speech and the vehemence with which he had scourged the common enemy of both sects, the Jesuits ("Those who destroyed Port-Royal are the same people who were the ardent persecutors of the Protestants"[44]) raised paranoid fears. Even the normally detached editors of the *Mémoirs secrets* denounced Saint-Vincent as a "stormy Jansenist," adding: "It is well known that Jansenism and Protestantism are first cousins."[45] One pious Catholic thought that he discerned in the magistrate's speech not just the coming together of Jansenists and Protestants, but the hatching of a far more comprehensive conspiracy, one which included the philosophes as well and which aimed at nothing less than the toppling of both throne and altar.[46]

Meanwhile, the objects of Saint-Vincent's solicitude were far from universally enthusiastic about his intervention. Those Calvinists who were willing to accept a guarantee of their social status without the right to worship publicly rejoiced, while those who remained inflexibly committed to that right were understandably critical.[47]

Years later, Rabaut Saint-Etienne suggested that the failure of Saint-Vincent's effort to induce royal action concerning the Protestants was due to Louis XVI's indignation at the effort of the parlementaires to take credit for legislation which he was himself intent on promoting:

> This body (the Paris parlement) which was beginning to develop a taste for playing legislator, resolved to request that the King grant a civil status to the Protestants; but the King felt that it ill fitted the parlement to dictate to him what he was already planning to do.[48]

The next opportunity for broaching the issue of Protestant relief came, hard on the heels of Saint-Vincent's speech, with the convening of the Assembly of Notables, which met for the first time on February 22. Lafayette, who was (thanks to Breteuil) one of the delegates, shared the hope of other liberals that the Assembly would urge the government to introduce a broad group of reforms, including the granting of Protestant toleration. His optimism concerning action in this last area, however, was modified by fear that clerical and lay reactionaries might combine to frustrate any action designed to sanction heresy. Writing to Washington about this potential difficulty on February 7, Lafayette noted somewhat sarcastically that, with or without the convocation of the Notables, nothing in French law prevented the King from acting unilaterally to give the Protestants a measure of civil or religious grief: "Since we have the inconveniences of power, let us in this instance have the benefits of it, all the more easily since the greater part of the clergy, if not consulted in the matter, will not throw obstacles in the way, and people at large wish for a more liberal system."[49]

Early in their proceedings, the Notables named several bureaux or committees to address the problems which were preoccupying the administration, most of which, as the new first minister Charles-Alexandre de Calonne made clear, were economic or financial in nature. The Second Bureau, of which Lafayette was a member, was presided over by the comte d'Artois, whose mind had been prejudiced against the granting of toleration by conservatives in the First Estate. Not surprisingly under the circumstances, the marquis had little opportunity to raise the Protestant question during the regular sessions of the Bureau. On May 23, however, two days before its final session, when the Bureau was about to approve or revise a report summarizing its activities, Lafayette pressed his colleagues to include in their final report a request that the King deal with two major areas of concern which had been all but ignored in their deliberations—the granting of civil rights to the Protestants and the reform of the criminal code. The marquis had prepared the text of a petition dealing with these two matters and was granted permission to read it aloud.[50]

When Lafayette finished his remarks, Artois suggested that they were, strictly speaking, out of order, since they introduced matters outside the purview of the Bureau. Nevertheless, the King's brother agreed to bring the questions raised by the marquis before the King if such was the wish of the Assembly. The bishop of Langres, a nephew of Malesherbes, then intervened in support of Lafayette, remarking that, as a priest, he would prefer to see Calvinists worship openly rather than illegally, in proper temples instead of simple houses of prayer, ministered to by trained pastors rather than by vagrant preachers.[51] Following these comments, the Bureau passed an all-but-unanimous resolution in favour of Lafayette's motion, even suggesting that a third item, the need for a revision to the civil code, also be drawn to the King's attention. Artois then agreed to set aside the following day for a more thorough discussion of the new issues.

At the conclusion of this special session on May 24, the Bureau formally endorsed Lafayette's motion after editing out a rather ironical comment about the tolerant views of the First Estate. ("The clergy, inspired by the great principles that the church fathers did themselves great honour by professing, will undoubtedly approve this act of justice") and substituting another wording "to appease priests and dévots." In the final version of their petition, the members of the Second Bureau acknowledged that some of the concerns which they were bringing before the King were beyond the scope of their original mandate; but they were confident that his sense of equity and his natural goodness of heart would bring him to give consideration to a matter "so significant to humanity, justice, the state's welfare and His Majesty's glory." They went on to say that, if toleration were granted, a large number of the King's subjects "would be relieved from an oppressive prescription which was contrary to the general intent of religion, to good order, to population, to national industry, and to all principles of morality and politics."[52]

The reading of this text having been greeted with vigorous applause, Artois agreed to transmit the views of the Bureau to the King, adding that he had already sounded out his brother in the matter and found him to be favourably disposed. Not surprisingly, the advocates of toleration now thought the battle won; Lafayette passed on the good news to his friends in America.[53]

In the end, however, the initiative of the Second Bureau evoked no immediate response from the administration.[54] The failure of the regime to respond to the Notables' gesture on their behalf exasperated the Calvinists. Although Lafayette continued to show concern for their problems, intervening at one point on behalf of a predominantly Calvinist group of manufacturers from Nîmes who were seeking trading privileges in Spain,[55] the Protestants considered that the overall cause of their emancipation had been abandoned. Meeting in late June 1787, delegates to the synod at Montauban felt that it was vital "to focus the attention of the ministry on our status again," and urged Calvinist communities throughout the nation to consult with one another as the best method of reactivating the campaign for toleration.[56] Rabaut Saint-Etienne, back in Paris after the disappointing July conference at Malesherbes's country property declared that, if nothing were done, he would return to Nîmes and circulate a general petition aimed at arousing public opinion, thereby forcing the government's hand.[57]

As it turned out, the sense of discouragement which began to pervade the Calvinist community in the spring of 1787 was to be shortlived. Fortunately, a series of developments inside and outside France during the late spring and summer provided the extra stimulus needed to bring the administration to commit itself at last to the cause of Calvinist relief. When this happened, the ministry could turn in confidence to the masterful briefs in favour of religious toleration which had been drawn up by the small band of men who had gathered around Malesherbes and Rulhière, beginning in 1784.

---

1. Rulhière's account of Russia's turbulent domestic politics during the early years of Catherine II's reign, which circulated in manuscript form among French literati, helped secure his election to the Academy in 1787. V. C.-C. de Rulhière, *Histoire, ou Anecdotes sur la révolution de Russie en l'année 1762* (Paris, 1797). With the aid of Grimm, the Russian court did its best to prevent the circulation of this work, which was first published under the Directory.

2. A full account of Malesherbes's efforts on behalf of the Reformed during this period is offered in P. Grosclaude, *Malesherbes, témoin et interprète de son temps* (Paris, 1961), pp. 411-41, 559-602.

3.   C.-C. de Rulhière, *Eclaircissements historiques sur les causes de la révocation de l'édit de Nantes, et sur l'état des Protestants en France, depuis le commencement du règne de Louis XIV jusqu'à nos jours* (2 vols.; Paris, 1788), Grimm reviewed Volume I in February 1788, *Correspondance littéraire*, XV, pp. 199-208.

4.   C.-G de Lamoignon de Malesherbes, *Mémoire sur le mariage des Protestants, en 1785* (n.p., 1787), p. 75.

5.   It would appear that Malesherbes transmitted copies of his memorandum not only to Breteuil but also to a number of Paris parlementaires sympathetic to Protestant toleration. In any case, in May 1785, Louis-Achille Dionis Duséjour received a draft proposal for comment which bears a striking resemblance to Malesherbes's text. Exception made of Alsace, the author of this parallel proposal suggested, the Catholic faith should continue to enjoy a monopoly of public worship; however, a number of pastors might be allowed into the country, provided that they obtained a special permit from the intendants and that they restricted themselves to officiating at private services indoors. All French children, whatever the faith of their parents, would be obliged to submit to Catholic baptism. Concerning marriage, the author of the proposal was prepared to suggest some concessions: a Calvinist couple could legalize their marriage, following the publishing of the banns before the local justice, by making a mutual declaration in the presence of the judge, his clerk and two witnesses. Mixed marriages would be permitted only after the issuance of special letters-patent in accordance with which the priest would be obliged to marry the couple or incur a penalty. Rehabilitation of 'Desert' marriages would also be by letters-patent granted by a special ad hoc committee. The burial of Protestants could be resolved more easily by the reissuance of the royal declaration of December 22, 1685. Calvinists who had fled the country would be given a period of grace during which they might return to France; their property, if still in government hands, would be restored to them upon their reintegration into the national community. Du Séjour, who had urged the case for toleration before his colleagues in 1778, prefaced his analysis of this proposal with a word of caution. No doubt recalling the rebuff which he and his fellow-magistrates had incurred for their earlier effort, he observed that the function of parlementaires was to endorse or modify rather than to propose new laws; they would not do the Protestants a good turn by proposing to a King already "ill-disposed" towards his non-conformist subjects an item of legislation which might well alienate him even further from them. Having sounded this hesitant note, Du Séjour nevertheless went on to criticize the proposal, the dangers of which he exposed in a somewhat syllogistic argument: civil toleration meant de facto recognition of the Protestants; permission to worship publicly was the inevitable if not the desirable corollary of such recognition; permission to worship even privately entailed the legal re-entry into France of Calvinist ministers, and this development would inevitably pit Catholics against non-conformists. The magistrate went on to note that the increase in their number which would follow the open acceptance of the Protestants might threaten the Catholic character of France, while the possibility of the Calvinists developing a commercial monopoly would give them an inordinate influence in the nation's foreign policy. V. "Objections de Dionis Du Séjour

concernant l'édit proposé" (addressed to Malesherbes), May, 1785, B.N., Ms Fonds fr., 10619, fols. 1-5.

6.   The young marquis had, of course, been raised as a Catholic, but as the years passed, his membership in the Roman communion became more nominal than real; to his American Episcopalian friend, Dr. Griffith, he wrote half in jest that in France he was "suspected of a strong tincture of Presbyterianism" ; and, in a letter to Washington some years after the triumph of the American cause, he characterized himself, by contrast with his pious parents, as Roman Catholic "or supposed to be, if anything, that is." V. Lafayette to Dr. Griffith, December 26, 1786, cited in L. Gottschalk, *Lafayette Between the American and the French Revolution, 1783-1789* (2d ed.; Chicago, 1965), p. 170; *Lafayette to Washington*, May 11, 1785; L. Gottschalk (ed.), *The Letters of Lafayette to Washington*, 1777-1799 (2d. ed.; Philadephia, 1976), p. 297.

7.   Lafayette to McHenry, December 26, 1783, Huntington Library, H M 157, cited in Gottschalk, *Lafayette Between the American and the French Revolution*, p. 171.

8.   Lafayette to Elias Boudinot, March 16, 1785, *New Jersey Historical Society*, cited in ibid., p. 162.

9.   Lafayette to Washington, March 19, 1785, *The Letters of Lafayette*, p. 294.

10.   Lafayette to Washington, May 11, 1785, op. cit.

11.   Gottschalk, *Lafayette Between the American and the French Revolution*, p. 176.

12.   J.-P. Rabaut Saint-Etienne, *Triomphe de l'intolérance, ou Anecdotes de la vie d'Ambroise Borély, mort à Londres; âgé de 103 ans, recueillis par W. Jertermann:Ouvrage traduit de l'anglais et trouvé dans les papiers de M. de Voltaire* (Geneva, 1799), p. 181.

13.   Rabaut Saint-Etienne, *Le vieux cévenol, ou Anecdotes de la vie d'Ambroise Borély, etc.* (Paris, 1784); *Justice et nécessité d'assurer en France un état légal aux Protestants* (Augsburg, 1788).

14.   Rabaut Saint-Etienne, *Hommage à la mémoire de M. l'évêque de Nîmes, 1785* (Paris, 1821).

15.   Rabaut Saint-Etienne, *Le roi doit modifier les lois portées contre les Protestants, Démonstration: Avantages que la France tirerait de cette modification* (London, 1784), p. 75.

16.   Rabaut Saint-Etienne indicated to Poitevin that, while Calvinists would clearly prefer to be married by their own pastors, they would accept a purely civil ceremony if that were offered. Mixed marriages should pose no problem except perhaps that the Protestants' rigorous moral code might discourage prospective Catholic spouses. The Reformed, of course, recognized baptism in the Roman rite; but they put little faith in the motives which led priests to administer this sacrament to their children. A simple decree authorizing separate Calvinist cemeteries would be welcome. Finally, the government should recognize the Protestants' unshakeable conviction that public worship was part of their obligation to the Almighty. Rabaut Saint-Etienne to Paul Rabaut, February 4, 1785, B.P., Papiers Rabaut, III, G. fol. 96.

17.   Poitevin to Rabaut Saint-Etienne, August 1, 1785, Anon., "Les promoteurs de l'édit de 1787 qui a restitué l'état civil aux Protestants de France," *BSHPF*, III (1855), p. 334.

18. Rabaut Saint-Etienne to Malesherbes, September 22, 1785; Rabaut Saint-Etienne to
     Breteuil, same date, Rabaut, *Lettres à divers*, II, p. 357, n.
19. Rabaut Saint-Etienne, *Lettres à Bailly sur l'histoire primitive de la Grèce* (Paris,
     1787).
20. Rabaut Saint-Etienne, "Lettre-rapport de Rabaut Saint-Etienne à MM. les Membres
     du Comité de Bordeaux," June 12, 1788, Arch. Cons. Nîmes, Rég. B 332, fol. 2.
21. Pierre Grosclaude has uncovered the extensive notes on all aspects of the Protestant
     question which Malesherbes began taking in 1779. Among other issues examined in
     these notes is the admission of Calvinists to public office. In 1787, Lacretelle
     furnished Malesherbes with advice on this delicate matter which he had received from
     two close friends. The poet and philosophe Saint-Lambert suggested that Huguenots
     be admitted to officer rank in the nation's armed forces, while the lawyer Target
     thought there should be no problem about Protestants in the legal profession. In an
     unpublished note found by Grosclaude, Malesherbes offers his own opinion in the
     matter: as of 1685, the ex-minister writes, the monarchy had effected the conversion
     of the most influential and prestigious Protestant families, thus removing from the
     Calvinist community any leadership which might challenge royal authority. There
     was therefore no longer any justification for excluding the Reformed from public
     office, something which it was in any case hard to defend in terms of natural law. At
     most, it might be argued that the Huguenots be excluded from the magistracy, the
     teaching profession and certain key posts in the King's Household. (Malesherbes
     remarked in passing that the practice of the monarchy since the death of Louis XIV
     had been to admit or at least to tolerate Protestants in high positions in the military,
     the financial life of the nation, and the cabinet).
         In comments about the highly sensitive issue of Calvinist religious freedom,
     Malesherbes suggests that Protestant public worship should be tolerated, adding that
     the administration might counter any lingering anxiety about the peaceful and
     patriotic nature of such worship by keeping the Huguenots' religious assemblies
     under surveillance; Calvinist temples, on the other hand, ought not to be specifically
     mentioned in any *projet de loi*. To prevent any recurrence of the civil unrest which
     had been stirred up by Camisard prophets, it would suffice that any pastors
     circulating inside France be known to the regime.
         It is clear from these notes that Malesherbes held out no hope for a change in
     attitude towards the Huguenots on the part of the Catholic clergy. The majority of
     priests, the ex-minister indicates, still believe that the conversions secured by force
     in the 1680s were sincere. Those few bishops who expressed skepticism about that
     mass conversion were afraid to express their opinion openly. Malesherbes goes on to
     judge his fellow magistrates almost as harshly, suggesting that they were opposed to
     liberalizing the laws against the Calvinists because they got a feeling of personal
     satisfaction (and of public applause) whenever they used their influence to back
     Huguenot appellants in their courts. Even the underground pastors, Malesherbes
     notes rather cynically, might react negatively if the law were amended since the
     reforms under consideration would deprive them of the very special role which they
     had come to play on behalf of their co-religionists. V. Grosclaude, *Malesherbes*, pp.
     581-602.

22. Malesherbes, "Conversions. Premier moyen: missions, exclusions des places, et grâces accordées aux convertis," B.N., MS 7047, fol. 662.

23. Malesherbes, *Second mémoire sur le mariage des Protestants, en 1786* (London, 1787), p. 40.

24. Ibid., p. 93.

25. Banns preceding these marriages would be published in the presence of the local justice; a mutual declaration of fidelity before the judge and four witnesses (who would later sign the judge's registry) would constitute the marriage ceremony. The king would be the ultimate authority to whom an appeal might be made by persons whose efforts to marry in this fashion were challenged.'Desert' marriages could be regularized by making a declaration in front of witnesses or by reference to the Protestants' own marital registry where such existed; in cases where there was no other recourse, possession of status or testimony before an ad hoc commission would suffice. Ibid., p. 123.

26. Ibid., p. 174.

27. Rabaut Saint-Etienne, "Lettre-rapport à MM. les membres du Comité de Bordeaux," fol. 4.

28. Paul Rabaut to Charles de Végobre, April 11, 1788, Rabaut, *Lettres à divers*, II, p. 368.

29. Grimm, *Correspondance littéraire*, December, 1787, XV, pp. 177-78. In a third, never published, memorandum destined for the ministry, Malesherbes went out of his way to emphasize that the Protestants wished only to be tolerated: they were seeking no privileges and would be content with the legal recognition of their births and marriages. Some of the disabilities which kept Calvinists out of the public sector might be retained, Malesherbes suggested, since these restrictions channeled the activities of non-Catholics into productive careers in cities such as Nîmes which had been made prosperous by Protestant enterprise. Oaths of orthodoxy should no doubt still be exacted from candidates for judicial office, but the election of local officials should be open to all. As far as the nettlesome problem of Huguenot pastors was concerned, Malesherbes suggested in this memorandum that the laws banning their presence under penalty of death be rescinded but that their movements be watched and measures taken to eliminate from their ranks all but men of substance who were French citizens. The magistrate concluded his comments by warning members of the administration not to consult the Catholic clergy about any prospective legislation affecting the Reformed since "it is an illusion to believe that one will even obtain from the clergy as a body any deliberation favourable to the Protestants." Malesherbes, "Mémoire sur les affaires de religion," A.N., H 1639, fols. 11-12.

30. Lafayette to an unknown correspondent, August 1786, Lafayette, *Mémoires*, II, pp. 155-56.

31. In 1777, for instance, Lacretelle pleaded the case of a group of Jews from Metz who had been refused patent rights by the city authorities as well as by the local merchants' guild. Although the case was lost, it established the reputation of Lacretelle as a champion of the underdog and an advocate of reform in the legal system. In time, the attorney came to befriend Turgot and Condorcet as well as

Malesherbes, all of whom admired his high-minded, disinterested views. During the year in which he joined Malesherbes's entourage, Lacretelle published a treatise in which he urged the reform of the French criminal code, a work which won him an award from the Académie française. V. P.-L. Lacretelle, *Réflexions sur la réforme des lois criminelles* (Paris, 1786).

32. P.-L. Lacretelle, "Lafayette," *Oeuvres* (6 vols.; Paris, 1823-24), VI, p. 118.

33. Rabaut Saint-Etienne, "Lettre-rapport à MM. les Membres du Comité de Bordeaux," fol. 5.

34. Ibid.

35. This long-drawn out court battle will be discussed in the next chapter. The case of the marquise d'Anglure is described in detail in J. Hudault, *Guy-Jean-Baptiste Target et sa contribution à la préparation de l'édit de novembre 1787 sur l'état civil des Protestants* (Paris, 1966), pp. 121-22.

36. Breteuil to the comte de Périgord, June 30, 1786, A.N., 01 486.

37. M. Turgole to Breteuil, April 1, 1786, B.N., MS 7047, fols. 610-12; Abbé d'Agoult of Dauphiné to Breteuil, 1786, ibid., fol. 631; M. de Moncan of Dijon to Lacretelle, April 11, 1786, ibid., fol. 616.

38. Breteuil, *Mémoire, ou rapport général sur la situation des Calvinistes en France, sur les causes de cette situation, et sur les moyens d'y rémedier*, October, 1786, cited in Ruhlière, *Eclaircissements Historiques*, II, p. 50.

39. Robin de Mozan to Breteuil, November 27, 1786, B.N., MS 7047, fols.552-73. Robin stressed the paramount importance of civil marriage for the Protestants, in part because it would stimulate the return of large numbers of Huguenot refugees.

40. Bishop of Alais, "Mémoire sur les mariages des Protestants," A.N., H 1639, ms. note.

41. Rabaut Saint-Etienne,'Examen de cette question: Doit-on constater l'état civil des Protestants par le ministère des curés? Pour dissuader M. L'archevêque de Toulouse de l'opinion qui y est discutée, September 4, 1787, B.N., MS 7047, fols. 656-59; Charles Pradel to Loménie de Brienne, October 1, 1787, *BSHPF*, XXXVI (1887), pp. 594-96.

42. Robert de Saint-Vincent, "Discours du conseiller Robert de Saint-Vincent dans la séance de Parlement de Paris du 9 février 1787," A.N., H 1639, fol. 3.

43. Ibid., fol. 27.

44. Ibid., fol. 16.

45. *Mémoires secrets*, March 2, 1787, XXXIV, p. 230.

46. Anon., "Réflexions sur le rappel des Protestants," A.N., H 1639.

47. Differences of view surfaced even in tiny Calvinist communities such as Tonneins. V. Rabaut Saint-Etienne to the notables of Tonneins, March 28, 1787, Papiers Rabaut, III, G, fol. 119; Calvinists at Tonneins to Rabaut Saint-Etienne, April 13, 1787, ibid., fol. 120; Letter of other Calvinists at Tonneins to Rabaut Saint-Etienne, May 15, 1787, ibid., fol. 122.

48. Rabaut Saint-Etienne, "Lettre-rapport à MM. les Membres du Comité de Bordeaux," fol. 13.

49. Lafayette to Washington, February 7, 1787, *The Letters of Lafayette*, p. 320.

50. Minutes of the second Bureau of the Assembly of Notables, A.N., C2, liasse 5, cited in Gottschalk, *Lafayette Between the American and the French Revolution*, p. 315.

51. Lafayette to John Jay, May 30, 1787, W.A. Weaver (ed.), *The Diplomatic Correspondence of the United States of America from the Signing of the Definitive Treaty of Peace, September 10, 1783 to the Adoption of the Constitution, March 4, 1789* (Washington, D.C., 1837), I, p. 452.

52. Minutes of the Second Bureau, May 24, op. cit.

53. Lafayette to Washington, August 3, 1787, *Letters of Lafayette*, p. 325.

54. Interestingly enough, news of Lafayette's initiative did reach a tiny Quaker community living at Congeniès near Montpellier which commissioned Jean Lecointe de Marcillac, son of the former Calvinist lobbyist, to write on their behalf to Vergennes. Lecointe informed the foreign minister that there were several hundred of the king's subjects who, being neither Catholic nor Protestant, deserved His Majesty's special consideration. Vergennes promised to consider this appeal but requested beforehand an exposition of Quaker doctrine so that the administration might weigh what special provisions might be made for French members of the Society of Friends in any new legislation. V. H. Van Etten, *Chronique de la vie Quaker française de 1750 à 1938* (Paris, 1938), p. 134.

55. Laurent de Villedeuil to Lafayette, June 20, 1787, A.N., F12, fol 156.

56. Minutes of the synod of the Montauban region, Hugues, *Les synodes du desert, III*, p. 522.

57. Rabaut Saint-Etienne, "Lettre-rapport à MM. les Membres du Comité de Bordeaux," fol.8.

J.P. RABAUD DE St ETIENNE

Ministre Protestant, Député de Nimes et ancien Presidt de l'Ass. Nle

De la Religion transmise par nos Peres ,
S'il ne professe pas le culte, et les mystéres ,
Son cœur en est il moins et juste et vertueux ?...
Quand on sert la Patrie, on est vraiment Pieux.

A Paris chez Madlle Bersuy Mde d'Estampes de S.A.S la Princesse Lamballe, rue du Coq St Honoré.

A.P.D.R.

Rabaut Saint-Etienne: A Protestant negotiator close to the court.

CHAPTER XIX

Spurs to Action: The D'Anglure Affair and the Dutch Crisis, 1787

The Calvinists' discouragement at the government's failure to act on their behalf in the spring of 1787 was short-lived. For one thing, the ministry formed by Loménie de Brienne following his appointment in May was more favourably disposed towards the Huguenots than any of its eighteenth-century predecessors. This sympathetic inclination was translated into legislative commitment as a result of two developments: the publication in July of a forceful brief by Guy-Jean-Baptiste Target in defence of the marquise d'Anglure, the child of a mixed marriage who sought to reclaim her inheritance in the courts; and, in September, an appeal for asylum from France's traditional allies in the Netherlands, the largely Calvinist Patriot party which had suffered a crushing defeat at the hands of invading Prussian troups. This second development brought the government of Loménie de Brienne to ask itself whether it was ready to grant these would-be refugees the minimal religious rights without which their going into exile hardly seemed worthwhile. Prodded into action by these two developments, the *conseil du roi* decided in mid-November to initiate the process which would at last lead to the granting of the edict of toleration.

The ministry brought together by Loménie de Brienne following his appointment on May 1 was overwhelmingly sympathetic to the idea of toleration. Malesherbes and Breteuil, as we have seen, had been waiting for an opportune moment to press the cause of toleration. The appointment in April of Lamoignon as chancellor had strengthened the liberal element in the ministry; and when Pierre Victor, baron de Besenval, joined the government as *garde des sceaux*, the two key men responsible for the overall direction of French justice were both pro-Calvinist[1]. The foreign minister, Armand Marc, the comte de Montmorin, who joined the government shortly after the dissolution of the Assembly of the Notables late in May wanted to repair the damage done the nation's prestige by Prussia's coup in the United Netherlands: the free admission of Calvinist Patriots might well go far towards achieving that end. The Navy minister, the marquis de Castries, had demonstrated his sympathy for the Calvinists during the American Revolutionary War; the man who replaced him in October, Charles-Henri, comte de La Luzerne, was equally well disposed. Guillaume Lambert, the controller-general of finances, like so many of his predecessors, welcomed a measure which might help the nation's economic and financial situation substantially.[2] The sensitive and scholarly duc de Nivernais, who had accepted a ministry without portfolio at the age of seventy-two, strongly supported the cause of Calvinist emancipation and did his best to influence the King in this direction.[3]

The only serious hesitation within the admistration about the proposed legislation came from Loménie de Brienne himself. This resistance was all the more perplexing because the King's chief minister had taken a very advanced position concerning church-state relations as a young theology student at the Sorbonne.[4] As the key figure in the new ministry, Loménie de Brienne turned out to be frustratingly vacillating, and provided little leadership at a time when major policy decisions needed to be taken; a serious illness which afflicted him soon after he took office further weakened his capacity to dominate events.

The much-publicized legal problems of the marquise d'Anglure confronted the government of Loménie de Brienne early in its existence. The marquise's Catholic mother had married a well-to-do Calvinist, the sieur Petit de La Burthe, in a 'Desert' ceremony during which he promised that any children whom they might have would inherit the Petit name and fortune despite the fact that their marriage was not recognized by French law. The marriage produced a daughter, Marie-Reine, who was committed to the care of the Ursuline sisters at the age of three, much to her father's chagrin. Marie-Reine stayed within the convent walls until her marriage to the marquis d'Anglure, a cavalry officer, in 1767. Seven months later, the marchioness was a widow. Her situation dramatically worsened, however, following her parents' separation and her father's decision to abrogate his wedding pledge and desinherit her, designating his nephews (who bore the family name) as his sole heirs.

The marquise was left with a grim choice: she could either accept the stigma of illegitimacy (as well as the poverty) which would result from the acceptance of her father's will or she could challenge it, knowing that her legal status was tenuous at best. The decision to follow the second course of action was to lead to her vindication, but it was to be a long and costly process. In March 1782, when she lost a first appeal to the seneschal court of Guyenne, she turned to the parlement at Bordeaux for redress, offering as evidence of her legitimacy the certificate of her Catholic baptism, together with attestations that her parents had lived together as husband and wife in the eyes of the community. The verdict of the parlementaires was crushing: the marquise was told that, as Protestant marriages were invalid in France, none of her evidence had any relevance.

More outraged than intimidated, the marquise appealed directly to the *conseil du roi*, retaining as her defence attorney the lawyer who had become most clearly identified with Protestant legal battles, Elie de Beaumont. Then, when Elie de Beaumont died early in 1786, his close associate Target (who was also familiar with the Huguenots' legal difficulties), agreed to take over the case.[5]

Target belonged to a distinguished upper-middle-class family with close links to the *noblesse de la robe*: he had been one of the many co-signers to the brief drawn up by Elie de Beaumont on behalf of the Sirvens; by the beginning of the 1780s he had become one of the most celebrated trial lawyers of the day (Mirabeau and Beaumarchais, among others, had retained him as counsel); he had close relations with many of the leading philosophes; and, in March 1785, sponsored by Malesherbes, he was elected to the Académie française. Target's agreement to defend the marquise d'Anglure brought him back to the courtroom for what would be his last and most famous case. In the draft brief which he intended to present to the *conseil du roi*, Target began by reviewing the long and complex history of French marriage law as it had evolved since the Reformation, noting that the arrangements designed to cover the marriage of Protestants were full of flaws and contradictions. The result had been that lawyers and judges had resorted to all sorts of dodges to evade the very statutes they were pledged to uphold. From about 1765 on, the courts had grown accustomed to dealing with the question of clandestine Calvinist marriages, usually approaching it obliquely by guaranteeing the status of the children of such marriages on the basis of testimonial proof and the acquired status (*possession d'état*) of the parents. But what defence lawyers had overlooked in their effort to find a legislative basis for their clients' rights was the Declaration of December 13, 1698, which reserved to the King and his council the resolution of all problems arising out of the civil effects of Protestant marriages.

By pointing to this particular piece of legislation, Target intended not only to reassure conservatives who were terrified at the prospect of challenging the legislation of Louis XIV, but even more significantly, to stress the desirability of secularizing the laws affecting all French marriages, as far as their civil status was concerned. One of the prime concerns of the state, after all, was the protection of paternal authority; nothing could be worse than that this authority be threatened or subverted by the cupidity of in-laws or collateral relations, as in the present case. The reigning monarch, like his esteemed predecessor, was clearly concerned at this aspect of the question:

> When it comes to separating the couple, to disturbing public peace, to rejecting acquired rights, to destroying status, to throwing children into the infamous state of bastardy, the conscience of the sovereign seems troubled.[6]

All the legal circumstances in the case weighed in the marchioness's favour, Target went on. In terms of natural law, marriage was a simple contract based on the consent of the two parties involved, and, if one looked at the case in terms of the regulations affecting mixed marriages (as lawyers for the collateral claimants had done), one could only conclude that the edict of 1680 forbidding such unions (which had been drawn up with a view to encouraging conversions) was anachronistic, since there were obviously many Protestants still in France. Target pointed out that Benedict XIV had in 1741 recognized the legal validity of mixed as well as purely Protestant marriages. For that matter, had not the mixed marriage which they were presently reviewing produced in the marquise d'Anglure a new convert to the Catholic faith?

Towards the end of his *Consultation*, Target had the marquise describe the circumstances in which her parents had lived and the selfishness and greed which had brought her cousins, the Petits, to disinherit her. In the course of this narrative the marquise mentions that, during her long ordeal, she had been consoled by young princesses of royal blood, who would clearly not consort with persons of dubious legitimacy. Finally, Target adds his own eloquent comment about the significance of the impending verdict for the Calvinist minority as a whole, which was waiting upon the King's grace for its release and which might still be open to conversion if only the state would adopt a more tolerant policy:

> Whether these sectarians are accorded public worship or whether they are simply tolerated, they must necessarily be freed from the dictates of a religion of which they are no longer the practitioners.... It is perhaps among the decrees of a good and just God that the errors of our brothers should slowly and imperceptibly dissolve away under the influence of a benevolent administration.[7]

One of Breteuil's close collaborators, Le Blanc de Castillon, who saw Target's *Consultation* in draft form, was convinced that its publication would give the government an ideal opportunity to come out strongly in favour of Protestant relief.[8] Following up on this, Target visited Breteuil on a number of occasions and was given confidential government documents which allowed him to buttress those parts of the *Consultation* dealing with the background of the Revocation policy. The result, when read by the King, would reinforce the case made by those in the ministry who had been trying to persuade Louis XVI that the Sun King had intended to make provision for the civil status of those not converted between 1685 and 1698. On June 20, Target signed his *Consultation* and sent it to the printers. In mid-July, the marquise, eager to hasten the process of her legal redemption, sent copies to those who were soon to be her judges.

Paris society had known of the case for some time and copies of Target's briefs sold well; the lawyer kept an account of the various responses to the *Consultation* in his diary.[9] Generally speaking, he noted, people found his defence admirable but the case in itself rather feeble. Louis Philipon de La Madeleine, a lawyer who had succeeded Elie de Beaumont as major domo to the comte d'Artois, wrote flatteringly to Target: "When opinion is guided by gifted writers like you, legislation must follow suit.... I confidently await the destruction of the wall of separation erected by fanaticism which politics had too much respected." On the other hand, the Catholic Linguet, a believer in only partial emancipation for the heretics, described Target's work as "a long, thick, heavy memorial, laboriously compiled to prove that one must give the Protestants unlimited freedom."[10] Meanwhile, clerical reactionaries had commissioned the abbé Nicolas-Sylvestre Bergier to draw up a reply to the *Consultation*. Bergier described Target's book as "a brief for Protestantism against the Catholic religion, or rather for *philosophisme* against all religion."[11] Despite what the Protestants' apologists said, it was natural rebelliousness rather than spiritual scruple which had kept them from accepting marriage at the hands of the priest. English Catholics conformed externally to the laws concerning civil marriage; French Calvinists could do the same.

Opposition to Target had come from the expected quarters; just as predictably, the Protestants and their allies rejoiced at the publication of the *Consultation*. La Harpe felt that Target had used the arguments most calculated to bring about Protestant emancipation and end the "terrible barbarousness of our legislation."[12] The *Mémoires secrets* surmised that Target, whose approach was described as "less that of an advocate than of a philosophe," inferred from the text that the author felt was pleading a worthy but lost cause.[13] On July 25, Malesherbes invited Target to collaborate in the drafting of the edict of emancipation because he foresaw that "it will be as a result of (your) brief that a motion will be made on behalf of the Protestant question in general."[14]

Meanwhile, during a series of visits to Versailles, the marquise received promises to attend the all-important hearing in her case from a number of ministers, including Castries, Montmorin, and Nivernais. Having learned that the King might preside over the judgment in person, she pressed Target to provide her with a summary of the *Consultation*; friends at court had hinted that His Majesty might condescend to have such a memorandum read to him in advance, something which could surely only prejudice things in her favour.

On August 25, Target was wakened after midnight by a colleague who told him that the Bordeaux judgment against the marquise had been unanimously overturned. The validity of her parents' marriage had been accepted on the testimony of witnesses, and the brothers Petit had been ordered to pay the 6 000 in lawyers' fees.[15] Target's inventive reference to the Declaration of December 13, 1698 had impressed the judge; the *rapporteur*, Albert, had done a splendid job, and, even more impressive had been the presence of the King who, having read the *Consultation*, had pronounced it to be "inspired by the highest patriotic feelings."[16] The vindication of the marquise energized the committee working on the edict of toleration. Target, the newcomer to the group, wrote to Rabaut Saint-

Etienne, asking for complete documentation concerning the French
Protestants' situation and suggesting that, if they were willing to submit a
requête to the government asking only for civil marriage, the King would
undoubtedly grant this. Rabaut Saint-Etienne, who had declared of Target's
Consultation that "the true principles concerning marriage are now stated,"[17]
relayed Target's views to the southern churches, suggesting that, in order to
profit from the government's favourable disposition, the elders should
inform the administration that they were quite accustomed to marrying in the
secrecy of their houses, that they relied exclusively upon possession of
status and not upon evidence of pastoral benediction for the validation of
their unions and that they depended wholly upon the King's condescension
in their quest for civil marriage.[18]

    These were remarkably conciliatory views coming from a southern
Calvinist; yet Rabaut *pére* made it clear that he rejected Target's proposed
terms categorically, arguing that the Protestants must insist upon religious as
well as civil toleration. In a letter to Breteuil, the elderly pastor declared that
the Protestants had been alarmed to learn that distinguished persons who
pretended to represent their interests at court wished to "dictate or extract
from them *requêtes* in which they are made to ask only the validation of their
marriages;" to such a manoeuvre, the Calvinists could only reply that
"according them satisfaction on this head alone was according them almost
nothing." Rabaut concluded bluntly: "As long as public worship is not
authorized, (we) will regard (our) status as uncertain."[19]

    Rabaut Saint-Etienne meanwhile reasserted the traditional southern
Huguenot position in the *Réflexions impartiales d'un philantrope sur la
situation présente des Protestants* whose publication, originally scheduled
for June, had been delayed out of a desire not to jeopardize the outcome of
the Anglure case. In this work, the young pastor redefined for the public the
Protestants' key demands including the right to public worship.[20]

    Given these views, the trial balloon launched by Target in his letter to
Rabaut Saint-Etienne turned to lead. Fortunately, the dialogue about
Protestant rights between Rabaut Saint-Etienne and Malesherbes which had
begun in the summer of 1786 was both more sustained and more
productive. By mid-summer 1787, the two men were engaged in twice-a-
week conferences to help work out a compromise on the toleration issue
acceptable to both the government and the Calvinists; Rabaut later described
himself as having "pleaded, argued, written and often groaned" his way
towards an agreed-upon text.[21] Rabaut Saint-Etienne received the final draft
of the bill on November 16 and commented that the problem of the
government was that it had not consulted objective observers concerning
public worship, all of whom would have stressed the importance of
formalized religious ceremonies and properly trained clergy for Christians of
all sects.

What Malesherbes's Huguenot interlocutor could not understand, not just as a Protestant but as a simple citizen, was the ministry's fear of proceeding with the toleration bill before the next Assembly of the Clergy. Like the rest of the 'conspirators' working for toleration, Rabaut Saint-Etienne was especially troubled by the attitude of Loménie de Brienne. He was convinced that the hand of the King's first minister must somehow be forced and he wrote Malesherbes on November 7, asking if the minister could arrange a meeting between himself and Loménie de Brienne at which he would identify himself not as a Calvinist lobbyist but as a citizen of substance who approached the toleration issue out of disinterested patriotism.

Happily for the Calvinists, a diplomatic crisis in the Low Countries in the fall of 1787 forced the government to give the toleration question its full and immediate attention. The crisis began when the Estates of Holland repudiated the claim of William V to the stadtholdership. Frederick William of Prussia, whose sister had married the stadtholder, felt impelled to mediate in order to shore up his brother-in-law's shaken prestige. When the stadtholder's wife was subsequently prevented from travelling to The Hague to rally her husband's supporters there, the Prussian King threatened war. In order to avert a general involvement of the great powers, France and England signed a convention on August 30, pledging themselves not to enter the conflict. After the signing of this agreement, Louis XVI named a new ambassador to The Hague, François-Emmanuel Guignard, comte de Saint-Priest, who, as son of a former intendant of Languedoc, knew the French Calvinist question at first hand.

Meanwhile, on September 8, 20 000 Prussian troops poured across the Dutch border, quickly defeating the Patriots and restoring William V to the stadtholdership. Saint-Priest, who arrived just in time to witness the rout of France's protégés, felt that the least his government could do was to offer sanctuary to those Patriots who might wish it. In a memorandum to Foreign Minister Montmorin, the ambassador urged that France's borders be opened to the largely Calvinist Patriots and that "freedom to practice their religion should be given high priority." A royal declaration might perhaps be published which would stipulate that a fixed number of refugees in any given locale be given an indoor chapel for worship and that those who settled in larger numbers would be authorized to build their own temples provided they had the financial means. Saint-Priest went on to suggest that, if the descendants of Huguenot refugees still living in the United Netherlands sought to take advantage of the offer extended to the Patriots, this would surely in part compensate for the diplomatic reverse which France had suffered as a result of the Prussian invasion. Turning to the question of the large Calvinist minority still living in France, the count concluded: "Perhaps it will be considered inconvenient to anticipate by such a measure the granting of freedom of Protestant worship throughout the kingdom? On the other hand, would such a disposition not be a fitting avenue of approach to the new law which, it is hoped, will be obtained in this area from the wise deliberation of the King and his council?"[22]

While the administration at Versailles reviewed the advisability of offering spiritual as well as political asylum to its Dutch Protestant allies, the Huguenots took advantage of the opportunity afforded them by France's diplomatic debacle to press their cause. Having heard from the Dutch embassy chaplain in Paris, Marron, that thousands of his fellow countrymen were anxious to take refuge in France, Rabaut Saint-Etienne passed on the news to Malesherbes, and, noting that a good number of the would-be refugees were French in origin, suggested that it would be highly appropriate at this point in time to welcome back those who had been victims of repressive French policy a century earlier.[23]

1.   Besenval was a rather unreliable colleague, more given to intrigue than to effective administration; but he was convinced that Protestant emancipation was long overdue and so seconded the initiatives in this direction taken by the chancellor. V. Pierre-Victor, baron de Besenval (ed.), *Mémoires de monsieur le baron de Besenval* (3 vols.; Paris, 1805), III, p. 317.

2.   Jacques Necker, out of office but anxious to make a political comeback, maintained a discreet silence about the advisability of new legislation favouring the Protestants at this stage. V. Necker, *De l'importance des opinions religieuses, Oeuvres*, XII, 386-87; Observations of D. J.-G. Gallot, deputy of Poitiers, to the Estates-General as related in L. Merle, "L'édit de 1787 dans le Bas-Poitou," *BSHPF*, 1932, p. 157.

3.   L. Perey, *La fin du XVIIIe siècle, Le duc de Nivernais, 1754-1798* (Paris, 1891), pp. 310-11.

4.   [Loménie de Brienne and Turgot], *Le Conciliateur, ou Lettres d'un ecclésiastique à un magistrat sur les affaires présentes* (Rome [Paris]), 1754.

5.   The career of Target and his involvement with the Calvinist question is dealt with at length in J. Hudault, *Guy-Jean-Baptiste Target et sa contribution à la préparation de l'édit de novembre 1787 sur l'état civil des Protestants* (Paris, 1966).

6.   G.-J.-B. Target, *Consultation sur l'affaire de la dame marquise d'Anglure, contre les sieurs Petit, au Conseil des Dépêches, dans laquelle l'on traite du mariage et de l'état des Protestants* (Paris, 1787), p. 67.

7.   Ibid., p. 101; p. 164.

8.   Le Blanc de Castillon to Target, May 14, 1787, cited in Hudault, *Target*, p. 174.

9.   The Journal of Target for 1787-1788 was first published in the *BSHPF*, XLIII (1894), pp. 603-607.

10. S.-N.-H. Linguet, *Annales politiques, civiles et littéraires du dix-huitième siècle* (19 vols.; London, 1777-1792), XIII, 161. Equally ambivalent comment came from Me Morea, an advocate with the Paris parlement who concurred in Target's feeling that "our legislation with regard to the Protestants is unjust, cruel and tyrannical," but who nevertheless insisted that the state must continue to exclude the Reformed from public office, deny them public worship, and give no recognition to their pastors.

All Protestants should be obliged to declare themselves before the local magistrates who would then be empowered to marry them. V. Me Moreau, "Lettre écrite à M. d'Amécourt sur le mémoire de M. Target et sur le mariage des Protestants, le 26 juillet, 1786," A.N., H1639, fol. 7.

11. Abbé N.-S. Bergier, *Observations sur la Consultation d'un avocat célèbre touchant la validité de mariage des Protestants* (Montauban, 1787), p. 4.

12. J.-F. de La Harpe, *Correspondance littéraire*, V, p. 170.

13. *Mémoires secrets*, July 18, 1787, XXXV, p. 336.

14. Malesherbes to Lacretelle, July 1, 1787, cited in *BSHPF*, XLIII (1894), p. 607.

15. Target, Journal, August 25, 1787, *BSHPF*, XLII, p. 606.

16. P. Boulloche, *Target, avocat au Parlement de Paris* (Paris, 1892), p.264.

17. Rabaut Saint-Etienne to Target, July 12, 1787, cited in *BSHPF*, XLIII (1894), p. 605.

18. Rabaut Saint-Etienne, "Mémoire sur les mariages," 1787, Papiers Rabaut, B.P., I, F, fol. 201.

19. Paul Rabaut to the baron de Breteuil, July 1787, ibid., fol. 203.

20. Rabaut Saint-Etienne, *Réflexions impartiales d'un philanthrope sur la situation présente des Protestants, et sur les moyens de la changer* (Paris, 1787, p.7. An anonymous Catholic publicist took issue with these proposals, arguing that, once their public worship was conceded and their marriages validated, the Protestants would no longer depend upon the government nor would refugees come streaming back to France if such concessions were made since they hated their former homeland. As for the proposal to establish Calvinist seminaries, it would only revive old civil as well as theological conflict. Surely France's Catholics had learned their lesson from the past? V. *Lettre d'un bon catholique en réponse aux Réflexions impartiales d'un philanthrope* (Rome [Paris] 1787),

21. Rabaut Saint-Etienne, *Letter-report to the Bordeaux committee*, February 12, 1788, fol. 12. P. Grosclaude has unearthed the correspondence between Rabaut Saint-Etienne and Malesherbes for the years 1785-1788 in the archives of the minister's collateral descendants. V. Grosclaude, "Malesherbes et Rabaut Saint-Etienne. Une correspondance inédite," *BSHPF*, CVI (January-March, 1960), pp. 1-16.

22. Memorandum of the comte de Saint-Priest to the comte de Montmorin, October, 1787, A.N., H. 1639, fol. 19.

23. Rabaut Saint-Etienne to Malesherbes, October 20, 1787, Grosclaude, "Malesherbes et Rabaut Saint-Etienne," p.6. Thousands of Dutch refugees had meanwhile poured across the border, many of them ending up at St. Omer. In certain cases, they were given help in establishing new businesses. Letter of Jean Lecointe de Marcillac to John Eliot, February 18, 1788, cited in Henry Van Etten, *Chronique de la vie Quaker française de 1750 à 1938* (Paris, 1938), p. 138; v. also H. de Peyster, *Les troubles de Hollande à la veille de la Révolution française, 1780-1795* (Paris, 1905), pp. 230-31.

Louis XVI, champion of toleration and reconciliation.

CHAPTER XX

Toleration Triumphant:
The Edict of 1787

Its favourable intentions concerning Calvinist toleration having been forced into the open by the Anglure affair as well as the crisis in the Netherlands, the administration of Loménie de Brienne finally resolved to act. Rather foolishly as it turned out, the ministry decided to couple its proposed edict of toleration (which it was assumed the Paris parlement would register out of genuine conviction as well as from a desire to appear supportive of popular causes) to a second measure authorizing the floating of a substantial loan to cover the government's increasingly desperate need for money.

In line with this strategy, Louis XVI appeared in person before a *séance royale* of the parlement (that is, in the presence of the princes and peers of the realm in addition to the usual magistrates) and presented both edicts for simultaneous registration. The first edict, launching a loan of 450 million livres, was accompanied by a promise to summon the Estates-General before 1792, something the parlement had been demanding for some time. When he came to the second edict, the King spoke of a project which he had resolved upon long ago, the provision of "natural rights, and what the state of society permits," to France's non-Catholic population. Chancellor Lamoignon added that it had become apparent to all enlightened Frenchmen that one must either enforce the proscription of non-Catholics or offer them a secure legal status. It was a "wise tolerance" which the King espoused, and not "a culpable indifference to all forms of worship," since the edict, which would bring France many advantages in the fields of population, commerce, agriculture, and the arts, also confirmed the commitment of France to Catholicism."[1]

After Lamoignon's speech, debate began, focussing quickly on the proposed loan. When the King signified his desire that the edict sanctioning the loan be registered, the parlementaires were about to comply when the chancellor committed a serious tactical blunder: by-passing the vote-count which was standard procedure during the regular sessions of the parlement, he conveyed to the King the purely formal expression of the magistrates' consent to the new edict which was the practice when the monarch presided over a *lit de justice*. The duc d'Orléans contested the legitimacy of this manner of proceeding. The King then withdrew, mumbling that the edict validating the loan was indeed registered because he had so willed it. In this tense atmosphere, the text of the edict of toleration was read and discussed; but by this time the magistrates had resolved on an attitude of non-cooperation and refused to sanction the measure. This resistance brought the temporary exiling of Orléans and two of his more ardent supporters.

The delay in the government's plans permitted a final, frenzied distribution of pamphlets for and against toleration. Linguet said of the negative broadsides that they were enough to inspire "terror in timorous minds."[2] The most "terrifying" and the most controversial of these appeared just before November 25 in the form of an imagined address to the King's council by a "patriotic minister." In this *Discours à lire au Conseil*, written by an ex-Jesuit (either Abbé Jacques-Julien Bonnaud or Abbé L'enfant in collaboration with Abbé Proyart), the traditional arguments of the conservative clergy were yet again trotted out: since the 1520s the Calvinists had inspired moral licence and political rebellion; now, in league with the philosophes and the Jansenists, and encouraged by misguided ministers, they were planning to undermine true Christianity and the monarchy.

The ex-Jesuit went on to note that the administration's decision to offer a civil status to the Protestants posed a number of problems. Would Catholics not be tempted to convert by an arrangement which recognized marriage as a simple contract? Would the state support a Calvinist pastorate and would it permit the revival of the Reformed ecclesiastical organization? Would Protestants be permitted to sit in the provincial assemblies which were currently under consideration? Since the answer to all of these questions, in the abbé's view, was bound to be negative, the proposed law must, he argued, be rejected without hesitation. The only admissible toleration was that which might be accorded to the heretics "as citizens"— but the abbé gave no indication of what he considered to be basic citizens' rights.[3]

Replies to the *Discours à lire au conseil* were quickly forthcoming. Linguet denounced the extravagance of the abbé's arguments and the inaccuracy of his historical data, noting that the edict, which left certain privileges in the hands of Catholics, in fact encouraged conversion.[4] Grimm, who denounced the bad faith and faulty logic of the abbé, was confident that the enquête would not delay the coming of toleration.[5] Paul Rabaut thought that the "horror and terror" inspired in those who read the enquête would help the Protestants by revealing the need to protect citizens still menaced by such fanaticism.[6] The *Mémoires secrets*, while denouncing the abbé's historical analysis, acknowledged that the work had a "vigourous, animated, warm style," and merited serious refutation.[7]

The ex-Jesuit had, like others before him, attacked what he saw to be a Calvinist-philosophe-Jansenist plot to overthrow church and monarchy. Two Jansenist apologists were sufficiently unnerved by this charge to write pamphlets in which they took pains to dissociate themselves totally from the Calvinist position. In one of these, the author of the enquête was denounced as "a monster when you impute to them (Jansenists) the seditious spirit of the Calvinists," adding that the ex-Jesuit had been right in maintaining that "it is not necessary to give the Protestants the dangerous legal existence

which is offered them."[8] A less defensive rejoinder was given the abbé by
the Jansenist abbé Lambert, who felt that, considering the Jesuit origin of
the enquête, it was not surprising that "ignorant women, bewitched by these
seducers, hawk their libels." What was most shocking was that "black
plots" should be imagined between the Calvinists and the Jansenists simply
"because a magistrate...wants to see the disappearance of a shocking
discrepancy between the law on the one hand and the conduct of the
government and the courts on the other, and because a multitude of
individuals who acquit themselves of the responsibilities pertaining thereto
should not be permitted to enjoy the rights of the city."[9]

One of the "ignorant women" referred to by Lambert was the
maréchale de Noailles, Lafayette's mother-in-law, who had been
instrumental in having the abbé pen his treatise in the first place. She helped
ensure timely reading of the enquête (which went through two publications
before the end of the year) by sending all the parlementaires a copy and
challenging them to write down any objections they might have, which she
would undertake to refute.[10]

The maréchale de Noailles was aided in her propaganda campaign by
the marquise de Silléry, a pious but well-read traditionalist to whom the duc
d'Orléans had entrusted the catechizing of his children. That the marchioness
took her responsibility seriously is apparent on every page of her anti-liberal
tract, *La Religion considérée comme l'unique base du bonheur et de la
véritable philosophie*, the preface of which she read to the duc de Chartres
on the eve of his first communion. Over the last forty years, the marchioness
warned the boy, the philosophes had been disseminating subversive and
sacrilegious notions in the upper reaches of society; their long-term aim was
the establishment of universal toleration, the inevitable byproduct of which
would be the open propagation of atheism, materialism, and
republicanism.[11]

While the two noblewomen went about Paris trying their best to hold
up the edict of toleration, popular rhymsters circulated the following quatrain
through the streets of Paris:

Noailles et Silléry, ces mères de l'église
Voudraient gagner le parlement:
Soit qu'on les voit ou qu'on les lise
Par malheur on devient aussitôt protestant...[12]

The appearance of the enquête and the proselytizing of the two
noblewomen were among the last deperate battles waged in a losing cause.
Nor was strength added to the effort to check the coming of toleration when
another cleric, the abbé Proyart, joined the fray.[13] Proyart admitted to
having no knowledge of the thirty-seven articles of the proposed edict except
that they guaranteed some kind of civil status to the Protestants. Instead, he

turned on the philosophes, charging that they were espousing the cause of the Calvinists because they knew all Protestants to be republican (if not anarchist) by nature. Why in any case should so much concern be made of these wretched heretics who enjoyed all the privileges of citizenship except that of forming a separate corps within the nation? The proposed innovations in France's marriage laws would lead to divorce and would tempt weak Catholics to convert. Like his predecessor's lengthy discourse, Proyart's sixteen-page pamphlet, which the Bachaumont journal dismissed as peremptory, was distributed to the parlementaires.[14]

Proyart was bitterly attacked for his defence of the old system of repression in a pamphlet entitled *Non-Catholiques en France*, whose anonymous author concluded with the query: "Is it not vital, then, that we give (the Calvinists) a legal existence...and break down a wall of separation erected by arbitrary authority?"[15]

Proyart was not, however, to be silenced; in a second letter, he defended the Revocation as having kept a dangerous minority in check while allowing it certain de facto rights. Rather than change this system, one should continue to act on the premise that all French citizens were Catholics. Unswerving commitment to this view would in time transform a presumption into a reality.[16] This letter, which the Bachaumont journal dismissed as empty rhetoric,[17] was parodied by an anonymous liberal pamphleteer who "shuddered" at the thought of what a tolerant society might be like and defended the Revocation as a necessary check on Protestant plans of "subversion."[18] A conservative commentator, meanwhile, reinforced Proyart's thesis that the Catholic church must keep all rival religions in a state of humiliation, since any concessions envisaged would only encourage the sectarians to show a new boldness. Since the nation's Jews enjoyed all the rights of citizens without having any legal existence, this writer argued, so might the Protestants.[19]

If the opponents of toleration profited from the delay caused by parlement, so too did the Protestants and their champions. Gilbert de Voisins' two memoranda written for the King's council in 1767-1768 now appeared and served as the basis for discussion and controversy.[20] *Le Conciliateur*, published anonymously in 1754 by Loménie de Brienne and Turgot, was reissued in the hope that the "shining principles and healthy patriotic views" expressed by its authors would help to bring the ministry and parlement to push through an edict of toleration. The ghost of Turgot provoked an angry rejoinder to this reedition from a writer who described the King's ex-minister as the worst example of that mentality, half-heretical, half-philosophic, which was currently subverting good order and government.[21]

Two works published by those directly concerned with the edict's preparation also appeared at this time. One was the second memorandum of

Malesherbes on the Protestant question which helped to "counter-balance in the public the impression which might have been produced by the various writings circulated against toleration."[22] The other was the first volume of Rulhière's history of the Calvinist question which appeared in mid-January 1788. In this study, the First Estate is exposed as responsible for "that long succession of laws which, every five years, that is at each periodic reconvening of its assemblies, it thus purchases (by its *don gratuit*) from the government."[23]

Rulhière had undertaken research for this work with the help of Rabaut Saint-Etienne, who was quite satisfied with the historian's interpretation of Louis XIV's religious policy. Delighted at this reaction and at the news that his book had been read with "great pleasure" by the Huguenots, Rulhière asked Rabaut Saint-Etienne early in February 1788 to review the manuscript of the second volume of his study. Later, when this volume was being published, Rulhière observed to his Calvinist collaborator: "It is thanks to you that I left in my text the opinion on toleration which I held as a philosophe, independent of the much more moderate view to which, as a government minister, I was naturally led by a thousand circumstances."[24] In this second volume of his *Eclaircissements historiques*, Rulhière informed his readers, he intended, not to set forth the case for toleration, but rather "to destroy all the principles upon which intolerance was based."[25]

Another piece of pro-Calvinist propaganda published early in January 1788 took the form of an imaginary conversation between a Capucin monk, a Protestant pastor, and an advocate of the Paris parlement. The advocate felt that "recalling the Protestants was the only means of restoring France's finances, of profiting from the troubles in the United Provinces, and of undoing England's policy," while the pastor referred to the harmonious cooperation of Protestants and Catholics in Alsace as ample guarantee of the benefits of toleration.[26]

The main target of propaganda during this period of last-minute advocacy was understandably the members of the Paris parlement. Three broadsides addressed to the parlementaires urged that they modify two of the edict's terms—the stipulation that the new measure should apply to all "non-Catholics" instead of specifically to Calvinists, and the regulation that the civil magistrate and not the priest be made the officiant at the proposed marriage ceremony.[27] Some writers tried to influence the parlementaires in the opposite direction. One advocate maintained that "the state will never enjoy perfect and assured tranquillity as long as religious acts are related to the civil existence of men."[28] Another champion of toleration, Du Closel d'Amery, went so far as to argue that complete toleration should be given all those who respected the principles of "natural religion."[29] Only one magistrate advised his confrères to reject the underlying principle of the proposed edict, arguing that it would "destroy the unity of the social compact and introduce anarchy and the republican spirit."[30] In the view of this writer, the philosophes, who were stirring up the Protestants to advance their own subversive ends, realized that the breaking down of the "wall of separation" between Catholic and heretic in France would destroy peace and order in both state and church.[31]

Conservatives at court hoped that this final propaganda campaign would produce a rift among the parlementaires and thus further hold up the coming of toleration.[32] The rift, however, did not occur. If the magistrates had modifications to propose to the King concerning certain provisions of the edict, their "hearts were for its registration."[33]

By agreement between the parlementaires and the ministry, discussion of the edict was postponed until the holding of a royal session, which was set for December 7. Louis XVI opened this sitting by informing the peers and princes in attendance that his intention in calling a *séance royale* was not, as Orléans had suggested, to deprive them of their proper voice in the deliberations of parlement, but simply to allow them to absent themselves should they see fit to do so. (In fact, only two of their number, the prince de Condé and the duc de Bourbon, were present when the *conseiller* Jacques Duval d'Espremenil, a long-term champion of toleration, rose to speak). The central thrust of the councillor's remarks was to attack the suggestion that the terms of the edict be extended to all non-Catholics, instead of simply to Calvinists; in the view of d'Espremenil, such indiscriminate toleration would be dangerous. The liberal duc de Mortemart then commented that it was "a trait of wisdom and profound political sense on the part of the government to have generalized the title, since there was no question of giving a civil status to the Protestants as such rather than as citizens and as men."[34] When the duc de Luynes seconded these remarks, the commission named to examine the edict set about preparing its final observations and criticisms for submission to the King.[35] The parlement having clearly indicated its willingness to agree to the registration of the edict, the enemies of toleration began to despair.[36] These fears were realized when, Mortemart having added his own comments to *conseiller* Ferrand's report on the edict, the *Remontrances* of the parlement were adopted for submission to the King on January 18, 1788.

In these *Remontrances*, the magistrates recommended that the benefits of the new law should not be extended to non-Catholics in general but simply to the Calvinists: above all, the edict should make it clear that the Catholic church would continue to enjoy a monopoly of public worship in France. It also stipulated that non-Catholics should be excluded from all forms of direct royal patronage, judicial and municipal office, from all teaching appointments, as well as from master craftsmanships. Certificates of Catholic faith, however, should no longer be required for membership in the trades and crafts corporations and provision ought to be made for the restitution of those goods and properties taken from the Calvinists which were still held by the government. The marriage question was handled as follows: priests who objected to publishing banns for non-Catholic weddings from the pulpit could publish them on the church door; Calvinists could have their marriages registered before a local magistrate instead of a sometimes distant royal judge. Finally, the parlementaires suggested that the punitive legislation of 1685-1724 be explicitly repealed.[37]

When Pastor Gal-Pomaret learned of the parlement's remontrance, he remarked: "In saving us from the jaws of the lion, the parlement wants us to be left to a certain extent in its claws."[38] Rabaut Saint-Etienne offered his criticism of the edict's provisions in a letter to Rulhière in which, among other things, he pleaded for the right of pastors "to enjoy all civil privileges, like all the other non-Catholic subjects of the King." As it stood, Rabaut Saint-Etienne suggested, the proposed law "limits itself to allowing Protestants to be silversmiths and wigmakers."[39] By early January, the Protestant negotiator was partially mollified, feeling that the law did, after all, imply repeal of the penal legislation directed against the Reformed.[40]

Malesherbes, meanwhile, supported the parlement's criticisms in the King's council.[41] On January 24, the government decided to withdraw the original text of the edict and to substitute another version which incorporated a number of the suggested changes proposed by the magistrates. Three days later, Louis XVI assured the magistrates that the religious toleration of non-Catholics was neither explicit nor implicit in the edict—the object of the law was to give Protestants a civil status, nothing more. As for the penal legislation of 1685-1724, the King intended to do away with it in time, but the laws which forbade other than Catholic public worship must remain on the statute books. Only if it proved necessary would the government make a ruling requiring oaths of Catholic orthodoxy from those seeking entry into trades, craft guilds, and corporations. The King would look into the question of *patronage*. The matter of goods confiscated from the Calvinists would be dealt with once the present edict had been promulgated.[42] Louis XVI, whose marginal notes to the parlement's remontrance attest to a new sense of personal conviction about the necessity and justice of the edict,[43] ended by urging the parlement to register the law without delay.

Having received this favourable reply, the magistrates met on January 29 to make their final decision. Twenty-four of the parlementaires were for presenting new objections and demands for modification to the King. When their protests were overruled, eight of these dissidents withdrew from the chamber before the final vote so as not to appear to participate in a motion which they did not favour. In the end, the edict of toleration was passed by a vote of ninety-six to seventeen.

In its modified form, the new law was a model of compromise. The preamble summed up its basic provisions:

> The Catholic religion...will alone enjoy in our realm the rights and honours of public worship; while our other, non-Catholic, subjects, deprived of all influence upon the order established in our states, declared in advance and forever incapable of forming a single body within our realm, and subject to the ordinary regulations for the observance of feast-days, will obtain from the law only what natural justice does not permit us to deny them, namely, the authentication of their births, marriages, and deaths.[44]

In its specific articles, the edict guaranteed French and foreign non-Catholics (the Protestants in Alsace and the Jews in various cities in France, already provided for in different legislation, were excepted from the legislation) the rights to property and to careers in commerce, the arts and crafts, and the professions, exception being made of public posts which carried with them judicial powers or teaching responsibilities. Non-Catholics would not be allowed to form a corporate group, nor could they perform a corporate act. Their pastors were not permitted to act as such in public, wear distinguishing garb, or issue certificates attesting to birth, marriage, or death. Despite its seemingly negative formulation, this article implied the presence in the nation of pastors, and the Calvinists took advantage of it.

The articles concerning non-Catholic marriage caused the most controversy. The edict provided that banns for marriage would either be published by the parish priest at the church door without mention of the religious faith of the contracting parties or that they would be announced by the clerk of the local justice in the judge's presence, after which a declaration would be affixed to the church door. Any legal problems arising out of Protestant marriages would be dealt with by civil judges. The marriage declaration—that the contracting parties "have taken and take each other in legitimate and indissoluble marriage, and that they promise each other fidelity"—was to be made before the local judge or priest in the presence of four witnesses. A record of the marriage would be kept in a double registry. There would be one year's grace in which to rehabilitate previously contracted marriages not recognized in law. Disputes concerning such marriages would be handled by the *baillis* or *sénéchaussées* courts.

Birth would be attested to by an act of Catholic baptism or by a declaration by the child's father and two witnesses before the local judge. Double registers would be kept, as in the case of marriage. The certification of deaths was to be handled in similar fashion. Local administrations would designate a separate burial ground, where interment might be conducted discreetly and without publicity. A slight tariff would be charged all non-Catholics for certificates delivered at the ceremonies of birth, marriage, and burial.

Such, then, was the compromise measure which the Loménie de Brienne ministry and the Paris parlement joined in making into law. Despite the favourable attitude towards the Calvinists of most cabinet members, it had taken the massive publicity surrounding the Anglure case and the crisis in the United Netherlands to bring the regime to initiate legislation which the nation's leading thinkers had been urging for a generation.

France's intellectual establishment celebrated the passage of the Edict of 1787 two years later when, as though to atone for the praise heaped upon Louis XIV in 1685, the Académie française offered a prize for the best poem hailing the arrival of Protestant toleration. At a meeting of the Forty Immortals in September, 1789, Secretary Marmontel (who had made his own contribution to the cause twenty years earlier with *Bélisaire*) announced that the first prize had been won by the poet Fontanes, who then declaimed his verse. The granting of civil rights to the Calvinists had a highly personal meaning for him, Fontanes began, because his own ancestors had been victims of the Revocation:

> Moi, né d'aieux errants, qui, dans le dernier âge
> Du fanatisme aveugle ont éprouvé la rage,
> Puis-je ne pas chanter cet Edit immortel
> Qui venge la Raison, sans offenser l'Autel?

What follows is the conventional Enlightenment version of the social and political catastrophe of 1685 in which Bossuet and Louvois are the villains, Fénelon is the lonely champion of human rights, and Louis XIV the well meaning but misguided prince:

> Pardonnez à son ombre, et ne l'outragez pas,
> Son siècle l'a trompé: qu'on le plaigne et l'honore.[45]

The new law which, Fontanes suggests, is only the beginning of the process of reintegration for the Protestants, will assure peaceful coexistence, even intermarriage, between Catholics and Calvinists. Then, in a sudden thematic shift, the poet invites the reigning monarch (whose reconciliation of his spiritually divided subjects follows in the noble tradition established by Henri IV) to summon back to office the Calvinist Necker, that "nouveau Sully." Grimm tells us that this part of the epistle received loud and sustained applause.[46]

Honourable mention in the same poetry competition went to the abbé Noël, a professor of *belles lettres* at the University of Paris. The abbé's contribution is a provocative *Epître*, a letter-in-verse addressed to a member of the refugee community in Germany by an elderly French Protestant who has witnessed much suffering for the faith inside France. How much tragedy, he begins, had flowed from that terrible lapse of judgment on the

part of Louis XIV in 1685; among other horrors, the forcible abduction of
children, the dragging of the remains of non-conformists over the ground,
the execution of Calas. Recent developments, however, promised an end to
this century-old cycle of repression and persecution. For one thing, France's
allies in Holland, the Patriots, had crossed the border in droves, promising
to reinforce the struggle against tyranny which the refugees in Germany
should join:

> De fiers Républicains, fuyant la tyrannie,
> Nous apportent déja leur or et leur génie,
> Et vouant à la France un amour filial,
> Vous donnent à l'envi l'exemple et le signal.[47]

In fraternal alliance with their enlightened King, the French citizens
who had stormed the Bastille in July were sure to triumph against their three
main foes—fanaticism, despotism, and feudalism.

Like the Bastille, the Revocation of the Edict of Nantes was one of
those symbols of the past which the delegates to the Estates-General sought
to erase from the public mind. The Bastille symbolized tyrannous royal
power and arbitrary arrest, even if it housed few victims in 1789; the
Revocation represented persecution and intolerance, even if they had ceased
to be part of government policy since the 1760s. What the French intellectual
community thought it was celebrating was the dawn of a new era of
religious freedom and spiritual reconciliation, the conditions for which it had
been trying for so many years to establish.

---

1. Linguet, *Annales*, November 20, 1787, XIII, p. 100.
2. Ibid., p. 319.
3. Abbé J.-J. Bonnaud (or Abbé L'enfant in collaboration with Abbé Proyart), *Discours à lire au Conseil en présence du roi, par un ministre patriote, sur le projet d'accorder l'état civil aux Protestants* (Paris, 1787), p. 269.
4. Linguet, *Annales*, XIII, p. 350.
5. Grimm, *Correspondance littéraire*, IV, p. 411.
6. Paul Rabaut to Charles de Végobre, April 11, 1788, Rabaut, *Lettres à divers*, ed. Dardier, II, p. 369.
7. *Mémoires secrets*, November 26, 1787, XXXVI, p. 220.
8. Anon., *Deux mots au discoureur, prétendu ministre patriote, January 6, 1788*, in *Ecrits sur les Protestants* (2 vols.; Montpellier, n.d.), p. 3.
9. Abbé Lambert, *Lettre de M...à m. l'abbé Asseline censeur et approbateur du libelle intitulé: Discours à lire au Conseil*, December 20, 1787 (Paris, n.d.), p. 69.
10. *Mémoires secrets*, December 31, 1787, XXXVI, p. 291.
11. Marquise de Sillery, *La Religion considérée comme l'unique base du bonheur et de la véritable philosophie* (Orléans, 1787), p. 218.
12. *Mémoires secrets*, December 31, 1787, XXXVI, p. 292.

13. Abbé Proyart, *Lettre à un magistrat du Parlement de Paris, au sujet de l'édit civil des Protestants* (Avignon, 1787).

14. *Mémoires secrets*, November 26, 1787, XXXVI, pp. 230-31.

15. Anon., *Réponse à la lettre à un magistrat, à M...* (n.p. 1788), p. 5.

16. Abbé Proyart, *Seconde lettre à un magistrat du Parlement de Paris sur l'état civil des Protestants* (Avignon, 1787), p. 14.

17. *Mémoires secrets*, December 13, 1787, XXXVI, p. 280.

18. Anon., *Lettres sur la révocation de l'édit de Nantes, à Madame de ...* (n.p., 1788).

19. Anon., *Non-Catholiques en France* (n.p., 1788).

20. Anon., *L'état civil pour les non-Catholiques de France justifié, ou Observations sur les mémoires de M. Gilbert de Voisins, conseiller l'état, concernant les moyens de donner aux Protestants un état civil en France* (n.p., 1788).

21. Anon., *M. Turgot réfuté par lui-même sur la tolérance civile* (n.p., 1788).

22. *Mémoires secrets*, December 16, 1787, XXXVI, p. 291.

23. Claude Carloman de Rulhières, *Eclaircissements historiques sur les causes de la révocation de l'édit de Nantes, et sur l'état des Protestants en France depuis le commencement du règne de Louis XIV jusqu'à nos jours* (n.p., 1788), p.47.

24. Rulhières to Rabaut Saint-Etienne, January 16, 1788, *BSHPF*, XXXIII (1884), p. 221.

25. Rulhières, *Eclaircissements*, II, p. 362.

26. Anon., *Conférence entre le frère Pancrace, capucin, le docteur Hothman, ministre protestant, et Me Robino, avocat au Parlement de Paris, sur la question: Est-il avantageux à la France de donner l'état civil aux Protestants? Considéré par rapport à la religion, à la tranquillité de l'état, et à l'intérêt public* (Fribourg, 1788), p. 23.

27. Anon., *Observations d'un magistrat sur un mémoire récemment publié concernant l'état civil à donner aux Protestants en France (n.p., n.d.);* H. Jabineau, *Lettre (et Réponse) à un magistrat de province à M.... (n.p., 1768);* Anon., *Moyen de constater l'état civil des Protestants. Droits et devoirs des curés à leur égard* (Geneva, 1787).

28. Anon., *Du mariage des Chrétiens, ou La nouvelle loi sur l'état civil des non-Catholiques en France, justifiée aux yeux de la religion et de la politique, par un avocat au Parlement de Paris* (n.p., 1788), p. 131.

29. Du Closel d'Arnery, *Vues sur l'intolérance, et le rapport essentiel qu'ont toutes les sectes ou religions avec les religions chrétienne et naturelle* (Brussels, 1788).

30. [C.], *Le secret révélé, ou Lettre d'un magistrat de province sur l'édit des Protestants* (n.p., n.d.), p. 3.

31. The same view was expressed in Anon., *Considérations sur l'édit au sujet des Protestants* (n.p., 1788).

32. G.-M. Sallier, *Annales françaises, depuis le commencement du règne de Louis XVI, jusqu'aux Etats-Généraux, 1774 à 1789* (Paris, 1813), pp. 135-36.

33. Linguet, *Annales politiques*, XIII, p. 183.

34. Nougaret, *Anecdotes du règne de Louis XVI, contenant tout ce qui concerne ce monarque, sa famille et la reine; les vertus et les vices des personnages qui ont le plus contribué aux événements, etc.* (6 vols.; Paris, 1791), V, pp. 339-41.

35. *Mémoires secrets*, December 8, 1787, XXXVI, p. 274.

36. Letter of Bergier dated January 1, 1788, cited in *BSHPF*, LXI (1892), p. 373.
37. *Remontrances sur l'édit donnant un état civil aux non-Catholiques, arrêtées le 18 janvier 1788*, J. Flammermont, *Remontrances du Parlement de Paris au XVIIIe siècle* (3 vols.; Paris, 1888-98), III, pp. 694-702.
38. Gal-Pomaret to Paul Rabaut, January 25, 1788, *BSHPF*, LXXIV (1925), p. 169.
39. Rabaut Saint-Etienne to Rulhières, December 6, 1787, ibid., XXXIII (1884), pp. 361-63.
40. Rabaut Saint-Etienne to the baron de Breteuil, January 9, 1788, ibid., Documents Rabaut Saint-Etienne, fol. 46.
41. Sallier, *Annales françaises*, p. 136.
42. Réponse du roi, du 27 janvier 1788, Flammermont, *Remonstrances du Parlement de Paris*, III, p. 701-702.
43. Comte de Boissy d'Anglas, *Essai sur la vie, les écrits et les opinions de M. de Malesherbes, adressée à mes enfants* (3 vols.; Paris, 1819-1821), III, p. 26.
44. *Edit du roi concernant ceux qui ne font pas profession de la religion catholique, donnée à Versailles, au mois de novembre, 1787, registré en Parlement le 29 janvier 1788* (Paris, 1788).
45. Fontanes, *Poëme sur l'édit en faveur des non-catholiques. Pièce qui a remporté le prix au jugement de l'Académie française en 1789* (Paris, 1789), p. 4, p. 7.
46. Grimm, *Correspondance littéraire*, September 1789, XV, p. 513.
47. Abbé Noël, *Epître d'un viellard protestant, à un Français réfugié en Allemagne, au sujet de l'édit en faveur des non-Catholiques, donné à Versailles au mois de novembre 1788* (Paris, 1788), p. 7.

Epilogue

Given the prolonged resistance of the ecclesiastical establishment to any form of Protestant emancipation, and given the major institutional crisis France was experiencing in the late 1780s, the Edict of 1787 was less than a full and explicit bill of rights. One can only speculate whether or not this half-measure would have served as an appropriate basis for the long-term reconciliation of the four groups most directly concerned—the administration, the courts, the clergy, and the Reformed. The fact that in the immediate circumstances, all four accepted the new legislation, however conditionally, is a tribute to the ingenuity with which the text of the law had been drawn up and to the forbearance of those who found the rights accorded the Protestants either too meagre or too generous.

The King in whose name the edict was promulgated was perhaps the most 'Fenelonian' of the Bourbons. His conversion to the cause of civil toleration for the Reformed had been a slow and subtle process during which Malesherbes, Rulhière, and Breteuil had helped him accommodate his conscience to his obligation as ruler of what was clearly no longer an all-Catholic nation. Although cynics might argue otherwise, the reference which Louis XVI makes to the Edict of 1787 in his *Appel à la Nation* (published as he was on trial before the Convention and written in part by Malesherbes) rings true: "I suffered at the injustice which had been exercised for so many years against the Protestants and thought that it was my duty to make reparation for the edict of 1685 by giving them a civil status."[1]

Two of the men most closely associated with the campaign on behalf of the Huguenots, Malesherbes and Lafayette, regarded the Edict of 1787 not as a definitive settlement but as a first step on the road to full toleration for the Reformed.[2] The parlement of Paris, as we have seen, registered the new law by an overwhelming margin. The provincial parlements reacted variously, some resisting or delaying the registration in order to emphasize their autonomy, others because their constituencies were still influenced by Counter-Reformation attitudes; but none was effectively able to block the implementation of the law.[3]

Some resistance to the edict was to be expected, of course, within the ranks of the Catholic clergy. Bishop F.-J.-E. de Crussol d'Uzès at La Rochelle urged his diocesan clergy not to comply with the new legislation but this intended spiritual subversion was quickly put down following an intervention by Breteuil. A number of ecclesiastical pamphlets appeared in which a Calvinist plot to undermine the nation's social and economic structure was alleged. In its official response to the edict, however, the First Estate adopted a fundamentally positive approach. In the *Remontrances* which they addressed to Louis XVI, delegates to the Assembly of the Clergy held during the summer of 1788 accepted the general thrust of the new law, agreeing with the provision that the civil magistrate was the appropriate person to solemnize Calvinist marriages but indicating that the baptism of Huguenot children was still the proper responsibility of the local priest.[4]

For their part, the leading voices of the Protestant community adopted a realistic, if somewhat cynical, attitude towards the new law. If the administration had granted them a measure of relief, they reasoned, it was not out of affection for the Reformed nor from any sense of remorse at what they had endured since 1685; the edict granted the Calvinists no more and no less than what was politically feasible.[5] Given these assumptions, compliance with the terms of the law offered the best hope of gaining further concessions. A few briefs were forwarded to Versailles urging the administration to make clear whether Protestant access to public office and the opening of Huguenot cemeteries were authorized under the edict.[6] Rabaut Saint-Etienne was particularly concerned about the reaction to the new law on the part of the simple folk for whom the regularization of marital status was less important than the permission for open-air worship.[7] The idea of convoking a national synod to review the overall situation was briefly considered, then abandoned when the summoning of an Estates-General was announced.

The Revolution would bring with it a series of spiritual shocks, some liberating, some devastating. The Declaration of the Rights of Man and of the Citizen established the general principle of religious liberty and broke down the last barriers preventing the Reformed from participating fully in the public life of the nation; the constitution of 1791 granted the Calvinists their own form of public worship and offered to restore citizenship to those who had fled abroad to preserve their faith; the Terror brought evidence of a radical decline of faith even among the pastors, some fifty of whom renounced their ministry and abjured their creed; the Napoleonic regime brought the Organic Law of 18 Germinal (April 7, 1802) which radically reorganized the Calvinist churches, placing them effectively under state control. At the end of the revolutionary experience, the spiritual renewal known as *Le Reveil* was thus very much in order.[8]

Meanwhile, Catholic proponents of counter-revolutionary ideology had been vigorously propagating the view that the Protestant minority, alone or in collaboration with other dissident groups such as Jansenists, philosophes and freemasons, had been responsible for the overthrow of both throne and altar.[9] A definitive scholarly rebuttal of this thesis was produced a generaion ago by B.K. Poland who pointed to the radical diversity in the ideological outlook of Reformed leaders during the revolutionary decade (Pierre-Joseph Barnave was a monarchist, Rabaut Saint-Etienne a Girondin, and Jean-Bon Saint-André a Jacobin) as incontrovertible proof that there had been no coherent Calvinist plot against the established order.[10] Nevertheless, anti-Protestant prejudice did not die out with the crisis of the 1790s; it would surface in rather virulent form as late as during the Dreyfus affair.[11] What is significant, however, is that this deeply entrenched hostility never again enjoyed official sanction. Freedom of public worship, access to public office, security of social status were henceforth guaranteed France's Calvinist minority. It had been a long and sometimes bitter struggle to change the public mind. Begun timorously and obliquely with Fontenelle, sustained vigorously by Prévost and Voltaire, fought persistently and in the end triumphantly by Malesherbes and Turgot, the battle for Protestant toleration had at last been won.

1. Louis XVI, *Appel de Louis XVI à la nation*, 1793, ed. L. Madelin (Paris, 1949), p. 101. The original text was published by J.-J. Rainville in Paris in 1793.

2. Boissy d'Anglas, *Essai sur la vie, les écrits et les opinions de M. de Malesherbes* (3 vol.; Paris, 1819-21), III, 95-96; Lafayette to George Washington, February 4, 1788, L. Gottschalk (ed.), *The Letters of Lafayette to Washington, 1777-1799* (Philadelphia, 1976), p. 338.

3. V. H. Dubief, "La réception de l'Edit du 17 novembre par les Parlements," *BSHPF*, CXXXIV (1968), pp. 281-295.

4. *Remontrances du clergé de France, assemblée en 1788, au roi, sur l'édit du mois de novembre 1787, concernant les non-Catholiques* (Paris, 1788).

5. Rabaut Saint-Etienne, "Observations sur l'édit de Louis XVI restituant l'état civil aux non-Catholiques, 1787," *BSHPF* (1864), pp. 324-44; Rabaut-Pommier, "Discours fait à l'occasion de l'édit du roi qui regarde les Protestants, février, 1788," B.P., Papiers Rabaut, I, F, fol. 248.

6. J.-B. Gallot to Jacques Necker, December 3, 1788, A.N., Ba 64.

7. Rabaut Saint-Etienne, "Instructions aux pasteurs de Languedoc au sujet de l'édit de tolérance, 27 janvier 23 février, 1788," *BSHPF*, XXXVI (1887), p. 548.

8. For a discussion of Le Réveil, v. D. Robert, *Les Eglises réformées en France, 1800-1830* (Paris, 1961).

9. V. J.M. Roberts, "The Origins of a Mythology: Freemasons, Protestants and the French Revolution", *Bulletin of the Institute of Historical Research* (May, 1971), pp. 78-97.

10. V. B. Poland, *French Protestantism and the French Revolution* (Princeton, 1957).

11. V. J. Baubérot, "La vision de la Réforme chez les publicistes antiprotestants (fin xix-début xxe siècle), in Ph. Joutard (ed.), *Historiographie de la Réforme* (Paris, 1977), pp. 216-238.

Selected Bibliography
Primary Sources (manuscript)

France, Archives Nationales. "Affaires de la 'Religion Prétendue Réformée.'" TT 3254, 440-42, 445A, 463.

_____. "Correspondance du Ministre de la Maison du Roi." E 3512. H 1639. 01 457, 473, 482, 605, 617.

_____. "Procès-verbaux des Assemblées du Clergé." G8 701, 702, 706.

France, Bibliothèque Nationale. "Collection de pièces authentiques sur les Protestans, depuis 1669 jusqu'au rétablissement de la tolérance en 1788." Mss. Fonds Fr. 7044-47.

_____. "Mémoires sur le mariage des Protestans, par L. de M. (Malesherbes)." Ms. Fonds Fr. 10619.

_____. "Mémoire sur l'état civil des Protestans, par L. de M." Ms. Fonds Fr. 10620.

_____. "Mémoire sur les Protestans, suivi d'un projet d'édit relatif à leur état-civil, par G. de V. (Gilbert de Voisins)." Ms. Fonds Fr. 10621.

_____. "Loix concernant les Protestans de France, 1685-1779." Ms. Fonds Fr. 10623.

_____. "Mémoire sur la démarche que Mssrs de la troisième Chambre des Enquêtes se proposent de faire au sujet des mariages des Protestants." Ms. Fonds Fr. 10624.

_____. "Mémoire sur le mariage des Protestans, fait en 1779." Ms. Fonds Fr. 10626.

_____. "Projet de déclaration sur le mariage des Protestans." Ms. Fonds Fr.10626.

_____. "Recueil de mémoires sur les Protestans, 1751-87." Ms. Fonds Fr. 10628.

France, Bibliothèque Protestante (Paris). Papiers Chiron. 3 vols. (Letters of Abraham and Etienne Chiron).

_____. Papiers Gébelin. 6 vols. (Letters and memoranda of Court de Gébelin).

_____. Papiers Rabaut. 20 vols. (Letters and memoranda of Paul Rabaut).

France, Bibliothèque de la Société de Port-Royal (Paris).

_____. Fonds Le Paige 557 ("Religion. Emile. Bélisaire").

_____. Fonds Le Paige 788 bis. ("Tolérance. Lettres des deux curés").

_____. Fonds Le Paige 827 ("Tolérance religieuse. France. Allemagne. 1782-84").

Primary Sources (printed)

Allamand, F.-L. *Pensées Anti-philosophiques*. The Hague: P. van Cleef, 1751.

Bachaumont, L. and Continuators. *Mémoires secrets pour servir à l'histoire de la république des lettres en France depuis MDCCLXII jusqu'à nos jours*. 36 vols. London: J. Adamson, 1777-89.

Baër, K.F. *Mémoire théologique et politique au sujet des mariages clandestins des Protestans de France, où l'on fait voir qu'il est de l'intérêt de l'église et de l'état de faire cesser ces sortes de mariages, en établissant pour les Protestans une nouvelle forme de se marier qui ne blesse point leur conscience, et qui n'intéresse point celle des évêques et des curés*. N.p., 1755.

Barbat Du Closel d'Arnery, C.-G. *Vues sur l'intolérance, et le rapport essentiel qu'ont toutes les sectes ou religions avec les religions chrétienne et naturelle*. Brussels, 1788.

Barbier, E.-J.-F. *Journal historique et anecdotique du règne de Louis XV*. Edited by A. de La Villegille. 4 vols. Paris: J. Renouard, 1847-56.

Basnage, J. *Instruction et lettre pastorale aux Réformés de France pour la persévérance dans la foi et la fidélité pour le souverain*. Rotterdam, 1719.

Bayle, P. *Avis important aux réfugiés sur leur prochain retour en France, donné pour estrennes à l'un d'eux en 1690*. Amsterdam: J. Le Censeur, 1690.

_____. *Lettres de M. Bayle, publiées sur les originaux*. Edited by Pierre Des Maizeaux. 3 vols. Amsterdam: Aux dépens de la compagnie, 1729.

Beaumarchais, P. A. Caron de. "Observation d'un Citoyen adressée aux Ministres du Roi (remise le 26 février 1779 à chaque Ministre du Roi)." *Oeuvres*. Edited by P.-D. Gudin de La Brenellerie. 7 vols. Paris: L. Colin, 1809, 4: 479-84.

Beaumont, chevalier de. *L'Accord Parfait de la Nature, de la Raison, de la Révélation et de la Politique: ou Traité dans lequel on établit que les voyes de rigueur, en matière de Religion, blessent les droits de l'humanité, et sont également contraires aux lumières de la raison, à la morale Evangélique, et au véritable intérêt de l'Etat*. 2 vols. in 1. Cologne: P. Marteau, 1753.

_____. *La vérité vengée; ou Reponse à la 'Dissertation sur la tolérance des Protestans', par l'auteur de l''Accord parfait.'* N.p., 1756.

Beausobre, C.-L. de. *Le Triomphe de l'Innocence, ou Particularités peu connues; aussi honorables aux Réformés de France, qu'elles le sont peu à leurs adversaires*. Berlin: J.-G. Michelis, 1751.

Benant, Abbé. *L'Intolérance éclairée, ou Lettres critiques d'un vicaire à l'auteur de la brochure intitulée: "Les Protestants déboutés de leurs prétensions."* N.p., 1777.

Bergier, Abbé N.-S. *Observations sur la Consultation d'un avocat célèbre touchant la validité de mariage des Protestants.* Montauban, 1787.

Besenval, P. baron de. *Mémoires de M. De Besenval.* 3 vols. Paris: F. Buisson, 1805.

Besoigne, Abbé J. *Réponse à une dissertation sur les mariages clandestins des Protestans en France.* N.p., 1756.

Blin de Sainmore, A.M.H. *Jean Calas à sa femme et à ses enfants. Heroïde.* Paris: S. Jorry, 1765.

Boissy d'Anglas, F.A., comte de. *Essai sur la vie, les écrits et les opinions de M. de Malesherbes adressé à mes enfants.* 3 vols. Paris: Treuttel et Wurtz, 1819-21.

Bonnaud, Abbé J.-J. *Discours à lire au Conseil, en présence du Roi, par un ministre patriote, sur le projet d'accorder un état civil aux Protestans.* N.p., 1787.

Bossuet, J.-B., Bishop. *Correspondance.* Edited by Urbain and Levesque. 15 vols. Paris: Hachette, 1909-26.

_____. *Exposition de la doctrine de l'église catholique sur les matières de controverse.* Paris: S. Mabre-Cramoisy, 1671.

_____. *Histoire des variations des églises protestantes.* 2 vols. Paris: Veuve S. Mabre Cramoisy, 1688.

_____. *Lettre pastorale aux nouveaux convertis du diocèse de Metz pour les exhorter à faire leurs Pâques et leur donner des avertissements nécessaires contre les fausses lettres pastorales des ministres.* Paris: S. Mabre Cramoisy, 1686.

_____. *Oraison funèbre de Henriette-Marie de France, reine de la Grande Bretagne (16 novembre 1669). Oraisons funèbres.* Edited by J. Trudel. Paris: Garnier, 1961: 111-43.

Boulainvilliers, comte H. de. *Etat de la France, etc., extraits des Mémoires dressés par les Intendants du Royaume, par ordre du Roi, Louis XIV, à la sollicitation de Mgr. le Duc de Bourgogne, père de Louis XV à présent regnant.* 2 vols. in 1. London: T. Wood and S. Palmer, 1727.

Bouniol de Montégut, Abbé. *La voix du vrai patriote catholique, opposée à celle des faux patriotes tolérans.* Paris, 1756.

Cairol. *Conférences de jurisprudence sur l'Edit concernant ceux qui ne font pas profession de la Religion.* Paris: Chez l'auteur, 1788.

Caveirac, Abbé J.N. de. *L'Accord de la religion et de l'humanité sur l'intolérance.* N.p., 1762.

_____. *Apologie de Louis XIV, et de son Conseil, sur la Révocation de l'Edit de Nantes. Pour servir de réponse à la 'Lettre d'une Patriote sur la tolérance civile des Protestans de France.' Avec une Dissertation sur la journée de la S. Barthélemi.* N.p., 1758.

_____. *Lettre du Docteur Chlévalès à M. de Voltaire, en lui envoyant la copie manuscrite d'une autre lettre à laquelle il ne paraît pas qu'il aît répondu.* Paris, 1772.

_____. *Mémoire Politico-critique, où l'on examine s'il est de l'intérêt de l'Eglise et de l'Etat d'établir pour les Calvinistes du Royaume une nouvelle forme de se marier.* N.p., 1756.

Chabannes, Bishop J.-C.-G. *Lettre de M. l'évêque d'Agen à Monsieur le contrôlleur-général contre la tolérance des Huguenots dans le royaume.* N.p., 1751.

Chaumeix, A. *Préjugés légitimes contre L' 'Encyclopédie' et Essai de Réfutation de ce Dictionnaire.* 8 vols. Brussels and Paris: Hérissant, 1758-59.

Christophe de Beaumont, Archbishop. *Mandement de monseigneur l'archevêque de Paris, portant condamnation d'un livre qui a pour titre: "Bélisaire" par M. Marmontel, de l'Académie française.* Paris, 1767.

Clément, P. *Les cinq années littéraires.* 4 vols. The Hague: A. De Groot et fils, 1754.

Collection complète de tous les ouvrages pour et contre M. Necker. 3 vols. Utrecht, 1781.

Collection des Procès-verbaux des Assemblées-générales du Clergé de France, depuis l'année 1560 jusqu'à présent. 8 vols. in 9. Paris: Guillaume Desprez, 1778.

Condorcet, M.-J.-A.-N. Caritat, marquis de. *Réflexions d'un citoyen catholique sur les loix de France relatives aux Protestans.* N.p., 1778.

Conférence entre le Frère Pancrace, capucin, le Docteur Hothman, ministre protestant, et Me Robine, avocat au Parlement de Paris, sur la question: Est-il avantageux à la France de donner l'état civil aux Protestans? Considérée par rapport à la Religion, à la tranquillité de l'Etat de à l'intérêt politique. Fribourg, 1788.

Court, A. *Histoire des troubles des Cévennes, ou de la guerre des Camisars, sous le règne de Louis le Grand; tirée de manuscrits secrets et autentiques et des obvervations faites sur les lieux mêmes, avec une carte des Cévennes.* 3 vols. Villefranche: P. Chrétien, 1760.

_____. *Lettre du curé de L*** à M. L'évêque d'Agen au sujet de celle que ce Prélat a écrite à M. le Contrôlleur Général contre la Tolérance des Huguenots dans la Royaume.* N.p., 1751.

_____. *Lettre d'un Patriote sur la tolérance civile des Protestans de France et sur les avantages qui en résulteraient pour le Royaume.* N.p., 1756.

_____. *Réponse à la lettre sur les assemblées.* Geneva, 1745.

Court, A. and A. Court de Gébelin. *Le patriote français et impartial, ou Réponse à la Lettre de Mr l'évêque d'Agen à Mr. le Contrôlleur-Général contre la tolérance des Huguenots, en date du 1 mai 1751.* 2 vols. Villefranche: P. Chrétien, 1753.

D'Alembert, J. Le Rond. *Lettre de M. D'Alembert à M. J.-J. Rousseau sur l'Article 'Genève' tiré du septième volume de l' 'Encyclopédie.' Avec quelques autres pièces qui y sont relatives.* Amsterdam: Z. Chatelain, 1759.

D'Argenson, R.L., marquis. *Journal et Mémoires du marquis d'Argenson.* Edited by E.J.B. Rathery. 9 vols. Paris: Veuve J. Renouard, 1859-67.

Delabroue, F.G. *L'Esprit de Jesus-Christ sur la Tolérance; pour servir de réponse à plusieurs Ecrits de ce tems sur la même matière, et particulièrement à l' 'Apologie de Louis XIV sur la Révocation de l'Edit de Nantes', et à la 'Dissertation sur le Massacre de la Saint Barthélémi.'* Paris, 1760.

Diderot, D. *Correspondance.* Edited by G. Roth. 15 vols. Paris: Editions de Minuit, 1955-70.

_____. *Oeuvres philosophiques.* Edited by P. Vernière. Paris: Garnier Frères, 1961: 1-49.

Dissertation sur la Tolérance des Protestans; ou Réponse à deux ouvrages, dont l'un est intitulé 'L'Accord parfait', et l'autre 'Mémoire au sujet des mariages clandestins des Protestans de France.' 'En France,' n.d.

Du Closel d'Arnery. *Vues sur l'intolérance et le rapport essentiel qu'ont toutes les sectes ou religions avec les religions chrétienne et naturelle.* Brussels, 1788.

Dupont de Nemours, P.-S. *Mémoires sur la vie et les ouvrages de M. Turgot, ministre d'état.* ' Philadelphie,' 1782.

Dutens, L. *Mémoires d'un voyageur qui se repose; contenant des anecdoctes historiques, politiques et littéraires, relatives à plusieurs des principaux personnages du siècle.* 3 vols. Paris: Bossange, Masson et Besson, 1806.

Elie de Beaumont, J.-B.-J. *Mémoire à consulter et consultation pour la dame Anne-Rose Cabibel, veuve Calas, et pour ses enfants.* Paris, 1762.

_____. *Mémoire à consulter pour Pierre-Paul Sirven, accusé d'avoir fait mourir sa seconde fille pour l'empêcher de se faire catholique; et pour ses deux filles. Annales du barreau français.* Paris: B. Warée, 1824.

_____. *Questions sur la legitimité du mariage des Protestans de France célébré hors du royaume.* Paris: L. Cellot, 1764.

_____. *Entretiens d'un évêque de l'assemblée avec un curé de Paris, sur les mariages des Protestants en France.* Geneva, 1786.

L'état civil pour les non-catholiques de France justifié; ou Observations sur un Mémoire de M. Gilbert de Voisins, conseiller d'état, concernant les moyens de donner aux Protestans un état civil en France. N.p., 1788.

Fénelon, F. de S., La Mothe de. *Ecrits et lettres politiques.* Edited by C. Urbain. Paris: Bossard, 1920.

Fenouillot de Falbaire, C.-G. *L'honnête criminel, ou L'amour filial, drame en cinq actes et en vers.* Paris: Merlin, 1768.

Firmin de Lacroix. *Mémoire pour le sieur Pierre-Paul Sirven appellant contre les consuls et communauté de Mazamet.* Toulouse, 1770.

Fléchier, E. *Oraison funèbre du très-haut et puissant messire Michel Le Tellier...prononcé dans l'Eglise de l'Hôtel Royal des Invalides, le 22 jour de mars 1686.* Paris: S. Mabre-Cramoisy, 1686.

Fonbonne, Chanoine. *Avis à messieurs les Religionnaires de France, ouvrage propre à leur instruction et à rappeller les Protestants à l'ancienne croyance. Et Dissertation sur le peché originel à l'usage de messieurs les Auteurs Anglais et des Traducteurs de leur Histoire Universelle.* Paris: Debure l'aîné, 1762.

Fontanes, L.-J.-P. marquis de. *Poëme sur l'Edit en faveur des non-catholiques, pièce qui a remporté le prix au jugement de l'Académie française en 1789.* Paris: Demonville, 1789.

Fontenelle, B. le B. de. *Discours de la Patience. Oeuvres diverses.* 8 vols. Paris: M. Brunet, 1715. VII: 299-332.

_____. "Extrait d'une lettre écrite de Batavia dans les Indes orientales le 27 novembre 1684 contenu dans une Lettre de M. de Fontenelles, reçue à Rotterdam par M. Basnage." *Nouvelles de la République des Lettres* (January, 1686): 87-90.

Formey, J.H.S. *Pensées raisonnables opposées aux Pensées philosophiques, avec un Essai de critique sur le livre intitulé 'Les Moeurs', et la lettre de Gervaise Holmes à l'Auteur de celle sur les Aveugles.* Göttingen and Leyden, 1756.

_____. *Souvenirs d'un citoyen.* 2 vols. Berlin: François de La Garde, 1789.

Gilbert de Voisins, P.-P. *Mémoires sur les moyens de donner aux Protestans un état civil en France. Composé de l'ordre du roi Louis XV (1765).* N.p., 1787.

Giry de Saint-Cyr, Abbé. *Catéchisme et Décisions de cas de conscience, à l'usage des Cacouacs, avec un Discours du Patriarche des Cacouacs, pour la Réception d'un nouveau disciple.* N.p., 1758.

Grimm, F.M., baron et al. *Correspondance littéraire, philosophique et critique, adressée à un souverain d'Allemagne, pendant une partie des années 1775-76, et pendant les années 1782 à 1790.* 16 vols. Edited by Maurice Tourneux. Paris: Garnier frères, 1877-82.

Guidi, Abbé. *Dialogue entre un évêque et un curé sur les mariages des Protestans.* N.p., 1775.

_____. *Dialogue sur l'état civil des Protestans en France.* 'En France,' 1778.

_____. *Suite du dialogue sur les mariages des Protestans; ou Réponse de M. le curé de ... à l'auteur d'une brochure intitulée 'Les Protestans déboutés de leurs prétentions.'* N.p., 1776.

Irail, Abbé S.-A. *Querelles littéraires, ou Mémoires pour servir à l'Histoire des Révolutions de la République des Lettres, depuis Homère jusqu'à nos jours.* 4 vols. Paris: Durand, 1761.

Jurieu, P. *L'Accomplissement des prophéties, ou la Délivrance prochaine de l'Eglise.* 2 vols. Rotterdam: A. Acher, 1686.

La Beaumelle, L.-A. de. *L'Asiatique tolérant. Traité à l'usage de Zeokinizul, roi des Kofirans, surnommé le chéri.* Paris: Durand, 1748.

_____. *Mémoires pour servir à l'histoire de Madame de Maintenon, et à celle du siècle passé.* 6 vols. Amsterdam: Aux dépens de l'auteur, 1755-56.

_____. *Qu'en dira-t-on. Mes Pensées.* Copenhagen, 1751.

_____. *Réponse au Supplément du Siècle de Louis XIV.* Colmar, 1754.

_____. *Vie de Madame de Maintenon, pour servir de suite à ses lettres.* 2d ed. Cologne, 1753.

Lettre d'un magistrat, dans laquelle on examine également ce que la Justice du Roi doit aux Protestans, et ce que l'intérêt de son peuple ne lui permet pas de leur accorder. Avignon, Paris: Gattey, 1787.

Lettres à M. l'abbé Raynal, sur l'histoire de la révocation de l'édit de Nantes qu'il se propose de publier. N.p., 1782.

Lettres de deux curés des Cévennes, sur la validité des mariages des Protestans, et sur leur existence légale en France. 2 vols. in 1. London, 1779.

Linguet, S.-N.-H. *Mémoire à consulter et consultation pour un mari dont la femme s'est remariée en Pays Protestant et qui demande s'il peut se remarier de même en France.* Paris: L. Cellot, 1771.

_____. *Mémoire à consulter et consultation sur la validité d'un mariage contracté en France suivant les usages des Protestans.* Paris: L. Cellot, 1771.

Loyseau de Mauléon, A.-J. *Mémoire pour Donat, Pierre et Louis Calas.* Paris: Le Breton, 1762.

Malesherbes, C.-G. de Lamoignon de. *Mémoire sur le mariage des Protestans, en 1785.* N.p., n.d.

_____. *Second mémoire sur le mariage des Protestans, en 1786.* London, 1787.

Mariette, P. *Mémoire pour Dame Anne-Rose Cabibel, veuve du sieur Jean Calas, marchand à Toulouse; Louis et Louis- Donat Calas, leurs fils, et Anne-Rose et Anne Calas, leurs filles, demandeurs en cassation d'un arrêt du parlement de Toulouse du 9 mars 1762.* Paris, 1762.

Marivaux, P. de. *Le Télémaque travesti, contenant les treize derniers livres retournés et réimprimés pour la première fois (1714)*. Edited by F. Deloffre. Geneva, 1956.

Marmontel, J.F. *Les Incas, ou La Destruction de l'Empire de Pérou* (1777), in *Oeuvres complètes*, Slatkine Reprints, 7 vols. Geneva, 1968: 3.

_____. *Mémoires d'un père pour servir à l'instruction de son fils.* 4 vols. Paris, 1804.

Marteilhe, J. *Mémoires d'un protestant condamné aux galères de France pour cause de religion; écrits par lui-même.* Rotterdam: J.D. Beman et Fils, 1757.

Maultrot, G.-N. and Abbé Tailhé. *Questions sur le tolérance.* Geneva: H.-A. Gosse, 1758.

Mercier, L.-S. *La destruction de La Ligue, ou La Reduction de Paris; pièce nationale en quatre actes et en prose* (1784). *Théâtre complet.* Amsterdam: B. Vlam, 1775-84. 4: 1-146.

Merlat, E. *Traité du pouvoir absolu des souverains. Pour servir d'instruction, de consolation et d'Apologie aux Eglises Réformées qui sont affligées.* Cologne: J. Cassander, 1685.

Montesquieu, C.L. de Secondat, baron de La Brède et de. *Oeuvres complètes.* Edited by A. Masson. 3 vols. Paris: Nagel, 1950-55.

Montezat, Abbé de. *Observations sur un mémoire qui parâit sous le nom de Paul Rabaut, intitulée "La Calomnie confondue."* N.p., 1762.

Morellet, Abbé A. *Mémoires de l'abbé Morellet sur le dix-huitième siècle et sur la Révolution.* 2 vols. Paris: Ladvocat, 1821.

_____. *Petit Ecrit sur une matière intéressante.* Toulouse: P.L'Agneau, 1756.

Noel, Abbé. *Epître d'un viellard protestant à un Français réfugié en Allemagne, au sujet de l'édit en faveur des non-Catholiques, donné à Versailles au mois de novembre 1788.* Paris, 1788.

Nougaret, P.J.B. *L'ombre de Calas, le suicide, à sa famille et à son ami dans les fers, précédé d'une lettre à M. de Voltaire.* Paris, 1765.

Observations d'un magistrat sur un mémoire récemment publié concernant d'état civil à donner aux Protestants en France. N.p., n.d.

Petit, E. *Dissertation sur la tolérance civile et religieuse en Angleterre et en France, à l'égard des non-conformistes à la Religion dominante.* Geneva and Paris: Knapfen et Fils, 1778.

Pey, Abbé. *La tolérance chrétienne, opposée au tolérantisme philosophique, ou Lettres d'un Patriote au soi-disant curé sur son Dialogue au sujet des Protestans.* Fribourg: Libraires associès, 1784.

Pluquet, Abbé. *Mémoires pour servir à l'histoire des Egaremens de l'Esprit humain par rapport à la religion chrétienne: ou Dictionnaire des Hérésies, des Erreurs et des Schismes.* 2 vols. Paris: Nyon, 1762.

Prévost, Abbé A.-F. *Les Campagnes philosophiques, ou Mémoires de M. de Moncal, aide-de-camp de M. le maréchal de Schomberg, contenant l'histoire de la Guerre d'Irlande.* 4 vols. Amsterdam: Desbordes, 1741.

_____. *Le Doyen de Killerine.* 6 vols. in 3. Paris: Didot, 1741.

_____. *Mémoires et Avantures d'un homme de qualité, qui s'est retiré du monde.* Nouvelle édition. Revue et considérablement augmentée sur quelques manuscrits trouvés après sa mort. 6 vols. Amsterdam and Paris: Martin, 1756.

_____. *Le philosophe anglais, ou Histoire de Monsieur Cleveland.* 5 vols. Utrecht: Etienne Neaulme, 1736.

_____. *Le Pour et contre, ouvrage périodique d'un goût nouveau...par l'auteur des "Mémoires d'un homme de qualité."* 20 vols. Paris: Didot, 1733-40.

Procès-verbal de l'Assemblée des Notables, tenue à Versailles, en l'année 1787. Paris: Imprimerie royale, 1788.

Proyart, Abbé. *Lettre à un magistrat du Parlement de Paris, au sujet de l'édit civil des Protestants.* Avignon, 1787.

_____. *Seconde lettre à un magistrat du Parlement de Paris sur l'état civil des Protestants.* Avignon, 1787.

Rabaut, P. *Paul Rabaut. Ses lettres à Antoine Court, 1739-55.* 2 vols. Paris: Grassart, 1884.

_____. *Paul Rabaut. Ses lettres à divers, 1744-94.* 2 vols. Paris: Grassart, 1892.

Rabaut, P. and L.-A. de La Beaumelle. *La Calomnie confondue, ou Mémoire dans laquelle on réfute une nouvelle accusation intentée aux protestants de la province de Languedoc, à l'occasion de l'affaire du Sr Calas, détenu dans les prisons de Toulouse.* 'Au désert', 1762.

Rabaut Saint-Etienne, J.-P. *Le roi doit modifier les lois portées contre les Protestants. Démonstration: Avantages que la France tirerait de cette modification.* London, 1784.

_____. *Triomphe de l'intolérance, ou Anecdotes de la vie d'Ambroise Borély, mort à Londres à l'âge de 103 ans. Recueillies par W. Jesterman. Ouvrage traduit de l'anglais, et trouvé parmi des papiers de M. de Voltaire; suivi de la Tolérance au pieds du trône.* London, 1779.

Raynal, Abbé G.T.F. *Histoire Philosophique et Politique des Etablissements et du Commerce des Européens dans les deux Indes.* 6 vols. Amsterdam, 1770.

Recueil de pièces intéressantes sur les Protestans. 2 vols. in 1. Paris: Lami, 1788.

Réflexions impartiales d'un Philantrope, sur la situation présente des Protestans, et sur les moyens de la changer. N.p., 1787.

Remonstrances du Parlement de Paris au XVIIIe siècle. Edited by Jules Flammermont. 3 vols. Paris: Imprimerie nationale, 1888-98.

Remonstrances du Parlement de Paris, concernant les non-catholiques. Arrêtées le 18 janvier 1788. Paris, 1788.

Réponse à une Dissertation contre les mariages clandestins des Protestans de France; ou Lettre à l'auteur d'un Ecrit nouveau intitulé: "Dissertation sur la Tolerance des Protestans," ou Réponse à deux ouvrages, dont l'un a pour titre: "L'accord parfait" et l'autre: "Mémoire au sujet des mariages clandestins des Protestans en France." N.p., 1756.

Réponse d'un bon chrétien aux prétendus sentimens des Catholiques de France, sur le "Mémoire au sujet des mariages clandestins des Protestans." N.p., n.d.

Richard, Père. *Les Protestans déboutés de leurs prétentions, par les principes et les paroles mêmes du 'Curé', leur Apologiste, dans son Dialogue, avec un Evêque, sur leurs Mariages.* Brussels and Paris: Morin, 1776.

Rou, J. *La Séduction éludée ou Lettres de Mr l'Evêque de Meaux, à un de ces Diocésains qui s'est sauvé de la Persécution, avec la Réponse qui y ont été faites, et dont la principale est demeurée sans Réplique.* Berne, 1686.

Rousseau, J.-J. *Correspondance complète.* Edited by R.A. Leigh. 40 vols. Geneva: Institut et Musée Voltaire, 1965-71; Banbury: Voltaire Foundation, 1972-75; Oxford: Voltaire Foundation at the Taylor Institution, 1976-82.

_____. *Jean-Jacques Rousseau, Citoyen de Genève, à Christophe de Beaumont, archevêque de Paris, duc de St Cloud, pair de France, commandeur de l'ordre du St Esprit, proviseur de Sorbonne, etc.* Amsterdam: M.M.Rey, 1763.

_____. *Jean-Jacques Rousseau, Citoyen de Genève à M. d'Alembert de l'Académie française, de l'Académie royale des sciences de Paris, etc.; sur son article "Genève" dans le septième volume de l'Encyclopédie, et particulièrement sur le projet d'établir un théâtre de comédie en cette ville.* Amsterdam: M.M.Rey, 1758.

_____. *Julie, ou La Nouvelle Héloïse* (1761). Edited by M. Launay. Paris: Garnier-Flammarion, 1967.

_____. *Lettres écrites de la montagne* (1764). Edited by H. Guillemin. Neuchâtel: Ides et Calendes, 1962.

Rousseau, M.T. *Précis Historique sur l'Edit de Nantes et sa Révocation; suivi d'un Discours en Vers, relatif à cet événement.* London, 1788.

Rouvière, P.D. *Essai de réunion des Protestans aux Catholiques-Romains.* Paris: C. Hérissant, 1756.

Rulhière, C.C. de. *Eclaircissemens historiques sur les causes de la révocation de l'édit de Nantes, et sur l'état des Protestans en France, depuis le commencement du règne de Louis XIV, jusqu'à nos jours.* 2 vols. in 1. Geneva: F.Dufort, 1788.

Saurin, J. *L'Etat du Christianisme en France, divisé en trois parties ou Lettres adressées aux Catholiques Romains; aux Protestans temporiseurs; et aux Déistes.* 3 vols. The Hague: P.Hussau, 1725-27.

Seconde Réponse à des Dissertations contre la Tolérance pour les mariages des Protestans: ou Lettre à l'Auteur de deux Mémoires, l'un intitulé: "Mémoire politico-critique" et l'autre: "La voix du vrai Patriote Catholique, etc." N.p., n.d.

Le secret révélé, ou Lettre à un Magistrat de Province sur les Protestans. Signé C***, avocat. N.p., n.d.

Sentiments des Catholiques de France sur le mémoire au sujet des Mariages clandestins des Protestans. N.p., 1756.

Simon, R. *Lettres choisies de M. Simon, où l'on trouve un grand nombre de faits Anecdotes de Littérature.* Amsterdam: Pierre Mortier, 1730.

Soulavie, J.-L. *Mémoires historiques et politiques du règne de Louis XVI, depuis son mariage jusqu'à sa mort.* 6 vols. Paris: Treutel et Wurtz, 1801.

Sudre, T. *Mémoire pour le sieur Calas Jean, négociant de cette ville, dame Anne-Rose Cabibel son épouse, et le sieur Jean-Pierre Calas un de leurs enfants.* Toulouse: J. Rayet, 1762.

Target, G.-J.-B. *Consultation sur l'affaire de la dame marquise d'Anglure, contre les sieurs Petit, au Conseil des Dépêches. Dans laquelle l'on traite du mariage et de l'état des Protestants.* Paris: N.H.Nyon, 1787.

Themiseul de Saint-Hyacinthe. *Lettres critiques sur La Henriade de M. de Voltaire.* London: J.P.Coderc, 1728.

Tronchin, J.-R. *Lettres écrites de la campagne.* Geneva, 1765.

Turgot, A.-R.-J. *Le Conciliateur, ou Lettres d'un ecclésiastique à un magistrat sur les affaires présentes.* 'Rome', 1754.

_____. *Les (37) verités opposées aux erreurs de Bélisaire.* In J. Tissot, *Turgot, sa vie, son administration, ses ouvrages.* Paris: Librairie Académique Didier, 1862: 461-75.

_____. *Oeuvres.* Edited by G. Schelle. 5 vols. Paris: F. Alcan, 1913-23.

M.Turgot réfuté par lui-même, sur la tolérance civile. N.p., n.d.

Vauban, S. *Le Pestre de Vauban. Sa famille et ses écrits, ses oisivités et sa correspondance.* Edited by Albert de Rochas d'Aiglun. 2 vols. Paris: Berger-Levrault et Cie., 1910.

Véri, Abbé dé. *Journal de l'abbé de Véri.* Edited by J. de Witte. 2 vols. Paris: J.Tollandier, 1928.

La vérité rendue sensible à Louis XVI. Par un admirateur de M. Necker. 2 vols. in 1. London: J. Peterson, 1782.

Vernes, J. *Lettres sur le christianisme de M. J.-J. Rousseau.* Amsterdam: Neaulme, 1764.

_____. *Lettres critiques d'un voyageur anglais sur l'article "Génève" du Dictionnaire encyclopédique, et sur la lettre de M. d'Alembert à M. Rousseau touchant les spectacles.* 3d ed. 2 vols. Copenhagen, 1766.

Villiers, Abbé M.-A. de. *Sentimens des catholiques de France sur le Mémoire au sujet des mariages clandestins des Protestans.* N.p., 1756.

Voltaire, F.-M. A de. "Avis au public sur les parricides imputés aux Calas et aux Sirven" (1766). *Oeuvres complètes de Voltaire.* Edited by L. Moland. 52 vols. Paris: Garnier, 1877-85, 25: 517-37.

_____. *Correspondence and related documents. The complete works of Voltaire.* Edited by T. Besterman. Geneva: Institut et musée Voltaire; Toronto and Buffalo: University of Toronto Press, 1960-. 85-135.

_____. "Défense de milord Bolingbroke par le docteur Goodnatur'd Wellwisher chapelain du comte de Chesterfield" (1752). *Oeuvres* (M) 23: 551-553.

_____. "Dialogues chrétiens, ou Préservatif contre l'"Encyclopédie'" (1760). *Oeuvres* (M), 24: 124-39.

_____. "Discours en vers sur l'homme" (1734-37). *Oeuvres* (M), 9: 378-428.

_____. "Epître à Uranie" (1732). *Oeuvres* (M), 9: 358-62.

_____. *Essai sur des moeurs et l'esprit des nations et sur les principaux faits de l'histoire depuis Charlmagne jusqu'à Louis XIII* (1756). Edited by René Pomeau. 2 vols. Paris: Garnier frères, 1963.

_____. *An Essay upon the Civil Wars of France, extracted from various manuscripts and also upon the epick poetry of the European Nations from Homer to Milton.* London, 1727.

_____. "Le Fanatisme, ou Mahomet le prophète" (1741). *Oeuvres* (M), 4: 91-167.

_____. "Les Guèbres, ou la Tolérance." *Oeuvres* (M), 6: 504-70.

_____. "La Henriade." Edited by O.R. Taylor. *The Complete Works* (Best.): 2.

_____. "L'Ingénu" (1767). Edited by W.R. Jones. Geneva and Paris: Droz, 1957.

_____. "Lettre à S.M. Mgr. le Prince de *** sur Rabelais" (1767). *Mélanges.* Edited by J. Van den Heuvel. Paris: Gallimard, 1961.

_____. "Ode sur le Fanatisme" (1732). *Oeuvres* (M), 8: 427-30.

_____. "Oedipe" (1718). *Oeuvres* (M), 2: 58-117.

_____. "Poème sur la loi naturelle" (1752) .*Oeuvres* (M), 9: 433-64.

_____. "Réflexions philosophiques sur le procès de mademoiselle Camp". *Oeuvres* (M), 28: 553-55.

_____. "Réponse à la critique de 'La Henriade.'" *Oeuvres* (M), 8: 364-67.

_____. "Seconde anecdote sur Bélisaire" (1767). *Oeuvres* (M), 261: 169-72.

_____. "Sermon des cinquante" (1749). *Oeuvres* (M), 24: 437-53.

_____. *Le Siècle de Louis XIV*. Edited by La Beaumelle. 3 vols. Frankfort: Veuve Knoch and J.G. Eslinger, 1753.

Yvon, Abbé C. *Liberté de conscience resserrée dans des bornes légitimes*. 3 vols. London, 1754.

Secondary Sources

Anger, H. *De la condition juridique des Protestants après la Révocation de l'Edit de Nantes*. Paris: A. Rousseau, 1903.

Anquez, L. *Histoire des assemblées politiques des Réformés de France, 1573-1622* (Paris, 1859). Geneva: Slatkine Reprints, 1970.

Barker, J.E. *Diderot's Treatment of the Christian Religion in the Encyclopedie*. New York: King's Crown Press,1941.

Barni, J. *Histoire des idées morales et politiques en France au dix-huitième siècle*. 2 vols. Paris: Germer Ballière, 1865-67.

Bergeal, C. and A. Durrleman. *Eloge et condemnation de la Révocation de l'Edit de Nantes*. Carrières-sous- Poissey: "La Cause," 1985.

Bersier, E. *La Révocation. Discours prononcé dans le temple de l'Oratoire à Paris le 22 octobre 1885*. Paris: Fischbacher, 1886.

Bessière, F. *Le mariage des Protestants au désert de France au XVIIIe siècle*. Cahors: A. Coueslant, 1899.

Bien, D. "Catholic Magistrates and Protestant Marriages in the French Enlightenment." *F.H.S.* 2 (1961-62): 408-28.

_____. *The Calas Affair: Persecution, Toleration, and Heresy in Eighteenth-century Toulouse*. Princeton: Princeton University Press, 1960.

Bonet-Maury, G. *Histoire de la liberté de conscience en France depuis l'édit de Nantes jusqu'à juillet 1870*. Paris: F. Alcan, 1900.

Bonifas, E.-C.-F. *Le mariage des Protestants depuis la Réforme jusqu'à 1789. Etude historique et juridique*. Paris: L. Boyer, 1901.

Bonnefon, D. *Benjamin Du Plan, gentilhomme d'Alais. Député-Général des Eglises Réformées de France, 1688-1763*. France: Sandoz et Fischbacher, 1876.

Borrel, A. *Biographie de Paul Rabaut, pasteur du Désert et de ses trois fils*. Nîmes: Librairie protestante, 1854.

Bourion, I. *Les Assemblées du Clergé et le Protestantisme*. Paris: Bloud et Cie., 1909.

Calmettes, P. *Choiseul et Voltaire, d'après les lettres inédites du duc de Choiseul à Voltaire*. Paris: Plon, 1902.

Champendal, E. *Voltaire et les protestants de France*. Geneva: Librairie Académique Perrin, 1919.

Coquerel fils, A. *Les forçats pour la foi. Etude historique 1684-1775*. Paris: M. Lévy Frères, 1866.

Coquerel, C. *Histoire des églises du désert chez les Protestants de France depuis la fin du règne de Louis XIV jusqu'à la Révolution française*. 2 vols. Paris: A. Cherbuliez, 1841.

Coutet, A. *Jean Calas, roué vif et innocent*. Musée du Désert en Cévennes, 1933.

Crocker, L. *Jean-Jacques Rousseau: The Quest, 1712-58*. New York: Macmillan, 1973.

_____. *Jean-Jacques Rousseau: The Prophetic Voice, 1758-78*. New York: Macmillan, 1973.

Cruppi, J. *Un avocat journaliste au XVIIIe siècle. Linguet*. Paris: Hachette, 1895.

Dardier, C. *Paul Rabaut. Ses lettres à divers, 1744-94* 2 vols. Paris: Grassart, 1892.

Dedieu, Abbé J. *Histoire politique des protestants français, 1715-1794*. 2 vols. Paris: V. Lecoffre, 1925.

_____. *Le rôle politique des protestants français, 1685-1715*. Paris: Bloud et Gay, 1921.

Delattre, A. *Voltaire l'impétueux*. Paris: Mercure de France, 1957.

Desnoiresterres, G. *Voltaire et la societé française au XVIIIe siècle*. 8 vols. Paris: Libraire Académique Didier, 1867-1876.

Dompnier, B. *Le venin de l'hérésie. Image du protestantisme et combat catholique au XVIIIe siècle*. Paris: Editions du Centurion, 1985.

Douen, E.-O. *La Révocation de l'édit de Nantes à Paris, d'après des documents inédits*. 3 vols. Paris: Fischbacher, 1844.

Douen, O. *L'Intolérance de Fénelon. Etudes historiques d'après des documents pour la plupart inédits*. Paris: Fischbacher, 1875.

Dubois, L. *Bayle et la tolérance*. Paris: A. Chevalier-Marescq et Cie., 1902.

Engel, C.-E. "Le véritable abbé Prévost." *BSHPF* 104 (1958): 255-56.

Fabre, M. *Voltaire et Pimpette de Nîmes*. Nîmes: Chastanier Frères et Almeras, 1936.

Faure, E. *12 mai 1776. La disgrâce de Turgot*. Paris: Gallimard, 1961.

Fay, B. *Louis XVI ou la Fin d'un Monde*. Paris: Amiot, 1955.

Ferrier, J.-P. *Le Duc de Choiseul, Voltaire et la création de Versoix-la-ville, 1766-1777*. Geneva: Boissonnas, 1922.

Flassan, G. de Raxis de. *Histoire générale et raisonnée de la diplomatie française, depuis la fondation de la monarchie jusqu'à la fin du règne de Louis XVI*. 6 vols. Paris: Lenormant, 1809, 6: 7-24; 263-70; 361-414.

Fontaine, L. *Le Théâtre et la Philosophie au XVIIIe siècle*. Versailles: Cerf et fils, 1878.

Gaiffe, F. *Le drame en France au XVIIIe siècle*. Paris: A. Colin, 1910.

Galland, E. *L'Affaire Sirven. Etude historique d'après les documents originaux*. Mazamet, 1910.

Gargett, G. *Voltaire and Protestantism. Studies on Voltaire and the Eighteenth Century* 188 (1980).

Gay, P. *Voltaire's Politics: The Poet as Realist.* New York: Vintage Books, 1965.

Gordon, D.H. and Norman L. Torrey. *The Censoring of Diderot's 'Encyclopédie' and the Re-established Text.* New York: Columbia University Press, 1947.

Gottschalk, L. *Lafayette Between the American and the French Revolution, 1783-1789.* 2d ed. Chicago: University of Chicago Press, 1965.

Goulemot, J.-M. *Discours, histoire et révolutions.* Paris: Union générale d'édition, 1975.

Grange, H. *Les Idées de Necker.* Paris: Klincksieck, 1974.

Grimsley, R. *Jean-Jacques Rousseau: A Study in Self-Awareness.* Cardiff: University of Wales Press, 1969.

_____. *Rousseau and the Religious Quest.* Oxford: Clarendon Press, 1968.

Grosclaude, P. *Malesherbes, témoin et interprète de son temps.* Paris: Fischbacher, 1961.

_____. "Malesherbes et Rabaut-Saint-Etienne. Une correspondance inédite." *BSHPF* 106 (January-March 1960): 1-16.

_____. "Comment Malesherbes élabore sa doctrine sur le problème des Protestants." *BSHPF* 103 (July-September, 1957): 149-70.

_____. "Paul Rabaut et Malesherbes." *BSHPF* 105 (January- March, 1959): 26-28.

_____. "Une négociation prématurée: Louis Dutens et les Protestants français, 1775-1776." *BSHPF* 104 (1958): 74-93.

Guéhenno, J. *Jean-Jacques. Histoire d'une conscience.* 2nd ed. 2 vols. Paris: Gallimard, 1962.

Haag, E. and E. Haag. *La France protestante,* 10 vols. Paris: J. Cherbuliez, 1856.

Hallys-Dabot. *Histoire de la censure théâtrale en France.* Paris: E. Dentu, 1862.

Haynes, R. *Philosopher-King: Humanist Pope Benedict XIV.* London: Weidenfeld and Nicolson, 1970.

Hudault, J. "Guy-Jean-Baptiste Target et sa contribution à la préparation de l'édit de novembre 1787 sur l'état civil des Protestants." Mémoire submitted to the Faculté de Droit et des Sciences Economiques, University of Paris, 11 October 1966.

Hugues, E. *Antoine Court. Histoire de la Restauration du Protestantisme en France au XVIIIe siècle.* 2 vols. Paris: M. Lévy frères, 1872.

Jacquart, J. *L'abbé Trublet, critique et moraliste, 1697-1770, d'après des documents inédits.* Paris: A. Picard, 1926.

Joutard, P. *Historiographie de la Réforme.* Paris: Gallimard, 1977.

_____. *La Légende des Camisards. Une sensibilité au passé.* Paris: Gallimard, 1977.

Labrousse, E. "Calvinisme en France, 1598-1685," in *International Calvinism, 1541-1715*. Edited by M. Prestwich. Oxford: Clarendon Press, 1986.

_____. *Pierre Bayle*. 2 vols. The Hague: M. Nijhoff, 1963-64.

"La Révocation de l'édit de Nantes et le protestantisme français en 1685. Actes du colloque de Paris (October 15-19, 1985)." Paris: *SHPF*, 1986.

Lauriol, C. *La Beaumelle, un Protestant cévenol entre Montesquieu et Voltaire*. Geneva: Droz, 1978.

Lemoine, Jean-Marie. *Les Evêques de France et les protestants, 1698*. Paris: de Chaix, 1900.

_____. *Mémoires des évêques de France sur la conduite à tenir à l'égard des réformés (1698), publiés avec une introduction, des appendices et des notes*. Paris: A. Picard et fils, 1902.

Lenel, S. "Un ennemi de Voltaire: La Beaumelle." *Revue d'Histoire littéraire de la France* 20 (1913): 101-32.

_____. *Un homme de lettres au XVIIIe siècle, Marmontel. D'après des documents nouveaux et inédits*. Paris: Hachette, 1902.

Léonard, E.-G. *Le protestant français*. Paris: Presses universitaires de France, 1953.

_____. "Le protestantisme français au XVIIIe siècle." *Revue historique* (October-December 1948): 153-79.

_____. *Histoire ecclésiastique des réformés français au XVIIIe siècle*. Paris: Fischbacher, 1940.

_____. *Problèmes et expériences du protestantisme français. L'urbanisation, l'embourgeoisement, les déviations ecclésiastiques, l'attrait catholique*. Paris: Fischbacher, 1940.

Ligou, D. *Le protestantisme en France de 1598 à 1715*. Paris: S.E.V.P.E.N., 1968.

_____. *Montauban à la fin de l'Ancien Régime et aux débuts de la Révolution française, 1787-1794*. Paris: M. Rivière, 1958.

Loménie, L. de. *Beaumarchais et son temps. Etudes sur la société en France au XVIIIe siècle, d'après des documents inédits*. 2 vols. Paris: Michel Lévy Frères, 1856.

Lough, J. *Essays in the 'Encyclopédie' of Diderot and d'Alembert*. London: Oxford University Press, 1968.

_____. *Louis, Chevalier de Jaucourt (1704-1780), A Biographical Sketch*. Repr. from Essays presented to C. M. Girdlestone. Newcastle-upon-Tyne, 1960.

Lüthy, H. *From Calvin to Rousseau: Tradition and Modernity in Sociopolitical Thought from the Reformation to the French Revolution*. New York: Basic Books, 1970.

_____. *La Banque protestante en France de la Révocation de l'Edit de Nantes à la Révolution.* 2 vols. Paris: S.E.V.P.E.N., 1959-61.

Mandrou, R. *Louis XIV en son temps, 1661-1715.* Paris: Presses Universitaires de France, 1973.

Marion, M. *Machault d'Arnouville. Etude sur l'histoire du contrôle général des finances de 1749 à 1754.* Paris: Hachette, 1891.

Masson, P.-M. *La religion de Jean-Jacques Rousseau.* 3 vols. Paris: Hachette, 1916.

Mazoyer, L. "La question protestante dans les Cahiers des Etats Généraux." *BSHPF* 80 (1931): 41-72.

McCloy, S. *The Humanitarian Movement in 18th-Century France.* Lexington: University of Kentucky Press, 1957.

Metra F. G. Imbert et al. *Correspondance secrète, politique et littéraire ou Mémoires pour servir à l'histoire des cours, des sociétés et de la littérature en France depuis la mort de Louis XV.* 18 vols., London: John Adamson, 1787.

Metzger, A. *La conversion de Mme de Warens.* Paris: Fetscherin et Chuit, 1886.

Moulin, H. *Les Défenseurs des Calas et des Sirven. Elie de Beaumont et Loiseau de Mauléon, avocats au Parlement, P. Mariette, avocat aux Conseils de Roi.* Cherbourg: A Mouchel, 1883.

Mours, S. and D. Robert. *Le Protestantisme en France du XVIIIe siècle à nos jours, 1685-1970.* Paris: Librairie Protestante, 1972.

Musset-Pathay, V.D. *Oeuvres inédites de Jean-Jacques Rousseau.* 2 vols. Paris: P. Dupont, 1825.

Nicolas, M. *Notice sur la vie et les écrits de Laurent Angliviel de La Beaumelle.* Paris: Cherbuliez, 1852.

Nixon, E. *Voltaire and the Calas Case.* London: V. Gollancz, 1961.

Noailles, P. duc de. *Histoire de Mme de Maintenon et des principaux événements du règne de Louis XIV.* 4 vols. Paris: Comptoir des Imprimeurs-Unis, 1848-58.

Orcibal, J. *Louis XIV et les Protestants.* Paris: Vrin, 1951.

Palmer, R.R. *Catholics and Unbelievers in Eighteenth-Century France.* Princeton: Princeton University Press, 1939.

Perry, E.I. *From Theology to History: French Religious Controversy and the Revocation of the Edict of Nantes.* The Hague: M. Nijhoff, 1973.

Peyrat, N. *Histoire des pasteurs du désert depuis la révocation de l'édit de Nantes jusqu'à la Révolution française, 1685-1789.* 2 vols. Paris: M. Aurel Frères, 1842.

Peyster, H. de. *Les Troubles de Hollande à la veille de la Révolution française, 1780-95.* Paris: A. Picard, 1905.

Pic, P. *Les idées politiques de Jurieu et les grands principes de '89.* Montauban: Imprimerie cooperative, 1907.

Pilatte, L. (ed.). *Edits, Déclaration et Arrests concernans la Religion P. Réformée, 1661-1751.* Paris: Fischbacher, 1885.

Poland, B.C. *French Protestantism and the French Revolution; A Study in Church and State; Thought and Religion, 1685-1815.* Princeton: Princeton University Press, 1957.

Pomeau, R. *La Religion de Voltaire.* Paris: Nizet, 1969.

Proust, J. *Diderot et l' "Encyclopédie."* Paris: Colin, 1962.

Puaux, F. and A. Sabatier. *Etudes sur la révocation de l'édit de Nantes.* Paris: Grassart, 1886.

Puaux, F. *Les Défenseurs de la Souveraineté du Peuple sous le règne de Louis XIV.* Paris: Fischbacher, 1917.

Queniart, J. *La Révocation de l'Edit de Nantes. Protestants et Catholiques en France de 1598 à 1685.* Paris: Desclée de Brouver, 1985.

Rabaud, C. Sirven. *Etude historique sur l'avènement de la tolérance.* Paris, 1891.

Rébelliau, A. *Bossuet historien du protestantisme. Etude sur l' "Histoire des Variations" et sur la controverse entre les Protestants et les Catholiques au dix-septième siècle.* Paris: Hachette, 1891.

Renwick, J. "Marmontel, Voltaire and the 'Bélisaire' Affair." *SVEC* 121 (1974): 9-175.

_____. "Reconstruction and Interpretation of the Bélisaire Affair, with an Unpublished Letter from Marmontel to Voltaire." *SVEC* 53 (1967): 172-222.

Rex, W. *Essays on Pierre Bayle and Religious Controversy.* The Hague: M. Nijhoff, 1965.

Robert, D. *Les Eglises Réformées en France, 1800-1830.* Paris: Presses Universitaires de France, 1961.

Robert, L. *Voltaire et l'intolérance.* Paris: Fischbacher, 1904.

Roddier, H. *L'Abbé Prévost, l'homme et l'oeuvre.* Paris: Hatier Boivin, 1955.

Rothrock, G.A. *The Huguenots: A Biography of a Minority.* Chicago: Nelson-Hall, 1969.

Schwab, R.N. "The Extent of the Chevalier de Jaucourt's Contribution to Diderot's 'Encyclopédie.'" *Modern Language Notes* 72 (1957): 507-08.

_____. "Un Encyclopédiste huguenot: le chevalier de Jaucourt." *BSHPF* 108 (April-June 1962): 45-64.

Scoville, S.C. *The Persecution of Huguenots and French Economic Development.* Berkeley: University of California Press, 1960.

Shackleton, R. *Montesquieu: A Critical Biography.* Oxford: Oxford University Press, 1961.

_____. *The "Encyclopédie" and the Clerks.* Oxford: Clarendon Press, 1970.

Schmidt, P. *Court de Gébelin à Paris, 1763-84. Etude sur le protestantisme français pendant la seconde moitié du XVIIIe siècle.* Saint-Blaise, 1908.

Stocquart, E. *Le mariage des Protestants en France.* Brussels: O. Lambertz, 1903.

Taphanel, A. *La Beaumelle et Saint-Cyr. D'après des correspondances inédites et des documents nouveaux.* Paris: Plon, 1898.

Van Deursen, A.T. *Professions et métiers interdits. Un aspect de l'histoire de la révocation de l'édit de Nantes.* Groningen: J. B. Volters, 1960.

Verdier, H. *Le duc de Choiseul. La Politique et les Plaisirs.* Paris: Debresse, 1969.

Woodbridge, J. "L'influence des philosophes français sur les pasteurs réformés du Languedoc pendant la seconde moitié du XVIIIe siècle." Typewritten doctoral thesis, University of Toulouse, 1969.

Index